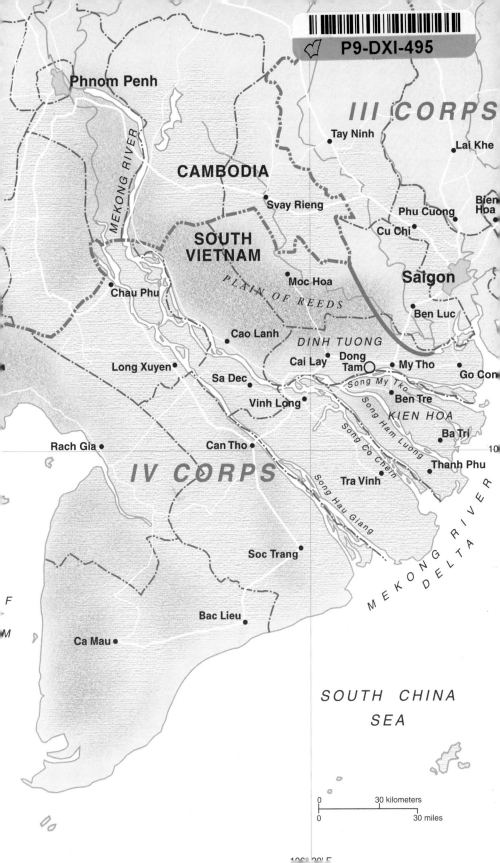

STEEL MY SOLDIERS' HEARTS

The Hopeless to Hardcore Transformation of
4th Battalion, 39th Infantry,
United States Army, Vietnam

by

COLONEL DAVID H. HACKWORTH

(U.S. ARMY, RETIRED)

and

EILHYS ENGLAND

RuggedLand

RUGGED LAND | 276 CANAL STREET · FIFTH FLOOR · NEW YORK CITY · NY 10013 · USA

RuggedLand

PUBLISHED BY RUGGED LAND, LLC

276 CANAL STREET • FIFTH FLOOR • NEW YORK CITY • NY 10013 • USA

RUGGED LAND AND COLOPHON ARE TRADEMARKS OF RUGGED LAND, LLC.

LIBRARY OF CONGRESS CONTROL NUMBER: 2002102090

CATALOGING-IN-PUBLICATION DATA

(PROVIDED BY QUALITY BOOKS, INC.)

Hackworth, David H.

Steel my soldiers' hearts : the hopeless to hardcore

transformation of U.S. Army, 4th Battalion, 39th

Infantry, Vietnam / by David H. Hackworth and Eilhys

England. — 1st ed.

p. cm.

ISBN: 1-59071-0029

1. United States. Army. Infantry Division, 9th

Regiment, 39th. Battalion, 4th--History. 2. Vietnamese

Conflict, 1961-1975--Regimental histories--United

States. 3. Vietnamese Conflict, 1961-1975--Personal

narratives, American. 4. Hackworth, David H.

I. England, Eilhys. II. Title.

DS558.4.H33 2002   959.704'34

QBI02-200183

Book Design by

HSU+ASSOCIATES

Maps by

BOB PRATT

RUGGED LAND WEBSITE ADDRESS: WWW.RUGGEDLAND.COM

MAY 2002

1   3   5   7   9   10   8   6   4   2

FIRST EDITION

To all the grunts and to all the guys in the sky and behind the tubes who served in Vietnam. And especially to The Hardcore.

PROLOGUE

Debt of Honor

Somewhere inside my head, I've constructed a bunch of double-locked doors to hold back my memories of Vietnam: the stench of swampy Mekong paddies, the angry snap of AK-47 rounds, the crump of incoming mortars; the billowing red and yellow flames of exploding napalm; the sour smell of gunpowder drifting in the black smoke; and the one-million-candlelight flares lighting up the battlefields where American men and boys, who knew the whole lousy enterprise was futile, fought and died.

Not something you want to dwell on. Not something you can ever forget.

In late January 1969, I helped a group of badly led, dispirited soldiers transform themselves into the Hardcore Battalion, probably the finest infantry fighting team in Vietnam. These men were not specially trained Rangers, Seals, Special Forces or other elite troops. Most were ordinary citizens—draftee soldiers who became great fighters because they found themselves in a war and figured out that the best way to stay alive was to become better than their enemy.

When I first became their commanding officer, a lot of them hated my guts. When they called me a GI Joe prick and "The Big Meat," they weren't far off the mark. To have a shot at getting them home, I had to be hard-nosed. Now, all these years later, I hope with all my being that the bottom line is that I led from upfront and never let them down.

The warriors of the Hardcore Battalion fought like hell. And they showed their country and the U.S. Army that there was a smarter way to fight in Vietnam. In telling their story, I want to honor every last one of these amazingly brave soldiers.

I salute you, my brothers-in-arms. This book is by you, about you and for you. What a privilege it was to lead you.

STEEL MY
SOLDIERS'
HEARTS

O God of battles! steel my soldiers' hearts;

Possess them not with fear; take from them now

The sense of reckoning, if the opposed numbers

Pluck their hearts from them.

HENRY V, *Act IV, Scene 1*

ONE

9th Infantry Division Headquarters
Dong Tam, Vietnam
15 JANUARY 1969

"It's a pussy battalion, Colonel. I want tigers, not pussies."

I had to hand it to Major General Julian Ewell. Twenty-five years after his kick-ass command in Bastogne, the old paratrooper was still firing for effect. He had sent stateside for me to fix one of his busted units—4th Battalion, 39th Infantry of the 9th Division—right then out in Indian country getting its clock cleaned.

"The 4/39th is the worst goddamn battalion I've ever seen in the Army, Hackworth. It couldn't fight its way out of a retirement home."

He thumped the desk in front of him.

It took some doing to keep a straight face. As a Lieutenant Colonel with over two decades of my life invested in the Army, though, I wasn't about to piss off General Ewell. You didn't spend a day in green without learning about his reputation for ruthlessness. He swung his ax with a high-pitched war cry: "You're gone. You're history." And you were.

We sat in his office in Dong Tam, half an hour by chopper from Saigon. The 9th Infantry Division's flagpole was planted—as if anything but rice could be planted in the Mekong Delta—just outside the general's window. *Ewell's* flagpole. *Ewell's* division. And *Ewell's reputation* at stake. And the poor, sorry 4/39th was letting him down.

He unconsciously jiggled his hand in a tight semicircle, thumb and pinkie extended like the hands of a watch, ticking off the points he wanted to emphasize.

"Pussy battalion." Tick, tick.

"I want tigers..." Tickety, tock.

His hand gyrated like a whirligig.

I'd known Ewell for years, a combat veteran gone long in the tooth, his days as a warrior behind him. Sure he was steamed, but if you looked closely you could see that the heat hadn't taken the creases out of his immaculately ironed fatigues. But before the starch, Ewell had earned a formidable reputation as a battalion and regimental commander with the 101st Airborne in World War II, serving under the legendary General Maxwell Taylor. After the war, he hooked himself to Taylor's coattails and took a peacetime trip up the chain of command to collect a shoulder full of stars. Right now he was a tightly wrapped, thin-lipped, hard-charging West Pointer who meant to drain the Delta before the Delta pulled the plug on him.

General Ewell and I were not alone. And the man standing a dog bone's throw behind him did nothing to improve my mood. Ira Augustus Hunt was a tall, good-looking bird colonel, as polished as a new Rolls Royce and—with his Ph.D. in engineering—about as useful in combat. The Army considered him one of its best and brightest. And just as Ewell had ridden upward in Taylor's jet stream, so Hunt was cruising in Ewell's, having served under him as commander of his engineer battalion in Germany and now as the 9th Infantry Division's chief of staff. The two made quite a pair. Between them they had more naked ambition than a Harvard Law School third-year hustling the Supreme Court for a clerkship.

My take on Hunt? A whiz with a slide rule and a dunce with a sidearm, or any other kind of weapon. I met him in Italy right after World War II, when I was Private Hackworth of the 351st Infantry Regiment and he was

Lieutenant Hunt of the Command's engineer company. Even then he was a piece of work. We were TRUST soldiers (Trieste United States Troops), so tightly disciplined that if a private even blinked at a sergeant he'd find himself running around the parade field with his rifle over his head shouting "I'm a big-assed bird" until he dropped. In Italy, I learned that exacting even-handed discipline is crucial when the bullets start flying, but Hunt worked overtime inventing infractions, gigging good troops and basking in his power. The GIs I knew who felt his lash or sting thought he was a first-rate bastard. Now he was General Ewell's consigliere.

I'd been back in-country less than three hours. Earlier that morning I'd stepped off a commercial charter jet in Saigon. The Army's own FTA flight, free trip to Asia. All expenses paid by the Department of Defense of the United States of America. Three times before 1969, I'd made the same eighteen-hour trip across the Pacific to Southeast Asia. Nothing had changed. The plane was full of FNGs, fucking new guys—nineteen- and twenty-year-olds, pink-cheeked, dry-mouthed, wide-eyed, eager but scared—one more load of fresh meat for the Vietnam grinder. I couldn't help wondering which of them the KIA Travel Bureau would be bagging up for the return trip home. Even the lucky ones, the ones who made it out alive, would never be the same.

At Tan Son Nhut, the U.S.-controlled air base in Saigon, customs greased me through like a four-star general, and I went directly to the Military Assistance Command Vietnam (MACV) helicopter pad, where a 9th Division chopper waited. The bird rose and veered to the southwest, Saigon fading behind under its haze of camphor smoke. I watched the chopper's shadow racing above rice paddies where tiny figures worked—men and women in black pajamas with naked children in tow, a few followed by the dark silhouette of a water buffalo.

Thirty minutes later, the bird circled Dong Tam. From the air, the place looked like a huge, dirty, nineteenth-century Nevada mining town squatting in its own tailings—prefab wooden buildings with tin roofs, dusty roads and miles of green sandbags, the bunkered 3rd Surgical Hospital, a PX and an outdoor movie theater, one short runway of perforated steel planking and a huge helicopter pad. Home away from home to rear echelons of ten infantry battalions along with aviation, signal, engineer, artillery and military police outfits and every other kind of logistical ash and trash.

To build the place, U.S. Army engineers had brought in a monster machine that sucked several square miles of silt from the bottom of the Mekong Delta to create enough solid land for the 9th Division to set up shop. Four hundred acres in all with the rest heaped into an earthwork berm that gave the perimeter the look of an ancient Roman encampment. Twentieth-century innards surrounded by second-century ramparts.

As the chopper dropped toward the pad, under the whump, whump, whump of the rotors, I saw a World War II – style ammunition dump in the middle of the base. Great call. One enemy mortar round, and the whole place would be history. I walked off the pad and jumped into a jeep with a kid behind its wheel waiting to run me over to General Ewell's headquarters.

The ride was an eye-opener. Nearly 10,000 rear-echelon motherfuckers—REMFs to the grunts out on the line—were stationed in Dong Tam surrounded by all the creature comforts. I saw a miniature golf course and a swimming pool. I caught a glimpse inside a barracks, decked out with clean beds under mosquito nets. These guys pulled down the same combat pay as the young soldiers in the bush who lived in the mud, watching their feet rot, burning leeches out of their crotches and laying down their lives.

Dong Tam crawled with Vietnamese civilians, doing chores, changing the sheets on the beds of the generals and colonels, shaving the brasses' jowls, ironing fatigues and shining shoes. It took only one sympathizer to report every U.S. burp and fart to the Viet Cong. But what really got my heart pounding was that ammo dump. What kind of commander would squat on top of his own powder keg?

General Ewell's briefing lasted half an hour, with Colonel Hunt bobbing his head in agreement every time Ewell spun his hand to make another point.

Tick.

Tick.

Tick.

After that, they sent me on my way.

I left that meeting unsure of myself, anxious. I wasn't sweating a sick unit or leading troops. I'd enlisted in the military before I finished puberty and in the two decades since, I had commanded two infantry battalions and nine companies—two rifle companies and two artillery batteries, and one each of raider, heavy weapons, armored cavalry, combat support and headquarter companies. But here, the chain and the terrain both spelled trouble. Pragmatically, I could do nothing about the chain of command and the tactical operational stupidity of Dong Tam. I'd be out of Ewell's and Hunt's eyesight soon enough, and worrying about how combat operations were being handled from above was a waste of time at best and got men killed at worst. There'd be ways around that. But the terrain was another matter. The Mekong Delta was an unknown to me—a vast swamp riddled with a tough enemy who'd been fighting in it forever and who had every furrow down cold.

I knew that I couldn't count on my earlier in-country combat tour to guide me. In the Vietnam Highlands, where I cut my teeth fighting the North Vietnamese Army (NVA), the enemy wore uniforms, there were few civilians in the jungle areas and the terrain, except for the coastal plains, consisted of mountainous, lung-busting jungle—a bitch, but a manageable one. The Delta, mainly flat and open, was turf made for a chopper war. Not only didn't I know much about using choppers, it had been almost two years since I'd smelled enemy gunpowder. Over and over in my mind I asked myself: Will I be able to handle it? Will I remember what to do when the bullets sing?

I tracked down and spent the rest of the afternoon with the 9th Division's G-2, Lieutenant Colonel Leonard A. Spirito, bringing myself up to speed on the intell coming out of Dinh Tuong Province. Dinh Tuong was the swampy home court of Base Area 470, the Viet Cong's Mekong stronghold. A capable intelligence officer, Spirito gave me the skinny on the basics of what the 4/39th faced every day—Enemy, Weather and Terrain. "Don't expect the enemy down here to fight or think like you do," he told me. "In the Delta, the enemy is strange, tough. He wrote the book on guerrilla warfare—and he just keeps adding new chapters."

Colonel Spirito backed up what I'd learned stateside. Before leaving Fort Lewis, where I'd been running a training battalion, I called up an old friend, Colonel Hank Emerson, who was back in the States recovering from severe burns after his chopper was shot down in the Delta. Hank was a legend in Vietnam, a warrior's warrior, the guy the troops called "The Gunfighter."

Until the crash, Hank had been commanding the 9th Division's 1st Brigade—he had, in fact, been the one who persuaded Ewell to send for me—and he knew the Delta the way he knew his own service record. "It's like fighting in the Everglades," he'd told me. "Except if you don't have your shit together, the VC take you faster than the 'gators. Everything there is an infantryman's worst nightmare."

The problem I had to figure out was how to "out-G the Gs," out-guerrilla these guerrillas. But regressing to General Ewell's—and the entire Vietnam chain of command's—visions of World War II – era glory days and tactics was not the answer. That evening, Ewell organized the most worthlessly theatrical show-and-tell I'd ever seen: starched briefers, maps, charts, sitreps, stats, kill rates, body counts galore; the whole deal, all of them shining brightly. All of them pure-grade crap that made it perfectly clear I couldn't take anything coming from Ewell and Company at face value.

I managed to button my lip until Ewell's boys trotted off. Then I told him my overall plan. I intended to steal a page from Hank, use his checkerboard tactics, Eagle flights and jitterbug strikes to fix and fuck the VC while adding a few tricks of my own.

"You just go ahead and do what you need to do," Ewell said dryly. Either tactics bored him or even he'd had enough of the dog-and-pony.

So much for defining the mission. But that night, I hit the sack knowing that my commanding general had given me what I needed most—enough rope to hang the enemy. Or myself.

The next morning I did more recon, but moved down the line to the point of the actual spear. I needed someone I could trust to help orient my compass, get my combat bearings. So I paid a visit to an old buddy who'd been running the 2nd Battalion of the 39th Infantry for over six months, Lieutenant Colonel Don Schroeder. A fierce, charismatic soldier, tactically brilliant but even better in the bush, Schroeder was the finest infantry battalion commander the 9th Division had. We'd been captains together at Benning and majors together in the 101st, where Don had served as Hank Emerson's battalion Executive Officer (XO).

Schroeder was a stud on his way to stars, every one of them well deserved. During the next six days, he taught me more about fighting in the Delta than I could have picked up from a year in a classroom. He also slipped me some priceless intell. Over a beer one night, he told me that after Hank Emerson's chopper went down, Colonel Hunt had cut Hank out of the burning bird and saved his life. Everyone respected Hunt for it and the men were ready to get behind him after he took over temporary command of Hank's Brigade. But the esprit de corps didn't last. "That son of a bitch rode us too hard and *always* put us away wet," Schroeder said. "He never knew when to stop. He's bad news." Pushing back his can, he sent up a million-candlelight flare over Hunt and Ewell.

"Watch your back," he warned. "They're a couple of rattlesnakes."

But by then I was raring to get out with my troops and walk the walk. Before I moved out, though, I made one last stop to see the new commander of the 1st Brigade. Colonel John P. Geraci was Ranger, Airborne, Special Forces and a grizzly, all-animal fighter. His radio call sign was "Mal Hombre"—loosely translated, "mean motherfucker." During the Tet Offensive, his 1/506th Airborne "Centurion" Battalion had racked up 1,294 VC KIA in exchange for eleven of his rock-hard centurions.

Geraci ate staff officers uncooked for breakfast, but the troops idolized him. "Here's what I've got for you," he'd tell them, laying out a mission. "Any questions? No? Good. Now go out there and knock their cocks stiff." Not a guy for euphemisms. When I asked him for the straight skinny on the 4/39th, he grinned and clapped me on the shoulder.

"Worst battalion I've seen in twenty-six years of service, Hack. You got your work cut out for you."

The 4/39th's area of operation, Fire Support Base Dizzy, was set on the Wagon Wheel, deep in bandit land where five canals converged like spokes on a hub. From my chopper vantage point coming in from Dong Tam, the place looked normal enough, but when I landed, I couldn't believe my eyes, or nose. The whole base smelled of raw shit and rotting morale. Toilet paper blew across the chopper pad, machine-gun ammo was buried in mud, and troops wandered around like zombies, their weapons gone red with rust.

These were the sloppiest American soldiers I'd ever seen, bar none. Unkempt, unwashed, unshaven, their uniforms ragged and dirty, hippie beads dangling alongside their dog tags, their helmets covered with graffiti.

Where did these troops think they were, a fucking commune?

In the middle of this shithole stood the command post (CP) of Lieutenant Colonel Frederick W. Lark,* the officer I would replace in a change-of-command ceremony the following day. He'd snuggled his CP next to a 155mm artillery battery at the hub of the wheel while deploying his four rifle companies raggedy-ass around the perimeter in defensive positions that would have melted away under a water buffalo's charge.

The firebase was loose as a goose. My brain went into overdrive, sorting out priorities, assessing problem areas and trying to keep cool. From what I saw in the first thirty seconds on the ground, I knew I'd need all the seasoned warriors I could find to turn the Battalion around. And I needed them now.

I meant to start by canning the outfit's S-3 operations officer and the 250-pound heavy drop Sergeant Major. To replace them, I'd sent for two men of my own. The first was Robert Press, who had served as First Sergeant under my command in the 101st. We'd also served together in the States as well as in Vietnam, and our partnership went all the way back to the same unit during Korea. Lean and mean, Press would be my new Battalion Sergeant Major, the noncoms' chief ass-kicker and role model.

I loved this warrior. He was smart as a whip, tough as a one-dollar steak, an NCO right out of James Jones's *From Here to Eternity*. From the time he was a teenager during the Korean War, he'd been training and leading soldiers, and he knew his job the way a master carpenter knows his toolbox. On the flight up, we divided the chores. He'd concentrate on the noncoms. I'd work on the officers. And we'd meet in the middle with the troops.

For my S-3, I'd brought in Major Neville Bumstead,* whose near-fluency in the Vietnamese language was a big plus. He'd served with me during an earlier in-country tour as a platoon leader and staff officer and I thought he'd make one hell of an operations officer. He was West Point, Airborne, a

*A pseudonym.

school-trained Ranger who'd seen combat in the Mekong Delta with the Vietnamese Rangers. Another two-dozen good men were also on the way.

Press came back from his first circuit of Dizzy shaking his head.

"I wouldn't even call it a firebase," he said. "I don't know what it is—it kind of looks like a picnic area. I mean, it's like some kind of outing with the local Kiwanis or something. I looked around and seen no one wearing helmets. No one carrying their weapons. Everybody in the CP group was sleeping above ground. I didn't see a foxhole anywhere. Sir, this outfit stinks worse than we thought."

"Top," I replied. "As soon as I take over tomorrow, I want you to have the company commanders and staff assembled. While I meet with them, how about you getting together with the first sergeants? They haven't been doing their jobs, or this outfit wouldn't be in this shape. Really smoke 'em. Between us, we'll get things straightened out."

He shot me a pitying look.

"Right, Colonel. You, me and John Wayne."

Press was right. We were in serious trouble, open to attack at any moment, with only a bunch of demoralized and badly led troops loitering on the perimeter to fight off any assault by the VC. If Dizzy were hit, we'd go down as quickly as a sandcastle smashed by high tide.

All that night, while Press worked the perimeter, talking to the NCOs and the troops, Bumstead and I sat back to back, pulling our own private stand-to.

We took up our position at a safe distance from Lark's brightly lit Tactical Operations Center (TOC), which was glowing like a circus tent in the darkness. The VC could have taken it out with a barrage of well-aimed rocks.

My mind shifted into overdrive as I went back through every combat trick I'd learned over the years. Throughout the afternoon, I'd scribbled ideas in a sweat-stained pocket notebook that was now overflowing. Bumstead began a new one.

"Remind me about automatic claymores," I'd tell him, and he'd duck beneath his poncho, click on his red-lens flashlight, and write it down.

We spent the whole night like that. Every now and then, there would be an enormous BAM, and someone would scream, "Medic!"

Just before sunup, Press came back. For a moment I thought he was going to blow away the TOC tent himself.

"You're not gonna believe this, Sir."

Colonel Lark had set Dizzy dead center in a Viet Cong minefield.

TWO

There are no bad troops, just bad officers—an axiom as old as the profession of arms. Through tightly clenched jaws, Press gave me a sitrep from his all-night recon. "There's no one to blame for the rotten condition of this battalion but Colonel Lark."

During the days that the Battalion had been set up at FSB Dizzy, eighteen soldiers had been wounded inside the perimeter from mines and booby traps. Morale, understandably, was lower than Death Valley. How could Lark put his firebase in such a dangerous spot? Hadn't anyone done a recon before the outfit deployed from Dong Tam? Why hadn't the engineers cleaned up the place? And if all the basics had been too hard for the guy, why the hell didn't he just *move* the Battalion?

The troops agreed that Lark was a decent guy, an officer with good intentions. But only a general like William Westmoreland—Lark had been one of Westy's dog robbers in the 101st—would have entrusted him with an infantry battalion in combat. In the fourth year of the war, Lark had arrived in Vietnam still scratching for his Combat Infantryman's Badge, a bare-bones combat distinction of having served in the line of enemy fire for at least thirty days; and his troops paid the price for his inexperience.

If you wanted a symbol of Dizzy, you didn't have to look any further than "Lark's Throne." That's what the grunts—the name comes from the sound an infantryman makes when he pulls himself up from the mud with a full rucksack and all his other gear—called the compact white portable toilet parked an easy amble away from the TOC tent. It had come in with the Chinooks that choppered in a battery of 155mm howitzers but no ammunition. Instead, they unloaded a jeep trailer filled with beer and ice—and the Colonel's own PortaPotti. Up on the forward edge where things were hairy, the grunts had no covering fire, while back at "B" Battery, it was Happy Hour and the commander had everything he needed to take a nice warm crap.

The results of his approach were recorded all too clearly on the outfit's "Dich Board." Dichs—"enemy dead" in Vietnamese—dinks, gooks, slopes were all racist slurs aimed at the VC. The slurs served a useful purpose, dehumanizing the enemy, which made it easier to kill him before he killed you. They also helped grunts blow off some steam when Charley—the handle for the Viet Cong came from the Army's phonetic alphabet, Victor Charley for the letters VC—sat out there in the darkness behind the tree line screaming: "Fuck you, GI! Tonight you die!"

Lark had tasked the Battalion Operations Sergeant with keeping track of casualties. When we arrived, the score Sergeant Jerry Slater had entered on the Dich Board looked like this:

Dichs 127 KIA

Friendly 32 KIA...307 WIA (Wounded In Action)

The reality behind the stats knocked me out. After six months under Colonel Lark, the 4/39th had suffered the equivalent of nearly 40 percent casualties without ever meeting a significant enemy force in open combat. Rockets, mortars, booby traps and friendly fire had done most of the damage.

In fairness to the man, according to my pre-taking-over-command homework, the 4/39th had started to unwind well before Lark took over. The 9th Infantry Division had been in-country since December 1966. Originally part of III Corps in the early stages of the buildup (Vietnam was divided into four Corps of operation with I Corps the most northerly and IV the farthest South; III Corps surrounded Saigon, but did not include the hellish Mekong), the 4/39th distinguished itself against Viet Cong main-force units. But the warm-up did nothing to prepare it for war in the Big Swamp. The trouble began the moment the 9th was sent into the Delta to take it back from Charley.

Again, the terrain was just a flat sonofabitch. "All armies prefer high ground to low and sunny places to dark," Sun Tzu wrote over 2,500 years ago. "Low ground is not only damp and unhealthy, but also disadvantageous for fighting. If you are careful of your men, and camp on hard ground, your army will be free from disease of every kind, and this will spell victory." I don't think General Westmoreland or the U.S. commanders running the war in Vietnam knew Sun Tzu from Sonny and Cher. If they had, the U.S. Army would not have been fighting in the Delta.

Dry season or wet, the place was a tropical hell where the grunts were always soaked, either from rain, wading across canals and rivers or from sweat. During the monsoon season, May through September, standing water greatly hampered airmobile operations. Mud from the waterway banks and swamps coated communications equipment, fouled weapons and made infantry operations a soggy, slow-motion nightmare. In just forty-eight hours in soaking jungle boots, foot rot set in. Mosquitoes zapped with malaria, leeches sucked onto balls and even up dicks and morale vaporized before Charley fired one shot.

Dinh Tuong Province, where Firebase Dizzy operated, was wide open except along the waterways, which were flanked by light jungle vegetation—single canopy trees and nipa palm thickets—and overrun with civilian-tended rice paddies. The low ground, flat as a surfboard, averaged only about two feet above sea level. With six major rivers connected by a maze of canals and streams making up the drainage network, water runoff was poor in the best of seasons. In the wet season, with the rivers and canals overflowing, it became debilitating.

The rice paddies themselves offered little concealment. But the paddy walls provided the VC good cover from direct fire weapons. The only way for a GI to get a clear shot at Charley was to scale the dike and hope he wouldn't get blown away by a lethal stretch of mines and booby traps planted in, out and around the paddies. Within the patches of jungle bordering the paddies, the VC, masters of camouflage, had excellent concealment from air observation. And the dense year-round Mekong undergrowth cut the grunt's field of vision to little more than the nose in front of his grimy, sweat-stained face.

Farther outside Dizzy's perimeter and in the patches of jungle bordering both the paddies and the actual Delta, the VC built fortified camps with their perimeters almost as bomb- and artillery-proof as the German Siegfried Line in World War II. If the VC chose to defend a position rather than slip away after an assault, which they rarely did, they could count on great natural cover augmented by wall-to-wall mines and more than enough of their own totally committed soldiers.

But even worse, there was no way to tell the good guys from the bad guys. Six million Vietnamese—nearly 35 percent of South Vietnam's entire population—lived in the Delta, caught in the crossfire of a cruel civil war. The VC in the Delta seldom wore military uniforms and intentionally mixed in with the population, most of whom tended to the thousands of shimmering rice fields. If surrounded, the VC ditched their weapons and military gear under water and, presto change-o, they came up looking like everyone else: just another bunch of hardworking rice farmers clad in black pajamas.

Conditions improved during the dry season, October through April, when the place became one giant, dusty landing zone. But no matter what time of year, early morning fog and low clouds interfered with Tactical Air operations (Tac Air) and chopper ops. It doesn't take a Napoleon to figure out that a straight-leg infantry unit's ability to maneuver is limited by the weather and terrain, or that dense civilian populations greatly restrict firepower. If it was tactically critical to send troops into those swamps, they should have been U.S. Marines with the equipment and experience to fight in an amphibious setting. Not draftee Army grunts.

The overall mission of the entire 9th Division under General Ewell was to control a big chunk of the seemingly endless Mekong waterways, rivers and canals, great natural supply routes from Cambodia to South Vietnam which the 9th was somehow supposed to take away from the tough folks who'd been using it—particularly at night—to resupply their fighting units for decades. Not exactly a slam dunk. Intelligence estimates from the show I got at Dong Tam put the number of VC operating within the ten-mile radius of the Division's headquarters at anywhere up to three or four thousand guerrillas.

Before I came on board, the 4/39th had the bad luck to draw the assignment of patrolling the VC "Rocket Belt" surrounding Ewell's headquarters—a mission that was a perfect example of the madness that went down every day in Vietnam. Here's how it worked. When General Ewell ordered, "Stop the rockets and shells from striking my base camp," his colonels replied, "It will be done, Sir." But while they were snapping off their salutes, the VC were busy protecting their gunners by planting even more mines and booby traps. To allow the brass and especially General Ewell to sleep better at night, grunts had to wade straight into a well-prepared hell.

Most 4/39th soldiers knew that each time they took a step they risked the ugliest of wounds. A bullet makes a hole, a chunk of shrapnel may take off an arm—but a mine turns a soldier into a splattered, shrapnel-punctured basket case.

Many troopers in the Battalion had concluded that waging war consisted of crossing a field, hitting a mine, calling for a medic, patching up the wounded, getting a medevac; then moving out again and hitting another mine. They also did the math and figured out that not many of them would be lucky enough to make it through the 365 days it took to rotate home.

"The very words booby trap bring back the smell of blood whenever I hear them," recalls Jim Robertson, a tall, lanky "C" (Claymore) Company squad leader from Long Island. "The damned things were so numerous, so varied, and Charley was so good at making and concealing them, that the feeling was that if you stayed in the field long enough, you were going to fall victim to a booby trap. It was just a matter of time."

In a firefight, the grunts knew they had a chance to fight back. If you got ambushed and you didn't get hit in the first burst, you could get your licks in. "But with a booby trap," Robertson remembers, "it was BANG, game over. Somebody was down. Sometimes more than one guy was down. And we'd get mad. But there was nobody to fight. That was the worst—the frustration and the helplessness." At least Robertson didn't have to deal with that form of frustration for his complete tour. Because of bad feet, he was eventually transferred to supply.

The VC used anything and everything to build their devil's devices. There were toe poppers—normally a single bullet no bigger than a pencil, set on top of a nail; step on it, and the bullet pushed down into the nail and fired through your foot. And grenades with trip wires, U.S. and Chinese claymores, Bouncing Betties, land mines, artillery shells, RPG rounds in cans filled with explosives. "All sorts of creations from hell," says "C" Company Squad Leader Jerry Sullivan, a six foot two regular soldier from Ohio, as gangly as he was gung-ho. "And they'd come up with new contraptions to bring us down every day, some as big as bombs."

The wounds were vicious. Young men blinded, legs and arms and dicks and balls ripped off, bodies punctured with dozens of bleeding holes. For the VC, mines and booby traps were economy-of-force weapons—easy to deploy, cheap to produce. Besides causing heavy casualties, they produced a lot of psychological stress. Soldiers never knew when they would lose a foot, a leg or a life, and the frustrating part was there were few ways to fight back. Many grunts concluded the civilians in the Delta helped set the mines, which fanned a widespread I-hate-the-gook mindset.

One study made by the 9th Division showed that the majority of all booby-trap casualties occurred when a soldier, plodding through slush and mud often up to his waist in steambath conditions, became tired and lost concentration. Roughly 34 percent of all booby traps were located along trails and rice paddy dikes, with another 36 percent in the jungle growth. POWs told us the VC commonly employed booby traps as a defensive measure around their perimeters and bunkered positions.

The biggest problems, besides tired soldiers who'd lost their alertness and focus, were from not keeping five yards and not yelling out "Hit it" and going for the ground whenever anyone heard the pop of a booby trap. Green troops were the worst. Too often, when they heard dread signature pop, they froze and got the crap blown out of them. Significantly— and tragically—throughout the Vietnam War, the Army training establishment never fielded an effective mine training curriculum or doctrine—or even something as simple as a training device that would go "pop" and "bang" to teach young soldiers about the apparatus that accounted for the greatest number of casualties.

Three out of four booby traps employed trip wires attached to grenades. Of these, the majority were Red Chinese. Nineteen percent of the mines and booby traps came from dud U.S. bombs and shells, the explosive material scraped out and then placed in C-Ration or coffee cans careless GIs left behind.

Generally, seasoned soldiers detected these visually and set them off with some sort of heavy Rube Goldberg grappling hook thrown ahead and dragged backward. Commo wire and 155mm shipping plugs also made good dragging devices for setting off trip wires as did claymore mines, M-79 grenade launcher fire or a dose of artillery fire and napalm along the avenue of approach.

Thirty-five percent of the booby traps were pressure activated. Found along dikes and trails as well as in the jungle, open fields and—during the dry season—in rice paddies, these were the real bastards, as you generally didn't know you'd tripped one until you heard that ominous pop or click, followed all too soon by an explosion.

Jim Silva, a "D" (Dagger) Company squad leader—a draftee from California, handsome, compact, a natural hunter with an attitude who became one of the Battalion's best—was moving to an ambush position when his point man tripped a booby trap. While looking for an LZ to bring in a Dust-Off Medevac, he found and destroyed three more booby traps.

"Four booby traps in 200 yards in an area where the day before there were no booby traps told me Charley wanted our asses out of there," Silva recalls. "As I was returning to the platoon to bring the wounded to the LZ, I heard, POP. I looked down and saw a puff of blue smoke. I whirled around, then leaped for all I was worth and at the same time yelled at the guys behind me to hit the ground. Then I started counting and praying. I'm not sure which came first. When I got to three, the explosion went off. Shit was flying all over the place.

"The wounded dude and the medic who were behind me jumped to their feet and asked if I was OK. I said I didn't know, the blast was so close to me—about two feet away—that my ears were ringing. Mud covered my legs. I thought they were blown off. The Doc carefully scraped some of the dirt away and I started moving my feet and by the goodness of God everything was still attached. When I got up, I looked at the crater next to my legs and realized that this was no grenade; it blew a hole about eighteen inches round and about a foot deep. We all agreed that it was a giant land mine. To this day, I always say a little prayer for the gook who put it there. I guess he didn't have the balls to put an instantaneous fuse on it, and that, in turn, saved all three of our lives. In fact, that was the only booby trap that I ran into in Vietnam that had a long fuse on it."

Silva wasn't so lucky a few months later when he was hit by an RPG. Or maybe he was since his wounds got him medevacked back to the States.

"The grunts loved to find a VC splattered across a trail when the booby trap he was setting went off prematurely," Division Intelligence officer Spirito told me. He saw this happen on three separate occasions, which probably explains why the VC didn't use a more complicated fusing system.

Ninety-four percent of all booby traps and mines weren't covered by enemy fire. This didn't mean the VC were not in the vicinity, but that they used them to keep our troops away from occupied positions and as warning devices to detect our movement. Since VC infantry seldom protected mines and booby traps by rifle fire and observation, which is normally SOP for a U.S. outfit, our troops learned they could take their time to neutralize the nasty mothers as they came upon them. And if our soldiers moved slowly and carefully they usually weren't hard to find—the VC signaled the presence of their booby traps to protect their own troops. They'd use a nipa palm tied in a knot or a straight stick pointing down a trail, or Tu Dai signs, Tu Dai being Vietnamese for "Kill Zone."

"We found these signs carved into gravestones and trees or written on a board nailed to a post or a tree," Robertson recalls. "Once you know what it means, you might think it's stupid to advertise something you want your enemy to blunder into, but Charley wasn't stupid. He knew that a sign on the side of a trail or road, most Americans would take to be the name of the next village. An inscription on a grave marker would probably be assumed to be the name of the departed. Charley had a diabolical sense of humor. It became sort of a game: finding the booby trap. We found a lot of major explosive devices and had we hit them, we'd all have gone up in smoke."

The signs meant "big danger"—and normally the troops would find mines within fifty meters. The next trick was to disarm, disable or destroy them, which was doubly dangerous duty because the VC booby-trapped many mines. One trap might be tied to another, and by disabling the one you found, you could find yourself in a world of pain from the other.

"Sergeant Morton was one of the best we had at spotting traps," Jim Robertson remembers. "The guy was positively uncanny. We swore he could smell them. He saved our asses more than once. I wasn't so skilled. I was walking point one day and ended up having to ford a stream. The embankment was steep and I was intent on my footing, trying not to slide into the drink."

"'Freeze, Robby,' Morton yelled.

"I instantly played statue and asked, 'What?'"

"'Trip wire,' Morton said. 'Don't move.'

"No problem. I was so scared I don't think I could have," Robertson says. "Morton came up behind me and pointed to a spot right in front of my face."

"'Right there,' Morton said.

"All I could see was the foliage overhanging the bank," Robertson says. "He had me back off and he pointed again.

"'Right there,' Morton said. 'What are you, blind?'

"I still didn't see it until he pulled me down and had me look up," Robertson says. "With the sky behind it, I could just make out a very thin line. It was monofilament, the kind we used for trip-flares, and it was at neck height. The VC had rigged it to snag some poor slob doing what I'd been doing—looking down as I entered the stream. If not for Morton's sharp eye, I would have hit the wire in the next step. We tried to trace the wire but it went into such thick stuff on both ends, we decided it was too risky and bypassed the thing."

Even Morton's expertise wasn't enough. He eventually tripped a mine, was badly wounded and evacuated to the States.

The brass, safe in the sky, too often failed to take the danger to heart. On one operation just before I took over, Sergeant Tom Aiken, a slight, wiry soft-spoken draftee who put as much passion into soldiering as into playing country guitar, lost seventeen of twenty-nine men from his platoon to booby traps without ever hearing a shot from the VC. "Hell, we were down to like twelve men left in the platoon," he recalls in his Georgia country drawl. "We'd doubled down with the equipment of the wounded men—none of the choppers would take the rifles or the packs, we had to carry those—and Colonel Lark came on the radio and said, 'Continue to sweep the wood line.'

"That's when my platoon sergeant, Toby Hager, grabbed the radio from me and said to Colonel Lark, 'You sonofabitch, I'm takin' what men I got left and I am goin' to the road because if I sweep this wood line one more time, there may not be a 1st Platoon in "A" Company,' and he handed the phone back to me and said, 'If he calls back, don't answer it.' Then he turned around and he looked at us and he said, 'I want every man to put their foot-step in my footstep and I'm going to try to lead us out of here and try to get us to the road.' And he did."

Booby traps usually didn't kill. Except for the big ones—coffee cans filled with explosives, artillery rounds, recycled rocket rounds. But most mines maimed. The 4/39th grunts, mainly nineteen- and twenty-year-old kids, weren't really afraid of dying. Most thought they were immortal, if not bulletproof. "Most of us, I think, were afraid of being maimed, of going home missing an arm or a leg, and I think most of us felt we'd rather die than go home that way," Jim Robertson says. "That's why we feared booby traps. You don't believe you are going to die, but you do believe you can be badly hurt."

During one operation Robertson's squad walked along a tree-lined dike. "We weren't supposed to walk on the dikes," Robertson says, "but you had to give yourself a break from the mud or you'd drop dead from a heart attack. We got to an intersection with the gap bridged by a log and we were about to negotiate the log when a sniper opened up on us. Everybody hit the dirt, but we had to get through the growth in the middle of the dike to get to cover on the other side. The smart thing to do was to drop and roll, and I'd been out there long enough to know that by then. Something made me dive *over*, instead of through, the bush that was behind me. When I came up to return fire, I was staring at a grenade tucked into a C-Ration can wired to the bush. The C-Ration can held the grenade's handle down because the pin was already out. The wire would pull the grenade out of the can and BOOM. If I'd done what I was trained to do, the thing would've blown up in my face. I couldn't even shoot back. I just stared at the thing with my mouth hanging open."

On another occasion, Sergeant Aiken, walking point, crossed a canal. "When I got to the other side," he says, "I looked up and there was a claymore mine five feet from my nose. I rolled back in the canal and started vomitin'.. I seen my mother, my daddy, my wife, my dog all in one flash. Hager slipped around and disarmed it. The mine was one of ours. Some lazy GI gave it to the VC and it almost snuffed out my life."

Dud five-hundred-pound U.S. bombs rigged along Route 4 were the Hardcore drivers' biggest worry.

"When I got off the line and drove a truck on Route 4," Jim Robertson remembers, "I always volunteered to drive the ammo and gasoline loads. Not because I was brave; quite the opposite. I had seen guys torn up by mines in the road, seen them ripped apart and still be alive afterward. I always felt if I were going to go, I'd prefer to go in one big bang. I didn't want to lie in the road in agony waiting for somebody to throw the pieces on a chopper for the surgeons to sew back together as best they could. I was more afraid of living maimed or paralyzed than of dying, and if I was going to die, I wanted it to be quick."

No one saw this mess more clearly than the 4/39th's Battalion Surgeon, Captain Byron E. Holley—a skinny young doctor almost always wearing a floppy green swamp hat when he wasn't in his helmet, no shirt, baggy green jungle fatigue pants and combat boots. His dog tags bumped against his stethoscope and the Colt .45 in his shoulder holster. He wore dark glasses, drove a jeep with "Super Quack" painted on the hood and used "Big Band-Aid" as his radio call sign.

The mismatch recorded on the Dich Board wasn't a matter of numbers to Doc Holley. In his field surgery and in the 3rd Surgical Hospital back in Dong Tam where the wounded lucky enough to get a chopper ride out of the bush were brought, the arithmetic transubstantiated into flesh and blood—a popular, nice kid from Alabama with a blob of gray brain matter protruding from a hole in his skull; a grunt with his aorta perforated by steel splinters; a boy rushed in from a dust-off chopper with a fractured tibia.

Hey, no sweat. Until the Doc looked higher and found that another round had turned the grunt's balls to mush.

"Mines composed a relentless unforgiving carpet virtually everywhere underfoot, so your guts were in your throat with almost every step," Holley recalls. "The terror and the anger they caused ran so deep that most of the men weren't even aware it was there. Until suddenly it would surface."

So it went, day after day of looking into the eyes of soldiers with missing hands and arms, mangled legs, sucking chest wounds. One night they brought Holley a gut-shot sergeant who'd been smoking a cigarette under his poncho liner, a perfectly illuminated target for the VC sniper who nailed him. Five grunts risked their lives to hump him out of the jungle, only to learn that he'd died. Out in the field, after a full day of cutting and stitching, Doc Holley would crash for a few hours on a litter—when he could find one that wasn't still wet with blood.

"It's a helpless feeling," he wrote to his fiancée, Sondra, back in the States. "You know that some gook is sitting out there in the tree line, lobbing miniature bombs in at you, and all you can do is lie there and pray that one doesn't land on top of you. The vets over here say that as long as you can hear them, not to sweat it because you never hear the one that kills you—some comfort, huh?"

One night Captain Paul Merlin came into Doc's tent to shoot the breeze. In the previous two days VC booby traps had cost nine wounded and one KIA. "He was so upset that he wants to get out of the Army and is asking for my advice," Holley wrote home. "The KIA was a real nice-looking young guy. He had found a wired hand grenade, and an officer told him to disarm it and throw it in the river. Well, he didn't mean for him to pull the pin, but the young soldier pulled it anyway. It literally blew his head completely off at the shoulders, including his right arm, right before their very eyes! In your wildest dreams you can't imagine the effect that something like that can have on you or the troops. The captain had tears streaming down his cheeks as he relayed the story to me. 'Doc, I don't believe in what we are doing over here anymore,' he said. 'I can't stand the thought of losing any more kids so needlessly.'"

Twenty young men from the 4/39th were killed just before I took over, from November 1968 until 20 January 1969:

Raymond Glenn Beam*	Calvin Lewis**
William Ernest Brown**	Michael Miller, Jr.**
Donald Richard Carlyle**	Lawrence Ortiz, Jr.*
Douglas Dupree**	Glenn Haskell Rollins**
Latney Dean Ferguson**	Robert Henry Sinclair, Jr.*
Leon Roy Field**	Charles Ernst Smith**
Richard Joseph Forte**	Francis Craig Sollers**
David Ernest Gardner**	Francis C. Sullivan, Jr.****
Richard Gerald Gillham**	Carlos A. Velazquez-Ortiz**
Robert Richard Hillard***	Ricky Lynn Wikle*

* *Casualty caused by small arms*
** *Casualty caused by booby traps*
*** *Casualty caused by illness*
**** *Casualty caused by drowning*

Source: 9th U.S. Army Infantry Division Report:

Roll of Those Who Gave Their Lives in Southeast Asia—1966 – 1970.

The tally of needless death in the 4/39th was well established before Colonel Lark took command. Lark's immediate predecessor, a gung-ho lieutenant colonel, drove the troops like indentured servants. One steamy day a company working its way across a rice paddy was plodding through several feet of water and muck, while overhead in the Command and Control (C&C) chopper, the colonel kept screaming "Faster! Go faster." It was never going to happen—the troops were already moving at max speed.

In a high lather, the colonel landed. Jumping out of his bird, he sprinted to a paddy dike and leapt on top of it to make his point. A supreme Mekong Delta no-no. And, when the almost instantaneous explosion blew him twenty feet in the air and he died immediately and needlessly, the ultimate ego trip, I was told the grunts cheered.

When Lark took command, he knew that he had to turn things around and he worked hard to do so. But with zero combat command experience and not enough time with troops, his good intentions meant less than nothing. Even the basics were ignored. He wore an Army-green baseball cap instead of a steel pot. Really cool. Except that the troops who followed his model and neglected their helmets wound up in Doc Holley's surgery with their brains running down their necks.

He was into good-guy fraternizing to build morale. A well-intentioned notion, but it made for bad news in the field. One night he invited the 4/39th's new XO, Major George Mergner, to go to the Officers' Club in Dong Tam for a beer. Mergner, a skinny-as-a-scarecrow regular Army officer from Michigan who cracked a very professional whip, was on his second tour in the Delta, his arrival in the Battalion preceding me by a month. The two men sat around a table with half a dozen other officers when, out of the blue, in the middle of the second can of beer, Lark informed Mergner that come sunup he was to lead a two-company operation. Mergner, who under the circumstances "would have preferred not to have had the beer," had little time to plan and no sleep—what a way to run a choo-choo train loaded with nitro .

While commanding the "Rocket Belt" detail, Lark sent his "A" Company on a three-day sweep of a wood line completely empty of VC, but a Ho Chi Minh wet dream of booby traps and mines. That was the day Sergeant Tom Aiken lost seventeen of the twenty-nine in his platoon without hearing a single shot. "All we were doin' was trippin' booby traps," he recalls, his voice trembling slightly. "There wasn't any enemy in there, no gooks at all. We knew it, but Colonel Lark kept sayin', 'Sweep the wood line, sweep the wood line.'"

More than thirty years later, Aiken made a list of the men in his platoon killed under Lark's command. When he finished writing it, his wife asked him, "How could you remember all those names after all these years?" His answer was simple: "How could I forget them?"

Other squad leaders felt the same way. "We'd hit another booby trap, call in another helicopter, dust those guys off and be told to 'keep moving,'" recalls Sergeant Bill Vandermay, a six-foot-five-inch giant. "So we'd keep moving until the next explosion, call in another chopper. What a waste of human lives."

No unit can take this kind of beating indefinitely. Bespectacled "C" Company commander Captain Gordon DeRoos, a total pro on his second tour, remembers that when he took over his company, the troops were walking around in a daze whenever out on a mission. "Several squad leaders acted as if being in charge was an extra, unwanted duty, and quite a few of them cooked up reasons to go back to Division base camp that I couldn't have worked out in a thousand years. And that was the leaders. The troops took advantage of their dereliction, of course, so out in the boondocks, the company was never over 50 percent locked and cocked. I had no problem with the mission to patrol the Rocket Belt. Someone had to do it. But the haphazard, hurry-up-and-get-it-done way we were ordered to waltz in quick-time through the woods really burned me up."

One time DeRoos was sent into an area of operation (AO) known to be infested with booby traps and given three hours to clean it up. "Like it was the same thing as getting ready for an inspection, for Pete's sake, or a regular Sunday walk in the woods. Most of the time, choppers were circling overhead, and I was being asked for sitreps or being told to speed it up. I had just finished loading out the medevac chopper with my wounded guys when I was told once again to get a move on. I couldn't believe it."

The brass sent the troops out to sweep the Rocket Belt day after day, only to find Charley's kids and wives. "And we knew they were the ones who were setting the booby traps. Didn't seem like we had a worthwhile objective. Nothing was ever accomplished except getting a lot of troops blown away."

Lark's S-3 (the staff officer in charge of operations and training) was an armor branch major named Templeton. The grunts called him "Simpleton," and it wasn't hard to see why. The fact that he managed to get himself smacked in the head by the tail boom of a LOH as it was taking off didn't help. "One day," according to S-4 (the staff officer in charge of logistics) Lieutenant Robert Johnson, "he ordered a good portion of the Battalion to saddle up for a special mission. A VC POW had volunteered to lead us into an active regimental area where there supposedly was a large cache of weapons. Templeton set up the mission and led it himself."

The turncoat VC led the unit through what could have been the most booby-trapped zone in Vietnam. And then he escaped. "When he got away, you should have heard the traffic on the command net. From Division on down, everyone went berserk."

Orders came down to find the runaway at all costs. To a lethal symphony of exploding mines and booby traps, the hunt went on for hours. Finally someone radioed word that the escapee had been found dead. Only he wasn't the same size and he was wearing a different color shirt—"Most of us believe that some poor innocent gook who just happened to be in the wrong place at the wrong time gave his life for a VC countryman he probably didn't even know"—but at least the discovery finally brought the chase to a close. At a cost of fifty casualties, all from booby traps. And just one more disaster not the exception but the rule under Lark.

On another occasion, Lieutenant Bob Knapp, a good-looking hard-charging West Point jock whose men loved him, was sent out on a similar mission. "It was a Brigade op and a real cluster-fuck," he recalls. "The VC knew we were coming and seeded the AO with booby traps. Our XO, Lieutenant Larry Neumann, and a 3rd Platoon Tiger Scout named Han, who was affectionately called 'Super Gook' because he was so aggressive, tripped a thirteen-grenade daisy chain in an open paddy that did a job on both of them as well as many other soldiers."

Mergner told me later that Neumann had assumed command of the company because Captain Merlin, the battle-rattled captain who'd decamped to Doc Holley, freaked out once again and was evacuated to Dong Tam. Mergner described Neumann as "a fine soldier who survived even though part of his torso looked like Swiss cheese." His final words to Neumann in the field hospital were, "Damn it, Larry, how many times have I told you not to walk point?"

"I suspect Brigade took over one hundred casualties in this op," Knapp said. "It smacked of the same stupidity and futility as British soldiers attacking German trenches during World War I."

DeRoos, Johnson, Knapp—it was a miracle Lark didn't get them all killed. He just didn't understand what was going down with the guys on the ground.

About the time Tom Aiken's "A" Company went for their bloody walk in the woods, a new captain just recalled from the Reserves turned up to join the 4/39th. The only recent active duty he had behind him was attending the Ranger Course. Mergner suggested to Lark they give the newbie a warm-up assignment before sending him to a line company. "I thought he needed some indoctrination."

Lark disagreed.

"The captain's been to Ranger School," he said.

A few days later, when the new man's company came under fire in a limited engagement out in Indian country, the captain bailed out as soon as the bullets started flying. He was immediately reassigned out of the Battalion. But then Lark ordered Mergner to see that the gutless captain was awarded the Combat Infantryman's Badge (CIB).

"He earned it," Lark said.

Mergner replied that the departing officer didn't deserve the award because it was given only for honorable service as an infantryman.

"Do it," Lark snapped.

Mergner refused. "Only time in my memory I disobeyed a directive from my boss."

I can't overstate how disastrous the leadership of a green colonel can be in a combat zone. Among other things, Lark decided that troops out in the Platoon Patrol Bases needed regular hot food. He accomplished this by ordering three deuce and a half trucks full of chow—the grunts called the convoy "Meals on Wheels"—to come in every day from Dong Tam. The trucks always arrived at noon. As precisely as a German train. You could set your watch by their arrival.

The setup worried Johnson. "Since I was S-4, I was responsible for this operation, and I was very concerned about rigid patterns."

Johnson went to Colonel Lark and told him about the dangers of holding to a set schedule or pattern, a key combat principle the Army teaches—and stresses—even in basic training.

"This battalion will not be intimidated by the VC," Lark snapped. "Keep the convoys rolling at the same time each day."

Draftee Dan E. Evans, a combat medic with a warrior's heart, built like the high-school running back he'd been, shared Johnson's misgivings. He'd begun to correlate the "abnormally high number of casualties" he was seeing with the "lackadaisical way" Lark ran the unit. In detecting the error, he was miles ahead of his West Point commander, who did nothing to correct it.

Three weeks before I arrived, an R&R party from the 4/39th's Platoon Patrol Base Cougar jammed itself into a jeep and trailer and headed down Widow Maker's Alley, the macadam road leading into Dong Tam.

The VC had planted an American-made claymore mine alongside the road.

"The world blew up suddenly in smoke and fire," Evans recalls in *Doc: Platoon Medic*, his blood-and-guts memoir of life with the 4/39th. "A wall of supersonic steel balls blasted the passengers, shredding metal and flesh."

From the bush, rockets swooshed down, lifting the jeep and trailer up into "an expanding fireball...[that tossed] mangled soldiers all over the road. Automatic rifle fire stitched every square foot of macadam as those few GIs still able made a run for...[an adjacent] water-filled ditch...Those left behind screamed and wailed and cried out. They crawled and pulled themselves around in the middle of the road like crushed bugs with limbs and pieces of their bodies missing...

"...'Teddy Creech used his elbows to claw his way across the road like a mangled worm. His hands were mutilated beyond recognition. His leg had been severed from his hip, except for a tether of bloody skin and flesh.....The jagged end of the detached bone kept digging into the road and staking him in place. He fumbled out his knife and, in the way that a trapped animal will gnaw off its own foot in order to escape, cut himself free of his leg."*

The survivors, making a fight of it from the muddy ditch, were joined by

*Daniel E. Evans, Jr. and Charles W. Sasser, *Doc: Platoon Medic* (New York: Pocket Books, 1997) pgs. 70-71

a platoon leader and nine grunts who came pounding in from Patrol Base Cougar, guns blazing. They held down the fort until Lieutenant Knapp led two platoons in for the rescue.

Ignoring heavy fire, Evans moved among the wounded and dying. "Creech's left leg, still wearing its combat boot, lay discarded in the road next to the mauled jeep," Evans remembers. "His other leg was twisted like that of a cloth puppet without joints. Blood and gray ooze gushed from his many wounds."

A sergeant looked at him and "started to move away. 'This one's dead,' he announced.

"Creech's eyes slowly opened in the bloody mask that was his face. 'I ain't dead yet,' he croaked. 'Give me a shot of morphine.'" He got his shot and lived to tell about it.

Richard Forte lay with a bullet hole in his belly. His bloated gut signaled heavy internal bleeding. His face was the color of old ivory.

"'It's all right. I'm OK, Doc,' he groaned. His face was the color of old ivory. 'Doc...the others...they need you. Go help my buddies, Doc.'" *

"Where did the Army get such men," Evans wondered, "thinking of others when they themselves were dying?" And what did they get in return? "The VC picked us off one by one," he recalls. "One by one. Day after day. The 4/39th was helpless and demoralized against a superior army of ghosts that could do to us what it wished."

To survive, the grunts had to improvise, and at times, outfox their own colonel.

The canals and rivers in the Rocket Belt were called "blues." At one point, Lieutenant Carl Hedleston received an order to "move along the blue," which entailed sweeping the sides of a canal on the lookout for enemy mortar and missile crews. Once he arrived at his objective, he was to set up an all-night ambush. "It was a horrible nightmare," Hedleston remembers.

*Daniel E. Evans, Jr. and Charles W. Sasser, *Doc: Platoon Medic* (New York: Pocket Books, 1997) p. 76

"There were more booby traps in the area than sand on the beach, and no one above platoon level seemed to care."

Hedleston's platoon sergeant, Ron Martinelli, a veteran with six months out on the line, came to him and said, "This is crazy. The area is filled with booby traps. We've been through there before and we always paid a high price."

Hedleston was between a rock and a hard place. He had to satisfy his captain, who wanted to please Colonel Lark, who wanted to please General Ewell, none of whom seemed to give a damn about the risks, since they so seldom took any firsthand. Command bunkers, the pleasures of the general's mess, choppers to keep them dry and out of range—what the hell did they know about what was going down on the ground?

So Hedleston employed one of the oldest tricks in a small combat unit leader's kit bag. He fiddled the order and did a "radio patrol." I would have done the same thing. In fact, I did the same thing when I was a company commander in Korea and the brass ordered me to have my soldiers conduct foot patrols in front of our defensive positions in twenty-degree-below-zero weather, a mission that guaranteed fingers and toes lost to frostbite.

Hedleston moved out a few hundred yards and set up. "We faked going through the area. That night, we set up in one place and never moved. We just sent in phony radio reports. I prayed all night that our own artillery wouldn't hit us because we weren't where I reported we were. I justify my actions to this day as taking care of my guys as opposed to following a dumb order. My guys knew I'd be court-martialed if I got caught. We knew if we didn't take care of each other, no one else would and we probably wouldn't survive."

That's a snapshot of the 4/39th on the night of 31 January 1969. The sun came up the next morning on an outfit that had been misled to the brink of mutiny—and close to utter destruction. And at Dong Tam that same morning, General Ewell climbed into his chopper and took off for Firebase Dizzy—to give Colonel Lark a medal.

No wonder the grunt's byword in Vietnam became "It don't mean nothin'."

THREE

Fire Support Base Dizzy
Dinh Tuong
01 FEBRUARY 1969

A scraggly bunch of Battalion soldiers assembled for the change of command ceremony. Undisciplined and dispirited, wondering what was going to happen to them next, they stood like characters in a police lineup where every participant was a perp.

With silver blades gleaming in the sun, a flock of brightly Simonized Hueys dropped from the skies over Dizzy. One by one, starched Army brass with an entourage of photographers strutted across the LZ, General Ewell leading the way—their fatigues pressed, their sleeves precisely rolled above their elbows into four-inch folds, their shoes polished to parade-ground perfection. To the grunts, they must have looked like aliens from outer space.

I stood soldier-straight and watched those from on high pay absolutely no attention to the assembled troops—men from their Battalion, their Division. For them, the boys on the line were beside the point, mere pawns to be ignored. It disgusted me. In the 9th Division the gap between the brass and the grunts looked unbridgeable.

The change-of-command ceremony itself was a joke. First, General Ewell handed me the Battalion colors, then he pinned a medal on Lark's chest. From the PA system, the Battalion Adjutant's disembodied tenor boomed out across the Plain of Reeds—"Lieutenant Colonel Frederick Lark is awarded the Legion of Merit medal by direction of the President, under the provisions of the Act of Congress for exceptionally meritorious conduct in the performance of outstanding service"—a blast of hot air that stank worse than swamp gas.

If the VC were listening and watching, which they no doubt were, they were probably too stunned by the bizarre spectacle to take a shot.

The Adjutant's booming rhetoric was matched by General Ewell's next exercise in medal inflation. He presented Lark a Silver Star, Second Oak Leaf Cluster—Silver Star number three for Lark. Just behind the Medal of Honor and the Distinguished Service Cross in the order of gallantry awards with which our country honors its warriors for battlefield heroics, the Silver Star is in no way a management medal. As a point of comparison, Audie Murphy, one of our most decorated ground-pounders in World War II, received only two Silver Stars for leading a squad, platoon and company from Africa to Italy to the Elbe, a march that put nearly four hundred combat days under his well-worn pistol belt.

XO George Mergner had been directed to hand-carry the award recommendation through the Division Staff Awards Committee. He recalled the G-5, Major Bernie Leofke, saying without reading the award recommendation, "For Fred Lark? Of course."

Out in the formation, I could see men rolling their eyes, openly snickering. Every man there knew that Lark's alleged deed of daring warranted only a Bronx cheer. He'd been in his chopper, way up there in the ozone on that particular day, nowhere near the dangers on the ground—the VC couldn't have shot him if they wanted to. When somebody in the formation started laughing, Lark's face turned beet red and he walked away. But that third Silver Star went with him.

The charade complete, the brass boarded their choppers, the blades turned and the birds took off, taking the bemedaled Lark with them to the alternate universe of Dong Tam and Saigon. With his ticket freshly punched,

Lark was about to leapfrog to the Pentagon, where he eventually, once again, became the right-hand man for then Army Chief of Staff General William Westmoreland.

The troops stared at me with a now-what? look that fell just short of hatred. I was their new designated tormentor.

Before the dust settled from the VIP liftoff, Press had the company commanders assemble for my first meeting. The young skippers quickly confirmed everything I'd seen and heard. The Battalion was on its ass. Not one combat leader or staff guy could remember a fight where the Battalion had come out on top. And they let it be known that the last thing Lark wanted was to relay the full Dich Board score to MACV headquarters. The official reports said that the 800-man unit had killed 127 enemy soldiers during Lark's six-month command tenure, adding up to fewer than one VC per day. The reports gave an honest figure for our dead—it's impossible to hide full body bags and metal caskets tagged with soulless bureaucratic stickers and forms—but underestimated the legless, the armless and other casualties by roughly 40 percent.

Each of the Battalion's four rifle companies was supposed to have 163 men; but on my first day not one had a "paddy strength" of more than sixty. Most of the NCOs were Shake and Bakes, bright privates selected during basic training and then rushed through a modified Officer Candidate Course at the Infantry School. After eleven weeks of NCO training, they became instant sergeants, prepared—in theory—to lead squads and platoons.

In practice, it takes at least three years to develop a good rifle squad leader. Most of the Battalion Shake and Bakes had less than twelve months total time in the Army. And few, I surmised, had the tactical savvy to keep their men alive on the battlefield. Until they became seasoned and relentlessly trained warriors, they amounted to the blind leading the blind up against a

Viet Cong with 20/20 vision.

Some command principles are just common sense. Good small-unit leaders make for good battalions. They are the cutting edge of a combat unit. It was no secret to me or to Press or Mergner why this outfit needed help. With a cadre of NCOs as green as the surrounding jungle, the 4/39th was in trouble the minute it poked its nose outside the berm at Dong Tam. You couldn't blame this on the grunts. The fault fell on the Army brass, who didn't know or had forgotten that small-unit leaders can't be mass-produced like rifles or tanks or golf balls.

Time for shock therapy.

As planned, I fired the incompetent S-3 and the heavy drop Battalion Sergeant Major on the spot and replaced them with Bumstead and Press. A thousand other changes needed to be made, but I didn't want to bury the company commanders or staff on our first day together. If I'd ordered all shortcomings squared away immediately, I'd have sent these leaders into overload, blown all their circuits. No one would've gotten anything right. So I approached this conversion from slackness to soldiering the same way I'd train a pup. Just a few tricks at a time.

"Starting now, we're going to follow the two-rule plan," I said. "I'll tell you what the two new rules are and you'll make them happen. Once your troops have mastered the first two rules, we'll add two more and we'll keep doing that until we're squared away. First we'll crawl, then we'll walk and then we'll run. Just stay with me—because we're gonna run faster and faster every day."

They shot me a prove-it look.

"These are the changes for today," I shot back. "We're always going to carry our weapons and they will be spotless. We will wear our steel pots at all times. Helmet covers will be reversed to disappear the graffiti. "

I didn't know it at the time, but I'd inherited one fine officer in Captain

Emile "Chum" Robert, the Battalion's artillery liaison officer. Chum looked like a movie-star and, as I soon found out, he was also smart, brave and a maestro with supporting fires. Years later, he told me that the graffiti order, which sounded Mickey Mouse at the time, produced an unexpected bonus. "Folks had shit written all over the camouflage covers—'We are the unthanked doing the unnecessary for the ungrateful led by the unqualified.' Hack said, 'Turn 'em over, we're not going to have anything written on 'em. It's degrading, disrespectful and it's not good discipline.' Folks responded, 'We can't do that because on the other side they're brown and we need them green in the lush green Delta,' and he said, 'I don't give a shit. It's better to be brown than to have all that crap written all over them.' And so folks turned them around. Before it was all over, the enemy soldiers we captured talked about bad-assed brown-hat soldiers, and those helmets became as distinct as fear itself. Charley always knew when we were the outfit on their butts."

The Battalion S-4 Lieutenant Robert Johnson was another shining light, a doer, a self-starter, a guy who made things happen—the perfect supply guy.

"Johnson," I told him, "this outfit's ass is hanging out. I want you to organize a couple scroungers and go pick Long Binh and Saigon clean," I said.

"You got it, Sir," Johnson said. "Any priorities?"

"Yep, jungle fatigues, jungle boots and as many Halizone tablets as you can get," I said.

"Halizone tablets," Johnson said. "Why so many?"

"We're gonna spend a lot of time way out in the boonies where it's just too difficult and dangerous to resupply by chopper. We're gonna drink what we find, live off the ground."

"On the way, Sir."

A few days later, after finding a very small soldier who told me his feet were killing him because he couldn't get any boots to fit him—they were all too big—I had a little discussion with the good S-4.

"Hack went ballistic," Johnson recalls. "He chewed out his chain of command from his squad leader to his company commander and then he got a hold of me. He made it very clear that I better get that man a pair of boots or all kinds of horrible things were going to happen to me. The Army did not make a men's boot small enough to fit this little guy. We scavenged the country and found a pair of women's boots that fit the bill. This taught all of us an important lesson, that Hack cared for the lowest of soldiers and he expected his commanders and staff to damn well look after them."

While I had my here-is-the-word talk with the company commanders, Sergeant Jerry Slater, the Battalion Operations Sergeant, passed a request from me to Colonel Geraci up at Brigade that we urgently needed a platoon of sappers to clean up the minefield where Lark had stuck the Battalion. Geraci came through like the old warrior he was. That same afternoon, a platoon of engineers flew in and went straight to work, clearing all possible mines and booby traps within our perimeter and closing off areas that were too mine-infested with white engineer's tape and signs marked MINEFIELD.

Hopefully, we'd lose no more feet or legs inside Dizzy.

But I was worried. If penetrated, we had little room to maneuver a counterattack force since mines still covered much of our center.

Chum Robert told me the 155mm howitzers were worthless for close-in defense. As he put it, "Unlike a 105, they're not designed for a direct fire role." Fortunately, before we'd left Dong Tam, Press had done some snooping around the Battalion's rear. He found and liberated some new 81mm mortars, far more responsive for countermortar fire, stowed in unopened containers. We set them up next to the howitzers and Chum had his artillery folks train the infantry crews on how to best use them. Soon

Press reported that the 81s had been zeroed in around our perimeter—they were "good to go."

"Great, Sergeant Major," I told him. "Now get rid of the Boy Scout camping stuff around here."

I pointed at the Coke and beer coolers, the cots, the portable radios, the tents, the footlockers—and especially at the white portable toilet. "Net it up and fly it out of here in the morning. We're going to be foot mobile. If they can't carry it, lose it."

After that, I cut every one of Lark's kinder-gentler privileges. Hot chow, fresh water flown in to forward positions and slack standards were suddenly history. "The more sweat on the training field, the less blood on the battle-field" was my mantra. That's why I needed Bob Johnson to scarf up all those Halizone tablets.

I knew that most of the grunts in the Battalion were draftees—true citizen soldiers who didn't want to be there and couldn't wait to get the hell out. A world of difference from my last in-country command experience back in 1966—a parachute battalion of all-volunteer regular troopers from the 101st Airborne. The men of the 4/39th were used to thinking for themselves and weren't about to take crap from anyone, including me. To them, Army service was a dangerous pain in the ass, something to survive, not a job to stick with until they got a gold watch. At the same time, they represented the same cut of citizen soldiers who'd won all of our big wars. If properly trained, properly motivated and correctly led, they'd fight as well as my regular Army paratroopers.

Another significant change from my first tour with the 101st was the availability of Tiger Scouts. Used in the Delta in rifle squads, Tiger Scouts—Hoi Chanhs—were former Viet Cong soldiers who'd defected. Most walked point. Old-timers in the Battalion told me that the Tiger Scouts' guerrilla experience and local knowledge made them invaluable. They said the scouts were first-class soldiers who knew the terrain, could commo with the local civilians and were worth their weight in diamonds.

I finished my first session with a set of orders that stunned the commanders.

"Here's the drill," I told them. "We're shrinking the perimeter tonight. I want you to recon your new positions. When it gets dark, each company will pull back. You'll maintain your old positions with half your force and by midnight I want those holes filled in. I want nothing left the enemy can use, particularly holes the VC can hop into if they attack. All your people will be at 100 percent stand-to, ready to fight in the new positions by midnight. I expect total light and noise discipline. Remember, nothing happens other than reconning until after dark. You've got to always remember that the enemy's out there in the bush watching our every move—and he's always looking for a weak spot to knock your cock stiff and close down the show. You'll call me at midnight from the new positions. Midnight. Understood?"

The commanders went out to brief their troops.

My orders went down like an iron kite. Preparing a fighting position is hard, sweaty work. Moving a fighting position is even more of a bitch because you have to fill in the old hole before digging in again. It sucks under any circumstances, but the Mekong Delta makes it worse because of the high water table. Digging in becomes trial and error. Some holes work. Many slowly fill with water and have to be filled in and dug again.. The grunts figured, "I've already worked my ass off digging out the last position, filled sandbags and stacked them around the trenches, put up overhead cover, cleared fire lanes, and put in flares and laid down claymore mines in forward positions to slow Charley down if he makes a direct assault. Everything's fine. What the fuck does this new asshole think he's doing? It's harassment. It's fucking Regular Army harassment!"

They hated my guts.

Not only did I have to get the Battalion to understand the new guy in charge came with a broom and that the old ways were dead and gone the moment Lark climbed on that getaway chopper, but I suspected Charley might be wondering what was up from all those incoming and outgoing Hueys. I had no intention of making it easy for him if he decided to probe.

While the grunts dug, Bumstead cracked the whip to get the S-2 and S-3 people together. I'd put both sections under his control to assure the necessary and often critical coordination. Too often, the S-2 intell shop worked in its own little world and the important hand-in-glove relationship between intelligence and operations got lost. This outfit was no exception—staff procedures of both sections were as slack as the rest of the Battalion.

At first glance, Bumstead was a GI Joe meets Rambo cartoon—a thin little guy weighing in at around 130 pounds who took his soldiering *very* seriously. He carried all the commando toys: a folding stock shotgun, a bone-handled knife upside down in a shoulder strap, jungle boots with Velcro fasteners so he could get in and out of them fast, web gear and load-bearing equipment weighed down by grenades and ammo pouches he hung around his waist. The right stuff if you were a rifle squad leader, but hardly the kind of gear needed as a Battalion staff officer.

I wasn't singling out the boys at the perimeter. Before dark, I had Bumstead strike Lark's tent—a target waiting to be destroyed—in the center of the base. From now on, the 4/39th TOC would be a sandbagged bunker, and all TOC personnel, regardless of rank, were ordered to dig individual foxholes around it. They'd live there when not on duty.

My TOC order had a twofold purpose. Having a bunkered command post made it much harder for Charley to take out the Battalion Ops Center with one well-directed round, which remarkably he hadn't already done. And if Charley hammered the Battalion with incoming fire or penetrated our outer line, we'd have an inner perimeter of staff weenies to hold off the enemy while we fought the good fight and called in supporting fires. Plus the staff would be setting a positive example for all the line soldiers. We'd live exactly like the grunts. We'd sleep on the ground like Stonewall Jackson did during the Civil War. No one would have a plush deal anymore.

Plush, of course, being relative. From the platoon command post back, life kept getting easier and safer. Platoon and company headquarters offered soft duty compared to that of the guys in the squads up on the forward edge. And farther and farther back to the rear—battalion, brigade, division, corps, Headquarters MACV in Saigon—life got exponentially more comfortable and a million times less dangerous. Needless to say, my policy did not win the hearts and minds of the TOC folks, but that tent came down and by nightfall those foxholes were dug. Now the bitchers really had something to move their lips about.

I like bitchers. I've always found it's healthy when soldiers moan and groan. It's also much easier to sleep. When the going's tough and the men are silent, watch out for a frag grenade to come rolling your way.

Precisely at midnight, with the new TOC operational, the company commanders called in:

"'A' Company—Up."

"'B' Company—Up."

"'C' Company—Up."

"'D' Company—Up."

All four companies had dug in to their new fighting positions in the reduced perimeter of Dizzy and were 100 percent on stand-to: every man in his battle position with his weapon pointed downrange, all radios on and manned. The Battalion was hunkered down and ready to fight. I was pleased. Good, I thought, they've got it right. And they did it without shooting each other. Or me.

Press and I were preparing to walk the perimeter, when the world fell in.

"INCOMING!"

The shouts ripped out of the darkness.

CRUMP, CRUMP, BEEEEEOWWWWW.

Mortar rounds. Recoilless rifle fire. Machine-gun fire.

"An RPG round screamed in," Chum Robert recalls. "Then all hell broke loose. Strobe lights—they had just become SOP at Hack's commanders meeting that afternoon—flipped on around the perimeter. The VC were hitting us hard, but we were ready. Wow. I thought, Stay close to this guy and you'll be all right."

I jumped into the TOC hole. For an instant, I was afraid I'd blow it when I brought in the flares to light up the battlefield, called in the gunships to blister Charley and worked the indirect fire. Or that I wouldn't remember how to orchestrate a counterattack. Those two years away from a battlefield had made me as rusty as the rifles I'd found that morning. Be cool, motherfucker. Nervous as a kid driving a car for the first time, I took a bunch of deep breaths. Don't fuck it up, Hack.

As Chum Robert predicted, the 155s were as useless against this attack as a machine-gun without ammo. "The Light Fire Team is coming up on your freq," I told him. "Lift the 81mms and have the guns hose down the area where the firing's coming from."

The new 81mm section saved us until the gunships got there. The strobe SOP I ordered that day defined the perimeter, and anything beyond our forward edge was fair game.

I told Nev Bumstead to call in Puff the Magic Dragon, the AC-130 gun-flare ship. We needed to light up the arena.

"Have the perimeter fire a Mad Minute," I said.

For the next sixty seconds, every weapon in the outfit scorched the bush, blistering Charley ass.

Reports on the enemy's location started coming in. We were hammering them. But I had to keep in mind that when you're using mortars or artillery and then adding gunship chopper fire, you have to be very careful because the choppers can run into the shells. You need to choreograph the firepower with the finesse of a ballet.

"Off mortars."

"Roger that."

"OK, gunships, make your run."

"That's a Rog."

After thumping the enemy for twenty minutes, I called off the strikes and the night turned quiet. I called for a sitrep. When the radio traffic stopped we learned that because the VC had been hitting our old positions, we had no friendly casualties.

About an hour later, I stood the Battalion down and let the men go to 50 percent—one man sleeping in the bottom of his hole, his foxhole mate sitting on the edge or standing in the hole staring out into the darkness. From one of the foxholes forming the TOC's inner perimeter, I heard a whisper:

"He's a mean sonofabitch, but he knows what he's doing."

I was back in the game.

At first light, I went out to meet the man behind the voice in the dark. "You the guy who said I was a mean SOB?"

The soldier didn't flinch. "Yes, Sir, I am."

"Then you're the first SOB I've met in this outfit who knows what he's talking about. What's your name?"

"Lieutenant Lawrence Tahler, Sir."

A New Yorker. I could tell from his accent. "Tahler, eh?" As I turned to go, I made a mental note to check him out. The outfit definitely had its studs. I just needed to find them.

FOUR

Fire Support Base Dizzy
Dinh Tuong
04 FEBRUARY 1969

After our first little scrimmage I realized I had to convince everyone in the Battalion that the Viet Cong were not ten feet tall, that we could beat them anytime, anywhere.

The challenge was to find a way to motivate the men. Even the dumbest trooper in Vietnam knew we were fighting a war with a moral justification that had gone AWOL. The average age of these soldiers was just a shade under twenty years old, so young they complained there was too much beer being issued and not enough soda pop.

For these men, William Westmoreland's "light at the end of the tunnel" was a Viet Cong Express coming straight at them. As rifle squad leader Jim Robertson puts it, "The 'older' guys in our unit, even some senior NCOs, told us the war was unwinnable because our government had handcuffed us with ridiculous rules of engagement. That left us with one simple mission as far as we were concerned: to survive for a year and go home. We never hid from the war—as we saw our ARVN counterparts do daily—but we didn't aggressively pursue it. There was no purpose in our eyes in dying for a cause that was not so much lost as an enigma."

Dawn was breaking as Press walked the perimeter. "Sir, some of the troops are saying you have your shit together," he reported. "They're talking about how you pulled them back." Maybe I'd made a few converts that night, but I knew I was a long way from convincing the grunts that they could hit Charley harder than he was hitting them.

Over the next four weeks, I talked to every swinging dick in the Battalion. I told all the soldiers, all the sergeants, all the lieutenants and captains in each platoon and company what was expected of them and why they were going to be the best.

When I spoke to the troops, I promised I'd take care of their butts and be right out there with them when things got hot. I wanted to get it into their heads that by stealing a page from the enemy's book we would take the war to Charley rather than waiting for him to strike.

There would be a huge payoff if the troops believed me: They would have a better chance of making it home. "C" Company Squad Leader Jerry Sullivan recorded my 4 February comments to his unit: "We're gonna kick some ass, take the war to Charley, cut his supply lines and take him out in his backyard. We'll ambush him by night and take him out as he sleeps by day."

That, of course, was easier said than done. Dinh Tuong Province was one of the least pacified provinces in Vietnam, one bad place to pick a fight. Its proximity to Cambodia made things worse, allowing the VC to run supplies from a safe haven in a neutral country. When things got hot, they could slip across the border and flip their pursuers the bird.

Base Area 470, the Viet Cong stronghold, occupied the Western portion of Dinh Tuong extending into the bordering Kien Tuong and Kien Phong Provinces. This ugly chunk of ground encompassed almost 450 square kilometers. It contained extensive VC installations, defensive positions and other facilities: base camps for training and logistics, as well as a launching pad for combat operations. After a 9th Division probe of the Area in 1968, the division's official report euphemistically stated that the operations "met with only limited success." My own sources told me, "We got clobbered." Just the thought of Base Area 470 gave me a gnawing feeling in my gut.

Quietly I hoped the 4/39th would have some catch-up time before we had to go hunting there.

The Viet Cong in the Mekong Delta were one of the most formidable infantry opponents the U.S. Army ever encountered. The vast majority were locals, women as well as men, though after their extremely heavy losses in Tet 68, NVA regulars came in to beef up their southern allies.

Most of the VC had cut their first teeth on war. Their older brothers, fathers, uncles, grandfathers and great-grandfathers had fought the French, the Japanese, the French again, Saigon's troops and now the Americans. A thousand years before these battles, they'd fought the Chinese, Cambodians, Thais and anyone else who tried to grab their rich lands and make them slaves.

Like Spartan warriors in ancient times, the VC bred fighters. Small kids started out helping their big brothers and sisters—the VC's on-the-job War Training Program. Young boys and girls grew up spying on their enemy, carrying supplies, working in gardens to grow food, setting out booby traps, caring for the wounded and burying the dead. By the time they were teenagers, big enough to shoulder and aim a rifle, they were trained in the basic skills of guerrilla warfare. At that point, they joined whatever village guerrilla unit protected their home turf and assisted any Main Force units in their area of operations. When these seasoned outfits needed replacements, the youngsters volunteered from their village units. Though some were dragooned into the ranks, most willingly joined what they saw as their own War of Independence.

Because the endgame was to get the people on their side, the VC had no scruples about sniping from a hamlet, hoping a U.S. unit would return fire and cause civilian casualties: "Look, the Yankee, he killed your daughter, your son." If other forms of persuasion failed, the VC used terror against their own people. One way or another, contrary to all the Pentagon and MACV Pacification reports, all the men I spoke to who'd fought in the Delta believed the VC had the people, willing or not, firmly in their camp.

I figured the VC's Main Force units were our biggest worry. But in the villages, the "local G"—armed with whatever weapons they could find—would also carry a lethal sting. Since the Army of the Republic of Vietnam (ARVN), our ally against the VC, wound up more often than not as their supplier, most of the VC village guerrillas were equipped with a combination of old French and U.S. weapons. They prepared the way for the Main Force units, conducting operations with them, building bunkers, doing recon, laying mines, and providing guides and trail watchers. They were all pros, deadly.

The Main Force VC battalions had AKs, machine guns (RPDs), grenade launchers (RPGs), recoilless rifles and mortars—identical equipment to the regular NVA—and the quality and reliability of their rugged Soviet-designed weapons was far superior to the made-in-the-USA junk we had the misfortune to pack.

But because of our superior firepower, our great airborne surveillance capability and the mobility our choppers gave us, the VC operated mainly at night. Under cover of darkness, their major tactic was to attack U.S. units with a lightning-like infantry assault, supported by standoff rockets and mortar barrages. By sunrise they tried to be well dug in, hidden somewhere deep in Base Area 470.

Their intelligence was excellent. Not only did they scope out U.S. base camps, they had spies serving as KPs, maids and houseboys, penetrating everything from firebases dumb enough to let them in to the U.S. Embassy in Saigon, where one of the ambassador's drivers turned out to be a spook.

VC spies had infiltrated ARVN from top to bottom. And in the Delta, because operations had to be cleared with the South Vietnamese to prevent our bumping into ARVN or Regional Force outfits operating in the same

AO, the VC knew most U.S. plans before the U.S. platoon and company leaders who executed them. The minute the request went in, a VC spy informed his handler, who'd relay word to the local VC commander.

Besides watching firebases and studying patterns—when patrols and Ops went out—the VC would assign a tail to an American or ARVN unit in the bush to report on its location, strength and vulnerabilities.

The VC were very detailed planners. But strict adherence to the plan was also their Achilles' heel—they almost always stuck to the scenario even when things turned to shit.

Clearly they could be defeated, but only by an outfit that didn't underestimate them, a fast and flexible outfit that had its act together.

The 4/39th did not qualify. Yet.

One of my early orders instructed all company commanders to read Mao's *Little Red Book* and to memorize the *Vietnam Primer* which I'd written for the Army with historian Samuel "Slam" Marshall back in 1967 after he and I had spent five months in-country conducting after-action interviews with troops fresh from the fight. The Primer—a handbook on how to best fight Charley—was my first serious sally against the Army's endemic disease, Can't Remember Shit (CRS); I knew the information it contained from past grunts who'd been there would be invaluable to those now on the firing line.

I also had all our leaders read a pamphlet of combat rules and tips from articles I'd written that I had put together as *Battalion Combat Leader's Guide*. I wanted them to get in their heads both how Charley fought and thought and how I fought and thought. I wanted to build an offensive team; to make Charley react to us instead of calling the shots as he was doing all over Vietnam. I stressed how we'd find him by being hardcore and agile, using stealth and cunning and how we could turn his very own tactics against him. Then we'd bring in our big stick—fighter aircraft, chopper gunships, artillery—and fly in reinforcements to surround him and whack his sorry ass with everything we had.

With the first part of my campaign in process—reinstalling discipline and basic fighting standards—I turned my eye to motivation. When the 4/39th deployed to Vietnam in 1966, it was, according to then "A" Company Commander Mike Mark, who later retired as a colonel, "the best infantry battalion in the division." So the 4/39th had a proud tradition to draw upon, but we'd add another chapter.

To kick things off, I brought back saluting, a sign of military discipline that had been swallowed up by the rice paddy mud. Then I added a twist. When a soldier saluted, I required him to sound off with a loud "Hardcore Recondo, Sir"—to which the officer would reply, "No Fucking Slack."

The salute, discipline aside, also built unit pride. The name "Recondo," a combination of Reconnaissance and infantry Doughboy, came from the rugged, hands-on training the 101st Airborne Division practiced at Fort Campbell, training modeled after the British Commando and American Ranger Courses. Hank Emerson had named the 1st Brigade the Recondo Brigade to make the unit feel elite, like an airborne outfit. Hitchhiking on his idea, I named the 4/39th the Hardcore Recondos.

Bob Press hired a machine shop in Saigon to make small black metal Recondo arrowhead pins, which the men quickly began wearing. We painted the Recondo insignia on the sides of our helmets and on all of our vehicles just below the windshield, along with a large white Hardcore. We painted the same insignia on Company and Battalion signs at the firebases and back at our rear area in Dong Tam. We also had sharp-looking Hardcore Recondo stationery printed up and gave it to the troops, and all outgoing mail was stamped with the Recondo logo. All of this said: We're different, we're not just plain old infantry, we're the best. Dig it: Hardcore Recondos.

We drove home the point that in infantry combat, the team—squad, platoon and company—was the primary instrument and inspiration. We stressed pride in self, pride in unit and to never let a buddy down. Rifle company designations were changed from the conventional Alpha, Bravo, Charley and Delta to Alert, Battle, Claymore and Dagger, which went down as "Mickey Mouse" until the troops got into it and thought it was very cool.

Hardcore soldiers wouldn't look like bums anymore, either. They'd shave every day, wear their gear properly and always be in camouflage when on ops. And the leaders made it happen by setting the example and being hard but fair.

This was all viewed as "chickenshit" at first and I was considered, to quote Doc Holley, "the original GI Joe lifer sent from Hell to burn their hides with fire and brimstone." As Claymore Company's Jim Robertson put it in a February letter to his parents: "Our new colonel is nuts. It would take a week to tell you all the nutty things he's done, so I'll make it short. Line companies are offering $1,600 for his dead body. He won't last long. He'll get zapped. He's stark-raving mad."

"Nobody liked Hack," Alert Company's Tom Aiken recalls. "I remember the guys from "B" Company talkin' about, 'We're goin' to kill the sonofabitch, we're goin' to put a bounty on him.' And I'm tellin' you the truth if I ever told it in my life, I turned around and glanced at one of them and I said, 'I'll throw in the first twenty dollars.'"

But each time they saluted, they gave themselves a little subconscious commercial, a brainwashing that they were Hardcore, and after a while, I knew they'd begin to believe they were the meanest mothers in Vietnam.

The men of the soon-to-be Hardcore Battalion hadn't seen anything yet. Threats or no threats, I continued to issue them a daily basic Brown Shoe Army ass-kicking and tightened both the discipline and standards more and more. Of all the many traits needed to survive and win on the battlefield, discipline is number one. Without absolute discipline, you lose. And these guys still had virtually none.

I had a simple conversion plan. We'd concentrate on the ABCs of soldiering and follow Vince Lombardi's great leadership example: Forget the Hail Marys and fancy footwork, just work on the blocking and tackling. Where the skills the men had learned in basic and advanced infantry training were concerned, we had to start from the ground up, beginning with the soldier, then the squad, then the platoon.

I started by telling all Battalion leaders, "If you take care of your soldiers, they'll take care of you." According to Battle Company's Lieutenant Carl Ohlson, an OCS draftee who was sharp as a Hinson custom knife, "The rules were simple: Check weapons, check feet, show that you care and let the troops know if we get into deep shit, help will be on the way."

I used every second of every day to train and instill discipline, beginning with something as basic as making sure every man wore his steel pot and carried his weapon at all times. We trained in the firebase, we trained on ambush patrol, we trained sweeping a patch of jungle, we trained searching for Charley. I stressed to all of the unit leaders that all of the drills must be executed over and over again until they became automatic. I wanted these soldiers to roll into a firing position or take counterambush action even in their sleep.

Close combat allows little time to think. Do it right in training and you'll do it right when the incoming slugs flash by. A soldier has to react like a boxer. Basic training back in the States was a cakewalk compared to what we were going to put the boys through now.

In the first days, the rifle companies conducted combat operations along with hard training outside of the "Wagon Wheel"—patrolling and ambushing the waterways and trails. When they got that right, we conducted Eagle Flights, infantry raids from choppers at VC targets. I very consciously made the soldiers of the Battalion sweat, endure bitching conditions and suck up a lot of pain.

These drills against a real opponent who shot back started early in the morning and ended late, just as the sun went down. All day, Press and I were everywhere, observing, critiquing and chewing ass. All corrections were made on the spot; we busted chops and ripped butts until they got it right. The men moaned and groaned, but sacrificing and suffering together gave them pride in taking "all that crazy bastard could throw at us," as Lieutenant Tahler describes it.

As night approached, the units returned and took up the basics of defense. They improved their fighting positions, they cleaned their weapons, they set out claymore mines, they assigned sectors of fire. We called frequent stand-tos and leaders walked the line checking out their troops.

Hot chow, routine under Lark, was now a blurred memory from softer days. My idea of looking after the troops was not to spoon-feed them, but to make them as hard as forged steel, deadly in their kill-or-be-killed trade. Eating C-Rations when everyone knew hot food could easily be flown in made the point better than ten lectures: The ways of the past were over. Stay Alert and Stay Alive.

You can't make a unit proud by praising it and you can't make a soldier proud by telling him how tough or good he is. That's the superficial stuff. No pain, no gain. They had to earn it.

The standard was perfection, and not just for the grunts; all Battalion support personnel—cooks, clerks, supply, drivers—were to be soldiers first. I told XO Mergner to shape up the folks who brought up the rear, to make sure they knew how to use their weapons, to check their training in other infantry basics. Rear-echelon violators who didn't change their sloppy ways would need those skills. And fast. The minute I caught them fucking off, they'd find themselves in a rifle platoon.

As for rear-echelon stoners, I came down on them with a hard fist and they never knew what hit them. Grass and heavier shit were easy to come by in Vietnam. Out in the boondocks, marijuana grew wild. "We used to go after it with the machine gun and set it on fire to destroy it," recalls Preston Lancaster, a standup grunt from the 2nd Platoon of Claymore Company. Anyone I caught doing drugs was out on his ass the same day, though the problem was never as bad as Hollywood made it out to be when the movies finally got around to doing Vietnam. The worst of it was in the cities and rear areas. Out in the field, it was different. For one thing, you could pick up the sweet smell of grass a mile away, so taking a toke meant you could be pushing your face right into a sniper's sights. "I never saw any guys smoke in the bush," Lancaster says. "We just didn't want anybody using that stuff around us."

A few undoubtedly did, but most of the grunts knew that if your head was bent, chances were good that you'd get careless. Out in Indian country, getting high could very quickly get you dead.

Regardless of my heavy schedule, I made sure to talk to every replacement, to welcome them to the Hardcore before they went out to their units. At night, I'd come back from operations late and Sergeant Major Press would have the replacements assembled and waiting. I stressed to each new man how important he was, how important it was to follow the basic fundamentals of the infantryman's trade. With the zeal of evangelists, all Hardcore leaders drilled into the new guys that when they joined the Hardcore, they were joining a special Brotherhood.

I made the code for these leaders simple and clear:

Fight smart. Never be in a hurry.

Lead from up front.

Set the example.

Take care of the troops before you take care of yourself.

Keep good commo going.

Follow the *Vietnam Primer* and *The Combat Leader's Guide.*

The troops continued to bitch, but that changed when they saw the tough love was for real. One day Mergner saw a soldier wearing jungle boots with the toes worn out and immediately gave him a pair of his own, which happened to be the right size. The story spread like wildfire—someone finally cared. Not long afterward Mergner went down in the C&C chopper to pick up a soldier wounded by a mine. As the medics slipped the wounded man onto the chopper floor, he looked up at Mergner, grinned, saluted and said, "Hardcore Recondo, Sir."

A new, gung-ho attitude started to take hold. One day, Private First Class Famous Howard's squad got into a firefight and killed several VC. As Howard was checking out their bunker, looking for documents and weapons, one of the "dead" VC reached up and grabbed him around the neck. Howard jumped back, pulling the VC out of the bunker, fired a mean right cross and coldcocked him. "I could have easily shot him," Howard recalls. "But the captain told us a live prisoner is worth a hundred dead soldiers."

Some days were better than others. Stand-tos in the morning and the evening were good times to walk the perimeter, talk to the soldiers, see their progress and take their pulse. In Claymore Company's sector, I spotted a familiar face: Sergeant Jerry Frazier, who'd been in my stateside battalion.

Frazier popped me a perfect salute, almost blowing out my hearing with a loud "Hardcore Recondo, Sir." Before I could respond, he started spouting off the Principles of Leadership.

"Hold on, young sergeant. What's this all about?"

This fine Shake and Bake draftee sergeant braced at attention. "Colonel, last time we met at Fort Lewis you caught another sergeant and me taking an unauthorized smoke break. You chewed us out for not being with our soldiers. You said, 'The next time I see you, I want you to have memorized the principles of leadership and I'm going to ask you for them.' Well, this is the first time I've seen you since then. Do you want me to continue, Sir?"

"Nope. Good to see you, Sergeant Frazier. You're one of the few guys I've met in this lash-up who has his shit together. If we all keep smoking the troops, this outfit will turn around. You've been down this road with the 'Stay Alert, Stay Alive Battalion'—you know the drill."

"Wilco, Sir," Frazier replied. I'll never know if he was happy to be with me again—others were certainly miserable—but I was sure happy to see him and I wished I had fifty more NCOs just like him.

Many combat vets come to think they know it all and start taking short-cuts. They blow off the basics and neglect the little things that keep them alive because they get cocky or think it's better for their men's morale. They build a fire at dusk, smoke at night, walk on trails, don't carry their weapons, goof off on security, don't safe their grenades or weapons, wear mosquito repellent on ambush or patrol, don't send out flank security on Ops. Shortcuts that get you killed.

It's been my experience that if you can get an infantry replacement through the first few months of combat, his chances of making it improve dramatically. The 4/39th Battalion had probably turned over thirty or forty times in four years. I had to get time under their belts.

"It's easy to understand why there was no institutional memory, why morale was so low and why the troops were disillusioned," Lieutenant Tahler recalls. "Few officer leaders knew what they were doing. The top brass were fighting another war and most of us junior officers were trained to take Normandy, not fight insurgents. The grunts knew what was happening, but few officers listened to them. 'What do they know? They're just enlisted men' was too often the prevailing attitude. The same mistakes were made month after month—and mistakes ended up being dusted off."

Individual replacements poured in. To the brass at Dong Tam looking at charts reflecting assigned strength, the Battalion was in pretty good shape. But the charts didn't tell the real story of a fragmented band of individuals with little skill, cohesion, spirit or teamwork; and half of those listed as assigned for duty were sick, lame, lazy or siphoned off for some other job.

In Vietnam, just as the soldiers were replaced individually, so were the officers—in a mad martial version of musical chairs. If a grunt was lucky enough to make it through 365 days in a rifle platoon, he'd have had six to ten different platoon leaders, four to six company commanders and two to three battalion and brigade COs. Above platoon level, the names of most of the leaders were a mystery to most of the grunts.

When I look back, it's truly amazing that in 1969 the grunts in Vietnam hadn't blown their senior leadership to hell. Too many of the senior brass just didn't serve them and, in fact, treated them as irrelevant and dispensable. What Vietnam usually meant to those sorry bastards was a vital combat command punch on their tickets and a chest full of People's Hero badges they didn't deserve.

So, it wasn't surprising that the soldiers of the 4/39th mistrusted their officers. And if they were suspicious of me when I first took command, they really had a royal hard-on for me now. They viewed me as just another "bird" whose mission it was to drop more shit on them and soon fly away.

Rifle squad leader Jim Robertson summed up the troops' point of view. "If we'd known that General Ewell was calling us a 'pussy battalion,' we would have resented it to the point of rage. By the time Hack thundered in, we all had our doubts as to the veracity of the term 'superior officer.' Back home, the mantra was 'Don't trust anyone over thirty.' On the line, the rule of thumb was 'Don't trust anyone over E-5—and that meant buck sergeant.'"

The Battalion mission seemed to change with the casual whim of every passing brass hat. "In the six months I spent on the line we were Mobile Riverine assault troops, Bushmaster ambush specialists, Dong Tam security, Airmobile shock troops and finally Hardcore Recondos. 'Higher Higher,' as

Division Command was known, sent us into the bush on some of the looniest operations imaginable," Robertson said. "We did everything from massive Battalion-strength sweeps to platoon-sized outposts in the most indefensible positions available, to a night raid on a VC village launched from rubber boats. There was a pervasive belief among us that if the Army could ever figure out what we were supposed to be, we might just have enough time to get good at it before we were either killed or rotated home."

"So, when a fire-breathing Screaming Eagle named Lieutenant Colonel David H. Hackworth descended upon us from the north and started kicking ass and taking names, the reaction among the troops was to wag our heads, exhale a collective sigh and mutter, 'Jesus! Now what?'"

FIVE

My Dien, Plain of Reeds
04 FEBRUARY 1969

As soon as the engineers reported that they couldn't clear all of the mines inside Firebase Dizzy's perimeter, I sounded off to Brigade Commander Colonel John Geraci about getting out of there ASAP. We were not going to continue losing legs just to follow Lark's dumb plan.

"I'll take it to Ewell," he said. "Get back to you pronto."

The next day he radioed, "Do you think that ragged-ass outfit of yours can handle an independent mission?"

"Fucking A! We can start moving yesterday."

"Division has intell that Charley's going to funnel in a lot of people and supplies from Cambodia to zap us at Tet. Ewell wants to stop it," Geraci said.

"I'd take a Search and Destroy Mission to the moon to get away from Dizzy," I said.

"Well, you're not far off—your AO's the Plain of Reeds. Your mission is to interdict enemy movement coming in from Cambodia. Go out there and blow 'em away."

The operation would give us a Task Force, as Geraci said, "with the whole ball of wax." We'd have an air cavalry troop, an artillery battery, an army chopper company, engineers—all the logistical support and all the heavy chopper lift we'd need for our 800-man light infantry battalion. It was a new commander's dream, a long shakedown cruise, fighting and training far from the flagpole. I could put my brand on the Battalion.

"Thanks, Mal Hombre, I owe you," I said, mentally running the numbers, estimating how soon we could move, what chopper lift we'd need.

"How long will it take to move your lash-up?"

"We can start at first light."

The Battalion Task Force was assigned an AO that would've kept General George Patton's entire Third Army flat out in World War II—bigger than Los Angeles County, with gangs twice as mean. It wasn't far from Ap Bac, the site of one of the early defining battles of the war, fought six years before. As usual, the intell officer who briefed us on the weather, terrain and enemy for the mission knew nothing of that battle nor that our new AO was the birthplace of the Communist insurgent movement in Vietnam.

We deployed initially to My Dien in the Plain of Reeds, a wide, flat stretch of marshland along the Cambodian border. The Special Forces (SF) team there had a good handle on the local history, the countryside and the enemy. The snake eaters were as happy to see us as early American settlers must have been when a U.S. Cavalry unit bivouacked at their homestead. And by setting up our CP inside their camp so we didn't have to secure ourselves, we gained an additional rifle company to search for the VC.

The SF team knew nothing of the enemy buildup that Division was in a lather about, but they did give us locations where Charley might be hiding. Every day I'd ask, "Where do you think we should stump around?" The best place to get intell is on the ground, at the lowest level possible. In Vietnam this meant an individual SF team or district adviser, so I relished the opportunity and sucked these great warriors dry. The higher you went, the more paper you got and the less valuable the intell. The same is true on the battlefield. If you want to know about the enemy, conditions, the situation, don't ask the brass or their staffers. Always ask the guys on the ground.

But just hours after we'd arrived at My Dien, I received a message from the Brigade TOC: Division Commander "Ewell wants to see Hackworth between 1100 and 1130 hours tomorrow."

That night the paranoia kicked in. I wondered how I'd managed to fuck up so soon. The next morning my gut was still churning as I watched Ewell's chopper land. He immediately drew me aside.

"Colonel Hackworth," he said, "we've gotten reports there's a bounty on your head. Some of your own men want to take you out. Do you know anything about this?"

I did. But when Bob Press, Chum Robert and others had told me the pot was then at $3,500, I dismissed it. Hell, I thought, if I know grunts, they'll do a lot more bitching and betting and the pot will go a lot higher. "Let me know when it reaches $10,000," I told them, and laughed it off.

Sure, the troops were pissed at me. Claymore Company commander Gordon DeRoos told me the day before not to fly over his company—he'd gotten reports that some of his soldiers had been taking potshots at my chopper. But I always had trouble when I took a new command. For the first couple of weeks the guys would think I was crazy, then they got used to my ways.

"It doesn't surprise me," I told him. "I've been pushing them pretty hard. But I've been taking their temperature and I think they're OK."

General Ewell had a different idea. "I want to put in a couple of CID agents as replacements into 'B' Company. We'll ferret out the ringleaders and take 'em away."

"That won't be necessary, General," I said. "It'll sort itself out."

"Play it your way," he said. "It's your life."

That's how we left it. I'd damn sure watch my back, but I wasn't about to change my MO.

I found out later that Ewell checked with a fellow West Pointer, Captain Billy Winston,* Alert Company's CO, who'd been with me in the 101st, to get his take on where I was coming from. Winston, tall, extremely conscientious and as meticulous as a neurosurgeon, told him, "He's a good man. He'll shape the Battalion up."

Every day for the next fifteen days, we moved. We'd establish a firebase, jump the troops all over the area, look for Charley, move on. The rifle companies were lifted by the 191st Army Helicopter Company, the Boomerangs; and the heavy stuff—mortars, artillery, ammo, CP junk and our supplies—was moved by the big choppers, CH-46s.

Lieutenant Bobby Knapp ran the air show, convincing me he was not just a West Point pretty face who happened to be a hell of a fighter, but that he had a good brain to boot. I made a mental note to keep my eye on that boy. Talented leaders like Knapp, focused on a clearly defined objective and pulling together, get the job done. The Battalion had the talent; the challenge was to identify those who had the right stuff, put them in the right slots and point them in the right direction.

I divided the 50-kilometer-by-200-kilometer AO into squares, using the checkerboard technique Hank Emerson developed long before Vietnam and sharpened in the 101st and 9th. "OK," I told my guys. "We'll work these squares today, those squares the following day, these squares the day after that. While we're working the squares, we'll take everything apart: everywhere the enemy could be hiding, every jungle area, every village, every canal. If there's a VC sucking air in that square, we'll find him."

I also borrowed Emerson's Eagle flight or jitterbug tactic. The idea was to give an infantry maneuver unit the choppers—the assets as they were called in the 9th Division—and a large AO to play in. First you pooped them up on intelligence, then you let them hunt. Covered by gunships, the Hueys would buzz along randomly inserting infantry, searching suspected areas, mainly in the bush or nipa palm along the canals. Occasionally, the gun or scout ships would rake an area, hoping some VC having a bad hair day down on the deck would be dumb enough to fire back or panic and beat feet and give his position away. Almost all of our AO was a free-fire zone with thumbs-up rules for engagement. C1/11th Arty, the artillery battery at the firebase, was always on call to put iron on the target.

At first, we found nothing except abandoned VC camps and way stations that hadn't been used in a long time. Charley was laying low, but he still drew blood with a most effective air force—hordes of man-eating mosquitoes.

The Battalion was still at the scrimmage stage, not ready to run any hard plays. And I still needed practice using all the fast-moving toys that came with the Task Force. Fortunately, the aviation commanders were savvy, and until I got the hang of it, they led and I copied.

The first four days of skipping across our huge chessboard allowed the rifle squads and platoons to operate independently, sharpening their very rusty infantry skills. The kids were good, just out of practice and sloppy. "We were damn slack," recalls Alert Company RTO Jimmy Hux. "People would throw away ammo, frag grenades and equipment they figured was too heavy to carry. Guys would get tired of humping a claymore and they'd just throw it in the bush for the VC to pick up and use on us later. All this came to a screeching halt out in the Plain of Reeds."

Ever so slowly, as we got our act together, I could see teamwork and unit cohesion starting to click. But the rifle platoons remained our weakest link. Grass won't get cut with dull blades, no matter how powerful the lawn-mower engine. I made it my first priority to hone the capability of the rifle platoons to a fine edge.

Press would go out with one unit, I'd hit the ground with another, walking with the company commander long enough to check him out. After that, I'd move down to one of his platoons and check out its leader, then join a squad for a look there. At the end of the day, a chopper would bring me back to our temporary firebase—going up amid moans and groans from the headquarters troops—where I'd plan the next day's operations. The CP boys had gotten used to staying in a fixed location and didn't like all the moves. Every time they got dug in and set up, down came the choppers and up went the bitching.

Assistant Operations Sergeant Jim Silva took these moves as personal harassment by Hardcore 6—me. To advertise his displeasure, he lined up large white rocks in front of the Battalion landing pad in letters that stood out as clearly as a neon sign on Broadway: a six-foot F.T.A.

Battalion Operations Sergeant Jerry Slater tried to convince me the acronym stood for "Fun, Travel and Adventure," the reasons I'd signed up. No way, Sergeant Slater. Silva's "Fuck the Army" was the same slogan scrawled on so many 4/39th helmets when I first took over.

I got the message, but so did Jim "Hi Ho" Silva. Before the sun set, he was a rifleman in Dagger Company. After that, the FTA white-rock graffiti disappeared. Silva got wounded six months later as a Platoon Sergeant; he returned to the States with more medals than a Russian general and a new reputation as one Hardcore dude. "All the moving around seemed to be kind of stupid," Silva recalls. "Filling sandbags and digging in 110-degree heat wasn't a lot of fun. But once I got to a rifle company it didn't take long to learn that Hackworth was right. My first day there, a guy right in front of me tripped a booby trap and blew his foot off, and I was going like, 'Holy shit, this is a bad place.' Filling sandbags wasn't so bad."

I told the troops, "If we're gonna make you killers, you gotta be animals first."

"The first weeks were rough," Sergeant Jerry Slater remembers. "We'd dig in, which took some creative thinking in that we were mostly digging below sea level. Then we'd build overhead cover and then we'd move. We were tired, hot and pissed off. It wasn't long before we became killer animals."

These troops had seldom seen a colonel before except high in the sky in a helicopter telling them to move faster or sitting safely back in the rear. From Leonidas to Alexander the Great to Wellington to Stonewall Jackson and to Rommel, the very core of leadership has always been to set the example and let soldiers see that their leaders care about them, share the same risks and conditions. In the old Army Horse Cav, the leader's creed was: "Take care of the horses first, then your men, then yourself." The best way to get this message across is by living as the troops do, leading from up front, and always, always setting the example: first up, last to eat and last to lie down.

We were now in the dry season. I could only imagine what hell these kids went through in the months before I got there when the monsoon rains turned the Delta into one oozing frog pond. You could get the leeches off with the lit end of a cigarette—but even one of those ugly motherfuckers sucking your back, chest, arms or neck made for a heavy mind trip, and where there was one there were thousands. Get out of the water, the red ants preyed on you; they considered the rare patches of dry land their property and fought fiercely to maintain ownership—VC ants. Just when a soldier thought he couldn't endure the heat, the humidity, the mosquitoes, the leeches and the ants, the night would explode in a summer storm, and suddenly his teeth would be chattering from the cold.

I watched how long the companies stayed out with more attention than a stockbroker supervising a Mafia don's portfolio. Immersion foot—trench foot in World War I—could knock a platoon or company out as fast as the nastiest minefield. S-3 Sergeant Slater actually kept a foot-count clock up on his Operation's map, which showed to the minute how long each rifle unit had been out.

"Our skin was always wet," recalls Jerry Sullivan of his old days ramrodding a squad in Claymore Company. "It broke down, leaving us susceptible to infection. Pieces of flesh fell off, leaving open ugly ulcers that could well have been caused by bullet wounds. The Delta was like one large sewer. We humped in it, ate in it, drank its water and fought and bled in it. The terrible heat and humidity of the day was replaced by bone-chilling cold at night. If war is hell, then the Delta was the Devil's own personal torture chamber."

I tried to make sure the rifle soldiers dried out for a few hours every day by lying up in the bush with their boots off and bringing them back to the firebase about every four days for a four-day stint of security duty.

The policy kept them combat ready and equally important, it showed their commander cared about them. Sun Tzu tells the story of a famous general who ate the same food, carried his own gear and shared every hardship with his men. "One of his solders was suffering from an abscess," wrote Sun Tzu, "and the general himself sucked out the virus. The soldier's mother, hearing this, began wailing and lamenting. Somebody asked her, 'Why do you cry? Your son is only a common soldier, and yet the commander in chief himself has sucked the poison from his sore.' The woman replied: 'Many years ago...the same general performed a similar service for my husband, who never left him afterward and finally met his death at the hands of the enemy. And now that he has done the same for my son, he too will fall fighting."*

At the Base the soldiers wore flip-flops from Saigon—prescribed in a smart move by Doc Holley and his number two, Lieutenant Bill Casey—so the sun could dry out their feet. Holley also recommended that the men on dry-out cut off the lower portion of their trouser legs, just below the side pockets. "This little gesture did wonders for morale," S-4 Lieutenant Bob Johnson remembers. "I still have my cutoffs at home in a trunk."

But the troops really had the red ass over how I handled resupply. Under Lark the unit had hot food flown in Mermites—insulated containers—at least once a day, often twice. Peachy keen for Boy Scouts on a campout, but not in a battle zone where the helicopter's landing would flag exactly where

*Sun Tzu, *The Art of War* (New York: Delacorte Press, 1989)

our troops were to the enemy hard at work trying to find them.

Constantly sweating in the hot, humid weather presented a severe problem. The water in the canals wasn't exactly Evian. "Drink it," I told the boys. "Add Halizone tablets." The nasty mix tasted like seawater flavored with iodine, but it beat a heat stroke from dehydration.

Gradually the men's attitude was changing. It had a lot to do with being off on our own independent mission—and the fact that we had taken few mine or booby-trap casualties since we arrived in the area. By the fourth day in the field, both Bob Press and I reckoned the unit was off its knees, taking its first wobbly steps. Morale was still not over the moon, and Press and I had not endeared ourselves to anyone in the Task Force. But I purposely remained old stone face, careful not to crack a smile; we had a long way to go.

My job was soldier simple: It began with leading from up front. I just followed Rule Six of the old Army's Principles of Leadership: Know your soldiers and look out for their welfare.

And, little by little, they got to know me.

Bob Press and I continued going out with the troops, spending time with each of the Battalion's twelve rifle platoons. When I felt they were ready, I stressed to all the leaders that we were going to take the night away from the Viet Cong—we were going to boogie day *and* night.

"We weren't too happy to hear about the new twenty-four-hour shift," Squad Leader Sullivan remembers, "but it worked. Soon we were ambushing the enemy at night and taking him out as he slept by day. We busted our balls day and night; and, instead of morale going down, it went up. Within a couple of weeks the Battalion became cocky, profane and proud."

On 18 February, I tagged along with Sullivan's squad. With the rest of Claymore Company, Sullivan was checking out a marshy area; intelligence indicated that the wet zone was a possible VC Way Station. We were in water up to our waists when the trooper in front of me set off a mine.

BWOOM!

The explosion sent shrapnel flying in all directions. Amazingly, it didn't wound anyone in the squad. Simultaneously, the point man saw half a dozen armed VC bugging out and took them under fire. The grenade was probably part of their alarm system.

Sullivan and his point man cut down four VC. The rest disappeared in the marshes. I tried to get in on the action, but the worthless AR-15 carbine—a modified M-16 developed by the USAF as a survival weapon, the same weapon I'd bad-mouthed back in 1963 when I tested it for General Pat Cassidy at Fort Campbell—jammed after I got off a few rounds. My stupidity in carrying that piece of garbage could have cost me my life. It was a cute little thing, a prestige toy. Colonel Lark had presented it to me along with his little white john. That sonofabitch didn't work at Campbell where Cassidy gave it thumbs down for the Division, and it didn't work now. Sexy but not GI-proof—I'd have done better throwing Lark's little white shithouse at the VC.

It wasn't until evening, back at the firebase, when I pulled off my mud-encased boots that I noticed a two-inch slash just above my left ankle. A piece of shrapnel from the booby trap had torn through my boot and buried itself in my leg. I hadn't felt a thing. Mud had sealed the wound tighter than a medical compress. Doc Holley cleaned it out, and by morning I was good-to-go with a new pair of boots and an easy Purple Heart.

The next night, Bob Press called from a night ambush just outside Moc Hoa with Dagger Company. He asked me to come out first thing in the morning and he was waiting when my chopper landed, as pissed as I'd ever seen him.

"What's happening, Sergeant Major?" I asked.

"Last night we had twelve VC walk past us. The CO said he didn't want to give away our position, so he didn't kill a single one of them. They were sitting ducks!"

He didn't want to give away our position?

A memory as vivid as the day it happened flashed in my brain.

January 1951. I was a squad leader in the 25th Recon Company in Korea. We were about twenty miles ahead of the front lines, doing our thing: delaying, deceiving and denying the enemy's scouts from fixing the frontline trace of the 25th Division. It was two A.M., turn-you-blue cold, and quiet as a VC sapper infiltrating a position except for the trainlike whistling of the battleship USS *Missouri*'s 16-inch giant shells hammering in front of us.

Suddenly I heard loud stamping, like a herd of elephants, coming at us. Then, as far as I could see in the half-light of the moon, I saw enemy troops, double-timing down the tracks, column after column of enemy soldiers with automatic weapons at high port.

When they got close, our machine guns and rifles started firing. The enemy scrambled off the trestle into the paddy, precisely in front of our rifle squad, whose M-1s and Browning Automatic Rifles chopped them down with short bursts of grazing fire interlocked with deadly plunging fire from our good old 1919 Browning .30-caliber light machine gun. As I waited for the tanks to start blasting with their antipersonnel canister rounds, I thought, We're going to whack these guys good. Right then, a green star cluster— hand flare—exploded in the sky, our signal to withdraw. We gave the enemy a final blast, hopped on the vehicles and hauled ass back through the American lines. The last guy out, rifleman Ken Sheldon, later estimated we'd killed or wounded several hundred Chinese soldiers.

It was light by the time we passed through the American lines and got back to our base camp at an abandoned schoolhouse in Chorwon. Wild with Irish rage, I sought out my platoon leader, who'd ordered the retreat.

"How come you didn't fire the main guns? We could've killed a lot more of those bastards."

He looked at me and said—you guessed it—"I didn't want to give away our position."

"You're a yellow-bellied sonofabitch. I should take you out right now," I snapped.

I think I would've killed him if I'd brought my rifle with me, but my platoon sergeant, Master Sergeant Charley Taylor, dragged me away. "Cool it, young sergeant," he said.

But I didn't. I went back to my squad, got my pack and my M-1 rifle and went AWOL to join the Eighth Army Ranger Company, just down the road.

Going AWOL wasn't an option this time around. With blood in my eye, I sought out the Company Commander. The first day I'd walked with his company, he'd gotten lost and was slow to react to a small contact. I figured him a lightweight then, but didn't sack him. I'd seen a lot of slow-starters turn around and become champions.

"Is this true?" I asked him. "You didn't trigger the ambush?"

"Yes. I didn't have enough men," he explained.

I got into his face. "If you're defending, the ratio is one defender to every three attackers. With your eighty men, you could have taken on at least a battalion of VC—and there were twelve of them. Twelve! And you had total surprise." I was burning. "You failed to do your fucking job. You're out of here!" I fired him on the spot.

Fall out.

I told him to get into my chopper and he was gone from the Battalion by noon. "We were happy to see that sonofabitch get fired," Lieutenant Carl Hedleston says. "Not only was he abusive and a coward, but he didn't give a shit about his men."

I discovered later that a few days before I sacked the sorry motherfucker, he'd given Hedleston's platoon a flamethrower. Hedleston argued that it was too heavy, no point in having a soldier pack it around. In the two months he'd been out in the paddies he'd never had to use a flamethrower even once. "Why don't we leave it back at the firebase and fly it in when we run into some VC in bunkers or caves?" Hedleston asked.

"Don't argue with me, Lieutenant," the captain snapped. "Do what I say."

Hedleston issued the ball-breaking heavy flamethrower to his biggest and strongest trooper. "He just strapped it on his back like a mule, plowed ahead and never complained. The evening before the captain was canned, I got a call to have the flamethrower man report to the company CP ASAP. Thirty minutes later he returned, outraged.

"'What's wrong?' I asked.

"'The captain made me kill ants with the flamethrower. For three fucking days I carried this monster and he makes me burn the area around his sleeping position so he could get a good night's rest.'

"The next morning, we're moving down a canal and my man rips off the flamethrower, tosses it in the canal, and screams, 'Fuck it, fuck it, fuck it.'

"I looked up and said 'Combat loss' and the platoon had a great laugh. We watched it go down like the *Titanic*."

When I'd been out walking with Dagger Company, one of the platoon leaders, a Citadel graduate who'd earned his officer's commission through OCS, John Roberson III, impressed me enough that I immediately made him the acting CO. He had only a few months of combat experience under his belt, but what mattered to me was what he had in his belly and head—a lot of fire and a lot of smarts. A natural leader, unlike his predecessor, he loved to mix it up with the enemy as much as he loved his soldiers.

The airfield at Moc Hoa, our staging base on the Vietnamese Cambodian border, was a dangerous place. Several NVA regiments were holed up just across the border in Cambodia, and the mercenaries hired by U.S. Special Forces were feuding with a local ARVN outfit.

The two groups hated each other as much as they hated the NVA nestled in their sanctuary across the border. The SF indigenous troops, mainly Cambodians, had been fighting against the Vietnamese for centuries. Both sides were armed to the teeth. At the slightest provocation they'd go at each other like Croats and Serbs. "I was in the Special Forces compound when I heard the chatter of automatic weapons fire," Squad Leader Jim Robertson remembers. "I grabbed my M-16 and made for my position. I took a peek over the wall and spied an ARVN armored car, the wheeled type, with a mounted machine gun on the gun-ring, cruising along just outside the barbwire apron that stretched around the perimeter of the camp. There was an ARVN soldier in the turret firing short bursts at our compound. The mercs were firing back with their Carbines and M-16s. It was a marvelous display of poor shooting, because no one was hitting anything. I was about to grease the guy behind the machine gun when a Special Forces sergeant ran up and told me to cool it."

"It happens all the time. It's a private thing. Stay out of it unless I tell you otherwise," he said.

"Bullshit," Robertson said, and took a bead on the machine-gunner.

"Stay out of it," the SF sergeant shouted, and knocked Robertson's weapon up in the air. "I mean it."

"If that sonofabitch hits any of my people, I'm going to blow him away," Robertson said.

"And you'll start a war with our friends down there," he said with a nod toward the ARVN compound. "Just wait, it never lasts long."

In about fifteen minutes the South Vietnamese shooters, tiring of the game or deciding they'd defended their honor to the satisfaction of their peers, drove down the runway in their armored car and disappeared.

Once the Battalion arrived in Moc Hoa, I slipped over to Battle Company for a surprise visit. What I saw blew me out: weapons strewn everywhere, including fragmentation grenades, Battle Company soldiers drunk or stoned, Cambodian whores running through the company area. When I went into the bush with them, I made a note to keep a sharp eye on their commander. He seemed as nervous as a whore in church.

The young captain, a regular, should never have been given a rifle company command. Weak, no fire in his belly, totally turned off by the war, he'd taken the company over a few months earlier when Lieutenant Larry Neumann was wounded outside of Dong Tam. Neumann had replaced Captain John Seeker a few days earlier, who while on a security mission inexplicably put his company CP in a sampan and was bushwhacked by the VC. They killed one of his RTOs, wounded another soldier, yet a third drowned, and Seeker himself took a gut full of slugs. He had been in command for one week.

Battle Company First Sergeant Thomas Dunn told Bob Press that the captain was a coward. "He always got sick when it came time to walk the Rocket Belt around Dong Tam," Dunn said. "The troops didn't like or respect him. He'd send his men out to Cloverleaf while he sat in his CP."

I decided to have a serious commander-to-commander talk with the guy and caught up with him on the strip in downtown Moc Hoa. I'd put that wild, wild western outpost city off limits because of all the shoot-'em-ups and detailed a 9th Division MP squad to make certain no Hardcore troops found their way into trouble.

The captain was partying with American Special Forces guys, bent out of shape. Meanwhile his troops were a drunken zoo. I hadn't come to Moc Hoa looking to get rid of him, but I fired him right there.

Fall out.

Battle Company needed a stud. Bobby Knapp's name popped front and center in my brain. Knapp had been a red-hot platoon leader and company commander in Battle Company under Lark until he put Bobby in the TOC, seeming to prefer excellent reports and smooth air-movement schedules to first-rate field operations. Priorities were about to change.

When I got back from Moc Hoa, I popped into the TOC. "I was just planning the next day's airmobile operation," Knapp recalls. "Hack in his typical way didn't say anything direct. It was more like, 'If he was the Battle Company Commander he wouldn't be sitting around the TOC.' I looked up and the S-3 was standing there saying, 'You can't leave.' I said 'Bologna'— or words to that effect. I was the Battle Company Commander and I was out of there."

Knapp knew his job and he knew me. "Hack was running the troops harder than they'd ever run before. It's a huge mental shift to go from an easy life to airmobile four or five times a day, walking twenty miles, not getting enough sleep and food. All of a sudden, guys are getting lean and angry. It was a huge change. It shocked everybody. These were teenage kids, nineteen years old, all draftees who didn't understand. In my company there were only two guys who'd been in the Army more than a year. Only two. That means every Squad Leader and Platoon Sergeant was a draftee. They had no maturity in judgment, no experience to take them into a military experience, to tell them what made sense.

"The night I took over the company, I went in and read everybody the riot act. I'd heard that there was a bounty on Hack's head and the bounty was being put up in *my* company. Fortunately, I'd only been away for three weeks and I was credible. When we were walking through minefields and everybody froze, I'd put out claymores and blow them in front of us and clear an area, so I was accepted. I didn't have to prove myself. I went in there and said, 'No more crap. The casualties are down, don't you guys remember when we were dusting off two or three guys out of here every day?'

"The squad leaders, the platoon leaders all looked at each other. Finally, someone said, 'Right. That's the way it was.'

"All of a sudden it was possible to demand that my soldiers shape up. I went through this speech...I said, 'If you're sleeping on guard I'm going to hit you over the head with a rifle butt. Nothing personal, but we're just not going there. The best way for us to get out of this alive and for you guys to go home is for us to be the most dangerous infantry company on the battlefield and that's where we're going. If you're not a big guy and you want to pick a fight, who's it going to be—a 500-pound gorilla or a 120-pound guy, who the hell are you going to punch first? The way we are going to keep the Viet Cong away from us is we're going to start killing them and we're not going to sit here and produce casualties for our side. We're going to produce casualties on their side...Does anybody have any questions or problems with what I said?'

"There was just silence. Just as I was telling them we were about to become a lean, mean fighting machine—I looked up and framed in the doorway in the dark was Hack. He'd come over to see what the hell I was going to do on my first night. I had given this fired-up speech and I saw him laughing, so I walked outside and he said, 'Shithead, what are you doing?' I took it as a term of endearment."

Knapp had been out of West Point sixteen months when he first took command of Battle Company. He was an inspiring, dynamic leader who never sat down, a piss-and-vinegar commander. The day after he raised all that hell with his troops, I walked with his company. About noon, Knapp's scouts spotted an enemy squad in a patch of jungle. He ordered the platoon I was tagging along with to set up a blocking position to the enemy's rear while he maneuvered the main force. I got a little in front of the platoon as it slipped into position, sort of daring some young hero to have a good look at my back.

I figured no one would shoot me in the middle of a fight—where every gun matters. In a firefight, everyone's so concerned with staying alive they don't have time for any crap. The other major factor? I walked with them. I wasn't some Perfumed Prince in a C&C telling them to sweep a minefield, I was a grunt in their platoon. They had to identify with me.

By now Knapp's force had stirred up a hornet's nest, and slugs were flying. When it was over, Battle Company had killed six VC. That little firefight caused the start of a major turnaround in the troops' mind-set. The "Let's Get Hackworth" campaign fizzled out flatter than hot beer. They no longer looked on me as their torturer, but as a leader who would be there when the bullets started flying.

Not long afterward, when we were moving the Battalion from Moc Hoa, Jim Robertson, now a supply guy, was controlling the chopper lift with a PRC-25 radio not far from the TOC tent. It was early in the dry season, very hot. Only a thin sheet of clear water covered the paddies now, while several inches of brown talcum-powder-fine dust had settled on the road. The paddies were firm under foot, solid enough to drive a truck over and for a chopper to land on, but from the air they looked very wet and, to a pilot, seemed like mush.

The Battalion CP was set up in a tent beside the road near the Moc Hoa airfield. The staff and I were inside planning the next phase of the operation when the first chopper, a huge Chinook, came down next to the CP like a tornado and almost blew the tent down. Maps, journals and gear went flying helter-skelter, and everyone and everything was covered with a layer of dust.

I told Lieutenant Larry Tahler to tell Robertson to put the choppers down in the paddies, not on the road next to the TOC.

Tahler returned and said, "I've given Robby the word, Sir."

The next three choppers landed in the same spot.

"When I looked up," Robertson recalls, "Colonel Hackworth himself was stomping across the paddy toward me. I stood up, put one foot up on the dike feeling for all the world like a star pitcher about to be unjustly pulled out of the game because the opposing team was using loaded bats."

"You're not doing your job," I told the highly righteous Robertson. "These people are supposed to go where you tell them, not wherever the hell they please."

"Sir," Robertson said, "with all due respect, those guys in those birds are officers. I'm an enlisted man. I tell 'em where to go and they ignore me because they outrank me. They say, "I'm not getting stuck in the mud because some stupid grunt says so. This ship is my responsibility and that paddy's too soggy to support it.'"

"If rank is the problem," I said, "rank is the answer. For the rest of this operation, you are a Lieutenant Colonel in the United States Army. Use my call sign. You are now Hardcore 6. Consider this a battlefield promotion. If those chopper pilots give you any shit, bust'em."

For the rest of the afternoon, Robertson had a ball. He threatened Warrant Officers and Captains and Majors with court-martials, running the most perfect air-movement operation known to history. Not one chopper pilot dared to land on the road while Lieutenant Colonel Robertson was in command.

When the move was finished and the last Chinook fluttered off, I walked over to Robertson to thank him for a job well done.

This draftee Spec-4 hotshot said, "Thanks, Dave," still playing the role I'd given him. My face went red, and Tahler had to jump between us. He seized Robertson's elbow in a powerful grip and steered him from the field. As they disappeared, I heard Robertson protesting to Tahler: "Sir, I didn't get a chance to ask him how much a Lieutenant Colonel gets for an afternoon's work."

"In this case," Tahler said, "living out the day should be reward enough. Make yourself scarce, Robby."

God, I do love draftees. They keep everyone honest—they're not afraid to get in your face. In times of war, the citizen soldier is the heart and soul of the U.S. Army.

In fifteen days of hard slugging on a blistering hot battlefield with no shelter from the sun, we took heat casualties every day. One afternoon, Dagger Company alone had eight soldiers evacuated by chopper with heatstroke or heat exhaustion. Overheating can be just as fatal as a slug between the eyes. "It was so hot, we cooked like flapjacks," recalls Sergeant Ed Reynolds, who was to become one of the best and most heroic squad leaders in the Battalion even though he didn't want to be a leader. Reynolds quit Benning's Shake and Bake NCO course just before graduating because he thought the training was inadequate and he didn't want to have the responsibility for any deaths.

To outflank the sun, I told the company skippers to try and operate only at night, early morning and evening. But with the air assets for jitterbugging available only in the daytime, any company with an airmobile mission had to take a chance on heat casualties.

We were locked in a strange kind of war with even stranger rules of engagement, and it left all of the guys in the Hardcore Task Force pissed off. We should have been able to slip across the border to do an eye-for-an-eye. How can a war be fought when the enemy can sit across an international border, take a whack at you, give you the bird, and you can't lay a glove on him? When our pilots spotted VC and NVA positions, equipment and personnel just across the line, we were told "hands off." Occasionally, the little bastards would take a shot at us, and we had to grin and bear it. On 11 February, after one of the 7/1st Air Cav scout ships took a snout full of machine-gun fire from Cambodia, I asked Brigade for permission to return fire. The reply was "No direct or indirect fire across the Cambodian border, and you cannot pursue across the border."

Considering the limited enemy contacts we had, the Task Force did damn well. During the fifteen-day mission, we killed 158 VC while losing one of our own—James Thomas Pence, Battle Company, killed 13 February by a booby trap.

While I shook the Battalion down in the Plain of Reeds, XO George Mergner did the same thing back at the Battalion rear at Dong Tam. He knew the drill and just needed my OK to fire up his chainsaw and cut some dead wood. Word got back to Press that the maintenance and administration folks and the sick, lame and lazy were having so hard a time with the XO's ass-kicking purge they called him Attila the Mergner.

Bob Press continued to be my right hand. Without him on the tactical side I couldn't have gotten the Battalion together so quickly.

But the other half of my team was coming up lame. Everything Nev Bumstead touched turned to shit. I'm still not sure whether the job was too big for him or I was pushing too hard. Maybe the problem was that he was newly married and lovesick. Whatever it was, he couldn't handle the pressure, he wasn't pacing himself. Operations Sergeant Jerry Slater caught him on the phone trying to reach his Army-nurse wife in Thailand, talking to her for hours, when he should have been doing S-3 stuff or sleeping.

While on the Plain of Reeds mission, Bumstead made a number of blunders that could've resulted in good men dying. One morning, I directed him to recommend a night ambush position for Winston's Alert Company. An hour or so later I asked him about it and had the distinct feeling he'd forgotten, but he said, "Working on it, boss. Waiting for the intelligence to come in."

When he finally made his recommendation, I told Winston to take our LOH and make a quick recon. Winston rang me from the air and said, "Are you serious? You want me out there with the company in the middle of an ARVN Regional Force outpost? Because that's where the ambush position is." Had Winston gone out there at night without that recon, he would've run into a South Vietnamese minefield and probably gotten shot up by the South Viets to boot.

A few days later, I tasked Knapp's Battle Company with conducting a night raid. The company was to infiltrate into their objective area in the darkness, then cross over a major canal using air mattresses and ropes. I told Bumstead to get clearance for the operation from Brigade. Thirty minutes before Knapp was to cross the canal, his objective was hit by a South Vietnamese Air Force strike followed by an ARVN helicopter combat assault. Had Knapp been on his objective, he and his guys would've been fried.

This time Bumstead's poor excuse was that one of his Ops people had dropped the ball and forgotten to get clearance from Brigade. The truth was, he himself had gone to sleep. By the time the Plain of Reeds mission was over, I knew I couldn't rely on him. More and more, I turned his operational chores over to my artillery officer, Chum Robert, who was Billy Winston's West Point classmate. Letting Chum pull the operational strings, I left Bumstead behind in the TOC to do the paperwork and catch up on his sleep and phone calls.

The shakedown cruise with its total operational freedom slammed the Battalion into high gear. It also allowed me to identify problems, determine the unit's capabilities and assess the strengths and weaknesses of its leaders. I kept careful notes of my observations of the twelve rifle platoons and got rid of the weak and incompetent lieutenants as fast as I could.

It's hard to overstate the incompetence of many of the Shake and Bake lieutenants I inherited. Bob Press told me about one of these lieutenants, who picked up a dud 105mm round. Press told him to freeze and got all his people down behind cover. Then he told him to set it down. Gently. The Lieutenant then moved out. "He was so intent on his map reading that he left his rifle behind," Press told me. I fired him the same day. Off he went to Brigade to be reassigned to another battalion, where he could kill someone else's soldiers.

Fall out.

Bad leaders, dumb leaders, incompetent leaders—what they all do is kill soldiers.

We came out of the Plain of Reeds in good shape. We'd gotten rid of a lot of flab and baggage and cleaned up our act. But we didn't find or clobber a large infiltrating unit. Contrary to intelligence reports, the VC weren't stepping up infiltration of troops and supplies in the AO. Instead, the enemy spent January reinforcing its units in South Vietnam from Cambodia to prepare for Tet 69. The spooks were again one large step behind our very clever opponent.

We did screw with the VC logistical pipeline and we destroyed several tons of rice and salt along with about 1,000 gallons of gasoline and many tons of ammunition and supplies. We also slowed down a lot of boat traffic—sampans—bringing supplies out of Cambodia.

On 17 February at 1800 hours, for example, I tasked Apache Troop 7/1st Air Cav—who worked with us every day—to fly down the Mekong River on his way back to his home base and have a look for VC sampans slipping down the waterway. Known as "The Blackhawks," the Air Cav wore the blue cavalry hats of the Civil War Union Army and painted large yellow cavalry cross swords on the front of their aircraft. They were pros with all the dash and daring of the old horse cavalry and a million times more firepower and mobility.

Ten minutes after the 7/1st lifted off from our firebase, the CO got on the horn to report he'd made good—he was attacking an enemy convoy of sampans loaded with troops and supplies. Though running out of sun, ammo and fuel, he and his boys had sunk about twenty sampans and gotten a number of secondary explosions.

In the dead of the night, 9th Division choppers picked up Billy Winston's Alert Company and Gordy DeRoos's Claymore Company from their night ambush locations and dropped them at each end of the river. They quickly sealed the enemy force the Cav had found between them. Charley wasn't going anywhere. In the morning they found about a dozen very dead Viet Cong soldiers and over thirty tons of supplies in the drink. Had choppers been available right after the Cav strike, we'd have had a much bigger haul.

The next morning, Brigade CO Geraci flew in and met with DeRoos and me at the edge of the river. Chunks of VC bodies and pieces of sampans were scattered all along the riverbank. Apache Troop had brought death and destruction, and DeRoos's and Winston's boys had finished the job.

"The goddamn 4/39th is a new outfit," Geraci growled. "You picked up in the dark, flew fifty klicks and executed a perfect fucking seal, then you blew the shit out of these jokers. I'm not sure the 101st coulda done this good. You and your motherfuckers are now beyond Hardcore."

Geraci's praise ran like electricity among Gordy's troops. "We all felt ten feet tall," says Squad Leader Sullivan. "We'd made the shift to Hardcore in a few harrowing weeks and the troops knew it."

Geraci was a tough SOB, mean as a pit bull, rough as sixty miles of gravel road, the perfect combat leader. I looked forward to working for him in Dinh Tuong Province. After a few cold beers, some hot chow, and a little mail from home, that's where the Hardcore was heading.

SIX

Fire Support Base Moore
19 FEBRUARY 1969

After the Plain of Reeds, Geraci said we'd move to Dong Tam for a few days of rest and refitting and then he'd give us a hot AO. Somewhere along the way, the plan changed and we were sent to FSB Moore, a large complex consisting of about six acres of sandbags, bunkers and supporters. Right in the center of this monument to World War I sat the 1st Brigade Headquarters alongside an artillery battery of eardrum-shattering 155mm cannons that barked almost around the clock.

Instead of a hot mission like hunting down and destroying a Viet Cong Main Force unit, the newly converted Hardcore's next assignment was to secure Fire Support Base Moore. I'd always hated being near the flagpole—and now my hard-forged fighters were the Praetorian Guard. It was like turning a finely honed FBI SWAT team into a bunch of airport security guards.

Securing what Doc Holley immediately dubbed "The Waldorf Moore" required one of the Battalion's rifle companies to man the perimeter; a second, deployed around the FSB, was tasked with stopping VC mortar crews from peppering this fat sitting duck.

"Moore was too close to the wood line," recalls Jim Robertson. "The VC would stretch an inner tube between the forks of a tree trunk and lob hand grenades from their homemade monster slingshot into our perimeter."

Flying grenades weren't the only problem. From the moment most of my troops got to Moore, they scarfed up creature comforts: hot showers, a cold beer ration, three hot meals a day, ice cream and even the occasional movie. I knew if I didn't get them away from the Waldorf in a hurry, all the sweating they'd done in the Plain of Reeds would slide down the chute.

The change wasn't Geraci's idea. If he'd been there, I'd have requested a decent mission and he would have gotten the Hardcore out of Moore faster than you could squeeze an M-16 trigger. But Geraci wasn't there.

I learned he'd left on emergency leave—his wife had died—in a weird way. Soon after the Battalion arrived at FSB Moore, I was out running a minor fight from my C&C when a strange voice came up on my Battalion command net, the frequency I used to contact my company commanders, and started giving orders.

The voice, identifying itself by Geraci's call sign, "Mal Hombre," started talking directly to my commanders—an infraction of the basic rules of command. If your superior orders around the people under your direct control, why are you there in the first place? To make matters worse, he was making absolutely no tactical sense.

"Unknown Station, I don't know who the fuck you are, but you sure as shit ain't 'Mal Hombre.' Get off my net."

The voice coldly replied, "I am the new 'Mal Hombre.'"

Now, let's face it. To call yourself a "Mal Hombre" you have to look like an animal, walk like an animal, *fight* like an animal. For all the above reasons, Colonel Geraci used the name as his radio call sign. When the Division Signal Officer told him this violated Signal Operating Instructions and that he'd have to pick an authorized call sign that changed every month, he said, "Fuck that. I'm 'Mal Hombre,' I've always been 'Mal Hombre'—and you can take your SOI and shove it up your ass."

So who was this phony on my net?

"Look," I said. "Get the fuck off my freq."

I'd set up an SOP within the Battalion that if anyone jammed our net, we'd simply "skip rope." That meant the company commanders would immediately change to a prearranged backup frequency.

"Skip rope," I said. And we all went back to fighting the war on a new frequency, leaving the fake Mal Hombre in our dust.

Not for long. The sonofabitch soon caught up with us.

"Geraci's gone," he said. "This is Colonel Hunt."

Oh, shit, I thought. My old TRUST Trooper buddy, the Division Chief of Staff, Colonel Ira Hunt, didn't have the grunt sense to jump into a foxhole when his position was being overrun. And now the Hardcore was stuck with him.

Major Jim Musselman, an old-timer who'd been with the 1st Brigade for almost a year, told me that when Hank Emerson got hit, Hunt had baby-sat the Brigade until Geraci came in. He had only six weeks to achieve glory, and he almost killed the baby. There was no pacing, no real planning, no maintenance of soldiers and equipment. If you're going to be a Brigade commander for the long haul, you pace your troops, you don't burn out your soldiers or choppers, you're careful and preserve your strength. You want the unit as strong—or stronger—on day ninety as it was on day one. But if you're a hotshot in there for just a short time, like Hunt, you care only about what's in it for you, not what happens to the command after you've left.

Hunt wanted to build a battle record for himself on the backs of the men that would prove him the equal of Douglas MacArthur and George Patton combined, and as a result he didn't give a shit about anybody or anything, including our own casualties. His agenda was all about proving to the world that Ira Augustus Hunt was a boy wonder on the battlefield.

After riding the Brigade hard for forty-four days, he left when Geraci arrived and returned to his job as the 9th Division's Chief of Staff. The

Brigade was a wreck. But Ewell, who seemed to love Hunt like a son, gave him a glowing should-be-general-next-week efficiency report for his brief stint and almost a dozen medals for his heroics as Brigade CO.

Hunt was the type of officer who sent a helicopter from Brigade back to Division with his enlisted aide every morning to fetch him a starched uniform, a highly polished pair of boots and a basic load of ice cream, when down at the fighting level the troops couldn't get birds for priority operational missions. Hunt and Ewell had a symbiotic relationship. They were two of a kind. Both were hated by the troops and neither had a compassionate bone in his body. A Division staffer later told me, "Ewell and Hunt deserved each other."

Ewell awarded Hunt a Silver Star for never getting out of his helicopter as it circled over a fight while he "calmly gave directional guidance to the pilot of his craft." He got a Distinguished Flying Cross "for repeatedly traversing the area of combat in low passes, relaying vital information of the enemy's location." He was awarded a Bronze Star for just "being there" during those forty-four glory days, along with two Purple Hearts—apparently for not bleeding! In one year in Vietnam, Hunt received thirty-five medals, including a second Silver Star for an action no one can recall. It was no coincidence that he was also the Chief of Staff, the officer ultimately in charge of awards and decorations for the Division.

And here he was again, back for another grab at glory.

The only saving grace at Brigade headquarters was Lieutenant Colonel Jerry Carlson, the Brigade XO, and Major Jim Musselman, the very squared away Brigade S-3, who assigned a small AO to what was left of the Battalion. At least we could keep two rifle companies out humping and practicing their skills.

Soon after we arrived at Moore, Captain Dennis Foley took over Dagger Company from Lieutenant John Roberson III, who remained with Dagger when he wasn't pinch-hitting at other companies whenever a skipper was absent.

Foley had been with me in the 1/327th. A savvy commander who'd seen a lot of combat, I'd snatched him from the II Field Force Ranger Company, where he had been Ops officer. Dagger Company, mighty thin at this point, needed him. Although it had an authorized strength of six officers and 158 enlisted men, as Foley himself reported in his book, *Special Men*, he never took more than three officers and eighty-six men to the field. Besides having a "paddy strength" of 50 percent, Dagger was the Battalion's weakest line company. It had been heavy weapons until November, when it converted to a rifle company—and the transition hadn't been smooth because of a succession of bad skippers. My plan was to have his company operate independently as a Ranger Company. Foley, with his 1/327th Long Range Reconnaissance Patrol (LRRP) and recent Ranger Company experience, was the perfect guy to convert the men to sneak-and-peek ops and turn the company around in the process.

One morning when we had the assets, I gave Foley the day's jitterbug mission. The Brigade intell officer assigned a half dozen targets based on hot skinny, and Dagger Company got set to boogie. But Foley wasn't happy. Never in his Irish life did he have any trouble sounding off to his boss, and when I briefed him on the assignment, he let me know in no uncertain terms he needed more time with his unit before drawing a combat operation.

I was not convinced. "Dennis, my lad," I said, "when the sun sets tomorrow, you'll know more about your company than you would after four weeks picking your nose around here. Be at the PZ ready to go at 0500."

"Old age and silver leaves haven't changed you, boss. 0500 it'll be. And by the way, what's my Top Kick's name?"

Foley both made his point and got in the last word too. I loved the guy. This is the beauty of working with people you know and trust. You cut through all the bullshit. There's no game-playing and time wasted feeling each other out. Because you understand one another, you get things done by shorthand. No one's afraid to challenge the boss and vice versa.

By midday, the men of Dagger had made five helicopter inserts and killed six VC. After a slow kickoff, the company was clicking like a team that had played together all season. A couple of hours later, the gunships spotted VC movement along a canal and we inserted Foley's force at both ends to seal their escape routes while the gunships raked down the middle. When the VC, running to escape that mean pummeling, stumbled smack into Foley's ambushes, he racked up twelve more enemy dead.

Foley was jubilant. "Hardcore 6, Dagger 6, got a POW for you. Bop down. Popping smoke. Need to have a powwow. And beware, boss, the place is wall-to-wall mines."

All of a sudden, a red light started flashing in my mind. Hunt was the type of commander who didn't give a fuck about a grunt's legs if it meant a higher body count. He'd demand that Foley sweep through the mined area. No question.

Hunt was as much a threat, as dangerous to the grunts as the VC, and I vowed not to let him screw up my Battalion or fuck over my men, especially Foley's boys now wading through that minefield.

I knew if I told Foley over the radio to pull out, Hunt, no doubt listening in on our frequency, would immediately accuse me of running scared: "He doesn't want to take a few lumps. He had the enemy by the short hairs. He killed eighteen when he could have killed six hundred." So I came up with a new game plan.

"Look," I said to Foley, "you'll fake your radio traffic to me that you're going through there and sweeping, but you won't actually do it. Wait about an hour, call and tell me you've swept the area—that it's cool. Then move to the PZ and we'll pick you up and move you to a new objective. You sure as shit aren't wading through those mines."

It worked. Just as Foley was moving to his PZ, Hunt's chopper landed and he stepped out in a rage.

"Pursuit! Pursuit! Pursuit!" he kept shouting.

Foley *was* pursuing—in the correct way—inserting his men where he suspected the enemy might be located and fighting him on our terms instead of tripping through the minefields. But Hunt was out for blood—anybody's blood—and he couldn't stand the idea that no more VC bodies had been piled up along the canal. He was six foot three or so and turning to fat, the worst kind of bully, and now he was in my face screaming and carrying on as if I were a boot and he a grizzled 1940s Marine drill instructor.

Foley walked up, witnessing our little "conversation"—even getting off on it, for all I know. And as Hunt continued his tirade, I could feel rage travel from my flushed face into my fists. Even though Hunt was my commanding officer, I was about ready to deck him—ending my Army career—when Foley saved it.

"Colonel Hackworth," he said, a twinkle in his eye, "did you mention to the Colonel that our POW might be a senior officer?"

Hunt and I had been too much into our confrontation to pay any attention to the prisoner Bob Press had tied up and was caretaking. But I took one look at Foley, grabbed his great pass and ran.

"Just look at this guy," I said to Hunt. I pointed to the prisoner. "Smooth hands and feet. Look at those weak neck muscles. He hasn't carried a ruck or done any grunt work in years. And those intelligent eyes. It wouldn't surprise me if this bastard wasn't a general."

Hunt was transfixed. In a nanosecond, he processed this new information like a supercomputer and shifted gears. Grabbing the POW, he ran to his chopper and off they flew. I'll bet he could already smell those headlines: U.S. COLONEL CAPTURES FIRST VC GENERAL OF THE WAR...

RICE PADDY DADDY NABS CONG BIGGIE. Mergner says Hunt gave himself the catchy media-friendly call sign Rice Paddy Daddy and that "it appeared in one of the many promotional articles about him in the 9th Division newspaper, which he no doubt strongly influenced as Division Chief of Staff."

For the rest of the afternoon, he was too busy trying to get his "general" to talk to pay attention to anyone else. By the time he discovered the joker was a first lieutenant VC nobody, we'd gone back to work. And by the time the choppers dropped Dagger off near their night ambush positions, they'd killed thirty VC for the day. On top of that, they hadn't tripped any mines or taken any friendly casualties.

And by that time as well, Foley knew his First Sergeant's name— William Ballentine.

Two days later, I visited Foley and his boys in an assembly area just outside FSB Moore. They'd been out four days. I'd asked Hunt to pull them because Foley told me his men's feet were in trouble and they needed a pit stop.

Hunt overrode me. "Remember, Hackworth, mission first, welfare of troops second," he said.

Foley and I walked through the platoon areas where the soldiers had their boots off and drying out, inspecting each soldier's feet. When a leader gets down on his knees and looks and touches his men's feet, it delivers a clear message: That commander cares. Despite all the gold-plated, exotic equipment of war, feet are what give infantry troops mobility—without good feet an infantry unit is like a patrol boat on a dry lake.

While we were checking the soldiers, Hunt choppered in and joined us for the rest of the walk-through.

"Colonel Hackworth," he said in a loud voice as we entered a platoon's assembly area. "Why are your men's feet in such terrible condition? You're pushing them too hard." He loudly repeated this same spiel as he walked through each platoon's area, obviously trying to put me down in front of my troops and make his point that the mission better come first—meaning either I was committed to his body count quest-for-glory bullshit or I'd suffer the consequences. Somehow I managed to bite my tongue, and Foley later got his company together and told the men we'd tried to bring them in sooner. Hunt was that kind of game player, one nasty sonofabitch. Despite his twisted leadership, all four Hardcore rifle companies were now under good skippers, and all were on the mend.

That night Charley lit up FSB Moore with incoming 82mm mortar fire, wounding seven soldiers. Two of these casualties were from Claymore, which was on perimeter security duty. Gordy DeRoos hustled his wounded to Holley's aid station and the Doc patched them up and got them on a medevac bird. The incoming fire continued on and off for about three hours before stopping around midnight. I'd just crawled into the sack when a berserk bull came charging into my bunker.

"Hackworth," Hunt bellowed, "how come those men weren't sleeping under cover? You know that my standing orders are that every soldier will sleep under cover. Your two casualties were sleeping on top of their bunker. There's no excuse for this. It's in direct violation of my orders."

"Colonel, the word went out," I said. "I'll check with DeRoos in the morning."

"Morning, hell," he said. "I want full details right now. Get your fucking ass on the move, mister—I expect you in my CP with a full report ASAP."

In the dim light of my CP, I could see his red face, the throbbing purple veins bulging out of his neck. Any second, I thought, this motherfucker will stroke out and there's no way I'll be calling Doc Holley.

I went to DeRoos's CP. He'd talked to the platoon and squad leaders. The platoon leader had told his troops what to do and followed through with a personal inspection. Everyone was sleeping under cover. The squad leader reckoned the wounded men later chose the cool air on top of the bunker to the furnace conditions and the "dog-sized" rats inside.

"Sir, they were told," DeRoos responded in his calm way. "The chain of command worked. I can't tuck every soldier in this company in bed every night and then make sure they stay in the rack."

"Maybe you can't," I said. "But your squad and platoon leaders have to. Someone should've been checking to make sure everyone on the bunker line was awake and the rest were sleeping in a covered spot. It's that or a fucking court-martial."

DeRoos, a straight shooter, tactically spot-on, had his shit together. I told him to sack out and not to sweat it.

I reported to Hunt as he sat in his sandbagged air-conditioned VIP trailer eating ice cream and explained what I'd found out. Between gulps of what looked like chocolate swirl, he managed to throw one hell of a hissy fit.

"I want DeRoos relieved," he railed. "He's the commander, he's responsible. You said yourself it was a breakdown in the chain of command."

I wanted to shove that big bowl of ice cream up his fat ass.

"Colonel Hunt, DeRoos took a route-step company and in six weeks made it the best in the Battalion. He's as good as they get. No fucking way will I fire him over such a chickenshit incident."

"Don't use obscenity with me, Hackworth. How can you call two of your soldiers being grievously wounded 'chickenshit'?"

Man, this guy could twist anything into a big deal—even a little all-American cussing. Any seasoned commander would have written the whole thing off to a fuckup, to the reality that soldiers would be soldiers, but not this bully. He wanted to break anyone who stood up to him.

"Colonel, if Captain DeRoos goes, I go. I'm the one who should've been out there walking the perimeter all night, not DeRoos. He's been going day and night for six weeks. He briefed his people, walked his perimeter, checked everything was OK and he sacked out."

Hunt glared at me. "We'll see about that in the morning. Dismissed."

I stood in the door for DeRoos for a lot of reasons. One was that I needed good men like him to make the Battalion well again. Another was that the only way to deal with a bully like Hunt is to call his bluff. And, finally, I've always believed that loyalty is a two-way street, up to the boss and down to the troops. The troops come first. If a CO doesn't stick up for his guys, then who will?

The next morning at the Brigade briefing—which I was obliged to attend since I was co-located at FSB Moore—Hunt never said a word about the previous night. He badgered the staff over trivia and was as usual the all-time meanest mother in the valley toward his subordinates. Just his normal routine sadism.

I concluded that his crazy rage the previous night over my two casualties had nothing to do with his concern for DeRoos's soldiers. But men wounded on his watch would make him look less than perfect when General Ewell was briefed the next morning. And I suspect making subordinates heel made him feel better. He probably pulled the same kind of controlling crap when he was a senior-class man at West Point—bullying junior cadets over a pair of shoes that weren't polished to his standards or a bed that wasn't drum tight.

I spent the rest of the day with Bobby Knapp and Battle bopping around the battlefield doing chopper inserts.. His boys killed several VC and one of his scouts found some old graves. I radioed Bobby to ignore them and prepare to be picked up to move to the next target area.

"Negative on that, Hardcore 6," boomed a voice on my Battalion command net. "I want your people to dig them up and count them." Hunt was back to monitoring our internal radio traffic while playing Great Squad Leader in the Sky.

"Wilco, Mal Hombre," I replied, having not the slightest intention to comply with this dumb and demeaning order and feeling sick that I had to call that wimp pretender "Mal Hombre."

"Battle 6, skip rope," I told Knapp.

Once Knapp came up on the alternate radio frequency, I told him to ignore Hunt's order, finish searching out the area a little more to burn up time and then move to his PZ.

Brigade XO Jerry Carlson, who flew with Hunt that day, told me when I got back to Moore that Hunt went nuts flipping through freqs trying to monitor us. Sometimes when you receive a dumb order or have a CO like Hunt, you have to use what I call selective neglect. You know, sort of reinterpret an order.

The 9th Division stressed body count over everything else. Pity the CO whose count consistently ran on the low side. Infantry battalion commanders were required to carry 3x5 cards with the month's body-count totals in their pockets, and they'd better be right up-to-date.

"Jack up that body count or you're gone, Colonel," Ewell would scream. And if they didn't deliver, they would be.

Body count was the way the score was kept in Vietnam. The sophistry was: "The higher the score, the better the unit." Units with high counts must have superior commanders. Ewell, with the highest in Vietnam, was obviously the best commander, a real winner who should be promoted over all those loser lower-body-count commanders. As Ewell's virtual number two—and master counter—Hunt, too, should be sped up the promotion ladder.

A lot of great leaders who simply had bad luck locking onto the enemy or refused to lie or place soldiers where the enemy and/or terrain were not in their favor, found their careers ruined by Ewell. On top of the body-count pressure on the commander, a lot of innocent Vietnamese civilians got slaughtered because of the Ewell-Hunt drive to have the highest count in the land. In a 1969 recommendation for the Presidential Unit Citation, Colonel Hunt cites the Division Friendly-to-Enemy Kill Ratio as 84.9 to 1 for April 1969; he compares this to the "Historical U.S. Ratio" in Vietnam as 10.1 to 1. Yet, the 9th Division had the lowest Weapons-Captured-to-Enemy-Killed ratio in Vietnam. As the troops in Vietnam said, "This says it all."

The 9th Division's "shoot-first-ask-questions-later policy" earned Ewell an accurate nickname: "The Butcher of the Mekong Delta." I reckon that made Hunt "The Butcher's Boy."

The Hardcore grunts weren't the only ones having a hard time with Ira Augustus Hunt. One afternoon Hunt charged into Doc Holley's aid station with a shot-up VC and demanded that the Doc patch him up. "The dude's leg was practically blown off," Holley told me later. "I could see the open, oozing end of his femoral artery. The clowns that brought him in hadn't even put on a tourniquet, so he was just about bled out. He was in agonal respirations; even his pupils were dilated and fixed.. His vessels were all completely collapsed, his blood pressure was 0/0, he had only a very faint, irregular heartbeat. I didn't think there was any way this poor sucker would make it."

Holley and his team of medics worked frantically on the prisoner. They put a tourniquet on his thigh; Doc performed a hasty ankle cut-down to set up a surgical IV and pump max fluid into him. But they weren't going fast enough for Hunt. Right in the middle of the emergency procedure he shouted, "Finish it up. I want to interrogate him now."

"For Christ's sake, the man is dying," Holley snapped. "Time is critical if we're going to save his life."

"I don't care about saving his life. I just want to get some information out of him."

"Get the hell out of my aid station. And if you don't let me do my job, I'm going to charge you for violating the Geneva Convention."

Hunt, purple veins bulging, threatened to court-martial Holley just as the VC died on the table.

"Help yourself," Doc replied coolly. "Maybe I'll get out of here a little early."

Later, Doc Holley heard that Hunt had called him and his medical team "more of Hackworth's smart-ass mavericks."

One late afternoon, I gave Bobby Knapp, one of my chief "mavericks," instructions for the night's ambush festivities—Battle had already become quite the ambush experts—before I hitched a chopper ride back to FSB Moore.

Nev Bumstead was waiting at the helicopter pad when I landed. He breathlessly informed me that Mal Hombre had given him pinpoint sites and ordered him to put out ambush patrols. "He thinks the VC will be hot and heavy tonight," Nev said, his voice quivering, a courtier with inside info from the Emperor.

There was just one little problem. Hunt's sites put Battle in the same area as Alert. Which meant a more than random chance that the two friendly forces would bump into one another and blow each other to bits.

I fought to control myself. Bumstead was *my* S-3, not Hunt's. "Did you pass on Hunt's orders?" I asked.

"Yes, Sir, I did."

The dam burst.

"Nev, you're a fucking idiot! No motherfucker issues orders to my units unless it's me. You're a goddamn staff officer and you had no right to take it on your own to do what you did. I was not exactly out of commo. All you had to do was run it by me on the radio. Then, if I approved, you could've issued the order in my name. That's how the fucking game is played in the United States Army! Christ, a fucking new corporal would have better sense."

We'd reached the TOC, I grabbed a mike, called Commander Billy Winston at Alert and told him to cancel the mission.

"We have our head up our ass right now," I told him. "I'm sorry. Out."

Pros don't fuck up like that. What if the operation hadn't been called off and two of our ambushes from Alert and Battle ended up in the dark at the same place shooting each other up? I'd seen friendly fire too many times in Korea and Vietnam. There's nothing friendly about the casualty lists.

Bumstead didn't seem to share my concern. "Sir, I was simply following Colonel Hunt's orders. What choice did I have?"

"Jesus," I said, my voice cold with rage, "you went to West Point. You went to Fort Benning. You've been here on the battlefield for four fucking years. A fucking Girl Scout would have better judgment. Hunt can't issue orders directly to subordinate units. If every senior commander did that, there'd be total chaos. You're just as hopeless as he is, and I'm about ready to kick your fucking teeth down your throat."

Bumstead should have known better than to go along with Hunt's micro-managing our unit—and known that I'd have backed him all the way. He should have said, "Got the mission, Sir," and then gotten me.

"Call Brigade and tell 'em I'm back and I've canceled Hunt's ambushes," I said, getting back to the crisis at hand.

Within five minutes, Hunt stormed into our TOC, eyes bulging, face fire-engine red, veins snaking purple along his neck. That morning it was "skip rope," then Holley got into his face, and now the worst sin of all—I'd dared to cancel his lousy order. His little martinet world was falling apart.

Hunt came thundering up screaming that no one, but no one, could cancel his orders and we went face-to-face. Mergner recalls my blasting back, "Colonel, you don't tell me how to fight my Battalion and I won't tell you how to build your fucking bridges." Then I suggested we leave the TOC. If I punched the bullying motherfucker out, it would be best if it were just the two of us—no eyewitnesses.

Once we got outside, I told him exactly what I thought of him and how his constant interference in my unit's operations put my men at risk.

"You don't issue orders directly to my subordinate units, and I'll be damned if I take your shit."

His face got even redder but his tone went sub-zero. "Let me remind you, Hackworth, that I'm your Brigade Commander and you're being insubordinate."

"You can pull rank all you want, Colonel, because no matter what you are, you're not a soldier."

"I could relieve you, Hackworth!" His voice rose several decibels.

"Yeah, well, go ahead. Before the sun sets tomorrow night, I'll be commanding another battalion in another brigade in another division right here in Vietnam. But if I leave the Battalion, I promise I'll take you with me, Colonel. We're talking about men's lives here, not your fucking career."

All the time we'd been shouting at each other I'd been standing next to a waist-high blast wall of dirt-filled nylon sandbags baked by the sun until they were as hard as furnace-fired bricks. As he stalked off for the shelter of his Command bunker, I glanced down to where I'd been pounding on one of the bags while I made my points with Hunt. The bag looked like a sixteen-pound sledge had crushed it to shit.

Twenty minutes later, the Brigade TOC called and ordered me to report immediately to Colonel Hunt.

Oh man, I thought, you've had it. And my paranoia was not inappropriate—I mean, what would you do if you considered yourself a Master of the Universe and a subordinate ripped into you that way? For sure, Hunt had gotten the green light from Ewell to sack me and now he was about to do the deal on his turf in a room filled with his witnesses. A voice in my head said, In one hour you and that motor mouth of yours will be on a chopper headed for Saigon. You'll never see the Hardcore again and your Army career will be dead as a slab of beef in a chill room.

In the U.S. Army nothing is as final as being relieved in combat.

As I walked, I ran Hunt's twenty-minute conversation with General Ewell—as I imagined it—through my head:

"Hackworth's out of his mind, Sir. Raging, threatening to kill me, pounding his fist on a sandbag like a madman." Once he had Ewell, his voice would go syrupy, feigning concern. "He's over the top, General. Classic case of combat fatigue. Got to get him to a shrink right away. The man's a danger not only to himself but to his command and our soldiers."

But damn it, I was right, and if right meant court-martial, fuck it. One way or another I'd take the Butcher's Boy down with me.

SEVEN

The moment I entered the 1st Brigade TOC, I knew something ugly was going down. Shockwaves of tension bounced across the large sandbagged bunker housing the Brigade's nerve center—that "shit's happening" vibe.

Captain Edward Clark met me at the entrance. He wasn't smiling.

"Sir, there's trouble," he said. "A LRRP team's in a hot LZ. Colonel Hunt's having kittens."

LRRPs were small all-volunteer recon teams, highly vulnerable, tasked with serving as the eyes and ears of the commander and slugging it out only when they had to. In short, one of the most dangerous jobs in Vietnam.

Clark took me to Hunt, who monitored the Brigade radio net. He looked like a stockbroker who'd just gotten word the market was in the toilet. I marched up to him still into court-martial mode.

"Colonel Hackworth reporting as ordered, SIR!"

Cadet Hackworth gave his acting CO one of the most exacting salutes he'd ever thrown, but Hunt was too preoccupied to notice. He pointed to a large map standing next to a bank of squawking radios.

"Colonel, we put a LRRP team in here," he said. "They're in trouble. A helicopter's gone down trying to evacuate the wounded, they're surrounded and they've taken heavy casualties—sixteen WIA out of eighteen men." He seemed on the verge of losing it. From what he'd just told me, he was probably flashing on his crashing career.

"We've lost commo. We don't know their exact location, only that they're somewhere in here." He jabbed his finger around a four-click area on the map. The lost LRRPs were members of the 9th Division Ranger Company—E/75th—damn good men. "We've got to get them out," Hunt said, leaving unmentioned his own role in getting them in.

So the sonofabitch isn't going to fire me, I thought. I felt as if I'd been unbuckled from the electric chair seconds before the switch. Or had I been?

Of course, he meant *you've* got to get them out. You. The Hardcore. A brutal mission—imagine the U.S. Coast Guard ordered to search for a swimmer lost at sea during a storm somewhere between Hawaii and California.

When I asked Hunt what aircraft we had to lift in reinforcements, he told me all that was immediately available was a Brigade LOH, a small bird with a pilot, co-pilot and room for two people in back. There were generally four LOHs at the Brigade Aviation Platoon, and each battalion would normally get the use of one for some part of every day. The LOH was the bird we used to make recons, run emergency missions and for C&C. But to use it to move an eighty-man rifle company to rescue eighteen trapped LRRPs and an aircrew? Why not hunt grizzlies with paint-ball guns?

I gave Hunt a look that said—loud and clear—I'm not going out there and doing anything with just a LOH.

"Musselman's working on getting more birds," he said quickly, reading my expression. The LOH gave me a C&C bird for immediate recon and to establish commo with the embattled LRRP team. I took another look at the map. They're about forty klicks away, I thought—twenty minutes to get there.

I asked Musselman to have the LOH fired up. Then I grabbed the TOC phone and called my CP to brief Bumstead:

"Contact DeRoos. Move him to a PZ ASAP. Tell him to prepare for a night insertion. I'll brief him once he's airborne."

After that, I gave Chum Robert a heads-up: "Grab your gear and meet me at the pad."

I asked Musselman to tell the aviation commander who'd be leading the air package to come up on my command frequency and work out DeRoos's pickup with Bumstead. Thank God Hunt hadn't fired my most experienced commander, DeRoos, that morning.

As I made for the bunker exit, Hunt rushed up.

"Colonel," he said, "do everything you can to extract them."

I wheeled around.

"Colonel Hunt, if I get these people out, you will never fuck with my Battalion again. You just tell me what you want and when you want it done, but keep off my ass when I'm doing it. Do you understand me?"

Hunt the bully disappeared. In his place stood a little boy waiting outside the principal's office for his turn to get the belt. Looking down at his polished boots, he slowly, wordlessly nodded his head.

The Brigade Aviation Officer, a captain, lifted off with me upfront beside him. Chum, with his backpack radio, buckled into the two seats behind us. Once airborne, I radioed DeRoos on the aircraft's FM radio to make sure he and his boys were heading to the PZ.

"Sounds like a royal rat fuck to me, boss. Over." Gordy, cheerful, irreverent, cool.

"Roger that, but we'll unfuck it. I should be over the contact in a few minutes. I'll find out what's happening and work out a plan. Call me once you're on the way and I'll fill you in. Over."

"Wilco, Hardcore 6."

I began to man the radio like an air traffic controller moving tin, flipping from frequency to frequency to talk to Bumstead at Battalion, to monitor DeRoos's progress and to listen to the distress calls coming from the

Rangers themselves.

"Mayday. Mayday. Mayday."

The Ranger radio operator was trying to get help, but his one-way calls for assistance did neither of us any good whatsoever. As long as he transmitted, he couldn't receive.

"Get off the fuckin' radio," I yelled. "Put on a leader. Someone who can tell me where you are, where we can land. What's the best way to get into this thing? I'm looking for you in the dark!"

All that came back were more "Maydays." But I did pick up one telling clue: whenever the RTO came on with his Mayday message I could hear a firefight going on in the background. Grenades or RPG rounds exploded and AK-47s and M-16s were on rock-and-roll. They were still alive, but from the sounds of the rat-a-tat-tats and booms, they wouldn't be much longer.

We'd been flying for twenty minutes, so I knew we were near the ballgame. And then I looked out to the east and saw a flicker, a barely discernible tiny red light.

There!

"Look over to the left at ten o'clock," I told the pilot.

It was now almost dark. He turned the bird and minutes later we saw the silhouette of the downed Huey aircraft, the red light flashing on top, sitting in what looked like a drainage ditch.

"Going nowhere anytime soon," Chum said.

Circling over the fight, I went from the Ranger freq back to Battalion freq trying to find out where DeRoos was, all the time hoping to talk to the LRRPs. But I got only "Mayday! Mayday! Mayday!"

DeRoos reported in. He was on his way.

"Great, Gordy. We've found them and we're looking for an LZ. I can't talk to the guys on the ground. You may have to go in cold."

I told him to have his pilot vector on my signal and come to us, then I flipped back to the LRRPs.

"Mayday! Mayday!"

"Looks like I'm talking to myself," I shouted to Chum.

I'd been in fights like this with the 101st, but never in a situation where I couldn't talk to a leader or RTO on the ground. A commander's in serious shit when he can't commo with the guys in the fight. The scene below was surreal—red and green tracers arcing in the sky underneath us, the mangled chopper with its blinking red beacon, gun flashes all around the bird. It was as if I were looking down on a Fourth of July celebration busted by the cops, a circle of blinking lights with that holy-shit beacon flashing dead in the middle.

"Work up a wall of steel around those cats." I told Chum. "Start way out and walk it back slowly until it's a couple hundred yards around the chopper. Then keep it up until I tell you to lift it."

I was applying another basic 101st SOP—blister the ground around the encircled force. There's nothing like well-directed artillery fire to discourage an attacker. Not only does it tear his ass, it also delivers the message his prey's no longer helpless, easily overrun. This trick saved several of our units during the Battle of Dak To, but it was dangerous, a round could fall short, strike within the perimeter. Hopefully, the fire would buy us the time to sort out what was going down on the ground. Maybe the Artillery God would be kind.

I tried the Ranger radio net again.

"Mayday. Mayday. Christ, someone help us."

Again the one-way commo. Surely the RTO could see our bird orbiting in the dark. Surely he knew I needed to talk to him. Must be his radio was screwed.

"Hardcore 6, this is Blue Jay 6. I'm about twenty minutes out. Got gunships and slicks. Request sitrep."

Music. A full-on fucking Army Marching Band.

Blue Jay 6 was the 9th Division Aviation Commander, Lieutenant

Colonel Bill Crouch. He'd performed a miracle by organizing the birds and picking up part of Claymore in an amazingly short period of time.

"Blue Jay, we're looking for an LZ," I radioed back. "Will brief you on the plan when you get here."

Blue Jay reported back that he had a Cav troop to do the heavy lifting. And as a plus, the Air Cav knew the terrain—they'd inserted the LRRPs earlier that evening.

About this time, Chum, an amazing map reader, reported that the artillery folks had just told him the LRRPs had requested a marking round and then gone off the air.

"They're a little north of the downed bird," he said. "Will fire my reference round." How he could know all this in the dark at a hundred miles an hour was simply beyond this dumb grunt's comprehension.

Suddenly right out of nowhere, the pilot said, "We've got to break off."

I turned. "What do you mean, 'break off'?"

"Yellow light. We're running out of gas."

Oh, Jesus! "How much we got left?"

"About five minutes' worth at the most."

"And how far out are the slicks?"

"Maybe fifteen minutes."

Fifteen minutes? I could have strangled the guy for taking off on a mission with his bird running on empty. I needed to be on station when the flight commander arrived with DeRoos's Company so I could tell him where to land his birds and DeRoos what to do once he got his folks on the ground. But long before then we'd be out of fuel.

I couldn't leave Gordy high and dry to come in blind. We'd found an LZ he could use, a large open rice paddy about 600 yards from the downed chopper. In just another few minutes I could brief Crouch or the Cav commander and either one of them could run the show while we refueled.

"We've got to break off now." The pilot's voice was tight with anxiety. "We barely have enough fuel to make it back to Moore."

I made the most risky decision I've ever made. It came more from my gut than my head—as if I were in a speeding car and suddenly there was a boy chasing a ball ahead and I had nanoseconds to avoid hitting him. There were four easy options: turning left, turning right, flattening the kid or, in this instance, turning around and heading back to the firebase.

And then there was option five, the hard way, landing in the center of the inferno.

God knows I wanted to see Hunt go down in flames—and if those Rangers perished, his career would die with them. Hey, man, you ran out of gas, a small inner voice whispered.. Let Hunt stew in his own juices. He stuck these men in this trap. He was the one who violated the most basic principles of LRRP employment. Now let him pay.

But then another voice said, Yeah, but he won't really be paying—not like those twenty-two boys down there.

"Get your shit ready," I told Chum. "We're going down."

"Fine by me. Sounds like fun."

The pilot was the only one with any horse sense.

"No way, Sir. I'm not gonna land. I *refuse* to land."

The man was no coward—just a smart kid who didn't want to barge in uninvited to a VC barbecue where he could very well end up as the main course turning slowly over a very hot grill.

"Think again," I said.

I laid the mean end of my pistol against the side of his helmet. "You're going to land this sonofabitch right now. Park this fucking thing or I'll blow your brains out."

If he'd thought it through, he would've known I'd never do it—I'd be committing harakiri as well as taking Chum and himself with me. Not so smart. But maybe the steel against his helmet stopped him from thinking. In the years since, I've often wondered what would've happened if he'd called my bluff. He could've replied, "Go ahead and shoot, but you'd better ask yourself who's going to fly this bird."

In any event, I got his attention. We went down like a runaway elevator, flared and hovered above and to the side of the downed Huey. Slugs zipped around the LOH like lightning strikes. When we got to maybe six or seven feet off the ground, hands started desperately reaching for and grabbing the skids as a few of the survivors tried to pull our little bird from the sky. They were actually shaking the bird. Both Chum and I started kicking them away.

"Jump," I yelled, and we both bailed out—to find ourselves stuck knee deep in mud as the LOH hauled ass up, up and away. Bet that chopper jockey needed a shovel to clean around his pedals.

I turned to Chum. "If Prazenka could see us now, he'd think we were both crazy." Chum knew the gospel according to Prazenka—simple, smart stuff from my reconnaissance platoon sergeant in Italy, my infantry leader role model. I could hear him loud and clear: "Never volunteer for anything in combat—and don't ever take a chance when the odds are not in your favor."

Chum gave me a look that said he had no doubt.

After unassing ourselves from the mud, we looked around and tried to figure out what the hell was going on. I'd been in shit storms like this as a squad leader and as a platoon sergeant, and I knew it wasn't hopeless if we got the lead out in a hurry.

The troops on the ground were bunched together in a tight cluster, seemingly leaderless. In the dark, I couldn't distinguish between aircrew and Rangers, but they all wanted one thing—a fast ticket out—and I couldn't blame them.

I'd seen such fear before, especially during the bad days of the Korean

War. If we didn't get a hold of these guys, get a little discipline and a defensive perimeter going in a hurry, we might find ourselves very dead. Very soon.

"Okay, Chum, bring the artillery fire in closer. Put it over and around the outer edge of the tree line while I get a perimeter together."

I grabbed Rangers and aircrew by the back of their jackets and seat of their pants, shouting and pulling and pushing until we had a half-assed, 360-degree perimeter around the downed bird. Almost every man was wounded, but they were game.

On the battlefield when things are bad it takes only a few brave men to turn things around. It's been my experience in battle that out of ten men, only one or two are natural fighters. But once a fighter shouts, "Follow me" and charges, the rest are inspired to follow. In this instance, the Rangers—even bloodied—remained fighters to a man.

The downed Huey occupied about a third of the clearing, leaving more than enough room to bring in single choppers. Beyond the clearing were trees and nipa palm, and from the gun flashes I reckoned a small force of VC were scattered out there among them. Chum's artillery whistled over and splashed in, for sure the most joyous sound the men had heard in a spell.

BWUMP. The VC had to be thinking, uh-oh, they've got reinforcements in there.

BWUMP. They've got the big stick.

BWUMP. They're using it.

BWUMP. Better make tracks.

The enemy fire seemed to shut off as if we'd flipped a light switch.. Chum was busier than a one-armed juggler at a circus: adjusting artillery fire, spraying the nearby bush with his M-16, and switching our one radio from his artillery to my infantry frequency.

Just then Stogie 21 checked in on my freq. The Air Cavalry had arrived!

"Hardcore 6, Stogie 21. Five minutes out. What are your instructions? Over."

I told Chum to get ready to close down his artillery.

"Stogie 21," I yelled. "Hose down the outer north-south tree line with your Cobras as soon as we shut down the arty and be prepared to insert one lift ship at a time on my strobe when I yell. We're tightly wrapped around the downed bird. You can see its red light flashing. Keep your fire to the outer edge of the tree line. OK, here we go, we're shutting down the arty now—the last rounds will be Willy Peter."

I gave Chum his radio and he flipped back to his arty freq and gave them their shut-down instructions.

Hell is a burning chopper inside your perimeter with fuel and ammo exploding left, right and center. I knew the landing was going to be hairy. The LZ next to the downed chopper was some twenty yards long and fifty yards wide, about the size of a small parking lot. But then there were those trees. If we lost another bird, the game was over. But, like bringing in the artillery fire, it was a chance we had to take. The gain—the rescue of the trapped men—overrode the risk.

Another problem was visibility. There wasn't enough light for the pilots to see their way down, and the LZ was now blacker than a serial killer's soul. After we got the artillery shut off, I took the radio from Chum, strapped it on my back, and put my strobe light inside my steel pot and held it upside down over my head as though it were the Olympic torch. Now the Cav pilots could see the strobe light, but the VC couldn't.

I changed back to the infantry freq, then, still holding my pot on high, walked to the center of the field.

Stogie 21 said he had the strobe in sight.

"Stogie 21, we'll do one bird at a time. Have 'em approach from the west at 600 feet and when they see the strobe, flare and come straight down. I'll talk each aircraft in. Lotta mud here. Keep your Cobras hammering the woods to the north."

"Claymore 6, you set to bring in your grunts?" I asked DeRoos. "Make sure they know they've got friendlies on the deck and once they unass the birds they'll be escorted to their seats—just like at a play."

"Wilco, Hardcore."

I'd worked this same maneuver a fair number of compared to those we had up in all those trees and mountains. But the Highland pilots were used to small landing zones, while here the pilots kept telling me there wasn't enough room on my LZ to set a bird down with a sick chopper splayed across it. It was too dark. Too risky. Too many trees and a bad approach. They wanted to go for a large LZ in a rice paddy off to the west.

While the final decision to land belonged to the pilots, I killed the idea. Their LZ wasn't secure—Gordy's guys could be landing smack on top of a VC unit.

The lead pilot was twenty-one-year-old Warrant Officer Dan Hickman, who fortunately had the balls to go for my plan. He was flying Stogie 21, a Huey slick, and was accompanied by two more Stogie slicks, two Cobra gunships and—according to my Battalion log—a 9th Division slick tasked with the job of getting out their downed aircrew.

"I couldn't see the LZ and do a normal approach," Hickman said. "I had to line up where I thought it was and drop down blacked out and wallow across the top of the jungle till I saw your strobe. Then I dropped straight down, which was tough, as we were heavily loaded with your troops and a full load of fuel."

"Come left. Come right. You're dead over us now. Drop, drop, drop," I radioed him. He hit like a sledgehammer, but didn't get stuck in the mud.

Out jumped DeRoos and his RTO, followed by a squad of grunts led by Jerry Sullivan from Rex Fletcher's Claymore White Platoon. "The concept of going into someplace that we didn't know about, in the dark, had a pretty high pucker factor," Sullivan recalls. "I remember approaching the LZ and seeing the strobe light and tracers and thinking, We're all going to die."

After Hickman's brave example, Stogie 26 flown by Warrant Officer Elmore Jordon and Stogie 24 piloted by another Captain followed. The Stogie crews—"B" Troop 3/17th Cav—were magnificent. The Hardcore worked with them around FSB Moore and they lived up to their reputation that very bad night when they fearlessly flew through a sky full of machinegun fire and bitching flying conditions. One by one, choreographed as precisely as the Rockettes, the birds dropped off grunts and took off into the night. Hickman actually had his crew chief remove his pilot's door so he could lean way out and get a better look.

"Not sure if I could have spotted that tight LZ if I hadn't leaned out," Hickman told me.

When I asked if the ground fire was heavy, he replied, "There was shooting when I got there, but during my approach I was so intent on missing trees and not killing anyone by crushing them that I honestly couldn't say."

From my end, the noise was wild. THUMP, THUMP, THUMP, the rotors beating time to the WHOO-CRUMP of the Cobras' rockets hitting the outer tree line. But once the Stogie Cobras worked over the jungle and after Hickman and his pals got in with the first insert, I heard no more enemy fire.

"We were scared shitless," Sullivan remembers. "Not only that, we really didn't know what we were getting into. I mean, we knew there was a LRRP team in trouble but really didn't know if they were surrounded by a thousand VC or fifty, or if the whole team had been wiped out. When we first went in and we were taking a lot of fire, some of us were talking about whether or not the gooks had gotten the M-60s off the downed ship and, if so, we might be in serious trouble. When we got down on the ground, I found out that not only had they not taken them, but our guys already had 'em in the perimeter."

"Reinforce the perimeter," I told Gordy as Hickman lifted out. "Send the Rangers and aircrew back here as you put your people in and when you've got your company squared away, slowly push your perimeter out."

Again, Gordy unflappable. "Wilco, Sir. Can I keep the Rangers?"

I grinned. "Nice try, Gordy. But no, most of 'em need to see a Doc. Send 'em over to Chum—he'll back-load 'em. And button down the perimeter—get it STRAC. Yell if you need help."

I gave Chum the job of bringing in the rest of the birds and evacuating the wounded men as they reported in from the perimeter. A new bird would land, Gordy's troops would debark, and Chum would load the wounded for the flight back to the hospital at Dong Tam.

A quick study and cool under fire, Chum was also one strong mother. When a guy was slow to get on an outgoing bird, Chum just picked him up and tossed him into the aircraft as if he were a sack of potatoes. He was the kind of guy I'd be happy to have in my foxhole anytime, anyplace.

After that it was a yawn. About halfway through the job, after the aircrew and the Rangers evacuated, DeRoos and I walked the perimeter.

"Good job, DeRoos," I told him. "I know you're organized for ambush but you'll have to stick here till morning. They'll never try to evac that bird in the dark. I'll set up a radio relay and make sure you're covered."

"Roger, Sir. Get us some water and rations in the morning. I brought a Two Niner Two so we can get a commo check with our guys at Moore ASAP."

"Affirmative. Have your arty FO get the firing data from Chum—we're going out on the last bird. And in the morning, try to figure out what caused this rat fuck."

Although he wasn't on this mission, thirty-two years later, long after the smoke had cleared from the battlefield, E/75th Ranger Bill Cheek tracked down five of the seventeen survivors and pain-stakingly reconstructed what happened that night. According to Ranger Cheek, earlier in the day, the 1st Brigade scrambled a strong Hunter Killer force for a "hot intell" mission. The gung-ho Rangers up for the task "jokingly referred to the operation as a 'Superman Mission.'"

At dusk, two Huey slicks escorted by a pair of Cobra gunships dropped the Hunter Killer team into an LZ in an open rice paddy, just to the west of where Chum and I landed two hours later. It was a cold LZ.

"Sergeant David Stone was point man and the team leader for the Hunter team," Cheek recalls. "On landing, Sergeant Stone noticed many places on and around the LZ where the reeds were bent over as if someone had recently been sitting on them. He reckoned a large enemy force had just vacated the area because the reeds were bending back up as he watched."

Most likely, it was a large infiltrating enemy force coming out of Cambodia with orders not to get decisively engaged. They were probably taking ten when they saw the insertion birds, realized the LRRPs were on to them and hightailed it into the woods.

Something gave Ranger Stone an uneasy feeling. The terrain did not jibe with the map, and the matted-down grass bothered him. His sixth sense, developed during dozens of such missions, shouted: danger, danger, danger. A veteran patrol leader, he quickly moved the force off the LZ into the nearby woods and stopped when they came to a clearing. He then wisely called for a marking round to check his position. In case he was in the middle of a large enemy force, he'd be able to bring in the artillery big stick.

Just at that moment, Sergeant Wes Watson, who was at the rear of the column, saw an armed enemy soldier dressed in khaki about fifteen meters away. But before he could take him out, the guy disappeared into the darkness.

Then a single shot was fired.

Sergeant Stone realized the team had lost surprise and prepared for the world to fall in. He set his force up in a tight perimeter and waited for the artillery marking round. "Suddenly four dinks walked into the clearing. A Ranger yelled 'La Dai Motherfucker,' and when they ran, they joined the ranks of the KIA."

Sergeant Stone threw a grenade. It hadn't gone more than a foot when an explosion went off behind him and blew him out of the wood line into the clearing. Hit in the back by shrapnel and momentarily stunned, his shocked brain tried to connect his grenade with the explosion that came from the opposite direction.

Then more explosions clobbered the perimeter.

Thirty-two years after the saga, Ranger Watson, who had taken his Advanced Individual Training (AIT) in my "Stay Alert, Stay Alive" battalion back at Fort Lewis, said the minute the team landed, a VC LZ watcher spotted them. "A few minutes later, we started taking heavy small-arms fire," he recalls. "We returned fire and that brought a barrage of RPG fire aimed at the trees above us, creating air bursts—which is what caused so many casualties so quickly."

The RPG was a pee-bringer of a shoulder-fired weapon, deadly effective—with all the punch of a 90mm recoilless rifle and deeply feared by our grunts. In a strict infantry fight, the VC AK-47 and RPG outgunned the U.S. M-16 rifle and LAW, the shoulder-fired Light Anti-tank Weapon. Without U.S. Tac Air, chopper and artillery fire, American infantry in Vietnam would have sucked hind tit every time.

The Rangers blasted back with three M-60 machine guns, an XM-203 Over and Under—a combined M-16 and M-79—and a dozen M-16s. The enemy backed off fast.

Even though Sergeants Stone and Charles Chesser were both hit, they worked on the other wounded Rangers. Ranger Warren Lizotte had a serious head wound with part of his brain exposed, and Sergeant Stone tended to him while Sergeant Chesser patched up the others. Lieutenant Robert Hill, the mission leader, was very badly wounded along with Sergeant Jerry Wilson. All told, sixteen Rangers were hit, but all except Lizotte, who was down for the count, bravely manned their weapons and hammered the enemy with heavy and sustained fire.

The incoming fire had knocked out every Ranger radio. One PRC-25 had a light glowing in the Frequency Indicator box. Stone, hoping it could still transmit, started the one-way chant I picked up while on my way to the scene: "This is U.S. Forces calling any Allied Forces. Mayday, Mayday, Mayday, Mayday, this is U.S. Forces calling any Allied forces. Mayday, Mayday."

With the radio able only to transmit, Stone had a hot mike. He couldn't bring in artillery or direct other supporting weapons. He was talking only to himself.

Back at the Dong Tam Ranger TOC, Huey pilot Warrant Officer LaPotta picked up the Mayday call, raced to his chopper and took off, not even waiting the required five-minute engine warm-up time in his rush to fly to his besieged Ranger buddies.

Sergeant Stone turned on his strobe when he heard the circling bird. "LaPotta turned on his landing lights and came in hot on the small clearing. About twenty feet off the ground, the bird clipped a tree with its tail rotor and went into a wild spin, crashing on its side. The main rotor went flying, and the turbine roared out of control. The crew unassed the chopper, yelling, 'It's going to blow' to Sergeant Stone and Dennis McNally as they raced over to the downed bird to help."

When things settled down and LaPotta figured the bird wasn't going to explode, he returned to the aircraft and shut it down. The crew then removed the ship's weapons and ammo and joined Stone's people on the perimeter.

Ranger Warren Lizotte died a few hours after he was evacuated back to Dong Tam. Lieutenant Hill, Sergeant Wilson, Ranger Richard Shimel and a few other badly wounded Rangers never returned to the company.

Huey pilot LaPotta was almost court-martialed for his heroic, but unauthorized and, some thought, reckless flight. Ranger CO Captain Dale Dickey went to General Ewell and got the charges thrown out with the best possible defense: Screw the regulations, he was trying to save my men.

For their gallantry, both Stone and Chesser were awarded the Silver Star.

So the rescue went smoothly, except for one hitch. All during the ground phase of the rescue, Bumstead kept radioing from the TOC, "King David, you're doing a hell of a job" and "We have a cold beer waiting for you, King David. King David, you're a hero."

I wondered whether he'd raided Doc Holley's Benzedrine supply. Finally I told him to get the fuck off the radio—that I needed it to run the show, not start a fan club. I suppose he wanted to get into the act, live vicariously. Or suck up after he'd blindly followed Hunt's dumb orders to deploy Winston's troops. To me, it was one more instance of my S-3 making an ass of himself, but I was too preoccupied—or too dense—to catch yet another warning signal.

As Gordy and I walked the extended perimeter, S-3 Jim Musselman rang and said, "Only sixteen Rangers are accounted for at the hospital. Are the two missing men with you?"

DeRoos did a check. No Rangers had attached themselves to his platoons. We worried they were captured, dead or lying in the bush too shot up to sound off. In the confusion of DeRoos's people coming in and Rangers and aircrew going out in the darkness, neither Chum, DeRoos nor I had done a head count. Gordy ran a few small patrols out beyond our perimeter, but still no sign of the missing men.

With only three aircraft in each lift, it took three turnarounds to bring in all of Claymore. Meanwhile, Stogie Cobras circled our perimeter. It was slow going—a platoon would be dropped off and then the slicks would return to the PZs near Moore to pick up another. While we were waiting for the last platoon to come in, Musselman radioed back. "All the Rangers are accounted for. The two that were missing walked from the 3rd Surgical Hospital helipad back to their barracks at Dong Tam—they weren't wounded."

What a good man Musselman was, I remember thinking. Here he was with dozens of worries on his plate, running a six-thousand-man Brigade with a highly intelligent and superambitious—the worst combination for a combat arms officer—loose-cannon skipper; yet he still found time to chase down the missing men and let us know they were OK. Musselman, who clearly had his soldiering priorities straight, well earned the two stars he eventually wore.

DeRoos established good commo with my TOC back at Moore and USAF Captain Joe Connor, Tamale 14, agreed to keep a FAC (Forward Air Controller) aircraft over DeRoos all night to provide radio relay and fire support if needed.. So as the last bird dropped off its load of grunts, Chum and I climbed aboard. From womb to tomb, the complete rescue phase of the operation took exactly four hours.

Appropriately enough, Dan Hickman, Stogie 21, first in after Chum and me, took us out. When he dropped us off at Moore, I got Hickman's name and service number and put him in for a combat decoration. As is so often the case in war, my recommendation got lost somewhere along the way and Stogie 21 never got his medal. My apologies, Dan, and thanks for the ride. The Rangers and the Hardcore both owe you one big time.

DeRoos reported a brief exchange of gunfire when his troopers pushed out the perimeter and then all was quiet. He fine-tuned the perimeter, put out claymore mines and settled in for the night.

In the morning before the bird was lifted out, DeRoos's patrols found trails and places in the tall grass that were matted down and a fair amount of bloodstains. One patrol killed one VC and took two POWs. One of the prisoners told us, "There are three VC company-sized base camps in the vicinity."

"There were a bunch of bad guys here," DeRoos later said. "The Rangers were damn lucky they didn't get snuffed out."

Several weeks later, on a visit to Gordy's Claymore Company base camp, I noticed two aviation M-60 machine guns on his perimeter.

"I know where those came from," I said.

Gordy smiled. "The spoils of war go to the victor. And besides, we paid for them. That was one miserable night."

EIGHT

On Toward Danger
01 MARCH 1969

I didn't realize the importance of our shakedown cruise until after the Ranger rescue. I kept asking myself why it had gone so well—why did the aircrews, the infantry and the artillery click so beautifully together? The answer was that we were no longer individuals, but rather a single team, welded together in the heat and muck of the Plain of Reeds. Without the hard training sessions hopscotching along the Cambodian border, insignificant as each separate skirmish was, we might not have become one, all parts of the machine operating in perfect sync, and the Ranger rescue mission might have had a vastly different outcome.

I was proud of Claymore. A rested crackerjack unit could have rehearsed the operation a dozen times and still screwed it up because of its sheer complexity, all the unknowns. Looking back, I see now how that night was pivotal in the Battalion's transformation from hopeless to Hardcore.

Apparently it also sent the men a message that they had a commander who'd walk the walk with them and for them. Throughout the action, Doc Holley monitored the radio traffic at Moore so he'd be up to speed on incoming casualties. "It was a total change in mind-set," he recalls. "A month earlier everyone in this outfit wanted Hackworth dead, and here he was making a night insertion out in the boonies filled with gooks to save some soldiers he didn't know. We knew right then we didn't want him to get waxed. My medics and I sat around the medical bunker as if we were listening to a football game on the radio. 'Right on, Chum. Right on, Hack.' Everyone was cheering. Damnedest thing I ever did see."

While at FSB Moore, Battle Company killed four VC. But before Bobby Knapp could leave the field, he had to respond to an honor violation charge from West Pointer Hunt. Only minutes after Knapp had called in the four kills, Operations Sergeant Slater got a call from the Brigade TOC officer:

"Rice Paddy Daddy doesn't believe Battle's body count. He wants proof."

Once again Colonel Hunt was playing squad leader. For one West Pointer to question the truthfulness of another is a big deal. Fortunately, old soldier Slater, who worked closely with and respected Bobby Knapp, was not a man to be fucked with. He contacted a friendly Dust-Off pilot who was in the area and wanted to know if we needed anything.

This particular pilot was so fond of the Hardcore that he always dropped his medevac call sign, "Dust-Off 56," when he operated in our area and became "Hardcore 56."

"Affirmative Hardcore 56," Slater replied. "How 'bout picking up some dichs at Battle Company and dropping them off at the Brigade pad?"

"Wilco, Hardcore three, Alpha, on my way. Out."

Two hours passed. The Brigade TOC officer rang Slater to confirm the delivery.

"OK, we believe you," he told Slater. "We got the bodies. Now Rice Paddy Daddy wants 'em hauled away."

"You got 'em," Slater shot back. "They're all yours." He now says, "You better believe Brigade never again challenged a body-count report during the next four months I was Ops Sergeant of the Hardcore."

About the same time, another Hardcore soldier, former Claymore Company squad leader turned supply man Jim Robertson, had a different kind of VC body problem. One day he was told to report to Sergeant

McGuire at FSB Moore.

"What's up?" Robertson asked.

McGuire pointed at the truck and said, "Got a present for you."

Robertson looked in the truck bed, where he saw a dead VC.

"What do you mean, a present for me?" he asked McGuire.

"That's Luke the Gook there. Got himself killed in a firefight with our guys today."

"Yeah. So?"

"So, S-4's job is to bury the sonofabitch."

"Bullshit! Who says so?"

"Sergeant Major Press."

"What about Graves Registration?"

"That's for us, not the enemy," McGuire said.

"No way in hell am I burying this bastard."

"Look, Robby, I agree with you. Do you think I enjoyed driving a one-man convoy up here to turn this dead little shit over to you? It'll be dark soon and I'll have to stay here for the night and I don't feature that."

Everyone present at this exchange was a line soldier or an ex-line doggie and it really went against their grain to bury the enemy. "We hated these people because they'd killed and maimed so many of our friends," Robertson remembers. "This guy was a run-of-the-mill VC. I could tell when I looked down from the frozen scream on his face to the filthy peasant rags."

Closer inspection showed one wound, entry through the kneecap and the exit wound right behind where a six-inch chunk of his leg had been blown out. There wasn't another mark on him, and from the look on his face, shock and massive blood loss had killed him.

"Let's take him down the road and throw him off the bridge," Robertson suggested.

"Fine by me," McGuire said. "You want to bury him at sea, you do it."

"No problem, you drive and I'll chuck him over."

McGuire nodded and they took off for the nearest bridge. But an MP halted them. When they told him their mission, he turned them back. At the firebase, they cracked open a couple of beers and pondered their options. Everyone agreed burying the body was out of the question. "In our minds, there was something sacrilegious, irrational as it may sound, in doing this simple Christian task," Robertson recalls. "When I suggested we blow him up, the rest of the guys looked at me as if I'd flipped but all of them asked how I intended to do it."

"I told them we'd take him out into the wire and pack a couple of pounds of C-4 under him," Robertson said. "Use enough and he'll be vaporized."

"Why not?" someone said.

But this time they didn't get past the gate. An officer gave them hell for even thinking of what they were about to do and once again they turned back. By now, it was getting late. Robertson wondered if he could sneak the body out in the dark.

"You'll have to carry him," McGuire said. "I ain't doing no night driving with one truck. That's asking for trouble."

Just then Sergeant Major Press drove up. He glanced into the bed of the truck and snapped, "Which one of you dickheads is from S-4?"

"That would be me, Sergeant Major," replied Robertson.

"And why is this body still in this truck?"

"Because I ain't burying no goddamn VC, Sergeant Major," Robertson said.

"Colonel says it's your job."

Robertson didn't answer.

"That man's a soldier, son. An enemy soldier, sure, but a soldier who died fighting for what he believes in. Show a little respect."

"The Sergeant Major was right, of course," Robertson now says. "We were too blinded by hatred to see it until then. I buried the man in a shallow grave outside of the firebase. Even said a silent prayer for Luke the Gook's fucking soul."

Feelings toward the Vietnamese who were supposedly on our side weren't much better. Most of the Hardcore troopers believed the South Vietnamese Army were a bunch of slackers. "We fought their war while they watched from their bunkers," Jerry Sullivan said. "We'd go into an area and wade through wall-to-wall mines and booby traps and fight Charley from sunup to sunup. They'd go into the same patch of jungle and not fire a round. This 'search and avoid' cowardice built a wall of hatred between our guys and their South Vietnamese counterparts."

Doc Holley hit it right on the head when he said, "It was their country, their war, but they didn't want to pay the price to save it. In the end they lost to their brothers, who did pay the price."

Almost everybody in the Hardcore hated ARVN—just as most everyone in the 1/101st had hated ARVN—and for the same reasons. In particular, the Hardcore soldiers hated the ARVN soldiers who operated in our AO. Day after day, our guys would watch them go out and seldom find the Viet Cong. Yet if we followed in their tracks, we had to fight every step of the way. If ARVN saw a contact brewing, they just ducked, weaved or walked around it—clearly they had an unspoken "You don't shoot us, we won't shoot you" deal with the enemy. The Hardcore soldiers took all this in and when the medevac ships were carrying away their buddies while ARVN sat back and let us fight their war, it bred tremendous hatred.

One night in the TOC, a Hardcore lieutenant popped through the blackout curtain.

"Hardcore Recondo, Sir," he said. "How's the body count?"

"Middlin'," I said. "Why, young Lieutenant?"

"Got three more for you, Sir," he said. "Zapped 'em on Route 4 on the way in."

"Far out. Way to go," I said, and told the TOC NCO to report the kills to Brigade. But before he got on the horn, Brigade called and asked if we had any jeeps out on Route 4. The NCO looked at me. I grabbed the mike and asked why.

"An American jeep ran an ARVN roadblock and killed three ARVN soldiers," the voice at Brigade said.

"Been all quiet down our way," I said, and signed off.

"They shot first, Sir," the lieutenant said. "And if they were Marvin the ARVN, they were probably VC anyway."

"Don't report the lieutenant's body count," I told the NCO. "Wrong side."

"You'll stay here tonight," I told the lieutenant. "Gonna give your ass a little class on identification—like how to tell friend from foe."

Such incidents didn't do much to encourage U.S.-ARVN love fests or help our overall relations with the South Vietnamese people.

There was the time a VC mine blew up a civilian bus and an ARVN soldier, instead of helping the Hardcore medics patch up the wounded, stole the bandages. Meanwhile, our guys had to fire shots in the air to keep the civilians from robbing their own wounded and dead.

Another time, three teenage girls selling soft drinks to GIs on the side of the road triggered a vehicle ambush. One minute they were pretty, smiling hustlers and the next minute they were VC agents responsible for killing and wounding ten soldiers. "Most of the time I enjoyed helping the people. But on days like [that] I just felt like shooting them all," said Battle Company medic Dan Evans, who frequently risked his butt doing the regular medical Civic Action Program, MEDCAP, visits to the isolated villages as part of the U.S. "Win the Hearts and Minds" campaign.

"Whenever we set up in an ARVN compound, you'd have to guard your stuff because the Vietnamese soldiers would steal you blind in a New York minute," Jim Robertson said. "The first night we operated from one compound, we didn't leave anybody behind to watch our stuff. We came back in the morning and we had nothing left. You could go to their leaders and talk to them until you were blue in the face, they'd grin at you and shrug like they knew nothing—we came close to shoot-outs a couple of times." One night, Robertson's squad set up near an ARVN compound. "We figured if the VC came down the road toward the compound, we could ambush them," he said. "Suddenly, the VC attacked the compound. I started to call in artillery fire. But we were so mad at these guys for cleaning us out and generally fucking us over, we just took our sweet time about requesting fire. We let Charley work them over pretty good before we brought artillery in. It was payback time."

"There was an ARVN compound near our base. ARVN soldiers were always taking potshots at our convoys when we passed," said Robertson. "On more than one occasion I saw rounds come right out of that compound directly at our vehicles. And, hey, we were supposedly on the same side. Whenever we were anywhere near that camp, everybody had their fingers on their triggers."

At Moc Hoa, a Vietnamese girl no more than seven years old was spotted setting up a U.S. claymore mine at the edge of the runway. One of our cooks, on perimeter guard, saw the girl and lined her up in his rifle sights.

"That's a kid, asshole," a sergeant snapped, and jerked the rifle from his hands.

"She's VC," the cook said. "Look what she's doing."

They watched for a while and then the sergeant went out, took the mine away from her, smacked her on the butt and shooed her back to her mother.

Back at Dong Tam, Jim Robertson was in charge of building an ammo bunker using civilian labor. "I noticed this one mama-san who was placing one foot in front of the other, heel to toe, measuring the distance from where the sandbag pile was to the bunker. I pointed this out to Sergeant Stack."

"She's pacing us off," Stack said. "She's a goddamn VC spy."

"We grabbed her and turned her over to the MPs. She turned out to be a VC. Stuff went on like this all the time," Robertson said.

To avoid this kind of sabotage, I allowed no Vietnamese—civilian or military, regardless of rank—inside any of our firebases. I didn't trust a single one of them not to be a VC and the fact that none of our bases was ever attacked by enemy infantry or sappers made a good case for the rule.

We did allow a civilian barber to cut hair outside our front gate. He was good at his job. But I always felt a little queasy when he'd pull out his straight-edge razor, sharpen it to a fine edge with a leather strop and then shave the back of my neck. Then one day he didn't show up for work—and the next morning he was recognized among a pile of VC killed in a Hardcore ambush. My throat tingled for a week.

There were many reasons Hardcore troopers hated the people. It wasn't just that the South Vietnamese soldiers with whom we shared our AO were "search and avoid" experts or thieves or lazy bastards. Add to the mix that almost all of the Hardcore's other contacts with the people of South Vietnam came from dealings with the dregs of Vietnamese society—corrupt soldiers, bar girls, whores, pimps, hustlers, dope peddlers and clip-joint operators—and we're talking serious negative baggage. The cultural differences only increased the alienation and animosity.

Then there were the mines and booby traps, which we knew were placed by the genuflecting, cheering civilians we'd supposedly saved. They waved and smiled at us from the side of the roads and went back to setting their deadly surprises as soon as we were out of sight.

Right or wrong, most of the Hardcore soldiers looked upon the Vietnamese people they encountered as VC who were doing all they could to assist their pals with AKs hanging around their necks to do a number on us.

The Army kept trying to overcome this prejudice by promoting their tired commercial of "Winning the Hearts and Minds" of the people. But being total realists, the grunts—who faced life-and-death situations hourly, seven days a week, 365 days a year—felt the best way to deal with the Vietnamese was to grab them by their balls. Then, they knew, their "Hearts and Minds" would follow.

The Hardcore troopers wore their black metal Recondo arrowhead pins with pride, but as I found out recently the VC sometimes had the misfortune to wear the Recondo pin too. The Recondo Brigade had a calling card they left with an enemy body. The paper slip bore a Recondo insignia and a message in Vietnamese explaining how the dead VC met his fate and telling the reader that he'd make the same trip unless he surrendered. All well and good until some of the Hardcore soldiers decided to make a more lasting impression. "We used the Recondo pins to let Charley know we took them out," a Hardcore Platoon Sergeant says, "we hammered them into VC dead bare chests and sometimes their foreheads.

"Combat makes you numb," he adds. "Once, after a fight where we killed a few gooks, we turned one over and used him as a table. Four of us sat around him on our steel pots and used his bare belly for our C-Ration cans. Thirty-one years later, I'm not proud of it, but that's what war does to you."

Squad leader Sullivan says, "One night we killed five VC in an ambush. In the morning before we moved out, I saw our boys cutting off ears and tacking Recondo pins in dead gooks' eyes. I didn't understand the hatred then. But the longer I stayed, the less these kinds of acts bothered me. It was part of that ugly war."

The VC were not looked upon as humans by many of the Hardcore soldiers—even the name *gook* was part of the dehumanizing process. I reckon that's how grunts in Vietnam coped. And if the VC weren't humans, then there was no problem wasting, zapping and otherwise terminating them. Often with extreme prejudice. But interestingly, the "kill" word was seldom used by those who did the deed.

Lady Luck must have heard my plea for action, because the day after the LRRP rescue mission, Lieutenant Colonel Carlson called. "You're moving out," he said. "General Ewell ordered Colonel Hunt to get the Hardcore Battalion over to Giao Duc ASAP. Figures the hunting should be good there."

I'm sure the call made Hunt's day as much as it made mine—the word was he couldn't wait to see our "maverick" asses move out from his CP. "Hack, you have a real way of winning folks over," Carlson told me.

I laughed. What Hunt considered punishment was an answered prayer for me.

Giao Duc, in the extreme western portion of Dinh Tuong Province, was real Indian country, a VC stronghold dead center of War Zone 470, the home of Charley's Main Force units.

In Giao Duc District three tactical and two political zones bumped each other. In the military sense, boundaries used to mark a particular unit's area generally run along a river or a road or some other easy-to-recognize natural landmark. Firing or maneuvering into another unit's boundary is a big no-no. You don't mess with someone else's backyard; to do so most often brings casualties from your own fire. Three Vietnamese units—the 44th Special Tactical Zone, the 7th Division, and the 9th Division—all had their AOs intersect there and each gave the other a wide berth, resulting in large chunks of seldom-searched turf.

Guerrillas always operate out of neglected areas, marshes, mountains and urban hideouts—places that are hard to get into. The Giao Duc border areas offered the VC the perfect such base. And they not only had ARVN boundaries down cold, they had spies in every South Viet unit who told them what the outfits were up to even before the South Viet COs knew.

To hit the ground running, we needed to get our new permanent fire support base combat-ready ASAP. Word came down from Dong Tam that it was to be named Dickey.

"Dickey?"

Jesus, it sounded as if we were into toilet training, not fighting. No way were my Hardcore Recondos going to wage war out of a joint called Dickey. Never happen. I radioed Major Musselman.

"Jim, you gotta get Division to change the damn name!" I said. "How about Danger? That's what we're going to be deep in the middle of from now on."

Changing the name of a firebase wasn't exactly high priority in the grand scheme of things, but the major said he'd make a few phone calls. Poor Musselman—even though he was a good staff officer, I must admit I gave him the same hard time I gave most staff weenies. As a rule, staff officers are obsessed with having everything lined up, checked off, fairly distributed. They don't like anyone messing with their neat little plans. Since I was a big-time messer, Musselman and I had plenty of shoot-outs. And Musselman wasn't always wrong.

Several years after he and I left the 9th Division, Major Al Hiser, one of my former company commanders in the 1/327th, asked Jim to rate me as a leader. "If I'd been Brigade commander, I'd have fired him on several occasions," Jim replied. "To me, his aggressiveness and his inability to cooperate with others overrode his ability as a commander. Personally, I'd rather have a person who's not quite as flamboyant and outspoken but does what you tell him to do."

Then Hiser asked him, "How would you have considered him as a leader had you been one of his company commanders?" And Jim, straight-shooter that he was, said, "As a company commander, I'd probably have loved him because he got more support for his companies than anyone else could. But in getting the support, he'd go against SOPs and not cooperate with other battalions that were trying to do similar missions. We'd send something to the 2nd Battalion and he would divert it in the air, direct the guy to bring it to his battalion."

Guilty as charged. I wasn't big on sharing. I wanted every possible asset that would keep my boys alive and help us go for the gold. In my own defense, I should point out that the Army's built on competition and I've always been a competitor. In every outfit I've ever led, from Italy to Vietnam, I've scrounged, stolen, broken regulations and wheeled and dealed to get whatever I needed to take care of the troops and make the unit number one. Once the troops shape up—once they are Numero Uno—you have to accentuate the positive, make them feel proud, different from the herd. Tell an outfit that's making an effort why it's special long enough, show them the way, and they become special. You can call it brainwashing or mind-fucking, but it works. Especially with teenagers who might get snuffed out any minute, who need something positive to hang on to.

Now Giao Duc would give the Hardcore an even better chance to prove just how special it was.

Before we moved out, the Brigade Assistant Intelligence Officer, Captain Clark, gave my staff and me a first-class briefing on the enemy situation in the district. Clark impressed the hell out of me with his detailed knowledge of the battlefield, and after the briefing, he came up and asked if I'd autograph his copy of the *Vietnam Primer*. I stood there wondering what an Airborne-Ranger-Infantry type was doing as a staff weenie in the Brigade S-2 section. With his obvious smarts and gung-ho attitude, he'd be a good man to have in our company commander ready-rack. As I was mulling this over, Clark suddenly said in his soft Alabama drawl:

"Sir, I'd sure like to get down to the Hardcore. The Colonel said I could get out of here in a few weeks."

Man, what luck. I said, "Tell you what, Clark. I'll have a talk with Colonel Carlson. If we can pull it off, you'll start off in a staff job and if you work out you'll get a company down the track."

Two days later Clark reported for duty.

We were almost there, but I still felt the 4/39th lacked the motivation to go out and mix it up with the VC. We needed a win or two for the troops to realize how good they were. A few small victories would prove to them how well our new tactical concepts worked, that the best way to stay alive in Vietnam was to kill the VC before they could kill us.

As soon as Hunt gave the order, I flew out to Giao Duc. There were few good roads in Vietnam, but I saw we could locate the new firebase—Danger thanks to Musselman—right on Route 4. The VC called it "People's Road,"but I meant to make it ours, so supply trucks could move back and forth and we wouldn't be forced to depend solely on air resupply. Between fights, we could also truck the grunts back to Dong Tam, where they could get paid and maybe, if they were lucky, get their rocks off.

On 1 March, the Battalion, less Alert Company, which was back at Dong Tam for special ambush training, piled on trucks and—with security provided by a mechanized platoon from the 2/47th Mech Infantry Battalion and a Light Fire Team of gunships flying overhead—moved without incident to the Hardcore's new killing field.

Bobby Knapp's Battle Company had just completed a four-day operation near FSB Moore. It was dry-out time for them, so they got the mission of building the firebase. Bobby was certainly a savvy combat infantryman and I knew he was a West Point – trained military engineer, so he seemed the perfect guy to ramrod the job. Years later, he told me he'd almost flunked engineering at the Point.

We walked the perimeter, working out where each bunker would go, starting with foxholes in the berm the two mighty Division bulldozers had pushed up.

Battalion XO George Mergner, knowing the terrain and locals from a previous Delta tour, trucked in plenty of barrier and fortification stuff— Pierced Steel Planking (PSP), sandbags, metal culverts for instant overhead cover, wire mesh, barbwire and steel stakes for our wire barriers—enough to build a mini – Siegfried Line.

Bobby and his men hardened the fighting positions, sandbagging walls and the PSP roofing and installing wire mesh in front of the bunker's aperture to ignite B-40 rockets before they struck home. Each day we added another layer of protection, following the maxim that a defensive position is never finished. Wall-to-wall double apron barbwire fences with patrol gates stretched from the berm line out 500 meters. At every corner of the roughly rectangular-shaped firebase we built towers twelve to fifteen feet above the ground and posted 24/7 snipers who had a 360-degree line of fire stretching out from the base for several klicks. Eventually we put personnel radars in each of the towers. The radar operators plotted all after-dark movement on a large sheet of acetate, which they transferred daily to a special S-2 map. Once we had a detailed mosaic showing enemy movement patterns, including rendezvous points, we could bide our time until the target was ripe. Then we'd snipe, ambush or attack.

As soon as the convoy pulled into Danger, DeRoos and Foley were assigned their night ambush locations. All the Battalion key players—company commanders, separate platoon leaders and staff officers—reconned our new AO in the LOH we had for the day. This way DeRoos and Foley could eyeball their night ambush locations and figure out the best way in and everybody else got a good look at the battlefield.

While on aerial recon, at 1815 hours, Sergeant Julio Mendoza, the acting Battalion 4.2 Mortar Platoon leader, spotted three VC. He called the target back to his tubes and had the distinction of making the first three VC kills at Danger.

The losers Sergeant Major Press had discovered hiding in the rear when he first got to Dong Tam now started to earn their keep. "No wonder the line companies were operating with only half-strength," he recalls. "Initially I had over one hundred of these sick, lame and lazy clowns."

Press moved his "F" (for "Fuck-off") Troop—forward to Danger and put them to work, bestowing on them a green guidon with crossed pick and shovel and assigning them every mean job in the outfit. At night he sent them out to fill in on firebase perimeter security. "I treated them like the World War II Germans treated their penal units," he remembers. "I flat worked their butts off cleaning and burning out the shit drums from the latrines and using them as hard labor at the firebase."

Within a few days the Fuck-offs started showing up at Doc Holley's setup, asking to be taken off light duty, actually volunteering to go back to their units. Combat was beginning to look good to them. It sure beat the hell out of Press's slave labor schedule.

At Danger, the flying picks and shovels of "F" Troop were greatly augmented by the 15th Engineer Battalion bulldozers. They moved tons of dirt for the five-foot-high berm perimeter, which encased the base, raising its elevation by two feet to prevent flooding when the rains came. Then the engineers built what proved to be a pretty nifty drainage system. When I visited Danger twenty-five years later, it was all there, although the cannons and barbwire were gone. A modern six-pump gas station stood on ground the competition must have envied. But I still saw shreds of Army-green sandbags poking out through the hardtop.

At one stage of the work, one of the dozers uncovered a slightly moldy VC body, complete with an AK-47. I jumped down in the hole and yanked the AK out of the mud.

"Watch this," I said, "I'll show you how a real infantry weapon works."

I pulled the bolt back and fired thirty rounds—the AK performed as though it had been cleaned that day rather than buried in a marsh for a year. This was the kind of weapon our soldiers needed and deserved, not the M-16 that had to be hospital-clean or it jammed.

Demonstration over, we reported a body count of one, complete with weapon, to Brigade. In good 9th Division tradition, we didn't say both were encrusted with moss and mud.

"Engineer" Knapp was assisted by the Battalion S-4, Bob Johnson, a real engineer—and a damn good man—who was filling an infantry slot because of a critical shortage of infantry lieutenants. When I told Johnson to take off his Engineer insignia—which reminded me of Hunt—and replace it with Infantry crossed rifles, he refused.

"Sir, I'm an Engineer," he politely told me in his steady southern drawl, "I'm proud of these Castles. And even if you are called 'Mr. Infantry,' I doubt you have the authority to change my branch of service."

We'd see about that. I asked Mergner to call the Division G-1—Personnel and Administration—Lieutenant Colonel LeRoy Dyment, and have Johnson detailed Infantry. Two weeks later, he was wearing crossed rifles. A month later, he was awarded the CIB—and busting his balls as the new Headquarters Company Commander. Chalk one up for the Infantry.

Those first few days at Danger, no one in the Hardcore Battalion got more than four hours of sleep a night. We were in a race with the VC in an area they considered their own, and since I figured they were sure to attack, it was crucial to get the firebase hardened and ready. At the same time I wanted to put the Hardcore's footprints on our new AO through a series of ambushes and operations. We needed to send the VC the message that we might be new in town but we were a lean, mean fighting machine and we'd be sticking around.

The VC main force units were by nature cautious; tactically they spread out all over the landscape since they didn't want to offer a big target, like, say, FSB Moore or Dong Tam. They'd put a base camp here, another there and move frequently. Most of the time they put out recon elements to scout us and maintain a fix on our routine: guard changes; patrol patterns; CP, machine-gun and outpost locations; and alertness levels. We didn't realize how thorough they were until Lieutenant Larry Tahler took a journal full of copious notes on our strengths and weaknesses off a dead VC who'd been scoping us outside of Danger until Tahler scoped him—and an M-14 slug shut off his lights.

At the end of each day, I'd try to snare a LOH and fly from the outer ring of barbed wire in ever-increasing circles looking for signs of the enemy. Then, pilot willing, I'd go hunting. One day, flying around the wire, I looked down and saw a guy with green shorts and green shirt in the prone position right at the last strand of outer wire. Probably a scout, I thought. We circled around him to see if he had any buddies with him, and went down to a few feet off the ground as soon as I was sure we could scoop him up without getting our butts shot up. I jumped from the chopper, picked the guy up and threw him in the backseat of the LOH.

I can't imagine what he was thinking—one minute he was trying to crawl into an anthole, the next he was in some kind of flying machine with this wild-eyed American pointing a .38 pistol at him and telling him in English to sit quietly or he was dead. He must have been scared shitless because even with my pistol pointed at his head, he leapt from the backseat of the bird. "Geronimo"—a twenty-foot drop, and he took off.

I didn't shoot him as he was unassing the LOH: I worried that my slug would go through him and smack right into the engine. We flared down on him again, and he grabbed the skids and started swinging back and forth like a trapeze artist. The brave fucker must have thought he could pull us from the sky.. Then he dropped off and started running. It was getting dark and I realized we were going to lose him, so when Ken Carroll swung the bird around, I hit the VC square in the head. A 40-millimeter shotgun shell from my trusty M-79 grenade launcher peeled his face to the bone, leaving only a twitching skull. One more for the body count, but I'd lost a POW because I hadn't buckled him into the bird. I was pissed at myself. A POW was far more important than a faceless stiff, especially a scout who was probably from a recon outfit.

Within a few days, FSB Danger was hard as a brick, sharp as a Ranger's trench knife and ready for all comers—we'd won the race with the VC— even as DeRoos and Foley went out on their nightly ambushes, sowing as much fear into the enemy as they could. That first night at Danger, for example, while Battle Company and the rest of the boys worked on the defenses, DeRoos's Claymore Company nailed four VC in an ambush along a canal, and at first light Foley's Dagger Company, on a jitterbug mission, hit targets all over our AO. Within the first twelve hours, we'd put our paw on our new turf.

In the center of the base, a half battery of howitzers from C1/11st Artillery Battalion gave us three 105s ready at a moment's notice to blast Charley. The howitzer gunners, led by Lieutenant Ken Strong, a West Point classmate of Knapp and a good man, always put iron on the target. Never in the thousands of missions they fired in support of the Battalion were they less than deadly responsive. As important, they never had a short round or hit any of our troops. In all of my combat experience, Strong's boys and later Chum Robert's "A" Battery were the only cannon cockers who didn't drop rounds on my soldiers somewhere down the line.

Each day we added a little more protection to Danger and a few more tricks such as fifty-five-gallon drums filled with napalm in the outer barbwire that could be ignited by pulling a wire and exploding a white phosphorus grenade. Bob Johnson swapped a few AK-47s for several cases of one-million-candlelight Air Force flares, which we set up around the perimeter. All a grunt had to do was yank a wire, and instantly night became day.

Everyone at the firebase had an assigned battle position—the rotating rifle company drying out provided the main security, augmented by the Headquarters Company and artillery folks—with regular stand-to's at dawn and dusk where every soldier manned his assigned battle station and was at 100 percent alert. Stand-to's were also called randomly throughout the night. Within a few days, Danger was locked and cocked, set to defend itself and to control and support Hardcore units deployed around the firebase.

Every soldier slept under cover—in a bunker or a culvert covered with sandbags. Failure to comply was an automatic court-martial—no quarter given. Soldiers always try to beat the system even if their "doing their own thing" means getting killed or fined. On one day alone in early March, I court-martialed and fined ten soldiers for failure to sleep under cover. Even Jerry Sullivan, my platoon sergeant candidate, was caught sleeping in the open by his "designated tormentor," Lieutenant Rex Fletcher. Fletcher, an OCS graduate, was the longest-serving rifle platoon leader in the Battalion. Sullivan will go to Heaven sore at him for being so STRAC, but he was a first-rate combat officer who cared about his troops. According to Fletcher's former CO and greatest fan Gordy DeRoos, "Rex was the best."

Considering Sullivan's potential, I fined him fifty bucks but didn't bust him. "The fresh air and pissing off Lieutenant Fletcher was worth it," Sully said as he smiled, saluted and left. Another Irishman who always had to get in the last word. But the troops got the hard message and like good little groundhogs, they slept under cover—or got thumped with a court-martial.

The Hardcore began to hum. Between the Hardcore grunts, the Boomerangs, Bounty Hunter's gunships, the 7/1st Air Cav's Comanche troops and Tahler's Snipers, the Hardcore racked up forty more VC before we spent our first twenty-four hours at Danger. Along the way, Foley's boys captured a new VC tractor and three fifty-five-gallon drums of gasoline. Again, no U.S. KIAs. We were rolling and now we even had a new tractor to pull the load.

On our third night at Danger, the VC paid a visit, throwing everything at us but the kitchen wok. But for them there was just one problem: Not one round of perhaps a hundred mixed mortar and recoilless rifle shells struck within the perimeter. Charley's incoming resulted in blowing up a lot of rice paddy outside Danger but didn't cause one Purple Heart. Before the second round thudded in, every Hardcore trooper was at stand-to in his fighting position, kind of hoping Charley would follow through with a ground attack.

Press said later, "I reckon the gooks were just so afraid of us they couldn't even shoot straight. You can bet your ass some VC leaders got their butts ripped over that fuckup. Imagine, toting all that ammunition all the way from Hanoi and then flat missing the target."

I remember thinking at the time that maybe they blew it because they knew we were the Hardcore. Maybe they'd heard of the pain we'd inflicted around FSB Moore. Maybe their scouts had reported just how professional and alert we were. Maybe they'd told their commanders about our brown helmets and our HARDCORE RECONDO insignias and figured we were special dudes, just like I'd told our guys. Whatever, their half-assed attack further strengthened the Battalion's morale. At least some of the men began to believe we really were the best and couldn't be touched.

Foley quickly turned around Dagger, our weakest company. Within three weeks, he had them functioning close to his old Tiger Force in the 1/327th Airborne. Late on the afternoon of 10 March, Dagger was headed back to Danger to replace Battle Company and to dry out, when we got a flash intelligence report, a radio intercept, indicating that a VC force with a number of recoilless rifles—perhaps the same guns who'd tried to nail us the night before—had set up in a nearby village. Because the unit closest to the target was Foley's, I told him to turn around and go for it.

At first, for just a moment, Foley fought my decision. He said his men were beat and needed to dry out. They'd been wading through mud, water and slush for four days. "If we stay any longer, we'll have serious foot problems," he insisted. "Our feet are all fucked up."

"I know," I radioed back, "but there are no air assets and you're only two hours away by foot. It's top priority. We've got the mission. You've got the job. Get cracking."

"Sir—" Foley started to try again. But I didn't have the time or patience to go another round. I had no intention of arguing with him over the mission.

"Either you go," I said, "or your replacement will."

I loved Foley like a brother, loved his attitude, his courage, his honesty, his distaste for bullshit. We went back a long way together—I knew him, he knew me. Neither of us had anything to prove to the other. We could operate by shorthand.

"Wilco, out," he snapped, knowing any further protest was useless.

Dagger Company began the trek to the village. As Foley approached the target, his point element slipped up on three VC and took them out. Then, he recalls, the company started running into "a mile-long stretch of toe poppers." Posting a stay-behind patrol that killed a VC soldier tailing the company, Foley continued to move along a canal through thick vegetation that provided good concealment. But the VC got lucky when Foley and his RTO, Farley, didn't see a trip wire. A VC booby trap—a large coffee can filled with explosives and small rocks and wrapped with barbwire and nails—blew them sky high.

I was flying to the target area in a Brigade LOH when I got word that Foley and Farley were down. By the time I got over the unit, Platoon Sergeant Mike Kidd had taken command. He popped smoke to identify their location and while my pilot Ken Carroll was circling, he lobbed an LAW at an enemy bunker. "The round deflected off the hard mud covering and came so close to the chopper, it scared the hell out of me," Kidd remembers.

Carroll came down as close to the scene as possible, in the rubble of a bombed-out hooch. And as soon as he touched down with one skid, I jumped off while he went back up and circled.

"Freeze, Colonel," yelled Dagger medic Billy Scott. "You're right in the middle of a minefield!"

No one could get to Foley or Farley, his wounded RTO. Across the field, Foley was badly hit, bleeding as though he'd whacked his leg with a chainsaw. When I saw Foley's blood pumping out of his body, I took off as if I were going for the gold, grabbed him and carried him back to the hooch. Carroll did another of his one-skid landings, and after stuffing Foley into the front seat with his shattered leg sticking out, I ran back for Farley, then told Carroll to fly both men directly to Dong Tam's 3rd Surgical Hospital.

"If that choppuh had not appeared out of nowhere," medic Billy Scott said in his soft Carolina drawl, "the Captain would've died. There was no way I could've saved him. He'd lost too much blood and was goin' into deep shock...and I'm not sure Farley woulda made it either."

While I was stuffing Foley, already flying on morphine, into the LOH, he looked at me blearily and asked, "Who's going to take command of my company?"

"I am."

Even through the dope haze he looked stunned.

"You don't think I remember how to run a fucking rifle company, Captain?"

Foley grinned, I grinned back—and I got to play Company Commander for a spell. After slogging through a couple of klicks of knee-high water, we finally encircled the targeted village. But either the intell from Division had been wrong, or the VC, who probably saw us coming from the time we medevacked Foley and Farley, had hauled ass. So the result of the mission was zero. There was no one in the village but old men, women and children. They knew nothing. Typical.

Musselman organized enough choppers to fly the Company back to Danger just as the sun went down. While waiting for the birds to pick us up, I called the TOC and told Captain Bruce Spurlock* to take over the Company once it set down at Danger. Ed Clark would replace him as the Battalion S-2, one step closer to a command spot.

I felt damn guilty about Foley getting hit. Angry words from a skipper can have very destructive results. Yes, ass-chewing is sometimes necessary to get the job done and Foley could take it. But my admonishment might well have caused him to move too fast. I was probably unusually curt and abrasive because of short rations in the sleep department—no excuse since none of us ever got enough sleep—and, looking back, I realize that I came down on him too hard. It was the old truism confronting commanders since the rock was the basic infantry weapon: Hotheaded exchanges ratchet up the casualty lists.

When I visited Foley in the hospital, he just gave me another happy morphine smile. I was relieved to find out he'd be OK, but from the bandages and tubes, I could tell he wouldn't be coming back. And I was right. His wounds took him to Walter Reed and almost cost him his leg—it looked like it had been run over by a platoon of soldiers wearing golf spikes instead of jungle boots. He'd be damn hard to replace.

I tried to have one spare rifle Company commander up my sleeve on the Battalion staff, grooming him to take over if a skipper went down. Next up was Bruce Spurlock, who had little hands-on regular infantry experience, which was why I'd put him in as S-2, the Intelligence slot that I liked to use as a company commander ready-rack. The S-2's job was to know the enemy, but by working in the Battalion TOC, he also got to know the Battalion's tactical SOP, how the companies operated and what was expected. In the days that followed while Dagger ran local operations around Danger, I could see he was no Dennis Foley, whom I'd recruited specifically to turn our weakest company around. But with Foley blown away, Dagger needed a skipper right away and Spurlock was it.

A green but highly motivated volunteer, Captain Spurlock came to the Battalion from Brigade where, on his second tour in Vietnam, he served as the Headquarters Company CO. Brigade XO Carlson gave him high marks as a leader. On the downside, most of his service had been in the Reserves and he had little line time with regular troops. But at thirty, he was a lot older than his peers, which has always been a plus in my book. All too often in 1969 the majority of infantry company commanders in Vietnam were barely drinking age.

In Vietnam, a rifle company skipper frequently commanded right up front playing squad and platoon leader where the bullets fly and people die. Not the kind of job that promoted longevity. Nothing in battle goes down as neatly as it does in classroom war games at the Infantry School.

My intent had been to send Spurlock out with the rifle company commanders as his workload permitted so he could get some seasoning from these veteran skippers. I knew that after several visits with Foley, Winston, DeRoos and Knapp, topped off by a few weeks with the Aussies, where he'd get some OJT training from the best jungle fighters in the world, he'd be better prepared to run a rifle company when one became available.

Now, to compensate for the change in plans, I spent as much time with Spurlock as I could spare while his company was standing down, chalk-talking him through the tricks I expected him to use heading up one of the Battalion's two companies that would operate independently like Korean War Ranger units. I wanted to spoon-feed him, pass on my knowledge about fighting a rifle company in a guerrilla environment. To that end, I assigned him local day missions just outside of the base—on-the-job training at its best, hands-on against a real live aggressor on a kill-or-be-killed battlefield.

I just tagged along, provided guidance and on-the-spot corrections as Dagger slipped through the bush north of Danger. The exercises gave me a good feel for how Spurlock handled his unit and allowed me to check out his small unit leaders and soldiers while they eyeballed me. The men of Dagger were solid, with a lot of potential. As Platoon Sergeant Kidd now says, "We were tired of milling around in minefields, getting the shit blown out of us and never bloodying Charley." John Roberson had begun the process of turning them around, Dennis Foley had further sharpened them. Now I hoped that Bruce Spurlock, an eager, fast learner, would take them the rest of the way.

Within a few days of establishing Danger, we started to run into mines and ambushes along Route 4. The VC, following their standard tactics, tried to close down our ground pipeline. The idea was to force us to tie up a lot of troops securing the road instead of hunting them. A 1 March 1969 Division report said, "The most dangerous stretch of road (Route 4) in the Division AO was between My Tho and Cai Lai..."

Fire Support Base Danger was right smack in the middle of this shooting gallery. "Most ambushes were a quick thing," recalls Jim Robertson of his reassignment to a truck-driving detail. "You caught a few rounds and if you got through it, it was over. If you stopped, they kept at you, so we tried to keep moving, hit the gas and go like hell. The guys in the back of the truck were supposed to shoot back, but even the experienced guys didn't. Despite Battalion standing orders, the instinct was to just get your head down and get out of there."

So Route 4 was not a road you went on for a pleasant Sunday drive. If mines and ambushes didn't drive you crazy, ARVN drivers with road rage did. One day an ARVN driving a two-and-a-half-ton truck went ballistic after one of our jeeps returning to Dong Tam from Danger cut him off. He pulled up behind the jeep, took out his M-16 rifle, fired and killed Specialist Maxwell Smolla,* the driver for Lieutenant Gary Ellis, Hardcore's S-5.

It was supposed to be Smolla's last day in the field. The following morning he was to start processing to go home. Instead, he was KIA. Try explaining that to his family.

Between Dong Tam and Firebase Danger seven bridges rose about fifteen feet above the crossings to gain height over tides that came up as much as twelve feet during the rainy season. Robertson says, "We were most nervous driving through populated areas—you had to slow down because of the fear of hitting people—and fifty-five miles per hour was our preferred speed. We knew there wasn't a rangefinder on any type of VC direct-fire weapons that could track a vehicle going that fast. Twenty miles per hour and you were bazooka bait. Because the bridges were narrow, just a few inches on either side of the truck, if you judged it just right, you could floor it, go up on one side and land on the down ramp without even touching the top of the bridge."

But the VC had other ways to take out moving targets. They'd slip in at night and dig mines into the road's shoulders and then attach a wire running into some nearby bush where they'd hide. Some of their mines weighed in at three or four hundred pounds of explosives—getting most of their bang, ironically, from dud Air Force bombs and artillery shells. Their triggerman would wait until a fat target rolled over the mine and when it was in the right spot to sustain max damage he'd set it off.

One of our trucks with some of the Battalion cooks in the back hit a mine on its way to Danger. The explosion didn't blow the truck off the road, but it blew the transmission right through the floorboard almost into the driver's lap. The driver ended up badly wounded with large pieces of steel in his legs and feet. After the explosion, the VC came out of the tree line and walked up the road, getting ready to finish everyone off, when the wounded driver

 *A pseudonym.

attacked them and blew them away with his M-16.

The driver was a former line doggy who had his shit together. He was awarded the Silver Star for his gallantry. Without him, the Battalion would have been back on C-Rats because the cooks proved that day that they weren't yet Hardcore. "They all turned as soft as putty," Robertson recalls. "They went to ground."

But as we settled in at Giao Duc, the troops became harder, ready to play the game I had in mind. One company, Alert, would do long-range ambushes; another, Claymore, short-range ambushes; a third, Dagger, would operate as a Korean War Ranger Company; while Battle would do airmobile and Ranger operations. Winston, you go here; Spurlock, there; DeRoos, this is your assignment; Knapp, you're jitterbugging. And at the end of the operation, we'd all come together as one.

Alert and Claymore companies set up their own firebases, both several klicks from Danger. These units operated with a half company out on operations and the other half at their firebases, drying out, training and resting. This gave the soldiers and leaders a break from their unending 24/7 schedule. Another advantage was that if Charley attacked, any of our three firebases could scratch each other's backs with artillery and mortar fire from the others. Our 81mm mortars were placed with Alert Company at its firebase, called Tombstone Territory—right in the middle of a Vietnamese cemetery—and DeRoos kept things simple by naming his base, set up at an abandoned South Vietnamese school, Claymore. We put the Battalion's 4.2 mortar platoon with the nearby U.S. district advisers at Giao Duc along with our cooks—hot chow was back on the menu for breakfast and dinner for everyone except the boys in the bush.

Every four days I'd pick a Battalion target. "On the third day out, I want you to be here," I'd tell DeRoos, stabbing my finger at the map. "And on your fourth day, you'll be set up here." I gave similar instructions to the other commanders. "On the fourth day I want your company to be ambushing here." They were to advance using stealth and surprise. Then, coming from their different directions on the fourth day, we'd encircle our opponent like a giant steel bear trap.

CLICK.

I wanted them to learn from past mistakes. Too often in this war, our troops telegraphed their presence to the enemy: too much aerial reconnaissance, helicopter resupply, medevac and C&C flights drilling holes in the sky over the target or just sloppy grunt work. Seeing our punch coming, the VC ambushed us or put down booby traps or just hightailed it.

The VC wanted no part of a fight with superior forces. My idea was to silently approach them from 360 degrees all around their positions. By the time they sensed our presence and started to say, "Oh, no; Americans. We're out of here," they were going to run right into our waiting ambushes—and burn a little incense.

During the first eleven days at Danger, with supporting air and artillery, we ran airmobile operations, amphibious operations with the U.S. Navy, combined operations with Vietnamese units, and scores of ambushes and Ranger operations. Along the way, the Hardcore racked up a body count of 252 enemy. We had no friendly KIAs.

Early on, Ewell and Hunt choppered in for a visit. George Mergner remembers the moment: "The four of us were walking around the FSB when Ewell says to Hunt, 'Don't we have something for Dave?' Hunt pulls a Silver Star out of his briefcase. Ewell says, 'Read the order.' The medal was for the LRRPs' rescue, but Hunt had dropped the ball. He said, 'We don't have the order.' Ewell: 'I said, READ the order.' Like a little marionette, Hunt starts up with 'Attention to orders. Headquarters, 9th Infantry Division, etc, etc.' He goes through the whole thing, making it all up. Ewell pins the medal on you and says, 'Well, Dave, your second?' And you say, 'No, Sir.

That's a silver oak leaf cluster. It's number six.'"

When George e-mailed me the story, the scene came flooding back. Ewell stood there looking at me and I was thinking, Hack, you stupid shit. This isn't exactly the right time to correct the general's math.

"Very good," Ewell said.

Then I blurted out, "Oh, not so. MacArthur had eight."

Mergner told me he had to bite his lip to keep a straight face. "What a total gig!" he says today. "Great entertainment. Where were those two guys from?"

Hunt never again brought up the LRRP fiasco with me. Too embarrassed, I suppose.

But more important than math and medals, on the forty-first day after I took command, the Hardcore was damn near ready to walk the walk. We weren't perfect—no unit ever is—but we'd come a long way from that shit-hole Dizzy.

"If Colonel Lark had returned," Larry Tahler says, "he wouldn't have recognized the Battalion. We were a different outfit. We'd gone from stumbling to steamrolling."

No more toilet paper blowing in the wind.

NINE

Fire Support Base Danger
11 MARCH 1969

On 11 March at 1400 hours, while I was hiking along with Dagger Company outside Danger, Sergeant Slater called. "We just got a warning order to conduct an airmobile op," he said "The 2/39th's stirred up a hornet's nest. The hot skinny is there's a whole bunch of bad guys in there. A LOH is on its way to pick you up."

The 2/39th, our sister battalion, was the outfit I'd taken my OJT with when I first hit the 9th Division, scarfing up whatever knowledge I could while hanging with my old 1/101st buddy Don Schroeder. If there was any other battalion in the Brigade that I knew well apart from the 4/39th, this was the one. My week with them had convinced me they were a well-run, battle-tested outfit, no big surprise with Schroeder at the helm. But when Don was killed in early February, Lieutenant Colonel Robert Sullivan, a guy I didn't know, replaced him.

I hustled back to Danger, where Ed Clark briefed me.

"The 2/39th's stepped into a buzz saw. A platoon inserted into an LZ near My Phouc Tay, the company piled on and now they're getting seriously chewed up. Brigade estimates Sullivan could be in contact with a main force Battalion."

Bumstead told me that Jim Musselman was working the air assets for our move, since Hunt wasn't running the show. The reason was that Hunt was over in My Tho, the provincial capital, commanding the Brigade from afar while enjoying a fancy lunch at a top restaurant.

But Hunt scooted back fast. And once he arrived on the scene, he quickly convinced himself that Sullivan's boys had found a large VC force. Grabbing at the chance to play field marshal, he told everyone in sight, as if he were Erwin Rommel himself, that he intended to surround the enemy and then destroy him.

I told Alert Company's acting CO John Roberson and Claymore Company's Gordy DeRoos to prepare for action. There was no Huey C&C available—Sullivan had one bird and Hunt the other—so I got my favorite fearless pilot, Ken Carroll, to grab a LOH and we hightailed it over to the hot LZ near My Phouc Tay.

The fight was on the Kinh Tong Doc Loc canal, a "blue" running east-west near the village of Thanh Phu. As the LOH came in, I could see that the dry marsh grass adjoining the thick green vegetation near the waterway was on fire. A blanket of smoke was blowing into Sullivan's battalion; its units seemed to have been tossed on the battlefield as randomly as dice in a crap game. Mines and booby traps exploded from the fire and from Sullivan's advancing soldiers.

The brushfire blinded everyone on the ground. Together with the burning sun, it generated so much heat that those of Sullivan's troops who weren't coughing themselves sick keeled over from heat exhaustion.

When the fight first kicked off, heavy automatic fire from three sides had pinned down Lieutenant Richard Fisher's 2nd Platoon of "C" Company. As the fight developed, Fisher got hit. He went into shock from blood loss, four of his soldiers were wounded by booby traps, one died, and the platoon medic, who was patching up soldiers all over the battlefield, passed out from the heat. By this time, the smoke had gotten so bad the gunship pilots couldn't tell the good guys from the bad guys and had to check fire.

As I circled making my initial recon, Jim Musselman came up on the radio:

"Hardcore 6, your mission is to move to the north side of the Kinh Tong Doc Loc canal, link up with Sullivan's forces and complete the encirclement of the enemy."

The idea was that the Hardcore's two companies augmented by Company "A" 6/31st Infantry—made OPCON to the 4/39th—would work up to the canal while the 2/39th, with reinforcing companies from other battalions, would seal from the south. Musselman told me Chinooks would lift Alert, Claymore and A6/31st to the Special Forces Camp at My Phouc Tay, about five klicks away from where they'd air-assault by Hueys to the LZs I was to pick on the north side of the canal.

I didn't mind operating out of a LOH instead of a C&C bird, but I badly missed not having Chum Robert with me working the artillery and operating as my S-3. He'd been shifted from the Hardcore to Brigade just when we were clicking, replaced by a captain whom I didn't know and couldn't yet trust.

From the number of enemy machine guns spitting out green tracers, I estimated at least a company-size enemy force entrenched along the south bank of the canal. Since air strikes had blown holes in the foliage and napalm had burned away a lot of the underbrush, I was able to scope out a string of enemy bunkers that appeared to have good fields of fire—protected, I suspected, by a carpet of mines and booby traps. Black geysers from VC mortars exploded among Sullivan's deploying units.

Gunships and TAC air were temporarily shut down because of the smoke. The timeless rule that prior planning prevents poor performance paid off when early in the fight, Artillery CO Lieutenant Colonel William Hauser moved his "B" Battery—1/11th Artillery Battalion (105mm)—by road from FSB Moore to the Special Forces Camp at My Phouc Tay. At Moore, his

Redleg cannon-cockers would have been out of range to help. But now, when the smoke shut down our air cover, they saved the day by blistering the enemy from My Phouc Tay. And Sullivan's grunts desperately needed it. On the open flat terrain in front of the VC positions, they were as exposed as balls on a billiard table.

By 1700 hours, the tree line that ran parallel to the canal and concealed the enemy force started to look like it was hit by a tornado. But I'd learned the hard way how artillery fire and Tac Air could blow an area to smithereens with not a tree left standing—and still the VC or NVA would survive thanks to their amazing shovel-work and deep bunkers.

The no-fire line between the Hardcore and Sullivan's battalion was the "blue," so we faced the risk of friendly fire as well as the decidedly unfriendly enemy fire coming from across the canal. With the full picture in my head, I flew to My Phouc Tay, where my skippers were assembled and outlined our plan.

"Roberson," I said, "you'll go in first, in the center, followed by Reynolds, who'll go in on the LZ to your west. DeRoos, you're last and you'll go into the LZ to the east. I'll be running the show from the LOH. When I'm off station and not on the ground, Gordy DeRoos will be in command."

I told the skippers I wanted them to use Tiger Scouts well forward as the points and to brief their guys to expect wall-to-wall mines. "The points will use grappling hooks and claymore mines and M-79s to blow a path to the canal. Just take your sweet time and don't blow yourselves up—we're in no hurry here," I said. "Before Roberson goes in, we'll dust each company's approach to the tree line with artillery. Hopefully, this'll give us a path clear of mines right to the canal."

Before my companies inserted, I took some time to follow the action on the south side of the canal. All the while, Hunt, his glory-lust whetted by the "battalion" we were about to surround and then decimate, was jamming the radio giving detailed instructions directly to Sullivan's Companies and Platoons. He was running the ground maneuver, the fire of the artillery, TAC air and gunships, far too busy micromanaging every detail to bother with briefing a subordinate commander—me—who'd be running half the battle.

From my perch high in the air, Hunt's deployment made little military sense. The units he'd air-assaulted on the south side of the canal seemed to have no tactical purpose. The 2/39th's "C" Company Platoon that triggered the fight now had more than 60 percent casualties and was no longer combat effective. When the rest of "C" Company piled on, they became wrapped around the axle extracting the initial platoon's dead and wounded instead of engaging the enemy. It looked as though Sullivan's "C" Company commander had lost control of the unit, since the relieving grunts were milling around like ninth-graders at their first dance while the VC blasted the shit out of them.

Like everything else Hunt touched this terrible day, nothing went right. Bravo Company 2/39th inserted next, its mission to move to the canal and seal it from the east. But Bravo overshot their objective and got lost, and by the time the company finally got into position to block that easterly escape route, the VC slipped away.

To make the situation worse, Alpha Company 2/39th, the third rifle company of Sullivan's battalion—skippered by Captain Sherman Williford—couldn't accomplish the mission to seal from the west. After air-assaulting onto an LZ, they had to approach their objective—the canal—through a mile-long vicious carpet of mines while the VC pummeled them with mortars and machine-gun fire to keep them from closing the door. By nightfall, they were pinned down in an open field.

Hunt fumed that Williford wasn't moving faster. He came up on "A" Company's internal frequency screaming, "Get those people moving. I want you to close on that canal now!"

Williford, a hardened Airborne-Ranger on his second tour in Vietnam as an infantryman, knew that to charge across that open mine-laced ground into a well-entrenched enemy would be suicide.

"If you want to lead my company in an attack," Williford told Hunt, "come down here and do it, 'cause I sure as hell ain't going to."

Hunt didn't take the challenge—he just continued fucking up from 3,000 feet.

His next act of tactical genius was to insert "C" Company, 6/31st Infantry Battalion commanded by Captain George Maudlin on the same ground where "C" Company 2/39th had already been chopped up. The reinforcements got bogged down by mines, then pinned by very effective enemy machine-gun fire.

It was obvious from the bedlam below me that "Rice Paddy Daddy" didn't have a clue about what he was doing. Meanwhile Sullivan, probably too new and in shock over Hunt's overpowering style, seemed more than OK with Hunt taking command of and tearing up his fine battalion.

Throughout the fight, Chum Robert sat right next to Hunt in the Brigade C&C bird. As Chum remembers the fight, Hunt "not only micromanaged TAC Air and gunships, but also the slick inserts. He had no concept of unity of command or even that things look a little different from the ground than they do from 3,000 feet. He just started putting slicks on the ground wherever he saw some sort of trouble with no thought to who was in charge on the ground or what the men were supposed to do when they got there."

Hunt continued to short-circuit the chain of command by talking directly to individual gunship pilots and company commanders, tying up the company radio nets and confusing young leaders in a nightmare situation. In the sky over the battle area where fighter aircraft, helicopter gunships and artillery rounds were playing tag, it was nothing short of a miracle that we didn't lose gunships to our own artillery fire and that the jet fighters weren't ramming the choppers.

Luckily for Hunt and all the rest of us, Chum Robert shut off the cannons before our own artillery shells ripped through the gunships. Chum would listen to Hunt directing the gunships, then cut off the arty while they came in and made their passes. By listening closely to Hunt's manic orders, he could intervene and shut down the cannons quickly. "The problem was I only had control of the arty," he recalls. Hunt unfortunately controlled everything else.

"The place looked like O'Hare at Thanksgiving with all the air controllers stoned out of their minds," Ken Carroll remembers. While Carroll carefully orbited far from the deadly flying circus, I war-gamed how to take care of our own end of the battle.

My overall objective was clear: to make contact with Colonel Sullivan's forces at the canal and lock in the seal. Normally when a VC Main Force unit established a base near a canal, it would come in by sampans, then fill the boats with rocks and sink them to hide them. When caught in the buzz saw, they'd abandon their sampans and try to swim away underwater, using nipa palm reeds for breathing hoses. Or they'd hang on to the roots of the nipa palms along the sides of the canals just below the surface and try to work their way out, hand over hand.

DeRoos and Reynolds took in concertina wire to stretch across the canal. That and the occasional frag grenade made the VC's avenue of escape rough going, especially with Hardcore troopers spraying every floating nipa palm. The water around many of the palms turned red and then bodies would pop up.

At 1700 hours, Chum Robert hammered the tree line on the north side before walking his artillery fire back to my LZs. At the same time, Brigade FAC Joe Connor—radio sign Tamale 14—had a set of fighters with no targets so he pounded the canal south of Roberson's objective with 500-pound bombs. Connor reported seeing several machine guns in there, and we wanted them turned to junk. "It was a very frustrating day for the Air Force," Connor recalls. "We flew cover continuously all day and into the night. We had access to unlimited fighters, but because of the sheer chaos on the ground and in the air we did not put in nearly as many air strikes as we should have. It was very difficult to get a fix on where our troops were and the smoke from fires made the visibility problematic at best, perfect conditions for my worst nightmare, a short round."

After dark, a particularly troublesome antiaircraft weapons position finally gave Connor "a clean and worthy target." Green VC tracer rounds, almost impossible to see from the air during the day, became beacons at night.

"The skies were unusually crowded even for a major battle," Connor says. "To identify the fighters diving on the target from those climbing above it after their strikes, aircraft turned on their wing lights and taillights. The VC gunners quickly reminded us that silhouetting ourselves in range of automatic weapons wasn't exactly approved 7th Air Force procedure, not too healthy, but it was effective in clearing the airspace. As a bonus the VC tracers marked their positions for the F-100s."

"These VC were real professionals and they didn't go down easy," Connor said. "As soon as the lead F-100 dropped his napalm, they'd direct their fire at his afterburner as it blazed skyward. Their weapons only fired briefly while the aircraft was most vulnerable and stopped before the wingman could use them to adjust his strike. Unfortunately for them, they picked on the wrong guys. The flight leader was equally crafty. On his third pass, he directed his wingman to decrease his spacing between their aircraft from forty-five seconds to ten seconds. While the VC were still firing at the lead aircraft, the second F-100 was in perfect position to lock in on them and splash them with good old American napalm. That closed down their gun."

A few minutes later, Roberson's Company air-assaulted into its LZ without incident and moved carefully to their initial objective. Two hours later they were sitting on the canal, having killed five VC soldiers with no friendly casualties.

DeRoos and Reynolds landed and then moved to their objectives, killing about a dozen VC trying to slither out of the trees under the combined pressure of the bombardment and the squeeze from our forces on the south side of the blue. "I got the dubious honor of walking point," Claymore's Jerry Sullivan remembers. "The artillery had plowed that field pretty good. We didn't hit one booby trap, and I expected them to be wall to wall. The VC we ran into were spooked and getting ready to bug when we ended their little run." Again, no problems, everything so far had gone as smoothly as a sand table training exercise.

Then came Hunt's friendly fire.

"We caught a couple gooks on the run and sent 'em to their maker in a hurry," Alert rifle squad leader Tom Aiken recalls. "It would have been a walk in the sun 'cept for all the shit our own guys was throwin' at us from the other side of the blue."

At this point, the biggest danger for the Hardcore wasn't enemy fire, but fire from Colonel Sullivan's troopers on the south side of the canal and Hunt's wrong-headed use of supporting fire. Red tracers, 40mm M-79 rounds and M-16 slugs were coming our way fast and furiously from Sullivan's boys. The troops in DeRoos's Company took especially heavy incoming friendly fire, making it difficult for them to close on the canal. "Until we got it shut off, it was a flat bitch. It was about the worst incoming I'd weathered in two tours in the 'Nam," DeRoos said. "This wasn't the way they taught at Fort Benning how to do encirclement."

By 2100 hours, Colonel Sullivan and I had worked out how to be downrange of each other and make it through the night without taking a lot of lumps. The Hardcore now had its three companies in position lined up west to east—A/6/31st, A/4/39th and C/4/39th. My skippers reported little incoming enemy or friendly fire and from my perch in the sky I saw no more VC green tracers.

My guess was Richard Fisher's Platoon had made contact with a large enemy force, possibly a battalion that morning, but by now the VC main body had beat feet and escaped along the canal. What we were bumping into in the woods were small detachments of Viet Cong fighting a determined rearguard action designed to delay and deceive us, buying time for their main body to get out of Dodge.

Other than city fighting, slugging it out in heavy woods is the nastiest and most costly kind of an infantry shoot-out. Especially in woods laced with mines. The VC were slick and quick. If they weren't sealed immediately, they were like cockroaches caught for a second on the kitchen floor—gone. I had a hunch that Brigade had moved too slowly, that we'd been holding a near empty bag since the sun went down.

But Hunt evidently couldn't believe the obvious. He poured in more rifle companies, reinforcing failure, until at 2200 hours five companies from three battalions on the south side of the canal lurched around in the dark, stumbled on mines and shot into one another. Grass fires lit up the battlefield, silhouetting the moving soldiers and making them targets for the VC rear guard.

Then Hunt radioed me to say he was going to employ gunships by the canal at the inside edge of my Battalion's positions.

"Jesus," I shouted. "No. No! I don't know exactly where my forward trace is."

I had visions of my elements being chopped into mincemeat by our own rocket and minigun fire. At the best of times gunships are not the asset of choice for real close-in support—to even contemplate using them in the dark, with all the smoke and confusion on the ground, was criminal lunacy. If *I* didn't know where my forward trace was, how in hell could the gunship pilots know?

I put down my mike, thinking Hunt had gotten the message.

Then, almost instantaneously, two Cobras began attacking.

At 1,000 feet, the sight of those awesome aircraft spitting death knotted my gut. Imagine what it was like for the Hardcore grunts on the receiving end of all this firepower. Alert and Claymore instantly reported taking fire and I saw a Cobra gunship, miniguns and rockets blazing, making a run right at the center of both companies. I got on the LOH's air-to-air freq to tell the Cobra pilot to break off, only to see him turn around and start to make another run.

"There was no cover," Sergeant Aiken remembers. "We didn't take any casualties from my platoon, but the CO and some other CP guys behind us got hit. A guy from my squad and I hid behind a little tree no bigger than a broom handle. It was a bad, bad scene."

Medic Vernon Iddings explains what it was like being on the receiving end of our own stuff. He says, "Man, I was never so scared in my life as when those tracers whipped in. It was like watching a big red snake coming at you from out of the sky and cracking down all around you like lightning."

Roberson's RTO Jimmy Hux, who'd won a Soldier's Medal for saving a drowning grunt, was now swimming in minigun fire and made-in-the-USA chunks of red-hot shrapnel. He hugged the ground next to Roberson while the Cobras attacked. "It was the scariest night of my life," he recalls. "If you've ever been on the wrong end of a minigun, you'll never forget it. It sounded like a giant meat grinder. The rockets hit close, throwing mud and water all over us, and then the minigun bullets hammered in."

"Lieutenant Roberson yelled, 'My hand's gone,'" Hux said. "The bullets took off his fingers when he was talking on the radio. He was damn lucky they didn't take off his head, which was only inches away. The other company RTO cracked up and started screaming, 'I'm not coming out anymore. I'm done with it.'"

I didn't know what was going on down on the ground. I got on the horn and radioed Roberson, "Turn on a strobe so I'll know exactly where you are." He did, and I asked for a sitrep.

"Yes, Sir," he replied. "We've got four, maybe five wounded."

I noticed a crack in his voice. "How about you?" I asked.

"Just a scratch, Sir."

"The shrapnel chopped off his two middle fingers on the left hand and cut up his arm," recalls medic Charlie Wintzer, who patched him up. "Lieutenant Roberson refused morphine. He said he had to keep his head together to command his company. He was in incredible pain, but he was just so cool. He kept saying as he would rub his left thumb and forefinger together, which was about all he had left on that hand, 'I'll still be able to fly-fish. I'll still be able to fly-fish.'"

I told Carroll to take the LOH to about forty to fifty meters above Roberson's strobe and flip on the chopper's navigation lights. The gunships would have to blow our chopper out of the sky, or break off—and in fact they did break off just as they turned to make another lethal run.

Wintzer took care of the rest of the wounded and called in a medevac, but Roberson refused to leave his company. He stayed until daylight.*

"The Cobras took off once the LOH set down on top of us and then the VC tried to shoot down the colonel," Hux recalls. "A machine-gunner named Azar stood up in all that fire and let go with a burst of at least forty rounds. Even though Lieutenant Roberson was wounded, he kept yelling at Azar to get down. But he didn't. He just kept blasting and laughing like a madman.

*Roberson committed suicide in 1989, only two months before I was able to track him down. Some say he never got over the war, particularly that lousy night at Thanh Phu. It's still a major regret that I didn't find him sooner.

The VC stopped shooting."

About this time Claymore reported four casualties, all light wounds. The Docs said they wouldn't need medevacking till morning. "But believe me," DeRoos radioed, "this kind of shit ain't good for morale. It may kick up my insurance premiums."

I was killing mad. I told DeRoos to take command of the Hardcore and hightailed it with a now exhausted Carroll—who had over sixteen nonstop hours behind the wheel plus refueling—to My Phouc Tay, where that motherfucker Ira Rommel, having returned from his exploits above the battlefield, was busy holding court.

When we landed at the Special Forces Camp, I saw the sonofabitch standing by the Camp's chopper landing pad talking to Colonel John Hayes, the officer just coming in to replace him.

I'd known and admired John Hayes since we were captains together in Germany in the late 1950s. A soldier's soldier, he was with the 10th Special Forces Group when I was a staff weenie at the U.S. Army's European Headquarters trying to get into his damn fine unit. Up from the ranks like his dad, who'd been a distinguished warrior in WWI and WWII, he'd fought in Korea for two years as a tank platoon leader and a rifle company commander—where he was wounded five times.

When Hayes took over Recondo Brigade he already had five years' combat duty in Vietnam under his pistol belt. His first tour was early in the war, in 1962, when he formed and trained the first Ranger Battalion in the Vietnamese Army. Then he went on to serve in Special Forces commanding Project Delta and a Special Forces company, then he commanded a battalion-sized task force and was a brigade XO in the 1st Infantry Division. And after that he served with Special Operations Group running covert operations in North Vietnam. At the fighting level, you name it and he'd done it, and now he would soon be our skipper. Thanks to the big Ranger in the sky, the

Hardcore would at last have a leader who understood the nature of the war and how to fight it.

Hayes, professionally, was a lot like John Geraci, but without the bluster and roar. They were both extraordinarily capable combat leaders who brought enormous experience to battlefield But where Geraci was a loud, profane house-wrecker, Hayes was quiet, careful, methodical and introspective, not unlike the insurgent with whom we were slugging it out.

He not only had a keen understanding of the Asian mind, he also understood me. Luckily for all parties at that particular moment—as I got out of my chopper and stormed across the pad.

"Goddamn you, Hunt, you stupid sonofabitch. I told you no fucking gunships. You acknowledged my message and you still put in the strike. You shot up my soldiers, you asshole."

He looked up like a deuce and a half was bearing down on him, but I gave him no chance to reply.

"You're a no-good phony incompetent motherfucker!" I shouted as I reached for my .38 pistol, so crazed with fury that I was ready to blow this tinhorn imposter away and dump his fat body in the nearest canal.

Colonel Hayes, a martial-arts expert, struck like lightning. Before I knew it, he had my pistol and was throwing me back in my chopper.

"Hardcore Recondo, Hack," he said. He looked over at Carroll. "Take him up to 3,000 feet so he can cool off, then fly him back to the fight."

Nearly thirty years later, Hayes told me Hunt had filled his pants that night, then run inside the Special Forces command bunker shaking like a palm tree in a tropical storm. Hayes said Hunt knew he fucked up when I radioed him in his chopper right after the gunships hit my boys.

For most of the battle, Hunt flew well above the action at "oxygen-starvation altitude." Colonel Hayes, supposedly understudying the maestro in action, sat next to Hunt in his chopper. "He was yelling and screaming over the radio and asking for the latest body count or directing fire onto an enemy no one else in the C&C helicopter could see and then fabricating a body count which he pulled right out of the air," Hayes said. "I wondered what I'd gotten myself into by coming to the 9th Division. I had five years in Vietnam at that time and had never seen such a mess, and I'd seen a few messes."

Hayes is a deadly mimic. "Hunt totally panicked and tried to get reassurance from me. 'John,' he said, 'don't you think I did right?' I'd just ignored him. I never witnessed such a fuckup in my entire nine years of combat."

By the time Carroll ferried me back to the fight, mayhem ruled around the canal. "A" Company of the 3/39th was firing into "A" Company of the 2/39th, which was firing into "A" Company of the 4/39th, which was firing back into A/2/39th. Any infantryman worth his CIB knows that under such conditions—pitch-black night, mines, a determined enemy rear guard, and exhausted infantry fighters—you don't move, you squat. But Hunt had set up a kill zone and put our Brigade right in the middle of it. All for a shot at instant personal glory.

Eventually Reynolds—A/6/31st—linked up with B/2/39th south of the canal and stretched concertina wire across the "blue." DeRoos's Claymore and Williford's "A" Company were supposed to put the final nail in the enemy's escape door. But after plowing through acres of mines, enduring enemy and friendly fire, Williford and his brave soldiers couldn't close the seal. There was a gap of 500 to 1,000 yards.

General Vo Nguyen Giap, North Vietnam's answer to Sun Tzu, once said, "If I have an opening big enough to pass a mule, I can move an army." The VC SOP in case they got caught was to have prepared fallback locations and rally points, places they could reach by sampan, foot—or dog paddle. Based on the small amount of enemy fire between 1800 hours and dawn, the enemy's main body had started pulling through that huge gap just as soon as it got dark. By daylight, Hunt's seal was in place. The problem was, there were few enemy left—he sealed it twelve hours too late.

At first light on a deadly quiet and foggy battlefield, a sweep was started on both sides of the canal. Williford's "A" Company swept the contact area to the east, uncovering two bodies; some blood trails were spotted and two more bodies were found, then A/3/39th discovered a deserted bunkered enemy base camp with no enemy dead. Later in the morning, they linked up with Williford and swept abreast to the east until they linked up with C/6/31st, who'd searched the area where C/2/39th had received such brutal punishment at the beginning of the fight. They found at least twenty-five RPG rocket tail fins, but no enemy dead on a sweep that was slow and dangerous going—the place was littered with mines and unexploded U.S. ordnance.

To recap the enemy dead: On the north side, DeRoos's, Reynolds's and Roberson's troops accounted for seventeen VC by actual body counts. Add that to the KIA figure reported on the south—and by gunships, air strikes and thousands of artillery rounds—and the grand total was forty enemy dead and seven enemy weapons captured. This at the cost of fifty American soldiers wounded or killed and the exhaustion of a Brigade of infantry with all of its supporting elements.

"The operation was a crock from the beginning to crooked end," DeRoos told me. "We should all have stayed home."

To Hunt, on the other hand, the crock was a pot of gold. When he-of-the-full-pants returned to the Brigade TOC, he called Division and said there'd been a mistake in the body-count figure—the earlier reported forty enemy dead magically jumped to seventy-two. Only a dual-hatter Brigade CO/Division Chief of Staff could get away with a fudge like that. What Division staff officer was going to say, "Pardon me, boss, but on what authority have you changed the figures?"

As the sun rose on the still smoking field of chaos, two Huey slicks chock full of reporters set down. Hunt had ordered the Division Information officer to fly in the press and cameras so he could brief them at the site of his "great battle." He gave them the old razzle-dazzle, then flew them back to Saigon convinced he'd demolished a VC battalion of some 400 men.

While the choppers whizzed the media around Hunt's field of glory to get their scoop, neither Sullivan's nor the Hardcore's soldiers could get a single bird to bring in water or supplies. Finally the bone-weary troops moved to PZs, where they were picked up by choppers and returned to their starting positions.

When Hunt got back to being the Division's full-time Chief of Staff, he supervised the official report on the battle and authorized the following tapestry of lies, giving the generals, the service secretaries, the politicians and the White House the hot skinny on how "victory" was achieved at Thanh Phu on 11 and 12 March 1969:

This was a big day for the 1st Brigade and an especially active one for 2/39th Infantry. A bushmaster by 2/39th resulted in eleven enemy dead during the early morning hours before daybreak and at first light the battalion redeployed to conduct cordon and search and airmobile operations. While sweeping the ground following one insertion, C/2/39th Infantry contacted an enemy force, later determined to be the 261B Main Force Battalion, in fortified positions. Before the day ended 1st Brigade had executed the biggest encirclement of the cited period and provided a classic example of the "seal" and enemy destruction that was the goal of all 9th Division air and foot-mobile search tactics. In action lasting into the early morning of 12 March, the Brigade Commander, Colonel Ira A. Hunt, Jr. directed the air insertion of eight infantry companies and commanded a combined effort which reduced the Viet Cong Battalion to combat ineffectiveness.

The kicker from Field Marshal Hunt's glitzed-up report was that "gun-ships had been used with great finesse." Not sure Roberson and DeRoos and their soldiers would agree with him about the "finesse" part.

Colonel Carlson, then the Brigade XO and later a distinguished battalion commander of the 6/31st Infantry, described the battle as only a good grunt could: "One of the great cluster-fucks of the Vietnam War."

Chum Robert, who'd been over the fight from the first shot as the Brigade fire support officer, tells the real story: "Hunt screwed up Jim Musselman's initial plan. If he'd had enough sense to let Jim work the plan he had in place, he might indeed have had a real victory to celebrate. When he returned from My Tho, he nitpicked Jim's plan asking ridiculous questions. He wasted a lot of time and didn't close the loop early enough. He bullied Sullivan, put troops on the ground in random order rather than in accordance with Jim's plan, and the rest is sad history. "

As for me, it all confirmed everything that had been obvious to Private Hackworth twenty-three years before in Italy, and I still feel outrage whenever I hear Hunt's name. Those who suffered under him on the Division staff at Dong Tam called him "The Beast of Delta Tango." He was all of that in spades.

The next day, after three weeks as acting commander, he turned the Brigade over to Colonel John Hayes.

TEN

Co Co Canal
13 MARCH 1969

The loss of three company commanders in four weeks left Dagger Company drifting like a battered warship without a rudder. The company desperately needed a seasoned commander. By 13 March, Bruce Spurlock had been commanding Dagger for only three days. He was learning, but he was still at the crawling stage. I kept urging him to lean on his veteran small unit leaders, men who might not have logged much time in the Army but had just what Spurlock lacked—one hell of a lot of combat experience in Delta fighting.

That night, Spurlock had set out three platoon-sized ambushes around the north/south Co Co Canal. Operating independently, Dagger's 2nd Platoon was ambushing in the south, and the 3rd was in the north, separated by a large irrigation ditch running east/west perpendicular to the north/south canal. Spurlock's TAC CP was co-located with the 2nd Platoon's CP in a patch of woods. A rifle squad set up just behind the CP, pulling rear security.

The 1st Platoon, ambushing farther to the southwest, was supposed to rejoin the company before dark, but got delayed when it picked up two women from a small hooch observing its movement. The Platoon's Tiger Scout ID'ed the pair as VC or the wives of VC soldiers. "We knew if we didn't take them with us, they'd tell the VC we were in the area," recalls

Platoon leader Lieutenant Joel Wolfrom. The two VC women quickly became an "uncooperative anchor" that "bogged the platoon down."

Wolfrom radioed Spurlock, reporting that he could not close his position until well after dark. He recommended finding an ambush position for the Platoon and spending the night there. Spurlock approved the plan, then told Wolfrom to link up at first light.

He also told acting 3rd Platoon leader Sergeant Martinelli—a much-admired Shake and Bake who'd been with Dagger Company since its days as a heavy weapons company, to set up an ambush position along the canal. "His guidance was pretty vague," Martinelli recalls. "'Set up there,' he said, pointing to the canal bank on the other side of the ditch."

Martinelli recognized the danger of the ditch that divided the two platoons and instructed his 3rd Squad leader, Sergeant Ed "Gomer" Reynolds, to fishhook his squad's flank and cover it with a machine gun and claymores. "I put all three squads up, put the Platoon CP right on the canal bank, and made sure that claymores were put out—I was a fanatic about claymores. I always made sure they went out."

"It was a dark quiet night," recalls Alan Jensen, a hard-charging 2nd Platoon machine-gunner who'd taken his Advanced Infantry Training in the "Stay Alert, Stay Alive" Battalion at Fort Lewis. Jensen was with Spurlock and the 2nd Platoon squad securing the rear. "The guys in the Platoon were not happy—our positions were the worst we'd ever occupied."

At about the same time, Wolfrom started to move the 1st Platoon across a canal that ran behind Spurlock's position. But when the point man, Tiger Scout Ang, spotted mines and trip wires on the opposite bank, Wolfrom and Platoon Sergeant Eugene Lange wisely moved the Platoon to an alternative ambush position about 400 meters to the northwest of Spurlock, where they got ready for the night.

"Lange and I set our Platoon in high, dry grass at the junction of a feeder canal," Wolfrom remembers. While Sergeant Lange put the men in position and Ang quieted the VC women, Wolfrom studied the map by red flashlight under his poncho to conceal the light and talked to Spurlock by radio, fixing the location of the 1st Platoon.

Just after dark, a green replacement in Spurlock's position spotted a VC by the canal, fired at him from point-blank range with his .45-caliber pistol and missed with all eight shots. "The gook got away from us, and so did our surprise," says Bruce Peters, a bright, lanky Minnesotan who was Spurlock's RTO that night.

For the next eight hours it was quiet. With Wolfrom in the 1st Platoon, Squad Leader Steve Elgin, a tough draftee from Boise, Idaho, thought they were into a non-event. But around 0300 hours, shit started to happen. "Our OP heard movement," recalls Elgin. "It turned out to be a lot of gooks moving up the canal toward the 2nd and 3rd Platoons' positions."

Sergeant Lange gave Lieutenant Wolfrom the word that a VC element was using low tide to move barefooted in the mud along the feeder to the main canal and had almost cleared 1st Platoon's position. "We heard Charley moving noisily, clanking weapons, talking, with smokes glowing in the dark, along the bank opposite our rather open position," Wolfrom says. "The high palm tree and nipa palm growth along the feeder canal hid the VC movement, but also concealed my Platoon's location from the enemy."

As the tail of the VC column crossed the canal intersection, Wolfrom told Lange to have the OP squad leader toss one grenade high in the air to get an air burst. The squad leader said no way. When Wolfrom made it a direct order, the squad leader lobbed a high hard one up, over and into the palms at the last three VC crossing toward Spurlock's position.

What followed, according to Wolfrom, was the single most frustrating moment of his life.

"While Sergeant Lange got the rest of the 1st Platoon men alert and ready to move, I repeatedly radioed and was repeatedly ignored by Spurlock. He most certainly was sleeping. I was whisper-screaming on the radio to wake the Captain and tell him he'd soon be attacked. I repeated this at least three times and demanded the RTO tell me that he'd told the Captain. I threatened him with court-martial if my instructions weren't followed exactly and immediately."

The only feedback Wolfrom got was from the RTO, who said, "The Captain says that as long as you know where you are, it's OK with him."

"Obviously, Spurlock was referring to our earlier conversation when we defined our precise locations," Wolfrom recalls. His grenade signal, designed to alert the men of the 2nd Platoon to the enemy's exact position, was ignored.

And as the warning disappeared in the darkness, the night itself exploded.

Charley's attack plan was as brilliant as it was horrific. At low tide, the VC attack column had moved into a defilade position snug against the bank of Spurlock's ambush position. Next, the VC triggered the attack by floating a small empty sampan past Spurlock's Platoons. The decoy drew fire that gave away Spurlock's position. Without running any risk to themselves, the VC knew exactly where Spurlock's men were.

"The last thing I remember is the Captain was sitting up monitoring the radio," says Sergeant Michael Kidd, a steady-as-a-rock West Virginian. "For sure, he was hit and down in the first few seconds. He never regained consciousness."

The enemy force hit the 2nd Platoon frontally, driving the Hardcore troops to ground. Simultaneously, the VC infiltrated a large force down the east/west irrigation ditch, got behind the 2nd Platoon and attacked from the rear from south to north.

"A flare popped," recalls RTO Bruce Peters. "We could see the Viet Cong crossing the river. This was one of the few times in Vietnam I actually saw someone I was shooting at and, God, there were dozens of them!"

"Within seconds we were in the middle of it—they basically overran us," Rifleman Landon Hale remembers. "It was crazy, really confusing, until they dropped a flare. That gave us a chance to see what was going on."

"The VC used the ditch that separated my Platoon from the 2nd Platoon and drove a wedge between us," Platoon Sergeant Martinelli says. "My left squad got hit hard, but hung on. When they hit, they seemed to come right out of the water. But only my left squad was seriously engaged."

Squad Leader "Gomer" Reynolds and his squad were hit by RPG and AK-47 fire coming out of the irrigation ditch and from their front. "They were close," says Reynolds. "Real close. You could hear them armin' their grenades. It was like we woke up in hell. I told the guys, 'If we don't get them off us they're goin' to kill us.' I almost burned up my grenade launcher fraggin' as many bodies as I could."

Two of Reynolds's men went down immediately. He got his squad members returning fire. With slugs snapping all around him, he crawled to his two wounded soldiers and pulled them to shelter behind the canal bank. Then he ran forward and under a heavy barrage of machine-gun fire, blew the claymores he'd set up in the ditch.

The claymores were lifesavers. "I was lying on the side of the bank next to Ron Martinelli," recalls RTO Tommy Pye. "I heard these gooks coming up the canal, sloshing around just like they knew what they were doing. Three of them stopped right in front of my claymore and I said to myself, 'I know what to do now.' They were fixing to come in on that side. I popped the claymore right in their faces and stopped them dead in their tracks."

From his own vantage point, Wolfrom could see the VC firing RPGs and lobbing grenades across the canal bank from their own close but concealed positions. Simultaneously, two bunkers, located directly behind Spurlock's position, each manned with a Soviet machine gun—the antiaircraft type with small steel wheels—started to lay down a deadly wall of fire one foot off the ground with their ghostly green-yellow tracers. Those weapons kept Spurlock's group pinned down while the RPGs and grenades did their awful work.

"Had my Platoon not moved over to the canal intersection earlier, we certainly would have been directly in the cross fire of those two guns," Wolfrom recalls. "There was no cover or protection between the bunkers and us. I knew we'd be forced to cross in front of them when we moved to relieve Spurlock."

Wolfrom got on the radio and succeeded in raising Spooky, the gun/flare ship, and the helicopter gunships. To mark his position, he fired tracer rounds on the bunkers as well as vertically into the air, and the gunships began delivering supporting fire.

"The air cover was magic," Martinelli recalls. "It seemed like in minutes gunships and Spooky were raining bullets all around us. There was no commo, just one hell of a lot of incoming and outgoing. The gunships and Spooky were firing so close that the brass casing from spent ammo was falling down on top of us."

Rifleman Hale says,"This guy stayed over us in his chopper shooting up Charley for so long we could actually see his barrels glowing,"

David Wagner, a Canadian who volunteered for Vietnam duty—he'd swapped a safe clerk's job back in the rear to be a grunt—"awoke to the sounds of explosions, green tracers going over my head." He rolled into a nearby ditch.

"Guys were screaming that they were hurt real bad," he recalls. "All of a sudden me and the guy I'm with hear, 'CLUNK, CLUNK, CLUNK' and a grenade rolls right between us. It kind of shocked me. I froze. The other guy grabbed it and threw it out. I knew right then if I didn't get control of my fear, I was going to be dead."

"I was in position with Mike Kidd and the Company CP," 2nd Platoon radioman Don Owings, a tall, easygoing Californian, recalls. "A burst of AK fire went through my rifle's handguard. I rolled over, killed a VC soldier with my shattered rifle, and joined Mike, and he and I lay there side by side knocking off Charleys."

There were plenty of targets to go around. The Viet Cong, who'd slipped behind the 2nd Platoon through the drainage ditch, descended like crows on fresh roadkill.

"Gooks came right out of that ditch and were inside our perimeter before the first shot was fired," says Owings. "They threw grenades and then attacked our CP. They were also using the ditch for their supporting weapons. Several rocket rounds hit the trees, blowing red ants all over the ground. Sergeant Richard Duran, who was badly wounded, screamed and I ran over to him. 'Don, get those ants off of me,' he yelled. Here was a guy dying and his last request was to get the ants off of him. I did what I could."

"Slugs were flying in every direction," says PFC Bruce Peters. "I didn't know the captain was hit. I thought he was talking on the radio until Billy Scott, our medic, asked me to hold the captain down while he patched him up."

While medic Billy Scott was working on Spurlock, a VC ran up, fired point-blank at Billy, and missed him. "He must've thought both Spurlock and I were dead, since I was in the prone position trying to hold the captain, who was convulsing," Peters said. "Before I could swing around and blast him, Owings zapped him."

"It sure did get my attention and scared me half to death. But I was too busy with the captain to pay it much mind," Scott recalls.

Ignoring the firestorm, the medic calmly worked over Spurlock—who'd been seriously hit in the upper neck with either an AK bullet or a RPG fragment. Billy was starting a tracheotomy when Spurlock, who was making terrible gurgling sounds and spitting up blood, almost bit off his fingers. Once he stabilized Spurlock, he started taking care of the rest of the wounded. "I'd been in a fair numbuh of battles before that night," Billy says in that unmistakable drawl, "but I must tell ya, I've nevuh been busier. I was doin' triage on triage."

In the middle of the fight, Platoon Sergeant Kidd took a little snooze— courtesy of the VC. "It was black as hell and bullets were flyin' in every direction," he recalls. " I ran forward and jumped in a hole by the canal bank where I found a wounded soldier. I gave him my steel pot. Then somethin' whacked me in the head, knockin' me out. When I woke up, my head hurt. Thought somebody had kicked me. But the fightin' was still going on hot and heavy. I didn't give it any more mind. When it got light, I found a big potato masher grenade. That's what clobbered me. It was lyin' there right next to me. Thank God it was a dud."

"Our boys stayed cool," little Billy Scott says. "They hunkered right down in their positions and fought like tigers. That's the biggest thing that saved us. No one got up and ran. The boys jus' hung in there and tore up ole Charley."

Private First Class Peters instantly became the acting company commander. He called in gunships that blistered the attacking VC while Spooky lit up the battlefield. Peters kept me informed back at Danger and handled the besieged company like an old pro. Without a damn competent draftee PFC who'd been smart enough to pick up Tactics 101 from his previous COs, the outcome of this fight would have been even more tragic.

Within Spurlock's location, the sole surviving officer was the Forward Artillery Observer, Lieutenant Timothy Nay, a hero in the midst of chaos. The RPGs and grenades had blown out his left eardrum. Bleeding from the ear, he directed a 105mm howitzer rolling barrage along the canal bank.

Because of his injury, he couldn't hear much, so he was not responding to radio pleas to not walk those heavy shells into Wolfrom's position.

Somehow Nay was doing fine half-deaf. While he dropped his rounds between the platoons with great skill and accuracy, Wolfrom and Lange saddled up the 1st Platoon and started carefully moving toward the 2nd Platoon. Elgin's squad had the point. "As we were moving, a flare popped in the distance," he recalls, "and I saw a dozen gooks run into a big bunker about one hundred yards away."

Spotting two gunships several klicks away, Elgin got hold of Lieutenant Wolfrom and told him to get them. Within a few minutes, the two men were marking the target with tracer fire as a gunship rolled in and blew away the bunker. After the airstrike, they moved out. When they got near their objective, Elgin put his squad in position, took off his pack and lay down. "Suddenly, I was downrange in a shooting gallery," he recalls. "Machine-gun fire from across the canal was zipping above my face. If my nose had been three inches longer, I'd have lost it."

Three or more enemy machine guns and four RPGs laid down a steady stream of fire. Elgin saw at least three RPG rounds explode in the trees behind the 2nd Platoon. A number of RPG rounds also smacked into the 2nd Platoon's forward positions.

The RPG fire into the trees was probably aimed at taking out the Company CP. Knocking out a platoon or company's command and control was always high priority on a VC commander's thing-to-do list. By destroying commo, the VC could overrun the unit without being thumped by U.S. firepower.

"Thanks to Nay, the artillery fire kept pounding away, running up a VC body count in the palms next to the canal," Wolfrom recalls. "It was at this point when my Platoon ran straight into Charley's withdrawal, as he probably decided to avoid the artillery killing field, as well as the slow plow back through the canal, which was now being filled by the rising tide."

At least a squad of VC smoking cigarettes and talking loudly was heading toward Elgin. "When they were almost on top of me, I let go right into them with a couple magazines of M-16 slugs," he says. "There wasn't any damn cover. Nipa palm don't stop bullets much. I ran to the canal bank and jumped into a slight depression in the ground. Man, with all the shit flying around, I wanted some dirt between me and it."

"There were VC running all through our position," Lieutenant Wolfrom says. "We were mutually surprised suddenly to be introduced to one another. It was at this juncture that I issued a desperately wild order. 'Anyone who's an American and can hear my voice GET DOWN! Now shoot anyone left standing up!' I yelled. Sergeant Lange tactfully but immediately reminded me and Scout Ang—who may not have understood the phrase—that we were the only friendlies left standing! Ang and I hit the dirt as the bullets began flying furiously from all directions!"

On a battlefield lit up by flares, 1st Platoon Sergeant Lange observed Elgin's heroic action. "He single-handedly mowed down a dozen gooks. It was like he was cutting grass with a scythe. They never knew what hit 'em." The VC lost thirteen men to claymores and small arms fire. Four of the enemy dead were packing RPGs.

After the exchange Wolfrom worked forward to Spurlock's position. "I'll never forget the hollow sight of dead Americans lying in the muddy ditches," he says. "Spurlock was writhing in his death throes, and the FO, Lieutenant Nay, was standing there with blood pouring from his ear."

Without the quick thinking of "Gomer" Reynolds, the unit's flanks would have been rolled up, too. And it is significant to note that he and every other hero directly involved in this fight was a draftee, a true citizen soldier.

The next morning Platoon Sergeant Kidd checked the perimeter and found that the VC had turned many of the 2nd and 3rd Platoons' claymores around, another one of their nasty little tricks. "They hit us so hard with RPGs that a lot of our guys didn't get a chance to use their claymores. If we had, we'd been really hurtin'," Kidd said.

At first light, Colonel Hayes and I flew in aboard his C&C ship with Bob Press and Ed Clark, and I put Clark in command. He and Press reorganized the Company while I saw to the evacuation of the wounded and the dead, including Spurlock—thanks to the skill and dedication of Billy Scott, he was still alive along with eighteen other wounded. But two days after he was evacuated to Long Binh Hospital, Bruce Spurlock died.

When the dust from the fight settled, we counted thirteen enemy dead; in all probability, another twenty to forty had been dragged off. Dagger had taken three dead and nineteen wounded, three seriously. With rifle platoons running fifteen to twenty men, at least 30 percent of the company's paddy strength was lost. A very bad exchange.

Clark immediately dispatched several patrols to try and track down the enemy. Brigade sent a LOH and I gave it to Clark to recon the battlefield for signs of the enemy's withdrawal route and to have a good aerial look at the ballpark in which he and the men of Dagger would be playing for the next few days. Replacements and supplies were flown in and before noon, a rebuilt Dagger Company—granted, a bit shaky—moved out under their new captain in pursuit of their attackers.

"An hour after Hardcore 6 came in, General Gunn arrived to find out first-hand what happened," David Wagner recalls. "The general told us what a good job we'd done. It didn't compute. We got slaughtered, and no one asked why we were set up in such an indefensible place."

Frank Gunn was no Ewell. He knew the score. His veteran eye saw that the 2nd and 3rd Platoons tactical deployment had been unsound and that they were defending bad ground. But he also knew Spurlock was green and that the brave men of Dagger at exactly that moment needed praise, not an inquisition.

General Gunn presented a Silver Star for gallantry to Sergeant Reynolds, Bronze Stars for valor to Sergeant Kidd and Billy Scott and comforted the men. But he sternly said to Clark and me, "There are many lessons to be learned here."

None of them easy. Infantry combat is strange. Experience is a great but hard teacher. As in Spurlock's case, as in most instances of infantry combat, if you don't get it right the first time, you're dead. If Spurlock had been more seasoned, he would have listened to his small-unit leaders and shifted to another ambush spot after losing surprise; he would have deployed his Platoons smarter, set up better security, set out listening posts to provide early warning, insured that all of his troops booby-trapped their claymore mines with frag grenades and trip flares. And if the FNG had not given away the 2nd Platoon's position unloading his clip, we might have been ambushing the VC rather than the other way around.

On the flip side, if the 1st Platoon hadn't spotted the VC and Wolfrom hadn't decided not to reinforce Spurlock, Elgin and the 1st Platoon wouldn't have been in position to cut down the VC encircling force. It might well have finished off the 2nd Platoon. If Peters had not taken command and brought in gunships, we might have lost the 2nd Platoon completely.

If only Spurlock had acted on Wolfrom's warning, the nightmare that befell the 2nd Platoon would have been delivered to the VC. It occurred to me that Spurlock might have been talking in his sleep to the RTO who answered Wolfrom's call, not an uncommon fuckup in combat where sleep deprivation is the rule. I have to admit I've done it myself. In Korea, as a company commander, I moved an ambush patrol in the middle of the night while asleep. My RTO said later I seemed wide awake and looked at him and said, "Move the squad from position Blue to Red." Fortunately, my patrol didn't run into trouble, but the next morning, when I found out what I'd done, I told him to never accept an order from me unless I was standing and could rub my head and pat my belly at the same time.

The morning after the fight, Sergeant Kidd took Sergeant Major Press aside and told him he wanted to be busted back to private because he considered what had happened his fault.

"What do you mean, it was your fault?" Sergeant Press asked.

"I'm goin' nuts. I lost almost everybody," Sergeant Kidd said.

"How does that make it your fault?" Press asked.

"I knew Captain Spurlock didn't have much experience. I told him we had to move to a better position. Our place was no good and we had lost surprise. I told him we had an SOP that experience had proven and that we always moved after dark in case the VC had been shadowin' us, but he wouldn't listen to me. He pulled rank and said, 'We're stayin' here.' I told him, 'OK, you're in charge. You can do whatever you damn well want to do.' And I let it go at that. I should have been more forceful when I told him that this was not the way to do it, that it was not safe. But I let him do what he wanted to do and I feel responsible for the loss of all these good men."

"You were not in command," Press told him. "You're a sergeant and a good one. You did all you could do. You are not at fault. You will remain as the platoon sergeant and get on with your job."

Though just twenty, Sergeant Kidd was, in fact, a sharp and talented soldier. A Shake and Bake out of Benning, he'd been a squad leader or a platoon sergeant since he arrived in Vietnam in September 1968. At the time, he followed Press's orders and went back to his unit. Now, thirty-three years later, he says barely a day goes by when he doesn't think of that night and ask himself, Why in the hell didn't I fight Spurlock harder? "You never understand unless you've been there," he says. "The questions never go away."

In war, there's always a sudden death, an unexpected ambush, a situation gone haywire, a reversal. The only thing a commander can do is to learn from the hit, rebuild and move out. Lamenting the losses and the defeats while on the line just gets a unit deeper into a purple funk and endangers the living. At times like this it's a must to "accentuate the positive, eliminate the negative and don't mess with Mr. In-Between."

When the final count came in, we lost four good men KIA—Richard Losova Duran, Clarence Andrew Earley, Albert Thomas Glanton and Bruce Cameron Spurlock. The enemy had lost perhaps fifty-five. To me, that was not an acceptable exchange rate.

Richard Duran, recovering from an earlier wound, had volunteered to go out with the company against the medic's wishes. "Richard was a really fine soldier and man," Sergeant Kidd says. "He convinced the Doc he was well enough to go out. He knew we were short people and out of loyalty to his Platoon and wantin' to keep the Platoon safe, he was there. He'd just been promoted to sergeant and I'm sure this added to his feelin' of responsibility to look after his guys. We all lost a special friend when he went down, especially me."

"It was a long night," Don Owings said. "Finally the sun came up. For me, when the sun came up there was always an emotional release. It was usually a time to let go of pent-up feelings."

I'm sure Don Owings summed up a lot of his comrades' feelings: fear, fury, relief. "That morning tears came," he says. "Like, the lights came on. We made it."

ELEVEN

Sniper Control Center
15 MARCH 1969

Even through bad stretches like the Co Co Canal, I now had an ace up my sleeve: the Snipers. They called themselves Snoopy and Scooter, Hillbilly and Mountaineer, John Wayne and the Red Baron. Pound for pound, they were our most effective killing machine, twenty sharpshooters under the eagle eye of Larry Tahler, the young officer who'd called me an "SOB with brains" in the darkness during my first night with the 4/39th.

Tahler was a draftee who'd gone to OCS to "get out of KP and away from all the hut, two, three, four stuff." He had a brother who eventually retired as a Navy Rear Admiral, but his own attitude toward the military was strictly a citizen-soldier's. He was of slight build, wiry and hard as a railroad spike. His troops, who he'd hang out with over a beer or two, would do anything for him. "Tahler was there for you if you needed anything or just needed to talk," recalls Sniper Sergeant Bob Jones, a guy who could part your hair at 500 meters with an M-14 round. "But if you made a mistake, you'd know about it."

To form the Snipers, Tahler selected volunteers from throughout the Battalion. Before he'd even look at you, you had to have the Combat Infantryman's Badge and you had to shoot Expert, and even then, it didn't mean you were good to go.

"Getting volunteers was never a problem," Tahler remembers. "I always had a waiting list. It beat slogging in the mud, taking a chance on mines and booby traps. Snipers felt special and they were treated well by everyone at Battalion Headquarters because they were Hack's pets. The living was easier even though the risks were higher. And they were motivated—here was a chance to make a visible difference in the war effort. With every one I killed, I always thought that's one who won't be able to kill one of ours. And all my Snipers felt the same."

Tahler trained his gutsy trigger-pullers at Dong Tam under a team of top Army shooters led by Major Willis L. Powell, the former marksmanship guru at Fort Benning. Hank Emerson had persuaded General Ewell to bring Powell over from the Infantry School's Marksmanship Detachment. Within a few weeks, Powell's crack instructors turned our Hardcore grunts into deadeye killers. They taught Tahler's men techniques and tactics using specially accurized M-14 rifles (the XM-21) with silencers and smokeless ammunition.

"There were two different personalities of Snipers," recalls Sniper Ed Eaton. "Some were terrified of the infantry trip and others felt like a hero, being a doer, not a watcher. By the time you graduated you could hole a target at 700 meters. I came out of that course really confident."

When the Long Rifle boys—the name came from a Battalion Tiger Scout who said a Sniper's M-14 with an attached silencer was a "lung rifle" and eventually "lung rifle" became Long Rifles—returned from training, I told Tahler to suit them up in distinctive uniforms so they'd be recognized as a special unit. He came up with a doozer: camouflaged fatigues back when the Army was still dressed in olive drab, and a Black Beret bearing the Hardcore Recondo insignia—a black arrowhead—on a red flash, a pocket insignia and a "Sniper" shoulder tab.

"Once we got that sexy uniform," Tahler says, "even more people lined up to join. Plenty of guys wanted in, but only a small percentage passed the hard-ass Sniper School and fewer still were able to squeeze the trigger on a fellow human being."

The Snipers witnessed their kills, the way an executioner does when he pulls the switch on a guy sitting in the electric chair, with a shocking immediacy even frontline infantrymen didn't experience very often if at all in Vietnam. I felt toward the Snipers as I did the guys in the 27th Raiders and the 1/327th LRRPs. They took huge risks that required extraordinary courage and, in the Snipers' case, they not only had their asses hanging out on independent missions with small teams, but their high-powered scopes brought the war right up close and personal. Too close. One morning Tahler killed six VC and the man with him took out another. "I turned my scope on this one," Tahler told me later, "and it was a girl. All I could think was how lovely she was." Young and beautiful, and packing an AK-47—not exactly a Donut Dolly. Tahler did his job and blew her away. "I still see her face," he says.

Psychologically, the gig was tough. "After the first couple kills," Tahler recalls, "several of my Snipers found they didn't have the stomach for the job and quit." Tahler was always on the alert for what he called "Combat Sniper Stress." If he found a Sniper who couldn't handle the strain, he shipped him back to his original company. "A lot of fellows got out of Sniper School and found they just couldn't watch a head blow up through the scope," says Sniper Jones.

Bob Jones was one hell of a warrior. Initially as a rifleman in Battle Company and later as a Sniper, he received two Silver Stars, one Distinguished Flying Cross, five Bronze Stars for Valor and one Air Medal for Valor. By our count, he had thirty-eight Sniper kills to his credit. In any given month, he'd kill more VC than almost any rifle company in the rest of the 9th Division.

"Before I volunteered to become a Sniper, I worried about it some," Jones recalls. "The very next day we went out on an operation and found three gooks holed up in a bunker. They were down in there holding the dadgum lid down. One of my buddies took a hand grenade and laid it on top of the bunker and blew them out. One was pretty bad and he shot him. One of the guys was so upset about it he cried like a baby. But I was sitting around just as calm as ever because it didn't bother me. It was then I knew I'd make a good Sniper. I'd lost all feeling for these people...I did my job. If there was an enemy soldier out there, I'd zap him. Does this sound hard? Think about it. I'm also helping my buddies. He could kill one of them if I didn't get him first. I'm not fussing at all.

"The machine-gunners, the Artillery folks or the flyboys kill VC, but it costs something like $4,000 for them to get one. It costs Uncle Sam 27 cents, the price of an M-14 round for me to zero one out. They don't zap more than me, they just make more noise. It takes a lot for them to do the job, but I'm trained to do it with just one shot."

Snipers operated around the clock, their sharpshooters covering the day and the darkness with Night Hunter and Pink Filter—an infrared light mounted on a jeep that sent out an invisible light, allowing the Starlight Scope to see anything within its beam. Normally they set up at fixed locations such as bridges, ARVN camps and at firebases.

Tahler was trail boss—he picked the Sniper missions and sites, personally inserted the teams, closely monitored them and, at the end of the day, picked them up. He called the plays, not some distant, disconnected staff weenie, working closely with the S-3 and me to insure his operational plans went hand-in-glove with everything else the Battalion was doing.

Tahler's radio code name was Night Hunter 6. On Night Hunter operations, he used one Huey C&C chopper and two gunships. Conducting the show from the C&C bird, he'd set up one Sniper to fire out of each side of the back of the slick. Using their night vision devices, they'd find and then mark the target with tracer rounds. Then the C&C's door gunners, using M-60 machine-gun tracer rounds, would lock on the Sniper's impact area. Simultaneously, the C&C bird, rising straight up like an elevator, would pop out an Air Force flare or flick on a powerful Xenon searchlight, lighting up the target. The two gunships flying blackout just above and behind Tahler's bird would then roar in with rockets and miniguns blazing, striking wherever the C&C's door gunner's M-60 tracers were marking.

"The only way we could identify the target and then put accurate fire on it was to fly low and slow," Tahler says. His C&C bird flew on the deck— from ten to twenty feet above the ground—moving at between sixty to ninety knots. Dangerous work.

In a letter home, Jones wrote about one of the early missions: "I went up on Night Hunter last night. We shot up twenty-one sampans, got thirteen kills and three secondary explosions. I saw one sampan that was camouflaged with leaves and stuff, so I fired a shot at it. The door gunner opened up with his machine gun. He put a few rounds in it and it exploded. We were flying around in a chopper with a big spotlight and it lit up another sampan. I fired a burst and there was another explosion. I spotted another one and fired a shot, and the same thing happened. We circled a few times and I saw one more. I fired, the gunner opened up and it blew up all over the place! We were one hundred feet up and it shook the ship! Charley must really have had a lot of ammo in that convoy. I'm glad we got to it before it got to us."

Geraci, who was still Brigade CO at the time, was so pleased with the results of this mission that the following morning he assembled the aircrew and Snipers and hung a medal on each man. "Night Hunter blew up several tons of ammo that would have thumped down on my boys. Damn, I'm proud of you," he told them.

After that night, Night Hunter was golden. Tahler got priority of air assets.

"We all loved Night Hunter missions," Sniper Ed Eaton says. "You're up in the air. You're not down on the stinking ground, you're clean, cool and, compared to grunt work, relatively safe. It sure beat sloshing through the paddies and we got a lot of kills."

But Tahler's on-the-ground Snipers gave the Night Hunter boys in the sky a good run for their money. They initially worked from the observation towers at Danger and then started going out with rifle companies on missions—except that too often, rifle company skippers tended to use them simply as riflemen. In another battalion, a company commander threw a Sniper with over forty kills in with the rest of the grunts for an assault on a wood line. He was killed. This was like using a Cadillac to plow the back forty. Tahler never sent his shooters with companies whose skippers didn't use them wisely.

Success made the Snipers bolder. "Had to stay sharp and be innovative to keep ahead of the competition," Tahler recalls. He started by hitching rides for his Snipers on aircraft that flew over the firebase. Calling the pilot of any Huey chopper in sight, he'd say he was in a bind and ask the pilot to do him a favor and pick up or drop off one of his teams. Sometimes he bribed the pilots with captured AK-47s or gave them VC flags. I found out later that Tahler's trading goods came from a factory Battalion S-4 Bob Johnson set up back at Dong Tam, where he churned out "genuine VC flags" by the jeep-load.

In short order, Brigade started dedicating a slick and a pair of gunships daily to insert and extract Tahler's teams. He placed them five to ten klicks around Danger, always within range of its 105mm guns. The insert aircraft would fly over a large area making phony insertions to confuse the VC, then pop down near a tree line, where the Snipers would roll out and be in the woods before the bird even lifted off. "We always had good info where we were going and what the conditions on the ground were," says Eaton.

"Tahler did his homework. You had the whole nine yards in your head. The hooch, the rice paddy, the distances, the tree line. You were prepared, but there was always a terrible loneliness. You weren't with a rifle company. You and your buddy were hanging out all by your lonesome."

Normally the choppers returned to pick up the Teams before darkness set in, always varying pickup times to avoid setting fixed patterns. On certain operations, they would spend the night with a rifle company. Sometimes they worked with Pink Filter. Frequently they made sniper kills out to 600 yards; when they spotted deeper or larger targets, they'd adjust TAC Air and/or artillery fire on the VC, driving their targets closer so they could whack them with those long rifles.

"One night I fired a tracer round at a single sampan," Ed Eaton remembers. "The two Cobras stacked above us immediately followed the tracer. I informed the pilots that the round was right on and no need for any adjustment on their part. As the Cobras came to minimum altitude their Xenon lights came on, illuminating the entire river. But instead of a volley of minigun fire and rockets the Cobras immediately turned off their lights and resumed their position above my slick. Later that night while refueling, I went over to the Cobra pilots and asked why they never fired on an obvious target. The answer I got was 'No reason to waste rounds on a guy who has a hole through his chest and is hanging headfirst in the water. That was one great shot, Sniper.'"

Snipers could never be sure what was coming at them. "One night while with a rifle company I was asked to go outside the perimeter and set up," Ed Eaton recalls. "The area was a large paddy with several nearby hooches. I was outside no more than 150 yards, when I stopped to scan the area with my Starlight Scope. And not more than fifty feet from me was a VC with an AK, squatting down with ears cupped, looking straight at me. While startled, I quickly realized he couldn't see me—his visibility was no more than ten to twenty feet—but it was obvious he'd heard something. I watched him for some time, scanning the area before taking him out with a round in the chest that knocked him back on his butt.

"Within only a matter of minutes after I shot him, people in the hooch behind him began blasting in my direction with automatic fire," Eaton said. "As I got down, I realized that the fire was twenty degrees to my right into another hooch. Then the other hooch opened fire. After the firing stopped I returned to the perimeter, where we could then hear an excited group of Vietnamese doing what sounded like arguing. The Vietnamese then started yelling at us requesting permission to come into our perimeter. Our Tiger Scout ordered them to quiet down and wait until dawn. Throughout the night, we could then hear movement of chains. It was all very strange. At dawn, we discovered a group of chained VC prisoners. They had taken advantage of me killing one of their guards and overwhelmed the remaining guards and took their weapons. We found out later, these were VC soldiers who were prisoners, one of whom was shackled because he'd been caught having sex with his VC CO's wife."

The Snipers endured eye fatigue caused by long periods of peering through their scopes and great physical pain from being frozen in one position under clouds of mosquitoes. "The place stunk," Eaton recalls. "It was like swimming in a sewer and the scary night noises made you think a VC was behind every bush. As the water level lowered when the tide went out, it made a popping sound that sounded just like footsteps coming toward you. Then you had the fucking lizards that went 'Fuck you, fuck you, fuck you.'

"We couldn't wear mosquito repellent because the VC would smell it, so you just got used to being bitten and put up with it." After one night mission, he counted the bumps on one leg and reckoned he had 2,500 mosquito bites on his body. His eyelids and lips were puffed up and his index finger was "so swollen that I actually worried about having enough sensitivity in it to squeeze my trigger."

"I shot a gook out of a tree!" Jones wrote home. "The idiot was up in a tree looking at me, so I shot him. He could have been fixing to shoot me! I saw him just before he saw me, and he shrunk down trying to get out of sight. It didn't help much. I aimed my rifle and he got down some more—I let him have it—BAM! No more VC. He was one dumb VC. The first thing they taught us at Sniper School was not to crawl up any trees."

There was also a sensitive side to Jones. He wrote to his mother a few days after this incident and said, "They played Haydn's Mass in B this morning over Armed Forces Radio and it was beautiful—an outstanding performance."

Very quickly our Snipers inflicted so much pain on the VC that Charley struck back with his own sniper-killer teams. Tahler responded to the VC countersniper effort by beefing up his two-man teams with three or four volunteers augmented with an M-60 machine gun. The technique gave Headquarters types at Danger the opportunity to get out and really earn their CIBs.

Even though the teams always maintained dual commo with the Battalion TOC and Tahler's Sniper Control Center so that any team in trouble could contact Tahler and the TOC simultaneously and be reinforced in a flash, "it was some scary duty," says Rich Miller, a TOC Operations sergeant who frequently found himself with the detail that beefed up the Snipers. "When I went out with them, I'd practically be on the shithole the whole night before. You'd find out a day or two before a mission and it would be, 'Oh God, I've got to go out with those guys in the middle of no-man's land.' Once we got on the ground, I got radio watch. I'd report to the TOC, 'There goes one,' and they'd pop 'em off.

"They were just like astronauts or fighterpilots—very calm, cool and collected. And they never missed. They always aimed for the head. They called their shots 'watermelon poppers,' because when they'd hit a target, it was just like they'd popped a watermelon.

"Truth to tell, I much preferred TOC duty."

On one typical morning, for example, at 1015 hours, a Sniper Team a few klicks north of Danger killed four VC at a range of between 250 and 300 yards. At 1715 hours, the team saw a VC force moving toward them, took them under fire and called for help. Within minutes, Air Cav gunships, supporting nearby Hardcore units, responded. The Snipers killed three more VC, the Air Cav Crusader zeroed out five more. Then a Dagger rifle Platoon choppered in. In less than an hour, the VC were all dead or all gone and the Sniper and relief platoon arrived safely back at Danger.

"It was executed with the finesse of the World Series," Rich Miller, who was with the Snipers on this ballgame, recalls. "The VC force never knew what hit them."

I'd inherited a Swedish K submachine gun from Dennis Foley when he was hit and during a Sniper award ceremony I presented the little 9mm beauty to Larry Tahler. In Vietnam, the thinking went, "If you have a Swedish K, Rolex watch and opal ring on your pinky, you're bad, real bad." This particular gun was considered the best in the west, the right stuff for the maximum stud, which Tahler and all his snipers in fact were.

"This weapon is to thank you guys for doing such a great job," I told them. "Businesses give gold watches, but since you're in the killing business, I thought your leader Night Hunter 6 oughta have the finest submachine gun going for you guys knocking off more VC this month than most U.S. Army battalions. We've got our scroungers out trying to police up more of these beauties as backup weapons for each one of you. You deserve them."

Despite their victories, the Long Rifles were not the most popular guys in the 4/39th. "The Snipers had an attitude and they didn't mix well with my guys," says Lieutenant Carl Ohlson, a Battle Company rifle platoon leader. "The ones who worked with my platoon had notches carved into their stocks for each kill. They came on kind of like Paladin. None of my guys would talk to them or even chow down with them. On one operation when Battle White had infiltrated deep into VC territory, one of our attached Snipers had forgotten his rations. I offered him one of mine."

"You don't give them food," snapped my Platoon Sergeant. "They're cold-blooded killers!'"

Sniper Jones didn't let it get to him. "We do have to put up with a few ignorant GIs calling us murderers," he wrote home. "But they're stupid anyway."

While I commanded the Hardcore, Tahler's Snipers accounted for 456 kills—roughly equivalent to an enemy battalion, or nearly 20 percent of all our kills. Not a bad score for a force of less than twenty men including Tahler and his Platoon Sergeant John Morales.

The Battalion's top Sniper, Sergeant Terry Mathis, had forty-eight kills. He also had the division record for the longest kill, made at 900 meters. One evening when I was walking the firebase perimeter, I stopped and talked to Mathis.

"Why do you look so sad, Sir?" he asked me. "Have we had a low body count today?"

"Yeah," I replied. "Six dichs. That's it all day."

"Well, how 'bout I give you three more, Sir?" he asked, and, leaning against the sandbagged top of the berm, he aimed his Sniper rifle at three South Vietnamese soldiers guarding a bridge about four hundred meters away.

I knocked the barrel of the weapon up in the air. "Hold it, man! They're South Vietnamese."

"A gook's a gook," Mathis said, smiling.

Whoa, I thought. Let's not go there. "Look," I said, "we'll get some dinks tonight, OK? Tahler will bring 'em in, so just cool it."

Even today most of these brave men don't want to open the mental compartments they nailed shut three decades ago. "I can see still the faces and still smell the fear," Jones says. "If I'd talked about this fifteen years ago, I'd have been a basket case."

There is no way to overstate the personal price the Snipers had to pay for their success. One day at Danger, Jim Robertson bumped into an old Claymore Company buddy who'd become one of Tahler's Snipers. Sitting on a bunker top watching the beautiful Vietnam sunset, the two pals did some catching up.

"Wow, you have only two weeks to go before you climb on that big silver Dust-Off and head back to the land of flushing toilets," Robertson said.

"I've killed too many people to go home," the Sniper replied. "I don't deserve to go home."

"Where do you get that shit from?" Robertson asked, but didn't really want to know. This wasn't the easygoing Californian he knew. The change frightened him down to his toenails.

"I've got more confirmed kills than I want to remember, Robby," the Sniper said. "You know what that means?"

"Means you're good at your job," Robby said. "So what? They're the enemy. They've killed plenty of us, a lot of our friends. Hell, we all shot them up when we got the chance."

"How many confirmed kills you got?" the Sniper asked.

"That hurt," Robby recalls. "I've been in firefights and done my job, but I'd never seen one go down and known for sure that I'd hit him. I'd been in a lot of shit. I'd spray the trees like everybody else and hope for the best. You know how it is. You almost never got to see the little bastards."

"As a Sniper, through my scope," the Sniper said, "I saw every one of their faces, usually at the moment of impact. You don't know what it's like to see the shock on their faces or the agony when the bullet strikes. One minute the guy's happy as a Surfer with great waves, not even aware I'm around. The next, he's dead. And I see every one of them now whenever I close my eyes. I'm a killer, Robby, and there's no place for me in the world."

"I sat in silence," Robby remembers.

No power on earth could heal the Sniper.

TWELVE

Thanh Hung
23 MARCH 1969

Eventually Charley's people saw that our defenses at Danger were too strong, our people too alert for them to launch a ground assault. The VC must have thought that mortar attacks against us were like going after a Tyrannosaurus Rex with a plastic spoon. So they went back to their drawing board and came up with a medieval goodie from hell: a catapult capable of flinging twenty to thirty pounds of explosives wrapped in canvas over our berm.

At 0330 hours on 21 March, the day they let that sucker sail, I woke up feeling like a Ping-Pong ball. As the air parcel post surprise exploded on the road right next to the TOC, I bounced all the way between my rack and the ceiling. Then the explosion smashed me through a little screen door, practically imprinting me onto a sandbagged blast wall. I wiped the blood away and counted my moving parts to make sure all were present and accounted for. Talk about rude awakenings!

Fortunately, a five-ton truck that belonged to the engineers took most of the blast. The satchel charge landed virtually under it. The TOC—two metal conex containers welded together, dug in and buried under multiple layers of sandbags supported by heavy wooden beams—was built to take mortar and rocket fire; but a direct hit from that mini-tactical nuke would have really whacked it good.

"I was sleeping between the TOC and the truck under a sandbagged piece of corrugated pipe with a blast wall of sandbags at either end," Major George Mergner recalls. "My feet were in the direction of the truck. The explosion lifted me and moved me while spraying me with dirt and debris. A couple hours later I developed soreness in the bottom of my foot and the Docs dug out a piece of metal."

I wandered over to Holley's aid station, where the medics were already hard at work patching up the wounded. No one required dusting off, but a few soldiers were cut up—mostly Snipers. The "bomb" landed twenty feet from their solidly built bunker. "The blast blew six-inch-by-six-inch beams apart like they were twigs and gave all of us a good rattling," Larry Tahler remembers.

He was skinned up and he had blood running out of both ears, but as usual, he remained his cool, cocky New York City self. "See, I told you we were hurting the little bastards," he said. "That bomb was aimed at the Hardcore's most dangerous weapon—the Snipers."

"The next morning, I stood in the crater," Tahler recalls. "It was waist deep—I spread my arms and couldn't touch both sides at once. It made that heavy duty truck look like a pretzel."

The surprise attack reinforced my policy of making everyone sleep under cover. Our soldiers didn't like sleeping in the tropical heat in badly ventilated bunkers or in the sandbagged half-culverts Mergner had scrounged and I didn't blame them. But without that precaution we'd have lost at least a dozen soldiers, including Sergeant Major Press, Op Sergeant Slater, XO Mergner and probably every member of the Sniper Team.

You had to hand it to the VC. They were fighting a superpower that could fill the sky with bombers, yet they came up with a primitive weapon that could have taken out the Battalion's Command and Control.

The truck had given us a lucky break. We'd gotten another one with the arrival of Captain Ed Clark, Dagger Company's new skipper. He took charge of the badly bent unit like a welder firing up his torch. Clark came from a long line of southern military men. His father, a true infantry hero, earned three Silver Stars in World War II; that meant Ed had a lot to live up to. He wasn't a big guy; he looked more like a scoutmaster—which he'd been—than a hard-ass soldier. But he'd become a tough, ruthless, resolute leader who'd mastered the hard lessons of 13 March.

Almost immediately after Ed reported in to the Battalion from Brigade, we received orders to conduct a joint amphibious operation with the Navy, an assault on an island that wasn't part of my overall battle plan. The Battalion was fully committed and I didn't want to pull a rifle company from a mission because some staff weenie with a wild hair over "hot intelligence" wanted us to do a mini-Inchon invasion, so I decided to do the op with a scratch force. I grabbed rifle platoons from "C" and "D" Companies, added some headquarters folks and gave the mission to my new S-2, Captain Clark.

"You're now Task Force Clark. Go do it," I told him.

It wasn't an easy operation. He had to form a combat team, liaise with the Navy, conduct an amphibious assault and encircle the suspected enemy force in a very nasty place. But under him, Task Force Clark clicked together like a well-drilled football squad—he acted like he'd been a commander all his life.

Clearly we had a keeper.

Clark was a gung-ho guy, always volunteering for missions. If I said, "Maybe we should check out this area," he'd say, "We'll go, Sir"—a habit that, along with his demand for exactness, did not endear him to his men. He reminded me of myself when I was a small unit leader, always out there ready to lock horns with the enemy—which my guys didn't think was such a swift idea either.

Clark soon had the Hardcore's M.O. down cold. "We'd start moving around twelve or one P.M.," he recalls. "We would check out the area. We were trying to intercept VC traffic. The main traffic was sampans on canals, so we moved slowly, tried to stay out of sight. We'd always move into the pre-night location just before dark and set up just as though we were going to stay there all night. But we'd send out patrols in different directions, at least three and sometimes four patrols. Their mission was to pick out a precise night location that we'd use for ambush. We wouldn't get into it until eleven or twelve o'clock at night."

Sergeant Jim Silva—or "FTA" as the warriors of Dagger Company called him when he got bounced down to the line for his attitude—was now a squad leader in the 1st Platoon. And he was damn good at his job. He'd gone to college before the draft got him, so he was older than most of his buddies. "They called me Grandpa," he recalls. "I decided I was going to be the best old man in the business or die out there. I'd fished and hunted all my life and I found it no different hunting for deer than it was hunting for people, except they shoot back."

On 23 March, just shy of dark, Clark, Silva and three other boys slipped out of the company's perimeter and went out to look for an ambush position. "We'd gone about 500 yards and we found the perfect spot," Silva says. "It had the right amount of cover, good canal access for our ambushes, and the back opened up into the rice paddies."

Clark remained with his RTO. Sending Silva back to lead the Company into the new positions, he deployed the 1st and 2nd Platoons in a killing zone along the canal with the 3rd Platoon wrapped around the rear to provide security.

"It was a moonless night, pitch black," recalls 2nd Platoon leader Mike Kidd. "We were set up in a tight box formation, river in front, wide clear firin' zone to the rear and a dry canal along each side. Grandpa Silva did good."

At 0345 hours, the listening posts (LPs) alerted Dagger Company that they heard enemy movement. John Bandel, Silva's foxhole partner, had just awakened him for his turn on guard.

"You hear that?" Bandel said.

"Hear what?" Silva replied. A few minutes passed.

"Don't you hear that?" Bandel whispered.

"I heard something," Silva recalls. "It sounded like a transistor radio. Then it got louder. It was gooks talking. They were headed to our position. They had no idea that we were there."

Everyone was 200 percent alert, fingers on the trigger, pins straightened on grenades, claymores ready. The artillery FO, still Lieutenant Tim Nay, now an old pro, quietly alerted the tubes back at Danger, where "C" Battery's gunners were prepared to put a red-hot barrage down around Dagger.

"Suddenly the shit hit the fan on the right side of the perimeter," Silva says. As the VC moved forward, Dagger's two LPs popped claymores in their faces. Confused because Dagger was not where the recon parties had said it would be, the VC began flailing at the air—punching an empty bag. All of Dagger's perimeter opened up. M-60 machine guns hosed down their sectors of fire. Riflemen blasted their M-16s and M-79s while artillery rounds churned in, slashing through their machine guns as well as their RPGs across the river. "In a matter of seconds it went from complete peacefulness to a shooting gallery. AK, M-16, M-60 and RPG rounds were flying all over the place. The VC had stumbled into us and we were kicking their asses. I saw a few gooks run through our perimeter, but I couldn't zap them because I might hit my own guys."

"We were set up with the 'blue' in the front, a wide clear firing zone to the rear, and a dry canal along each side," 2nd Platoon Sergeant Mike Kidd remembers. "The VC charged forward and hit the dry canal. The point element jumped or fell into the ditch and opened up on us with AK-47s. The initial burst of fire hit Sergeant Smith, who was layin' on my left. My RTO, Don Owings, and I both opened up at the muzzle flashes. Then we touched off our claymores. The VC moved about twenty feet right along the edge of my platoon and tried to cross the dry creek. Again, fire and claymores met them. They were stopped in their tracks."

Next, the VC moved parallel to Kidd's line—all the way to the paddy in the back.

"A squad of VC walked right into where I had my Claymore set up," 1st Platoon Sergeant Eugene Lange says. "When they got right into the center of the killing zone, I squeezed the firing device. It got them all. Just like a perfect bowling strike."

"We definitely caught them with their pants down," Kidd says. "We evened the score for 13 March."

Within fifteen minutes of the first shot, gunships from the 9th Aviation Battalion's Light Fire Team, which were airborne and on standby for just this kind of contingency, screamed in, thumping rocket fire on what was left of the enemy's supporting weapons and along his probable escape routes. Artillery flares initially lit up the battlefield and within five more minutes, Spooky, also on alert status and overflying the Division AO, turned night into day with its powerful flares. "The VC were as exposed as clay pigeons at a skeet shoot," Clark says.

Spooky made his first pass about 400 yards from Dagger's position. He had his running lights on. Thousands of red tracers plowed up the ground. "About thirty gooks started shooting everything they had at the plane," Silva recalls. "The plane circled and when it got back up over the same spot, the gooks opened up again. Spooky dropped the world on them. It rained red death. No one shot back. I think they were all minced meat."

"It was just madness," Clark says. "Boom, boom, boom. Claymores and grenades were going off. Slugs flying. Tree limbs falling and sparks and tracers. My guys hammered it to them. Charley didn't have a chance—which was the way we liked to do things in Dagger."

The VC, recoiling under the shock of the heavy fire, broke off the attack and tried to haul ass. Charley had taken the Hardcore bait—poor, beat-up Dagger Company, on its lonesome way out there in bandit country, vulnerable, exposed. Clark had hooked them good. He called for medevac to dust off two seriously wounded soldiers and asked the Battalion TOC to chopper in ammo and water. After the wounded had been dusted off and the warriors resupplied, Dagger was ready to reel the suckers in.

Brigade Commander Hayes swung by Danger in his bird, picked me up and we flew out to Dagger. After Clark briefed us, we agreed with his bottom line: The men of Dagger had knocked the enemy on its ass and now was the time to stomp him.

Hayes gave us his C&C ship so we could recon the battlefield and Clark could use it to bring in more gear. But first he made me promise not to take any chances flying too low in his precious flying machine.

With first light on 23 March at 0543 hours, Dagger's grunts moved out of their holes and policed the battlefield. More than forty dead enemy soldiers were stretched out in front of their positions. Enemy weapons and equipment littered the field. Dagger had taken two dead—Sergeant Leo Brian Smith and Sergeant John Robert Yarger, both from Mike Kidd's Platoon—along with two serious and two lightly wounded.

Abandoned equipment, bandages and blood trails led away from Dagger's perimeter. The reeds in the rice paddies were pushed down where the retreating VC had pulled their sampans, dragging away their dead and wounded.

"Our Platoon alone piled up close to thirty bodies," recalls Tommy Pye. "When we started our sweep of the area I crossed a little ditch—no more than three foot wide—and I stepped on a body. It had been weighted down under the water. They got out so fast they had to leave quite a few of their bodies around—with their weapons—something I never seen them do. They always policed up their own weapons and anything they could find of ours too."

Clark tasked Silva to take a patrol and follow the trails. "Blood was everywhere," Silva says, "even on the green leafy jungle parts. We'd put out so much firepower that we had actually cut the jungle down. When Clark asked me, I thought, If you think I'm going to take four men and follow a large group of wounded and battle-hardened VC, you must be out of your mind. But I said OK, and when my patrol was out of sight of the perimeter, we set up and kept calling back phony sitreps until Clark asked us to come back. I wasn't into suicide missions. My men came first."

Other patrols found the enemy's tracks and took a prisoner, a shot-up medic who said he was from the 261A Main Force Battalion.

The 261A—a bad-ass unit that had been the terror of the Mekong Delta for twenty years! As tough and experienced a group of soldiers as the VC could produce, the best the VC had in the Delta, the 261A had been on my list since I took over the Battalion. But since hitting "D" Company when Spurlock was killed, they'd become the outfit I most wanted to decimate. I figured if we could take them down, we could bust the chops of any Main Force unit.

Our POW said the 261A had taken many casualties and was headed north. Thirty minutes later, we took another POW, a platoon sergeant. After a Tiger Scout grilled him, he sang like Sammy the Bull to the FBI, giving us a general idea of his unit's withdrawal plan, rally points and post-attack hide positions.

The standard VC drill when an operation ended was to meet at Point X. If they got into bad shit, they'd meet at Point Y. No question they were swimming in shit—and now, thanks to our VC canary, we had Point Y.

Courtesy of Hayes, Troop C 7/1st Air Cav flew in, as did our old, bold buddies, the Boomerangs of the 191st Army Aviation Company, both of whom we'd been with in the Plain of Reeds. The Black Hawk Cav took off like hunting dogs on a strong scent and the Boomerangs helped us out with a little jitterbugging, inserting Dagger's Platoons along the VC withdrawal route.

Hayes also flew in tracker dog teams. We attached them to Clark's platoons and flew our POW platoon sergeant back to the CP to be worked over by his Vietnamese-speaking interrogators. In short order, we started confronting small groups of stragglers. At 1125 hours, the Cav killed three VC, another at 1126 hours and two more at 1145 hours. At 1205 hours, 1st Platoon of Dagger killed three VC; and at 1245 hours, the Cav killed fourteen more. They were all out in the open, hauling ass. It was as easy as stepping on ants at a picnic.

"All morning long we were taking down VC running out in the open," Bounty Hunter gunship pilot Ken Carlton says. "We'd insert in a Hardcore platoon and the VC would pop out and we'd mow 'em down. The enemy kept making a big mistake by running. We were catching a squad and a platoon at a time. We shot up one bunch and landed and picked up a dozen AK-47. Our door gunners used them as backup weapons so they didn't have to clean their M-16s. We used 'em until they jammed and then we'd throw them in the river."

At the same moment, Lieutenant Colonel Peter Wittereid, who'd replaced Bill Hauser as CO of the 1/11th arty Battalion, quickly shifted his "C" Battery from Danger by CH-46, getting closer so those mean 105mms could support our pursuit. I asked Hayes for two more rifle companies to pile on and seal the enemy once we'd fixed his positions. Hayes was right there. "Already working on it, Hack. Got one company for you now—A/6/31st Infantry—and looking for another."

We were having a great day until around 1330 hours. Then, like a crapshooter in Las Vegas whose luck's suddenly left him, we couldn't make a point. Every sign of them—the blood and bandages, the tracks, the bent reeds, all the signs we'd been following, just flat vanished. Somehow, with LOH Scout ships right on the deck looking in every crack and crevice, with rifle platoons jitterbugging all over the place, our opponent had pulled a Houdini.

I was in the Cav C&C flying at about 500 feet with two scout LOHs below me checking out a patch of jungle along an east-west river when, just for an instant, I saw the black silhouette of what looked like a head about the size of a coconut by a palm tree. But that was enough for my infantryman's brain— it was a VC soldier sliding down a spider hole at the base of a tree.

"Swing it around," I told the pilot, and "have the Scout ships look over there."

The LOHs immediately went down on the deck. "Shit," one of them reported, "there's foxholes all over here." They raked the area over with minigun fire, then lifted off and called in gunships, which whacked in a dozen or so rocket rounds.

Now, with some of the foliage blown away, the Scouts went back down and found a .51-caliber machine gun on a tripod in a foxhole. A gutsy LOH crew member grabbed the gun by its barrel, pulled it out of its hole and dumped it in the open. The gunships rolled back in and blistered the position again.

"Scratch one bad-ass antiaircraft machine gun," Comanche 6 told the Hardcore TOC. "Also scratch ten VC."

About this time, Tamale 14, Captain Joe Connor—the Air Force Forward Air Controller who'd been circling the AO—spotted "a platoon of dug-in VC with at least three machine guns at the northern end of this patch of jungle," north of where we'd uncovered the .51-caliber.

"OK to zap 'em with napalm?" he asked.

"Affirmative, Tamale 14," said Captain Bob Reynolds. The artillery liaison officer who'd replaced Chum had hit the ground running and was holding his own. "Then work over that strip of jungle to the north just at the bend in the river."

While John Hayes's POW interrogators were working on the captured VC sergeant to get him to confirm his battalion's defensive positions, I flashed on how the enemy was deployed and how he was going to fight. First "coconut head," then the .51-caliber machine gun, then the FAC's sightings—they opened my mind's eye so I could perfectly visualize the VC's defense positions. I can't explain it, maybe it was just an infantryman's gut feeling, but I *knew* in that instant where Charley was, how he'd fight us— and how we'd destroy him.

There was no doubt in my military mind we'd fixed at least the 261A. All because one VC soldier needed a little fresh air and thought he could evade that big eye in the sky.

If we blocked right there...and there...and over there...we'd have those guys roughly sealed—unlike Hunt's rat-fuck eleven days earlier.

I started moving my companies as well as the A/6/31st into those choke points. At the same time, Reynolds blistered the VC position with tons of Tac Air and red-hot artillery steel. The net was loose, but whether they tried to swim, low crawl or pogo-stick out, a bunch of them were sure to be caught.

From the air, the river and vegetation formed a perfect "W" running north and south for about a click. Connor's fighter jocks slammed in thirteen air strikes. Napalm, 750-pounders, 500-and-250 pound frags and 20mm cannon fire thundered down on the enemy. Reynolds coordinated the TAC Air, artillery and gunships from our bird. He also blistered the enemy's possible escape routes, making running a bad idea. The new cannon-cocker wasn't quite up to Chum's speed, but he more than got with the program. We sealed the enemy in by fire while we positioned our forces on the outer perimeter of the blazing steel donut we'd thrown up around him.

Moving by chopper, Dagger pinned the enemy from the south end of the river, the likeliest escape route. They had an old score to settle; they deserved the honor of administering the shot to the head.

Alert Company airmobiled into the northeast to seal off escape from that direction. Claymore Company also choppered in and set up in the south, while the OPCON Company, A/6/31st, sealed from the east. Back at Danger, Battle Company made sure no one could raid our house while we kicked ass but remained on alert in case we needed them to join the party.

I told the infantry commanders to wrap around the enemy, but not to close with him. "Let the firepower do the closing," I said.

This was breaking the rules. At Fort Benning, the Infantry School still taught the tactics of closing with and destroying the enemy—World War II stuff. Instead, I hammered into the Hardcore small-unit leaders' heads over and over that the name of the game was not banzaiing an enemy position, but fixing him so he couldn't move and then throwing everything we had at him. I kept stressing that Vietnam had nothing to do with taking terrain. It was about killing the enemy at the smallest possible cost in friendly casualties. "If you assault a bunker line, you'll pay a high price. And in a month it'll be rebuilt and reoccupied, and in the next assault you'll pay the same price. Put napalm on it," I repeated over and over again. "Don't play into the enemy's hands. Fry the bastards."

In the middle of the battle, I got a message from the Battalion TOC to release one of our Boomerang slicks.

"What for?" I asked, astonished. What could be more important than the battle we were waging?

"The helicopter's needed to pick up a USO Troop."

A USO Troop? This show was the only show in town.

"Fuck no!" I said.

The Brigade TOC officer fired back. "You must release the bird. It's by order of the Division Chief of Staff."

Hunt! Once again, the sonofabitch had his priorities ass-backward. In the middle of the fight, he wanted to jerk a combat asset away from a battle for a bunch of entertainers so he could "raise the morale" back at Division Headquarters for a bunch of REMFs stacking up the beans and bullets.

I radioed Hayes.

"Fuck Hunt," he said. "We're fighting a battle."

Thank God for Hayes. He understood the way to raise morale was to whip the enemy.

By 1530 hours we had our seal in place. The sealing units stretched concertina wire across the waterways and tossed frag grenades in the "blue" to discourage any VC swimmers. Air and artillery continued to pound mercilessly into the enemy's positions. For the VC, it must've been like sizzling inside a huge pizza oven while being pounded with grenades. "It was the damnedest thing I ever saw," says Sergeant Tommy Pye. "Every time a jet would come by, thirty or forty guys would jump up and run to other holes. The flyboys did a hell of a job. They put their bombs and napalm right on them. We were downwind and you could smell them burning real good."

At 1600 hours, Hayes sent us a helicopter equipped with powerful amplifiers and carrying a Vietnamese-speaking psychological warfare team. Soon an eerie voice from the sky was telling the VC to surrender.

When there were no takers, we hit them some more. Finally, some of the enemy soldiers could take the punishment no longer and tried to break out in broad daylight. Their first attempt was in the south, where they ran smack into the guns of Dagger Company:

"Hello, suckers. Surprise!"

"The whole thing was unbelievable," Sergeant Lange recalls. "I could see the VC and actually see the bombs and rockets tear into them. The VC were panic-stricken and running back and forth like water in a trough. Suddenly about twenty of them took off across an open field and headed straight to my platoon. A helicopter put a pair of rockets right in the center of the fleeing VC and got about five of them. My guys let them get right close and then we cut them down. We got 'em all. That was the way it was all the rest of that day and all that night."

Scattered groups tried to run to the east and west only to be zapped by Alert and Claymore or to be caught in the open by the rocket and minigun fire. At 1610 hours, Dagger cut down two enemy soldiers while both Claymore and Alert racked up five more. At 1627 hours, Air Force FAC Connor reported his Phantom jets had destroyed eighteen bunkers, killing twenty-five VC. Dagger spotted enemy soldiers dressed in black shirts and shorts running toward them, racing right into their waiting guns. Thirty-two more enemy dead.

The body-counters at Division would need an electric calculator.

"They were in the trees and we had great positions behind rice paddy walls," Platoon Sergeant Martinelli says. "Our fire really got to 'em. They came running, screaming, blowing whistles and trying to break out. We blasted away, cutting them down. Payback time."

By 2200 hours, the seal was as tight as we could get it. Throughout the night, artillery fire rained down hundreds of rounds of high explosives on the enemy's already burning positions and Spooky again made the battlefield bright as day. Small groups of enemy soldiers kept trying to break out—between dusk and dawn, Dagger alone killed twenty-two VC in five separate escape attempts, and Alert and Claymore added an equal number.

"It was as black as a coal miner's ass," Sergeant Pye says. "I seen five guys walking down that dike and they stopped right in front of me. One guy started to walk to the guy next to me as if he were going to tap him on the shoulder. The boy shot him. I tossed a grenade, killed two and we all ganged up and shot the other two."

"Some would run to get out of the napalm and our guys would cut them down with their machine guns," Silva recalls. "I fired at one guy who popped out of a bunker at 500 yards. Everyone yelled that I got him, but I didn't think so. Later, as we started searching the bunker complex, we drew a lot of fire from this same bunker. We put enough M-79 fire into that bunker to sink it and then all was quiet. During the night a number of gooks tried to bust out and we mowed them down."

Unfortunately, A/6/31st got hung up in a minefield and took two wounded. While moving them to an LZ for Dust-Off, the litter party hit more mines, killing three soldiers—Larry Eugene Bailey, David Stanley Harris and Johnny Young—and wounding two more. They spent most of the night extricating themselves and didn't get in on the kills. But their presence stopped the enemy from spilling out through that sector of the seal.

To minimize the number of holes in the seal, I brought in every rifleman I could scrounge from FSB Danger, including all of Larry Tahler's Long Rifles. Back at the firebase, only one Battle Company platoon, two squads of engineers and the headquarters folk were left to defend the perimeter, a job usually filled by a rifle company plus. I took a chance, which is what war is all about—we needed max combat power where the action was. I told Lieutenant Bradley Turner, acting CO of Battle, who was in charge of the defense of the FSB, that if Danger was overrun that night, the defense at my court-martial would be: "I employed the Principle of War, Economy of Force—and failed."

Throughout the night, we readied for dawn. Supplies were flown in, ammo was issued, leaders were briefed. Come first light, we'd hit the shell-shocked VC with a fresh serving of air and artillery fire. Then—at last—Hardcore troopers would move in with cold steel glittering.

"The VC tried to break out," Mike Kidd remembers. "But we laid down a steel wall of lead. We had a grenade-pitchin' contest with the VC. We must have tossed fifty grenades back and forth durin' the night. My boys were better pitchers."

At 0630 hours, the sky fell in on the enemy. We pummeled him with everything we had. After the last artillery shells whistled in and exploded, there was total silence, but I knew the troops had to be wary—the VC could live through bombardments that would level a mountain. There was every chance that some die-hard VC's hand would stick up from the muck like in some horror flick and drag some of our boys under.

"At first light we once again initiated the assault," Ed Clark says.

"There were bodies all over the place including the canal," recalls Sergeant Rich Polak. "One of the 'bodies' was face up in the water and as I approached him, he sat up with a weapon pointed directly at my gut! Scared the shit out of me. I emptied my weapon at him."

"We won because of a lot of sweat, skill and luck," says Sergeant Gary Dubois, a Dagger Company squad leader, who had more than a basic load of luck. While his platoon was blocking one of the enemy escape routes, a group of VC charged his position.

"They were firing like crazy and screaming. And we were firing back just as crazily. A burst of bullets or grenade fragments hit the dirt about six inches in front of my face. I felt something thump my chest and thought it was a chunk of dirt. I kept firing. The next morning, I was checking my ammo and one of my M-16 magazines was embedded with a piece of shrapnel. It cut the first round in half. Still have it. I was lucky."

After that, says Clark, "The air hung still and quiet and smelled of death. The VC were broken. There were a few isolated pockets of resistance, which the men of Dagger dispatched with ease. Bodies were everywhere. AK-47 rifles littered the ground. The earth was ripped, charred black and torn. Elsewhere the lush green jungle of yesterday was blackened and beaten to dust. A barren, scarred landscape greeted my tired troops. An arm, a finger, a half-buried body spoke of the fury of our firepower."

Hardcore troopers moved slowly through the still-smoking enemy positions. Initially no shots were fired—the VC were either dead or gone or deep in bunkers. Throughout the sweep, we killed only a few more VC and captured two. "We blew every bunker we found with grenades," says Silva. "We pulled a lot of dead gooks from the tree line. The place looked like what hell must look like."

Not only did the Hardcore destroy the 261A Battalion completely, we captured their Battalion Colors and Battalion Operations Journal, along with seven machine guns as well as a dozen mortars, recoilless rifles, radios and over sixty individual weapons. Sergeant Kidd recovered the M-60 machine gun the VC had taken on 13 March as well as the empty ammo box his gunner used to keep his stationery dry. "Charley must have thought he was takin' ammo," Kidd said. "Sure shows what scroungers they were."

We found company-size mess halls, training areas, billets, medical facilities and enough medical supplies to run a small hospital. Many of the supplies were stamped in English: "Donated by the University of California, Berkeley." I couldn't help thinking that between these "donations" and all the others Charley lifted from us, it's a wonder the war wasn't costing more and generating even more pork. We'd finally figured out how to supply both sides.

We blew up the whole works. Then we took their Battalion Colors and their weapons and set them up at FSB Danger. Hardcore Recondos, the display said, here's the World Series pennant. You won it!

The battle was written up in *Stars and Stripes* and by UPI: "4/39th 'OUT-GUERRILLAS' ENEMY, KILLS 163; VC FLEE INTO WAITING GI GUNS." We'd proved we could go up against Charley's best and beat the shit out of them.

The night after the battle, ABC reporter Craig Spence, who was tight with Rice Paddy Daddy, rang. He all but ordered me to give him a blow-by-blow account of the fight, implying that if I were uncooperative he'd go to his buddy and have my butt.

I disliked Spence. I'd met him back in February as I was running to the Brigade LOH when the Hardcore got the LRRP mission. He'd stopped me that night to demand a pre-mission interview and I'd told him to fuck off. He told me Hunt was his special friend and I better come through. If I'd had my trench knife, I would have cut off his nuts and handed them to him. He had a knack for rubbing me the wrong way.

"Gladly give you an interview," I now said with gushing sweetness on the TOC phone. "Pop in a Saigon taxi and come on down."

"You're kidding. Driving on Route 4 would be suicide—it's dark. Come on, Colonel Hackworth, I got a deadline."

"Don't have time. We're a little busy here. You know, fighting a war."

"Just give me a short quote and I'll get the rest from the wire services," he begged.

"OK," I said. "You set up?"

"Right, ready to record."

"You sure?"

"Absolutely. The tape is turning."

"OK. Let's see…You really ready?"

"I'm set!"

"OK. Here goes: War is hell but actual combat is a motherfucker. Got it?"

"I can't use that!"

"Pity. Good night, Spence." I hung up.

The next morning, the first thing I saw when I opened my eyes was a sign courtesy of Rich Miller over the TOC door: "WAR IS HELL BUT ACTUAL COMBAT IS A MOTHERFUCKER."

A lot more than luck accounted for this victory. The Hardcore soldiers and their magnificent support—Black Hawk, Boomerang, Tamale FACs and their daring jet jockeys, the Dust-Off crews and the cannon cockers of "C" Battery 1/11th Artillery Battalion, who'd all worked with the Hardcore since the Plain of Reeds—all of them were now clicking together like the New York Yankees.

Dagger Company had out-G'd the G, proving themselves to be guerrillas as dangerous and savvy as the best of their opponents. Alert and Claymore Companies, two platoons of Battle, Tahler's Snipers and the troopers of Alpha of the 6/31st had all moved noiselessly and swiftly and performed like total pros.

We'd fought the battle the way Hank Emerson had fought at Bu Gia Mop in 1966—working out early in the game that we were on to something big, then quickly surrounding the enemy. It was a battle that wouldn't have gone the way it did had I not learned from my own mistakes in 1966 at My Canh the high price of conventionally "closing" with a trapped guerrilla enemy.

If the Hardcore could blow away the meanest VC outfit in the Delta, I thought to myself, just imagine what the U.S. military could do if every U.S. infantry battalion in Vietnam copied our tactics.

THIRTEEN

Kien Phong Province

25 MARCH 1969

The Hardcore's triumph left the Battalion flatter than high school all-stars after an all-nighter. We'd worked hard and we were exhausted. But after only six hours' sleep in three days, I woke up on the morning of the twenty-fifth as revved as a sixteen-year-old on his first date with Miss Congeniality.

Right next to the TOC, Headquarters CO Bob Johnson set up a display of all the stuff we'd captured from the newly departed members of the 261A: recoilless rifles, mortars, machine guns, around one hundred AK-47s plus the 261A's Communist hammer-and-sickle battle flag with a photo of Uncle Ho pinned in the center. The battle loot was great for Hardcore morale, and I knew those AKs would make Johnson's scrounging program go a little easier. I also knew if we kept pushing we'd find a lot more booty and bodies out there in the bush.

The evening before, just as we pulled out from the 261A's graveyard, John Hayes flew in. Never one to let a unit sit on its butt after a fight, even a neat victory like ours, he wanted to know what I had in mind for that night and the next day.

To help with the hunt, we got the assets again on the twenty-fifth—the Boomerangs and the Blackhawk Comanche Troop, our deadly buddies. "Claymore will be picked up and inserted near their night ambush positions," I told Hayes. A/6/31st would chopper back to FSB Moore and revert to the

6/31st, and Alert, the two Battle platoons and the Snipers would return to their firebases and get ready for the next day's ops.

We discussed my plans for the next day. I'd give Alert the north of Danger with Palmer's Boomerangs, and the mission to check out a ten-click square near the spot where the 261A had made the mistake of tapping Dagger Company. That night at sunset, Palmer would insert half of Alert to work the ground and set up a deep ambush position while the Blackhawk Cav Troop and one platoon from Battle Company moved in closer to the site of our shoot-out with the 261A. I told Hayes Charley might come snooping around for his dead and missing, checking out what we'd done to his base camp. If that happened, the Battle platoon, my hammer, would slam the VC straight into the rest of Battle, the on-call anvil.

"Good," Hayes nodded. "But what about Dagger Company?"

"Sir," I said, "do you mind if I shoot Dagger back to Dong Tam? Let the boys get drunk, have a steak fry, do a little strutting around the base. Show the REMFs what combat soldiers look like."

The Rear Echelon Motherfuckers at Dong Tam outnumbered the grunts by a ratio of ten to one. In Vietnam, "motherfucker" was used either as a stand-up-and-fight challenge or as a term of endearment to your close buddies. Most REMFs did not fall into the latter category.

Hayes looked at me straight-faced. "You know it's against Division policy. They're supposed to stay here and get a body count."

I could feel my temperature rising. I'd concluded from day one with the 9th Division that Ewell and Hunt didn't care how many of their men were killed, or how tired or untrained the men were so long as the body count kept climbing. And I'd always been sure Hayes felt the same way I did.

"They've earned a break, John. They sucked in the enemy, chased the enemy, sealed the enemy, destroyed the enemy—it was classic! They've done more than enough fucking body count business to buy themselves a day off."

He grinned, pleased I'd taken the bait. "Do it," he said. "I'll get you the lift. Redeploy the rest of your Battalion per your plan and slip Dagger Company into Dong Tam."

Hayes was that kind of man, willing to go against policy for the greater good of his men. "Could you arrange for General Ewell to lay some impact awards on Dagger's troops tomorrow?"

"Jesus," Hayes said.

I knew what he was thinking—give this guy a grenade and he'll ask for an artillery battalion. But that night he called. "General Ewell agreed. But it means you and I've gotta be there, too. I'll pick you up around noon in my bird, OK?"

It didn't sound OK to me. I wanted to hunt for Charley. "I'd rather have Mergner go," I said. "He's already back at Dong Tam squaring away our rear."

"You're going. See you tomorrow around 1230 hours. End of discussion."

The next morning before the first rooster crowed, the Boomerang gun-ships, the Bounty Hunters, made contact, killing one VC. Alert Company took a POW. In the next two hours, the Bounty Hunters killed four more VC.

While Alert was getting in the first good punch, the Air Cav hunted with the 1st Platoon of Battle Company. At 1130 hours the scout ships spotted VC in the wood line near the 261A's trashed base camp, and the rest of Battle sitting on PZ's at Danger was put on high alert to reinforce Lieutenant Roger Keppel's 1st Platoon if they got into trouble or to act as the anvil.

Third Platoon Sergeant Ron Sulcer, a tall, thin-as-a-rail Shake and Bake with more common sense than there were cows in Texas, remembers the moment: "We were just going to have a stand down at the firebase, when all of a sudden we got word to get our gear together and get lined up—the helicopters were coming to pick us up. Then we were told the choppers weren't coming for a while. Hurry up and wait. So everybody just kinda laid back and relaxed and took their packs off and leaned up against them."

About that time, a helicopter landed with starlets from the TV series *High Chaparral,* four of them in miniskirts. Sulcer started talking to a tall, beautiful brunette from Temple, Texas, near his own hometown. "The Vietnamese Coke gal was having a fit," he recalls. "They told her to get away because the choppers were coming in, but one guy was lollygagging over his Coke, and she wasn't going anywhere until she got that bottle back. So I took the Coke bottle from the guy and threw it as far as I could in the direction that I wanted her to move to, figuring she'd just go and get it. And the USO gal kinda looked at me like I was crazy, like, what did he do that for?

"About then I got this weird touch on my shoulder like God put his hand there and told me that it was my day, that I was going to get hit but I wasn't going to die. It was the strangest feeling in the world, like cold went all the way through me, like I was there by myself for just a second. It didn't matter if there were twenty people around me, I was there by myself. There was no doubt in my mind that I was going to get hit—that was the premonition, like a direct telegraph to my mind."

Arles Brown was there, too, limping around in a cast—his gunner, L. J. Henderson, had accidentally dropped a twenty-two-pound M-60 machine gun on Brown's foot—not too happy that his company was going out without him. But when he saw the actresses, he made the best of what he considered a bad deal. "You guys take care of Charley," he said. "Ol' Arles will take care of the women."

Around noon, just before Hayes was due to pick me up, the Cav commander decided to insert Keppel to check out what his scouts had found. But I held back the rest of Battle, so Sulcer got a temporary reprieve and Arles Brown got a little more time in with his buddies.

In a chopper above the contact, Keppel got the word that his platoon was going in as the birds wheeled off toward the northwest. L. J. Henderson, chewing on a cigar, rode next to medic Dan Evans; across from them sat Larry Faulkenberg and Slim Holleman. Over the LZ, Henderson looked out at the fast-approaching wide field that was the drop-off point and had his own sort of premonition. "We lost four of us in a place open like this," he muttered, pointing to the LZ with his cigar. "I'm startin' to really get tired of this shit."

After the Cav gunships hosed down the tree line where the VC had been sighted, the slicks hit the LZ and Keppel's 1st Platoon burst out into the scorching day. The objective was bisected by a nearly dry streambed from which high weeds ran to the wood line. A long spell without rain had baked the paddy brick-hard.

Keppel quickly split the 1st Platoon—Battle Red—into two sections. One, led by Sergeant Donald Wallace, moved to the right of the weeds; the other, led by Keppel himself, went to the left while Cav Cobra gunships flew overhead, blasting and spraying the tree line with rockets and minigun fire.

"We moved out in a typical fashion with the point out front," recalls Keppel. "We didn't receive a lot of fire, just a few rounds."

"We were waiting as we always did while the choppers shot down into the wood line," Larry Faulkenberg remembers, "and there was bullets flying everywhere, tree branches flying off the trees. It was really noisy.

"I got hit almost right away, a sucking chest wound that went clear through my right side. It burned like fire. I tried to pull my ammunition jacket over it and as I did I saw blood running down. I tried to get up, but I think I fell forward and I started hollering for help. My lung collapsed. Then I tried to get up again and Frank Ellis shoved me right back down. He and another guy kept smacking me on the face because they didn't want me to go completely out. After that, I just thought about home for some reason. I thought about my mom and dad and I started praying that I could get out alive and just come back to the world.

"To this day I don't know how I got out in front of everybody but I looked around and noticed that I was the only one there," medic Dan Evans says.* "Everyone else was behind me flat on the ground or in the ditch. The helicopters were making so much noise I couldn't hear anything else, but I could sure see Lieutenant Keppel motioning me to get down. You better believe I hit the deck fast, and it was a good thing I did—there was a fierce firefight going on just on the other side of the weeds."

Evans low-crawled back to the streambed, only to hear that Faulkenberg was down and needed a medic fast. "There was no way I was letting Doc Evans go out there alone," Battle Company Platoon Sergeant Marty Miles said. "He took care of us and we took care of him. That was the way it was. 'Keep your fucking head down,' I remember yelling as I started out with him toward Faulkenberg."

Using the streambed for protection, Evans and Miles ran to about where they thought the wounded man was supposed to be. "I peeked my head up over the bank," Evans says. "Holy shit! Faulkenberg was directly in front of an enemy bunker—I could actually see the heads of the enemy soldiers from where I was behind him.

"Sergeant Gregory was thumping round after round into the bunker with his M-79 grenade launcher while Henderson and Reese were going at it with their M-60 machine guns, along with the rest of the squad on their M-16s. Somebody was spraying into the trees in case there were snipers. We crawled right through the center of their fire."

Faulkenberg was conscious, in shock, with blood all over his fatigues on the right side. Evans ripped his jacket off him, quickly patched the entrance wound. Then, as he rolled him over on his stomach to treat the exit wound, Faulkenberg spit out brown pieces of crud. Evans figured he was coughing up pieces of his lungs.

*See the book Dan Evans wrote (with Charles W. Sasser), *Doc: Platoon Medic*. We drew this account from the extensive and meticulous notes and advice Evans generously supplied us and from our own interviews with many of the survivors.

DIVISION BASE CAMP AT DONG TAM.
FOUR HUNDRED ACRES OF SITTING DUCKS. (COURTESY DR. BYRON HOLLEY)

HARDCORE CO, YOURS TRULY
(LEFT), BRIEFS DIVISION CG
MAJOR GENERAL JULIAN EWELL
(CENTER) AND CHIEF OF STAFF
COLONEL IRA HUNT (RIGHT)
IN THE MEKONG DELTA, 1969.
(COURTESY DAVID HACKWORTH)

VIETNAMESE WORKERS
AT DONG TAM.
(COURTESY VICTOR L. HENRY)

THE MEKONG DELTA FROM ABOVE. (COURTESY EDWARD CLARK)

A TYPICAL MEKONG
RICE PADDY.
(COURTESY DR. DAN EVANS)

ALONG THE "BLUE" — WITH A SAMPAN IN THE MIDDLE.
(COURTESY COLONEL GEORGE MERGNER)

HARDCORE GRUNTS LIVE THE NIGHTMARE
OF SUN TZU'S ADAGE "LOW GROUND IS
NOT ONLY DAMP AND UNHEALTHY, BUT
ALSO DISADVANTAGEOUS FOR FIGHTING".

BOOBY TRAPS WERE AS COMMON AS FLEAS ON A WILD DOG ALONG APPROACHES TO WATERWAYS. RIVER CROSSINGS WERE A FLAT BITCH. (COURTESY TOM SMITH)

BATTLE COMPANY RTO SGT. TOM SMITH AND HIS HARDCORE BRETHREN DUCK AS A BOOBY TRAP IS BLOWN. (COURTESY TOM SMITH)

DRYING OUT THE MORNING AFTER A HARDCORE AMBUSH. (COURTESY TOM SMITH)

CLAYMORE CO CAPTAIN GORDON DeROOS (ON RADIO) AND RTO SP-5 BARRY RABINOVITCH (LATER KIA) PUTTING OUT THE WORD. (COURTESY LT. COLONEL GORDON DeROOS)

MEKONG MUD SUCKS THE WIND OUT OF TWO HARDCORE GRUNTS. (COURTESY COLONEL BOB JOHNSON)

BATTLE COMPANY
RETURNS TO FSB DANGER AFTER AN EAGLE FLIGHT. (COURTESY LT. COLONEL BOB KNAPP)

TWO GREAT COMBAT LEADERS: LT. COLONEL DON SCHROEDER (LEFT) (LATER KIA) AND COLONEL HANK EMERSON (LATER WIA). (COURTESY DAVID HACKWORTH)

"PRIOR PLANNING PREVENTS POOR PERFORMANCE." (COURTESY COLONEL BOB JOHNSON)

HARDCORE'S SGT. MAJOR BOB PRESS, ONE OF THE U.S. ARMY'S BEST "FROM HERE TO ETERNITY" NCOs. (COURTESY CSM ROBERT PRESS)

COLONEL JOHN HAYES (LEFT) WITH HISTORIAN S.L.A. "SLAM" MARSHALL (CENTER) AND ME (RIGHT) WITH HAYES' DELTA FORCE—RESEARCHING THE *VIETNAM PRIMER*.

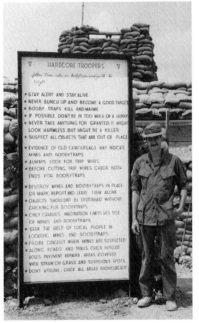

SGT. RICH MILLER STANDS TALL BY THE HARDCORE TROOPER RULES IN FRONT OF THE TOC AT FSB DANGER. (COURTESY RICH MILLER)

THE 4/39TH SIGN AT DONG TAM. AAA-O STANDS FOR ANYTHING, ANYWHERE, ANYTIME, BAR NOTHING. (COURTESY DR. DAN EVANS)

CAPTAIN ED CLARK INSERTING 9TH DIVISION RANGERS FROM A C&C CHOPPER IN THE MEKONG DELTA. (COURTESY EDWARD CLARK)

SQUAD LEADER JERRY SULLIVAN CHECKING OUT A DOWNED CHOPPER. (COURTESY JERRY SULLIVAN)

HARDCORE GRUNTS QUICKLY MOVE TO THEIR INITIAL OBJECTIVE AFTER CONDUCTING A COMBAT-ASSAULT. (COURTESY OF KEN CARLTON)

THE HARDCORE COMING IN HOT COURTESY OF THE BATTLING BOOMERANGS-191ST AVN.CO.
(COURTESY OF KEN CARLTON)

WARRIORS GETTING A LITTLE COOL AIR EN ROUTE TO REINFORCING THEIR BATTLE COMPANY
BROTHERS ON A VERY HOT, VERY BAD DAY, 25 MARCH 1969. (COURTESY OF KEN CARLTON)

FIRE SUPPORT BASE DANGER IS LOCKED AND COCKED.
(COURTESY COLONEL GEORGE MERGNER)

FIRE SUPPORT BASE TOMBSTONE, HOME OF HARDCORE'S
ALERT COMPANY. (COURTESY TOM AIKEN)

BATTLE COMPANY'S PLATOON
SGT. RON SULCER, WHO WAS
THE BUCKLE IN THE VC'S BELT.
(COURTESY RON SULCER)

CLAYMORE COMPANY EXPLODES OVER USO-SPONSORED INCENDIARY
VISIT FROM *HIGH CHAPARRAL* STARLETS. (COURTESY JERRY SULLIVAN)

A DAGGER COMPANY MEMORIAL SERVICE
AT FIRE SUPPORT BASE DANGER FOR THE MEN
WHO LOST THEIR LIVES AT THE CO CO CANAL, 13 MARCH 1969.
(COURTESY DAVID HACKWORTH)

TO THE VICTOR GO THE SPOILS.
VIET CONG'S 261A BATTALION'S CAPTURED GEAR
AT FIRE SUPPORT BASE DANGER, 25 MARCH 1969.
(COURTESY USAF CAPTAIN JOE CONNOR)

SGT. JIM SILVA, WHOSE "FTA" STUNT GOT HIM IN A
HARDCORE RIFLE PLATOON AND TWO PURPLE HEARTS.
(COURTESY JIM SILVA)

HARDCORE ALERT COMPANY BUDDIES
PFC ROBERT CHATUM, SGT. TOM AIKEN,
AND SP-4 JOSEPH SANCHEZ.
(COURTESY TOM AIKEN)

ALERT PLATOON SGT. TOBY HAGER AND BYRON "DOC" HOLLEY WITH CAPTURED AK-47s
AT FIREBASE DANGER. TWO OF THE HARDEST OF THE HARDCORE. (COURTESY DR. BYRON HOLLEY)

"THE ANIMAL," ME, ON THE LEFT AND "THE INTELLECT," MAJOR GEORGE MERGNER.
(COURTESY COLONEL GEORGE MERGNER)

CLAYMORE CO CAPTAIN GORDY DeROOS (LEFT) AND PLATOON LEADER LT. REX FLETCHER AT THEIR BASE CAMP. BOTH WERE THE LONGEST-SERVING OFFICER COMBAT LEADERS IN THE HARDCORE. (COURTESY LT. COLONEL GORDON DeROOS)

LT. BOBBY KNAPP, BATTLE COMPANY CO, A WARRIOR'S WARRIOR WHO ALWAYS LED FROM THE FRONT AND WHOSE TROOPS WOULD FOLLOW HIM TO "HELL AND BACK." (COURTESY DR. DAN EVANS)

BATTLE COMPANY'S SGT. DON WALLACE, THE BRAVEST OF THE BRAVE, WHO COLLECTED ENOUGH PURPLE HEARTS - 7 - TO BE CALLED "OLD MAGNET ASS." (COURTESY DR. DAN EVANS)

MEDIC "DOC" DAN EVANS, A HERO'S HERO, AWARDED THE DISTINGUISHED SERVICE CROSS FOR HIS "BEYOND THE CALL OF DUTY" ON 25 MARCH 1969. (COURTESY DR. DAN EVANS)

GREAT-GRUNT-TURNED-GREAT-DRIVER SP-4 JIM "ROBBIE" ROBERTSON AT DONG TAM WITH HARDCORE MASCOT, SNOOPY. (COURTESY JAMES ROBERTSON)

SGT. TIM "SUGAR BEAR" BAUER, A TOUGH FIGHTER, BEHIND A 50 CAL MACHINE GUN AT FSB DANGER. (COURTESY DR. DAN EVANS)

BATTLE COMPANY'S SP-4 L. J. HENDERSON, "THE BEST MACHINE GUNNER IN THE HARDCORE." (COURTESY TIM BAUER)

NIGHT HUNTER 6, LT. LARRY TAHLER,
A LEADER WHOSE TWENTY SNIPERS KNOCKED
OFF THE EQUIVALENT OF AN ENEMY BATTALION.
(COURTESY LARRY TAHLER)

COLONEL JOHN HAYES,
A GREAT WARRIOR-LEADER WHO LED FROM
THE FRONT AND TOOK CARE OF HIS WARRIORS
AT DANGER DURING THE BLOODY BATTLE OF
25 MARCH 1969.
(COURTESY JOHN HAYES)

PLATOON SGT. MICHAEL KIDD,
A GREAT SHAKE 'N' BAKE LEADER,
IS AWARDED THE BRONZE STAR FOR VALOR
BY BRIGADIER GENERAL FRANK GUNN.
(COURTESY MICHAEL KIDD)

A MEDEVAC DUST-OFF COMING INTO A HOT LZ.
(COURTESY DR. DAN EVANS)

M.G. HARRIS HOLLIS, GENERAL WILLIAM ROSSON, ME AND BRIG. GENERAL FRANK GUNN
IN THE HARDCORE BRIEFING TENT ON 24 MAY 1969. (COURTESY COLONEL GEORGE MERGNER)

THE HARDCORE
PULLING OUT OF THE DELTA
ON ITS WAY TO HAWAII.
(COURTESY VIC HENRY)

"Jesus," Miles said.

"They were really goin' there for a minute," Faulkenberg remembers with a glint in his eye, "until I told 'em it was just candies—butterscotch—my favorite."

The day of the mission, Faulkenberg had received a Care package from his mother and brother that included some candy along with the Kool-Aid they knew he liked. He'd put the sweet powder in his canteen to try to kill the taste of the Halizone and he was sucking on several lumps of butterscotch when he got hit.

The relief didn't last long. "I was helpless," Faulkenberg recalls. "I remember every time I took a breath, it bubbled right there in my back and I heard them guys say, 'Oh goddamn, that's bad.'"

Back at Danger, I got word from the Air Cav CO that Faulkenberg had been hit and reports from Alert Company that the hunt had suddenly gone cold. One casualty wasn't a threat to the mission, especially since it looked as if I might be right about the VC sneaking back, so I did some quick reshuffling. With Alert's AO off the boil and Battle's warming up, I told Nev Bumstead to bring Billy Winston and the Boomerangs back to Danger and stand them down. They'd be the reaction force if Battle ran into something—we didn't want to be dealing with two fights in two different directions at the same time.

Logistics also demanded the decision, primarily blade time. When we received a helicopter package, it came with only so much blade time for that day; to exceed the time limit meant getting rapped hard on the knuckles by Hunt's helicopter Gestapo, who policed how commanders used the birds. If you didn't manage them well and release them according to schedule, there'd be hell to pay and it could be a while before you got them again.

It was still too soon to know what Battle Company was really getting into. Since I was about to fly to Dong Tam with Colonel Hayes, Bumstead would be running the show. I figured if I made my instructions to him crystal clear, there'd be no fuckups in the few hours I'd be away. So I spelled out his assignment like a teacher explaining a lesson to a slow schoolboy.

"Get the rest of Battle Company out there to reinforce the 1st Platoon," I told him. "Scout out the battlefield. If you can knock off a stray, so much the better. But do not become decisively engaged under any circumstances."

The last thing I wanted was for him to get into a heavy fight—I didn't trust him as a combat leader. I'd become more and more convinced that the man simply was not equipped to fight a battle except with a grease pencil in a classroom at Fort Benning's School for Boys.

"You understand the guidance, Nev?"

"Yes, Sir," he assured me as he prepared to leave Danger in our C&C bird with a small TAC CP to take charge of the hunt. "I got it."

With my belly churning, I flew off with Hayes for Dong Tam. I was proud that General Ewell was honoring the soldiers of Dagger Company— Silver Stars, Bronze Stars and Army Commendations Medals for Valor—for their courage. They'd been the key players in the battle and deserved to be singled out. But throughout the ceremony my uneasiness kept building. I had three other companies in the field and my place was with them.

"Come on," Hayes said after the awards ceremony. "I'll buy you a beer."

"Thanks, but no, I gotta get back."

He stared at me for a couple of seconds, then said, "That's an order."

I could see he was playing with me, trying not to smile.

"Look," I said, "Charley's out there. I'm worried about Bumstead. I should've put Mergner in charge of the operation."

"Jesus, Hack, give it a rest. You look as if you could use a little R&R yourself."

Then he must have seen the look in my eyes.

"OK," he said. "Let's saddle up."

Dong Tam was about forty klicks to Danger. En route, I switched Hayes's chopper radio from his Brigade to my Battalion frequency and got hold of my TOC.

"Give me a Sitrep," I said, hoping for the best, expecting the worst. I smelled trouble.

A very sharp, steady and dedicated TOC NCO, Sergeant Craig Provin, said, "Battle Company's in contact. At 1250 hours, Battle Red 6—Keppel— estimated he was in contact with one VC squad. Major Bumstead inserted the rest of Battle Company at 1323 hours just to the west of Battle Red's Platoon. Battle 6 is on the ground. Comanche reports two machine guns and at least two RPGs in the wood line in front of Battle Red. Major Bumstead deployed Alert Company north of Battle Company at 1400 hours with the mission to seal the northern escape route."

Bad news.

I took a deep breath. Bradley Turner, Battle Company XO, was filling in for Bobby Knapp, who was on R&R in Hawaii with Doc Holley. Turner was running the show and no way did he have the experience to handle a hard fight.

"Any casualties?" I asked.

"U.S.: Battle, four wounded. Alert, zero. VC: thirteen dead," Provin said. "Alert took four POWs. One Boomerang gunship shot down. Crew OK. Bird's being lifted out."

This didn't sound to me like "Do not become decisively engaged." I called Bumstead.

"Give me a Sitrep."

"Everything's smooth." He sounded as upbeat as I'd ever heard him. No point pressing him for details.

"I'm in Colonel Hayes's bird. "We'll be at your position in one zero mikes. He'll drop me, you pick me up."

As we got over the fight, I could see that everything was about as smooth as the barbwire enclosing Danger. Battle Company was getting the shit kicked out of it.

We flew over a rice paddy bordered by a thick stand of trees. I could see the fight—Battle Company's guys exposed with little cover on about a 400-yard-wide field. Behind the tree line lurked the enemy, with good fields of fire. At the intersection of the paddy and the trees, two of my soldiers lay motionless; behind them was a small bunch of men hugging the ground; and farther back at least two squads lay flat on the open rice paddy or hunkered down in a long, deep streambed. The rear element couldn't go forward without getting shot up. The trapped advance guard couldn't pull back—if they tried, they'd be as visible as black bears on an ice floe.

It was obvious those VC motherfuckers were "Holding the Belt"—not giving away their positions until U.S. troops were right on top of them. A proven tactic. They'd start firing only once we were belly to belly. Our guys were so close to the enemy that we couldn't bring in our heavy stuff without killing our own men.

Most infantry engagements in Vietnam were fought under these conditions. Americans would stumble into such an ambush and be cut down, the survivors trapped under enemy guns. Then the fight would become exclusively about trying to extricate the trapped force—as it would be now.

Jesus, I wondered, how did Bumstead and the leaders of Battle Company fall for this old trick? More important, what the fuck were we going to do about it? I organized a place for Hayes to drop me off, and stood there in the middle of a big fucking rice paddy all by my lonesome. It was real pucker time. Then Captain Bruce Palmer, the pilot of my C&C, swooped down, I jumped in and we circled over the fight so I could get a closer look at what seemed a major cluster-fuck. I couldn't swing our big stick—air and artillery—without clobbering my own guys out on the point, so my first priority was to get the point sprung. But how? In my twenty-three years as a grunt, I'd never encountered a stickier tactical problem.

The situation had careened toward disaster after Faulkenberg went down and I was out of pocket in Dong Tam. "When Faulkenberg got hit, we stopped our forward movement," Keppel recalls. "Major Bumstead told us to hold where we were once we medevacked him." Once Faulkenberg was dusted off, Doc Evans and his litter detail returned to the streambed and recovered their gear. Then Keppel pulled the entire 1st Platoon back while Tac Air, artillery and helicopter gunships did their thing.

The South Viet Artillery unit supporting Battle Company fired wildly. Lieutenant Ross Sterling, Battle Company's FO—artillery forward observer—decided the ARVN cannon cockers were more dangerous than the VC. He wanted pinpoint accuracy, not friendly fire blasting into the company. Early in the battle, Lieutenant Colonel Peter Wittereid, the Artillery battalion CO, radioed a request to Dong Tam to move "C" Battery, located at Danger, forward by Chinook to be in range to support the fight. But Division, managing blade time big time, overrode his recommendation, telling him it was "premature." Sterling next tried to get the U.S. Navy into the act—with fire support from a cruiser with its big guns that were in range. They were as erratic as the ARVN gunners, so he told them to cease-fire and "go back to playing hearts."

But the USAF Tac Air was on the mark and Army gunships were also blasting the tree line, both wreaking their havoc.

"I was amazed the way bombs were exploding in the wood line and the power of the bombs," Keppel says. He took a look through a Sniper's scope and saw only devastation. "Fifty-foot trees flew around like they were twigs. I was lying there on that open ground and those 500-pound bombs were smacking into enemy positions," rifleman Tom Bevers remembers. "They were exploding and lifting me off the ground."

Soon after the rest of Battle Company landed, a single VC soldier with "weapon, black PJ bottoms and a dark shirt"—as Evans noted—ran screaming from the smoke and fire of the wood line. One of Larry Tahler's Snipers, Dan Conney, who was working with Battle Company for the day, drilled him through the heart at 400 yards.

Sergeant Miles figured the VC couldn't survive such a beating as did most of the men from Battle—that VC had to be the last man in the woods. There couldn't possibly be anything or anyone left but shattered trees, bomb craters and dead gooks.

On the ground, Turner got the order from Bumstead to sweep the objective and ordered Battle to move forward and take the wood line. Turner directed the 1st Platoon and the 2nd Platoon to attack on parallel axis with the 3rd Platoon bringing up the rear. Keppel told Sergeant Wallace to put two men in the point element, with an advance guard behind them; the rest of the Platoon would follow. This was a Battalion SOP formation designed to neutralize the VC's "hug the belt" tactics.

Doi, the 1st Platoon's Tiger Scout, and PFC Earl Hayes made up the very lonely point of the spear, far and away the most dangerous job in Vietnam. Sergeant Wallace, Ron Miller—his RTO—Mario Sotello and Jim Fabrizio walked some thirty yards behind; the rest of the Platoon, on Keppel's orders, stayed a good one hundred yards farther back.

Keppel saw there were only four men in the advance guard and told Wallace to add another soldier. Wallace chose Joe "Slim" Holleman, but Holleman rebelled, saying he'd walked point too many times before and wasn't about to do it again.

"Get up here," Wallace snapped.

"I ain't goin', man. I done did my share."

"Get with the program, Holleman," shouted Keppel.

Holleman finally went, dragging his rifle on the ground. "I thought at the time that the VC were probably watching all of this," Keppel recalls, "the typical American unit in front of their eyes"

Doi, still out front on point with Hayes just behind him, moved slowly toward the tree line followed by Fabrizio and Holleman, then Wallace, Miller and Sotello. Then came the rest of Wallace's squad, led by Tim "Sugar Bear" Bauer, moving parallel to the first squad, led by Sergeant Bill Gregory. In the gap between the first and second squads moved the CP group, including Keppel, RTO Bob Eaton, Charley Reese carrying an M-60 machine gun, Platoon Sergeant Marty Miles and Evans.

"We were spread out, really much more than the standard five yards between men," Doc Evans says. "Doi and Hayes were almost to the tree line while much of 3rd Platoon was still in the streambed—where Lieutenant Turner was directing operations. The 2nd Platoon was walking single file about twenty yards to our left, parallel with us."

Waiting silently in the smoking woods were as many as four hundred heavily armed Main Force VC under the control of the Dinh Tuong Province Headquarters. They came from the 279th Viet Cong Security Force, the remains of the 261A and 261B Battalions beefed up with NVA troops and probably elements of the 514C Local Force Battalion. This was one battle-scarred outfit. Hunkered down in its bunkers during the Tac Air and gunship strikes, these hardened troops now watched the twenty-four men of Keppel's Platoon approach, waiting for exactly the right moment.

Just as Doi and Hayes walked into the wood line, the VC grabbed the belt.

"They waited until they had us where they wanted us, where they could get us good," Evans says. "Somebody gave the order to open that ambush right then because they all started firing at the same time. Machine guns and hundreds of AK-47s. They shot at Doi and Hayes and they also shot at every-one else. Doi just kept getting hit, over and over. He must've died instantly."

Fabrizio told Doc Evans he saw the bullets go through Hayes. "Earl fell backward—he was dead before he hit the ground."

"Everybody grab dirt," Wallace yelled.

Miller's radio had been hit, and Wallace lost communication with Keppel. He couldn't tell if his point element was dead or alive. He told Miller to find "Sugar Bear" Bauer, his assistant squad leader, and put him in charge. Wallace and Sotello then started moving forward to try and recover the men on the point, operating on the assumption that they were all alive and trapped up forward. Every time the gunships swooped down and fired, he and Sotello would get up and sprint forward, leapfrogging until they reached Jimmy Fabrizio. Fabrizio told them he'd seen Hayes and the Tiger Scout get shot and die and that Holleman was just up ahead of them. So Wallace crawled forward until he reached Holleman, who was still alive, got him and crawled back.

"We were like sitting ducks," recalls "Sugar Bear" Bauer. "It was terrible. I was carrying an M-79 grenade launcher that day. We were pinned down with no cover, and I was afraid to shoot because the rest of the squad was in front of us. It was total bedlam. I kept lofting 79 rounds into the wood line, far enough away from the point—I didn't want to hit any of our own guys. I shot all of my rounds except three, which I was saving to take as many VC with me as I could in case it came down to that."

To the right of Keppel's 1st Platoon, the 2nd Platoon, now mostly in the prone, was spread out over 300 yards in column formation. No rice paddy walls or rolling terrain offered cover to protect the grunts from direct fire. At the same time, Battle's 3rd Platoon, still wisely hunkered down in the streambed, remained relatively safe. Bundles of harvested rice stacked across the open field offered concealment, but as protection they were even less effective than pillows in stopping bullets and RPG fragments. "I was hiding behind a one-foot-high rice stack," Platoon Sergeant Miles said. "I knew the damn thing wasn't cover, wouldn't protect me. It was like pulling a blanket over your head to protect yourself from an earthquake."

"I was in the dark," Keppel says. "I didn't have commo with my forward elements. This wasn't how the training scenarios went down at Fort Benning." Keppel told Miles to see if he could get a machine gun off to their right flank and lay down some fire to cover Wallace's withdrawal. Turning to PFC Charley Reese, the nearest machine-gunner, Miles told him to get cracking. But the enemy turned up the heat and Reese took a hit while putting his gun in place. Anyone even kneeling on that field was cut down like sugarcane at harvest season. Seemingly bulletproof, Evans somehow low-crawled over to Reese and started patching up his wound.

Keppel continued to crawl forward. Rising up on an elbow to ask if Reese needed a Dust-Off, he immediately caught a bullet in the chest and flipped on his back. "Mommy, Mommy," he mumbled as he felt a terrible weakness come over him. He was sure he was dying.

"Doc!" Miles yelled.

Grabbing Reese's M-60, Miles started raking the tree line while, under a sky full of enemy automatic weapons return fire, Evans began crawling to his next patient. Keppel's exit wound was large as a fist and he was making a gurgling sound.

"Doc," he called out weakly as Evans crawled near, "Doc, go back. I'm going to die anyhow."

Still, Evans inched his way to him. "Gotta get my people outta here," Keppel mumbled. "Gotta get my people ..."

Evans got up on his elbows trying to put a bandage on Keppel. "I kept pushing him away and saying, you're going to get hit," Keppel recalls. "Then, after a while, he kind of gave up with taping it because the bandage wouldn't hold anyway and I just stuck one into the exit wound and lay on my back to try to stop the bleeding."

Moving him was impossible, Evans concluded; they'd both be killed.

The medic told Keppel he'd have to wait for nightfall before they could evacuate him. Promising to return, he crawled off. Drifting in and out of consciousness, Keppel continued to give instructions to Wallace. But Wallace was pinned and pinned good, the buckle in the VC belt.

By now, the 2nd Platoon was also in deep shit. Enemy automatic and Sniper fire coming from the wood line and trees to the right of the 1st Platoon were raking them hard.

Eventually Evans and Rick Hudson, the 2nd Platoon medic, teamed up. Working together, one treated entrance wounds, the other exit wounds, both of them lying on the ground next to the stricken soldiers with bullets striking and skipping all around them. "We crawled around so much on that hard ground that we wore holes in our pants," Evans says.

Above the fight, Lieutenant Ken Carlton, a ballsy Bounty Hunter gunship pilot, stayed from start to finish. "The ground fire was wild," he recalls. "Enemy green tracers filled the air. My ship took a number of hits but I didn't lose one Bounty Hunter ship while I was in charge because we shot and didn't ask questions until later. I could see the point element maybe twenty meters from the enemy bunker line. I was infantry and damn well knew that the grunts down there were between a rock and a hard place."

Miles raised Carlton on his PRC-25 radio.

"Put fire on the bunker line," he said.

"We came in hot, hovered down," Carlton remembers. "I was on the minigun and started shooting right in front of the grunts, walking it into the tree line. Brass and links were falling on the grunts and they thought we were hosing them down and asked us to check fire."

Carlton's aircraft then swung around and approached the target from a different angle. "We flew parallel to the tree line. We blistered the target. I fired all 3,000 rounds of minigun ammo and the door gunners probably blew off a thousand rounds. The M-60 barrels were so hot I could smell them."

The VC then raised the ante, firing RPG rounds at the 1st Platoon. In the confusion, Wallace, Miller, Sotello, Holleman and Fabrizio tried to make a break. They began crawling, crabbing close to the ground. "Helicopters were still making runs so all four of us started making those leapfrog runs heading back to the company," Wallace says, "Sotello took off, then Fabrizio and I got up to run but when Holleman didn't, we jumped back down beside him. He'd been hit in the head, the gray matter was starting to come out of his head, sticking out behind his ear. He was still breathing."

The bullet with Holleman's name on it had gone through a package of Lucky Strike cigarettes he kept under an elastic band around his helmet. Passing through the helmet, it had exited behind his right ear.

"Slim," Wallace shouted, "don't you die on me. Listen to me, asshole, don't you dare die on me."

Wallace used his own pressure bandage on Holleman's exit wound. He found a clean pair of socks in Holleman's rucksack and stuffed them into the smaller entry wound. Somehow, he kept Holleman alive.

"Just then," Wallace remembers, "a round struck the selector switch of my M-16, sending fragments of metal through the palm of my left hand. If it hadn't hit the selector switch, it would've hit me. The rifle was more fucked up than I was."

As Wallace began wrapping a camouflage handkerchief around his smashed hand, Fabrizio felt blood running down his leg and started yelling for help. Wallace asked him how bad it was. Fabrizio said he still felt OK but thought he'd lost a lot of blood.

Wallace told Fabrizio to put a dressing on the wound.

"I'll probably pass out if I look at it," Fabrizio replied.

So Sotello and Wallace crawled over and started checking him out. Fabrizio kept screaming that he was "hit bad and bleeding all over the place."

Suddenly Sotello cackled.

"James, it's your canteen that's wounded, man. Not you."

The snap of bullets over their heads cut off their laughs.

Right in the middle of a red-hot frying pan, the men of Battle Company fought back fiercely. Sergeant Eugene O'Dell, one tough Pennsylvanian, toted a thirty-five-pound 90mm recoilless rifle, while many members of the 2nd Platoon carried the nine-pound rounds for his bunker-buster in addition to their other weapons and ammo. O'Dell and Artillery FO Ross Sterling— temporarily without a fire support job because he had no artillery to adjust— teamed up and set up in the open in kneeling positions as if they were at a stateside firing range and began pounding the enemy bunker line with round after round of deadly accurate 90mm fire.

As O'Dell sighted in on the enemy with Sterling's help, enemy slugs spit all around these two incredibly brave men and the equally valiant 2nd Platoon guys running ammo to them. By the time O'Dell and Sterling fired all of their 90mm High Explosive (HE) rounds, they'd knocked out three enemy machine-gun bunkers and destroyed a dozen fighting positions.

O'Dell was a mortar man—but just before the company moved out that morning First Sergeant Thomas Dunn had said to him, "Why don't you take the 90mm recoilless rifle with you? You're a weapons man! You know how to shoot it, right?"

"Well, I do, First Sergeant, and I don't, but I'll take it," O'Dell had replied. He'd trained on the weapon at Shake and Bake at Benning, but he'd spent all of his time in Vietnam with the 81mm mortars. At best, he'd be winging it. But good soldier that he was, he'd taken Dunn's cue, organized the 90mm ammo, checked out his blunderbuss and climbed on a chopper to reinforce the First Platoon.

After firing all of the 90mm HE rounds, both O'Dell and Sterling were again out of a job. Sterling went back to seeing if he could get artillery support. O'Dell had one canister round left that was different from the high-explosive shells—it shot razor-blade type projectiles over a wide area. "I loaded that there shell," O'Dell recalls. "And I left the 90mm down on the ground to use as a final resort if we were overrun and went after a couple of guys I seen were hurt or shot."

Running through a hail of bullets, he made three trips dropping the wounded off to the medics. On his fourth run, he himself joined the ranks of the bruised, battered and bloodied: "I got hit in the left leg by a green tracer just as I was picking up another guy to carry him to the Doc. Then, when I tried to get myself back up, I got shot again—under the right shoulder blade—and that knocked me down real good and flipped off my glasses. So I said to myself, 'Hey, you're not getting up again. You got hit twice and you're not getting hit a third time.'"

The enemy still wasn't finished with O'Dell. Charley zeroed in on the two grunts carrying him back to the rear. Bullets chewed the ground all around them. "The guys dropped me on my side and hit the ground just as two bullets slammed into my rear end at almost the same time."

That's when a round slammed into Frank Ellis. His helmet flew at least twenty yards in the air as a large-caliber bullet took off the top of his head.

"I was just lying there with my eyes shut trying to get myself together," O'Dell recalls. "I was having trouble breathing and nothing was going to get me to open my eyes. I was too scared—I'd heard more soldiers died from the shock of seeing their wounds than the wounds themselves, and I wanted to live."

Then, while Sergeant Craig and Freddie Downs tried to reach O'Dell and Ellis, Craig caught sight of about twenty men—in uniforms—making tracks through the woods. For a moment he thought they were American reinforcements, then saw "they were NVA regulars."

Sergeant Craig threw O'Dell over his shoulder and started running to the ditch. Melchor ran alongside him, holding his crushed arm, while Downs dragged Ellis, who was somehow still alive even though most of his skull was gone. They made it to the shelter of the streambed, rested and then ran to an approaching Dust-Off.

Then Downs, still clutching Ellis, turned away from the chopper dust to shield his eyes only to watch as a pair of green tracers hurtled down toward him. "One got me in the chest, the other one hit my wrist and just spun me right around before I went down—with Ellis on top of me."

Downs threw himself onto the floor of the Dust-Off, Ellis's body somehow ending up on top of him again. And then Craig shoved O'Dell into the bird.

As Craig tells it, O'Dell, though weak from his four wounds, "flashed me a thumbs-up as the bird lifted. I saw him kind of totter forward and for a bad moment I thought he was gonna fall right out that open door. But then he fell back inside."

"I had to hang on with my good arm or I would have fallen out," O'Dell remembers. "Just as I was about to lose hold, the medic grabbed me and pulled me in."

Battle Company medic Elijah Frazier bandaged the wounded as fast as they came in until a bullet put him out of action. Lieutenant Sterling was bandaging Frazier's wound when he witnessed a one-in-a-million. A green tracer bullet landed on Frazier's chest and began spinning like a top until Sterling flipped it off with his finger. He then picked up Frazier's aid bag and the FO-turned-90mm-assistant-gunner started his internship as a medic. Moving back to the battlefield, he began patching up and evacuating wounded soldiers.

"Medic! Medic!"

Third Platoon medic Mike Hill crawled to the sound of the wounded man.

"I think I sprained my ankle," the guy said.

"You stupid ass," Doc Hill exploded. "Guys are dying and you whine about a sprained ankle? What do you expect me to do about it?"

Suddenly, what felt like a bag of cement smashed into Hill's own leg. He fell down and tried to treat his wound, but he was losing blood fast and felt himself going into shock. Digging in his aid bag, he located some Darvon and whipped it down. When he woke up, Sergeant Craig from the 2nd Platoon was bandaging him up. "You know the old saying about no atheists on the battlefield," he says. "It's so true. I started praying, 'Lord, I can't think of a good reason why you should let me, but I'd sure like to live.'"

Out on the killing field, Marty Miles crawled thirty yards and took over Charley Reese's M-60 machine gun. From an exposed position, he fired belt after belt into the enemy's fighting bunkers, until running out of ammo, he grabbed the radio and asked a supporting gunship if he had any 7.62 machine-gun ammo to spare.

Carlton heard the call. "We were about to go off station to rearm and refuel," he remembers. "We received a message from the C&C that the grunts were low on ammo, so we got all our spare ammo together—about 400 or 500 rounds of linked 7.62, a half case of frags and smoke grenades and maybe a dozen M-16 mags. The grunts marked the drop with smoke, we came in fast, hovered and tossed everything out. We didn't stay long. It was hot as hell down there. VC green tracers were the predominant color."

Carlton's air-mail special delivery saved 1st Platoon's ass. "Manna from Heaven," Miles recalls.

At the same moment, Sergeant "Sugar Bear" Bauer and Sergeant Bill Gregory pummeled the enemy positions with accurate M-79 rounds. Sniper Dan Conney calmly lay out in the center of the open field, acting as if he were dead. Throughout the afternoon he knocked off six VC tree snipers, pretty good shooting for a corpse.

Bauer could hear steady bursts of machine-gun fire from his good buddy L. J. Henderson, a guy he considered "the best M-60 machine-gunner around." The tall black grunt was sucking one of the cigars "Sugar Bear" continually scrounged for him and he had a wad of tobacco, also courtesy of the "Bear," stashed away in a cheek for good measure. He continued to blister the enemy positions while Eusebio Fernandez, who was standing in for Arles Brown of the broken foot, kept the machine-gun belts coming.

"L. J. seemed to be permanently attached to the trigger," Fernandez remembers.

Lobbing M-79 grenades, Sergeant Gregory yelled to his squad, "People, goddamnit! Keep down but pull back!"

"Everything broke loose," Bauer says. "You were kind of in your own individual little world. You couldn't really poke your head up and you didn't know what was happening to the rest of the people. I shot off most of my ammunition.. Then I crawled around and scrounged some more ammo from some of the wounded guys."

The men of Battle Company were now in the same spot as the soldiers who fought at Gettysburg or went in on the early waves at Saipan and Normandy—out in the open with only their jackets for protection, fighting a well-entrenched enemy. As my bird wheeled over the paddy and tree line, I saw that they couldn't extract their point and with Wallace and his people still out there, I knew I couldn't use all my firepower effectively. I could also see that unless we figured out some way to turn things around fast, a lot more good men were going to die.

FOURTEEN

Kien Phong Province
25 MARCH 1969

Over the years I've found myself in some pretty tight spots and I've often felt only Lady Luck and my Guardian Angel pulled me through. As I looked down from the chopper, I prayed that both those Gals still had me on their A list—because Battle Company sure needed them now.

Bumstead, Turner and Keppel had bought into one of Sun Tzu's oldest, deadliest tactics, now a favorite VC trick: the lure. That single soldier sent running out of the woods during the air strikes was almost certainly a decoy used to suck our soldiers into a deadly L-shaped ambush. The Battalion battle log, recording progressive sightings of the VC, tells the rest of the story: "One enemy...two enemy...a squad."

Orbiting the fight, I could see that the two men on the point nearest the tree line were almost certainly dead. They lay on their backs, a telling sign, since wounded men on the battlefield almost always lie on their stomachs. But because the five soldiers in Sergeant Wallace's advance guard, one hundred yards behind the point, were on their bellies hugging the ground, I thought they just might be alive. If so, it wouldn't be long before they'd be joining Doi and Hayes.

At first, I couldn't come up with a quick fix on how to get those men out of there. My C&C ship, piloted by Captain Bruce Palmer, the skipper of the Boomerang platoon supporting us that day, had radios connecting me with my Companies, my Brigade commander, the artillery folks, the USAF Forward Controllers and supporting gunships. I knew I could bring in enough thunder to clobber Charley, but that might cost me the last chance to save what was left of Wallace's squad. All of that firepower and I couldn't use it. I felt like a gambler with a huge pile of chips who can't get his hands on the dice.

So I used what I could, beginning with whatever would not endanger the men of Battle Company. First I tried to put a wall of smoke between my guys and the enemy, using artillery white phosphorous and smoke rounds from "C" Battery that had finally been moved forward from Danger and then chopper-delivered smoke. But just as the smoke went down, the wind shifted, blowing it and the Willie Peter off in all the wrong directions.

The Air Force delivered bombs and napalm, and the chopper gunships put down heavy rocket and mini-fire, pounding as close to Wallace's pinned squad as possible. But they couldn't put their stuff squarely on the VC bunker line, because they might clobber Wallace and hit the rest of Battle Company. Still, I hoped our Tac Air would put enough heat on Charley to buy Wallace the chance to get the hell out. But Wallace wasn't moving. I didn't know Holleman had been hit and that there was no way Wallace was abandoning him.

The sun was fading fast, an ominous red-orange sliding toward the horizon. And in all probability, darkness would let the VC finish what they'd started and then escape.

Out on the point, Wallace stuck with Holleman. "As far as I knew, the company didn't even realize we were still alive. We couldn't leave Holleman there and we couldn't pick him up and carry him because we would've been moving too slow. I knew we'd be hit—there were too many rounds coming at us. The fire surrounding us was just too intense. I couldn't leave the man there, he was still alive. I couldn't abandon him. At that point I really didn't know what the 'F' to do."

While Wallace was sweating how he'd get Holleman out, I decided to roll the dice and called the front seat. "Palmer, looks like the only way we can do this is go down and get them ourselves. Will you ask your crew if they'll make the try?"

I ran the mission by my guys while Palmer, brave and combat-savvy, checked with his copilot and two gunners.

"Roger that, we'll do it," he said.

Nev Bumstead, Doc Schwartz, Bob Reynolds and RTO Billy McAllister all gave me a green light.

I had eight gunships combined from the Comanches and Bounty Hunters—Cobras and Hueys flown by daring and capable crews. "Here's what we're going to do," I told Palmer. "Our ship will land and do a quick snatch. You organize the guns to cover us. Pretend we're an infantry squad firing and maneuvering. Every second we're on the ground I want one gunship over us hosing down that tree line. And when that gun's out of ammo, I want him to break off and another to roll in immediately and pick up the slack. I want that tree line constantly blistered while we're down there. Got it?"

"Affirmative on that, Sir," Palmer snapped back.

The chopper guys had never seen or heard of any such aerial tactic before. No one taught it at Fort Rucker, the Army Aviation School. But it was, of course, common for infantrymen to cover their comrades on the attack with rifle and machine-gun fire—so why wouldn't it work with helicopters? I just needed the enemy to put their heads in the bottom of their holes and keep their fingers off the trigger while our bird landed virtually on top of them, scooped up Wallace and his people and hightailed it. My bet was we'd bring it off. We had shock, action and surprise on our side.

"Palmer, you squared away and ready to go?" I asked.

"Roger that, Sir." His voice was calm and steady.

He dropped down fast, hovering for a moment in front of the line of bunkers, aided in the maneuver because he was running low on fuel and had a lighter load. The VC, taken totally by surprise, responded by ducking instead of firing back. Rockets and minigun bullets from the gunships whistled all around us, smacking the VC positions.

Down on the ground, Wallace figured the situation was hopeless. "I didn't know what decision to make. And then, I looked up and here comes this damn helicopter down out of the air and heading straight toward us. I really didn't think he was going to land, but he kept coming down, heading toward our position and as he got fairly close, I saw that the Battalion Commander was standing out there on the skids with all the fire going on. I couldn't figure out what the hell he was doing. I mean, this is a man I was definitely afraid of—he'd eat your ass for no reason if you looked at him cross-eyed."

Tom Bever also looked up and saw the chopper coming down. "I didn't know who it was," he says. "Then someone yelled. 'It's the Colonel,' and I said, 'No that can't be.' It was like a scene in a movie. I couldn't believe anybody would do that."

Bever had a point. But this wasn't a movie and those were real bullets coming at us. And there were real men—not actors—getting the shit shot out of them down on that killing field.

When the ship was about six to eight feet off the ground I jumped from the skids and ran toward the pinned soldiers. Sergeant Wallace stood up, ramrod straight, a GI scarecrow with a leg wound and a bloody hand. He snapped a salute.

"Hardcore Recondo, Sir," he shouted.

I couldn't believe my eyes or ears. What the fuck did this idiot—this incredibly brave idiot—think he was doing? The VC were back to firing at us, bullets whizzing by from every direction—from our friends and our enemies, equally lethal—and here was Wallace sounding off.

"Let's get your boys in the chopper." I gave him a push in the right direction, toward where Holleman was lying on the ground. Wallace grabbed his feet, I grabbed his shoulders and we carried him to the chopper.

"There must have been about nine people already in that chopper—the pilot, the copilot, his two door gunners, I think the forward observer, an Air Force doctor and me and him and Holleman," Wallace recalls. "We put Holleman on the floor there and I turned around to go after my weapon even though it was no good at this point—that was training—and the Colonel grabbed me and swung me around into the chopper. Then he ran back and grabbed Fabrizio by the belt and shirt, picked him up and sat him up in the seat while he stepped on the skid of the chopper."

Any other time, no way could I have lifted Fabrizio so easily and carried him at double time a dozen yards and tossed him into the chopper. But with the adrenaline pumping through my body at battle pitch he seemed as light as a bag of marshmallows.

By this time, the VC were onto the game. Their guns zeroed in on our aircraft. When I looked inside, I saw Palmer ducking behind his console. "Tracers were going above and between the rotary blades and the body, and underneath the front and rear of the bird and through it," recalls Sergeant Gary Dubois. "All the gook machine guns out there were trained on that chopper. The Plexiglas windows in front were exploding. The chopper was smoking and shaking. I thought no way was that chopper going to lift out of there."

With the three additional passengers, the C&C was so full that I had to stand out on the skids. I grabbed my crash helmet and yelled in the mike, "Let's get this mother out of here."

I was so dried out I could only croak. Although I wasn't conscious of being afraid, my tongue was stuck to the roof of my mouth. Quickly,

I took a swig of water from my canteen and tried again.

"Let's get the fuck out of here."

This time Palmer got the message. He swung the Huey around just before an RPG round whistled in and landed where the tail boom had been. If he hadn't moved when he did, we'd have been a permanent VC firing range.

"Fabrizio and I reached out and grabbed hold of Colonel Hackworth," Wallace says. "I was afraid he was going to fall off the skid."

Inside the bird, Doc Schwartz, the acting Battalion surgeon, treated the wounded. He'd flown out with Bumstead that morning when the fight first started, figuring he'd be Johnny-on-the-spot. He had no idea that he'd become part of an air rescue so dangerous he'd have nightmares about it for the next thirty years.

"A soldier was stretched out on the floor," Doc Schwartz remembers. "He had a bad head wound. I kneeled down beside him and was attending to him and a burst of bullets ripped through the helicopter. I'd just opened a compress and a bullet tore it from my hand. Several more bullets cut through my webbing and jungle jacket. I couldn't believe what was happening, but I had men to take care of. Maybe that's what kept me calm."

At first we couldn't get fully airborne. The amount of lead coming at us from the tree line was so intense that unless the chopper moved and moved quickly, we'd all soon be as ventilated as a kitchen colander. Finally, the C&C managed a jump, and like a monster grasshopper, in one big leap we made a full five hundred yards away from the firing before we hit the ground with a jarring thump.

With all the shit that was happening, Fabrizio chose this moment to ask me for a smoke. He reached out of the cargo compartment and grabbed my webbing.

"Colonel," he said, "you wouldn't happen to have a cigarette on you, would you?"

That boy must have had one serious habit!

Five hundred yards took us out of the immediate VC killing zone. I quietly thanked my two Ladies for pulling off the miracle we'd needed. The Huey hopped another five hundred yards, then another, then suddenly we were airborne.

John Hayes, who was over the fight in his chopper, wasn't too happy. "You could see tracers flying through the chopper. I figured they'd all bought it," he said later. "It was pretty amazing when they made it off the ground."

"By this time, 'A' Company had been brought in, so Colonel Hackworth wanted to have the pilot land back behind the Company," Wallace says. "But the pilot told him he couldn't do that because he wouldn't be able to take off again because we'd taken too many hits. So we made a beeline for Danger."

The official battalion log reads, "1735 hours. Bn Cmdr bringing in three WIAs from battlefield to FSB Danger." Like all official logs, these words tell only the dispassionate facts, revealing little of the hair-raising circumstances.

At 1735 hours, we landed at Danger to unload Wallace, Holleman, Fabrizio and Doc Schwartz, who from the time we picked up the wounded worked frantically to keep them alive. Wallace had insisted on helping the Doc with Holleman, giving him mouth-to-mouth under Schwartz's supervision.

"Then they put Holleman on a stretcher and evacked him out," Wallace said. "And at that point I was told I couldn't go back out—the Docs grabbed me and started cleaning and bandaging me up."

Wallace's wound was his fifth. When he reached seven—and was still standing tall—his buddies started calling him "The Human Magnet" and "Old Magnet Ass."

The thing I remember most when we landed at Danger is the sight of a guy from Battle Company watching Wallace climb out of that shot-up bird.

"Fucking Wallace," the grunt said, shaking his head in awe and with a palpable pride that he too was part of the Hardcore Recondos, part of the toughest, most courageous group of mean-assed mainly draftee motherfuckers in Vietnam.

Doc Schwartz patched up Wallace and Fabrizio, and Holleman was evacuated to Dong Tam. As for Miller and Sotello, I eventually found out that they used the diversion of our landing to hightail it back to the rear and rejoin what was left of Battle Red.

Palmer's aircraft was a write-off. It looked like a madman had worked it over with an ax. Yet not one soldier sitting in that very shot-up, overloaded bird was even scratched during the snatch, which I found absolutely amazing. Bounty Hunter pilot Ken Carlton examined the aircraft later and said, "It had more bullet holes than screws. The belly was stitched from the nose to the end of the boom."

In the middle of all this mayhem, I'd raised Lieutenant Turner on the radio and told him to pull his people back to the ditch that Keppel had used and to reorganize, evacuate his wounded and redistribute ammo.

Lieutenant Turner told me they were still pinned down.

Fuck a lot of being pinned down, I thought. We had to get them out of there.

"Get off your ass and get moving," I shouted angrily over the radio. "Get your Company out of that field and back into the shelter of the ditch."

Five minutes after I deposited Wallace at Danger, I jumped into another C&C chopper with Palmer at the controls and returned to the fight. I discovered a few minutes later that in the brief time I'd been away, Lieutenant Turner had fatally attacked when he should have withdrawn.

Turner's RTO, Tom Smith, told me the lieutenant had gotten my order. But instead of pulling back, he'd stood up and rushed forward. Holding his steel pot on his head so it wouldn't fall off, he started running from man to man, ordering them to attack.

"Lieutenant Turner ran up and he was about even with me," Sergeant Tim "Sugar-Bear" Bauer recalls. "Sergeant Lester from the 2nd Platoon ran up and flopped down beside me."

"We're going to advance to the wood line," Sergeant Lester said. "Turner wants to make sure all the point element is out of there."

Turner ordered the 3rd Platoon to leave the ditch and attack. "It was like a movie scene from the Civil War," Sergeant Dubois said. "Guys banzaied out of that ditch and we were cut down like bowling pins. We didn't get ten yards. It was sheer madness."

"I yelled over to Turner that I was sure the Colonel's chopper had taken all the surviving point squad out," Bauer said. "He either didn't hear me or wasn't paying attention because he jumps up and says, 'Come on, everybody. Get up and attack into that wood line. They're not even shooting at us.'"

"We started moving forward and holy hell broke loose," Bauer says. "Sergeant Lester was on my right, he got immediately hit and spun and fell down."

"We were going to come on line and move out across this open field," Tom Bever remembers. "We took a lot more fire. Several guys were wounded. I was near Lieutenant Turner when he was shot through the chest with a burst of machine-gun fire."

"Lieutenant Turner had a large gaping hole under his armpit," Tom Bever adds. "And I was lying there myself along with a radio man, Dennis Richards, and Sergeant Bauer. I said, 'We got to get Turner out of here or he's going to die.'"

While enemy grazing fire swept the field, Sergeant Bauer hugged the ground, yelling at everyone to get down. "I could see a machine-gun bunker right in front of me," Bauer recalls. "It was blowing puffs of smoke as it was firing. It seemed like the gunship rockets were just bouncing off that bunker.

I remember seeing an LAW lying on the rice paddy ground when we were moving forward so I ran back and got it. When I hit the dirt again rounds were hitting all around me. I waited until the gunship made another pass at the bunker and while the machine-gun crew was distracted, I armed and aimed the LAW, popped up and let her fly. I must have hit that sucker right in its aperture because there was a large POW, a cloud of smoke and that damn machine gun didn't fire anymore."

Like Platoon Sergeant Ron Sulcer, Richards had told buddies he had a premonition that something was going to happen to him. "I'm going to get it," he'd said earlier in the day. He was right.

As Bever remembers the moment, "There was no stretcher near us so what happened, in all the confusion, was Dennis Richards ended up grabbing Turner underneath his arms. I grabbed underneath his legs. 'Sugar Bear' was helping out to get him back to the medics. ...Another barrage of shots rang out and hit Dennis Richards right in the throat and he spun around and went down. It hit him in a bad area there, in the artery and with every heartbeat, blood was coming out of his mouth and I said 'Just roll over on your side' and he did for a while and then he rolled over on his back and he died there."

"We were just about back to Doc Evans when I hear this crack," "Sugar Bear" Bauer remembers. "We all tumbled to the ground with Turner. I was covered with both Turner's and Richards' blood and when I felt it, I thought I was hit, too.

One of the medics called out, "Turner's dead." Bever lay on the ground thinking, "God, take care of them..."

Turner was too inexperienced for this very hot fight. He'd been a damn good Platoon leader and had done such a great job as Company XO, taking care of the bullets, beans and paperwork, that I decided he could handle things for the week that Knapp R&R'ed in Hawaii. It was a bad call. His inexperience cost him his life and was in part responsible for what happened to Battle Company. A skipper with more combat mileage like Knapp or DeRoos wouldn't have bought into Bumstead's let's-go-get-the-bad-guys gung-ho battle plan and also known there's no way to steamroll over a dug-in opponent without taking serious lumps.

Hearing that Turner had gone down, Ron Sulcer tried to get over to him. "About that time I felt rounds go past my head and I turned to see where they were coming from. There was a bunker off to the right, maybe thirty to fifty yards, and I saw a green tracer round coming at me. I went into a discussion with myself like, "Get out of the way, it's coming straight at you.

"The slow motion was unbelievable. The round hit me and just knocked the fool out of me. My weapon went flying somewhere. I was trying to get up and I couldn't get up. I don't remember anybody else around. I don't know how Turner got out of there. All I know is that suddenly I was by myself and I was trying to move and I couldn't. I got mad at myself. I just ripped open my jungle jacket and saw a little hole by the bottom of my rib cage. I started to give myself a hard time. I said to myself, 'Come on, get up.' I was afraid if I lost consciousness I'd die. I rolled over on my left side and reached behind me and that's when I felt a big hole. So I made a ball out of my jacket and laid down on it to stop the bleeding.

"All of a sudden as I was looking around I saw these VC in this really well-camouflaged bunker. I couldn't believe how close they were to me, so close that I could actually see their eyeballs and in what direction they were looking. We stared and stared at each other."

Sulcer's muscles tensed, waiting for the impact of a shot. "They started flipping me the bird, pointing their fingers at me, and every once in a while they'd kinda fire around me, laughing. But it wasn't too long before I realized they weren't gonna finish me off right then, they were gonna use me as bait. Then I got to wondering just what they were gonna do and when they were gonna do it."

Sulcer's never been sure just how long he lay out there, "a few hours anyway," but he'll never forget how every time they stared over at him, "I'd wonder if this was it, if this was gonna be when they were going to do me."

He says, "The guys told me that as the day wore on, they tried to take that bunker out—which I know they were doing because I saw gunships fire rockets—but they couldn't get the job done and that's when the jet jockeys came over. It was really strange. The aircraft were flying to my right and to my left, mostly parallel with the wood line, dropping their bombs, but not getting anywhere near that bunker. I'm lying there watching them and thinking, Are the VC gonna finish me off or wait for dark to come and get me or leave me there for three days to die slowly? And since I didn't have a weapon, I decided I was taking the two grenades I had left and holding on to them and the first guy that comes near me, we were going together."

About this time, Bauer saw an F-4 zoom over and drop a napalm bomb on the VC. It hit so close he could feel the searing heat. For an instant, "Sugar Bear" thought the F-4 was dropping the napalm on Battle Company, but the jet jockey found his mark and dropped the goods right on the VC bunker line.

As Sulcer recalls the moment, "Right then, this plane dropped straight down and he came in real fast from behind me and went over my head. I could just about have reached up and grabbed it, it was that close. That's when I just knew it was napalm and I figured I was gone."

The F-4 was flying parallel to the wood line to protect soldiers still on the ground from friendly fire. But then the pilot came in "low and straight at the bunker," according to Sulcer, and dropped a canister of napalm in a perfectly executed maneuver.

"He put it far enough in front of me and got enough in the bunker and I watched those two VC burn," Sulcer remembers. "I thought, Adios, motherfuckers. I think I even managed a cheer."

The air strikes continued, run after run.

As Doc Evans tells it, "This guy releases the bomb as he's coming in and I either fell asleep or lost consciousness and when I woke up there was nobody around me and I didn't know where I was because the wood line was gone. I actually spun around on my belly to try to figure out where I was until I realized that all the palm trees—everything—was gone. I think somebody must've checked on me at that time because later I found out I was reported as killed. Anyway, I finally got my bearings, I gradually became aware of Sergeant Miles back behind me talking to an Air Force FAC on his radio. I yelled and pointed over toward a big tree. 'There's a sniper in that tree,' I said. 'He's the one who got Dennis Richards.'"

"Let's give him the hot seat," Miles yelled back.

"The next air strike was for Dennis," Evans said. "It melted everything in front of me."

Evans was just pulling himself together when the message came—word-of-mouth from rear to front—to withdraw. "Best news I'd heard all day," he says. "I took off my rucksack and destroyed everything I didn't need. I just kept bandages, morphine, anything to treat wounds. I put all the medical supplies I could in those big pockets we had in our jungle fatigues. Everything else went, my food, my socks. Everything. Although I made sure it was all fixed so that Charley couldn't use it."

As the grunts pulled back, two guys from the 3rd Platoon stopped Evans. "They said, 'Ron Sulcer's still up there,' pointing forward and to my left," Evans said. "'He needs a medic bad.'"

Rick Hudson immediately volunteered to accompany Dan Evans as did the two grunts from the 3rd Platoon, who told the two Docs that Sulcer was lying directly in front of the bunker that was now filled with crispy critters.

Evans says, "I told those guys we were going to low-crawl and not run to Sulcer because with four of us on the battlefield, we were easy targets. So we crawled up to Richards and Turner, where we collected any ammunition we could 'cause everyone was low on ammo, and kept moving."

Sulcer heard Evans's voice calling to him. "He was crawling out and looking for me and I hollered to him to watch out, that gooks were still in the woods."

"Sulcer was lying face up," Evans says. "I don't remember any movement at all. I was worried he was paralyzed. I was actually relieved when I heard him yelling at us to stay back."

By now the sun was really low. Evans knew it would be dark in minutes. He patted Sulcer's shoulder. "Sergeant, we're here and we're gonna get you out. You're gonna do just fine now, I promise." He bandaged the entry wound, Hudson the exit wound with the teamwork they'd perfected.

"I believe you, Doc," Sulcer told Evans. "But I couldn't stop seeing those gooks," he says. "I kept thinking they were going to kill me—even though I knew they'd been cooked."

Sergeant Marty Miles crawled forward and yelled, "Doc, I've got a chopper coming in to lay smoke for you. Get ready to haul ass."

"So then Dan Evans and Rick Hudson rolled me over on one of those fold-up canvas litters. I seem to remember that they picked me up," Sulcer said.

"We'll try to give you an easy ride," Evans said.

"Do what you have to do, Doc," Sulcer said, "I'd give you my last C-Rat can of peaches even if you dragged me out by one foot."

The four rescuers grabbed the stretcher just as the smoke chopper made its first pass, laying a thick cloud of white smoke along the tree line between them and the VC.

"We jumped up and ran with him," Evans said. "But once I got to my feet, I could feel the wind on my face—blowing in the wrong direction. We were exposed and they were firing."

"All of a sudden rounds started coming at us," Sulcer recalls, "and they dropped me."

"Get down," Evans shouted—and they all hit the dirt.

"The Army always had a Plan B for everything," Evans says, "and this was no exception. While Hudson and I dragged Sulcer on his stretcher, a foot or two at a time, the two 3rd Platoon grunts and Sergeant Miles provided cover. We'd crawl backward, then grab hold of the stretcher and pull the sergeant on up to us and we kept doing that, until finally it got dark enough for us to haul ass over to the ditch, where we waited for the medevac."

So that's how things stood. Turner was KIA and his company was cut up pretty badly, but with Wallace and his men out of there and the Air Force napalming and bombing right on the enemy bunker line, it was a new ballgame. "It's our turn, motherfuckers," I said to myself.

I alerted Claymore and Dagger to be prepared to move to the battle area by chopper in one hour. Next, I asked Hayes to attach two rifle companies from other battalions to the Hardcore. My plan was to block all of Charley's escape routes while trying to pin him throughout the night with shitloads of air and artillery fire. I figured most of the reinforcing units would have to move in the dark, but we'd succeeded at the Plain of Reeds, during Hunt's phony battle at Thanh Phu and during the fight on 23 and 24 March. The fourth time around, I had no doubt we'd put it to the Cong without Vaseline.

I also contacted Winston at Alert, figuring I'd have him slip over to Battle, consolidate both units under his command, then put his beefed-up Company into a seal covering the VC's escape routes.

But Winston came off as flat goofy on the radio. Nothing he said made sense—he was raving, mumbling incoherent jibberish. Nev had told me earlier that when he inserted Winston by chopper, he'd given him his objective and told him what route to take, loud and clear. He said at the time that Winston didn't sound like he was playing with a full deck, but he was too busy running the battle to play shrink.

According to Sergeant Tom Aiken, Winston had been acting mighty strange all day. "He kept repeating on the company net to pop yellow smoke. He was saying, 'My wife is against me. My wife's mother and father are against me. They're all against me and they're all testing me. You got to pop yellow smoke.'"

So here was a good problem for a class at Fort Benning's Infantry School: two rifle companies on the field of battle, one leaderless and cut to ribbons, the other leaderless because its commander had lost it.

I got Bounty Hunters' gunships to blister the enemy bunker line again directly in front of where Battle Company's soldiers were pulling back. By this time, we had favorable winds and the smoke chopper could lay down a curtain between the blistered enemy battle positions and the open rice paddy.

While the ship was putting down the wall of smoke, I told Nev I was going to drop him off near Battle Company. He'd taken the S-3 RTO, PFC Billy McAllister, who was in the C&C for that very contingency.

"Nev, put Frank Angyal in command of Alert. I want what's left of Battle folded into Alert and I want these two companies combined into one to seal the enemy's escape route on this side."

While we weren't talking about a mission that required a charter member of Mensa, I hated to trust Bumstead with it—I was still smarting over his fuckup; but it was either him or PFC McAllister.

I also couldn't understand why Bumstead didn't realize Winston was hallucinating, if not in the morning at Danger, then surely when they talked during the fight. If he'd swooped in, taken Winston back to Danger and given him to the Doc, appointing Angyal in his place, much of the disaster might have been averted. But what it really boiled down to was that between 1200 and 1600 hours, we had an incompetent Bumstead, an incapacitated Winston, an inexperienced Turner and an AWOL Hackworth. And the result was tragic.

At least if Winston had gone directly to his assigned objective, his men would have had good cover and concealment, and their firepower would have clobbered the flank of the enemy. From that position, he could have put deadly fire on the VC, and the enemy might have withdrawn, or at least Battle Company would have had covering fire and not been in such a mess. In fact, Winston gave Frank Angyal the mission hours before to be prepared to go into the wood line, but the execute part of the order never came.

I knew Angyal—a solid lieutenant I'd brought to the Hardcore from the "Stay Alert" Battalion at Fort Lewis—could handle the job of skippering a combined Alert and Battle until I could bring in Captain Trent Thomas, who as the Battalion S-2 was next up in the skipper ready rack.

"I started the day as a Platoon leader and by the end of the day I was a Company Commander," Lieutenant Angyal recalls. "It seems to me we were dropped a few hundred meters back from where Battle Company's contact was. There was a strip of jungle maybe 100 to 200 meters away, and then everything else was wide open. Early in the night, somebody came to me and said, 'Yo, the old man's cracked up. You got to take command of the Company.'"

Since it was too dark for Angyal to move his men, he did the only smart thing—he ordered Alert Company to hunker down in place and set up a good defensive position.

Under the cover of gunship and air strikes and the chopper smoke on the enemy main battle position, my C&C ship set down without incident and dropped off Nev and Billy McAllister—with his backpack radio—near the ditch that provided the only decent cover on the field. As soon as we were airborne again, I had Reynolds pound the tree line with 105mm HE and smoke rounds from "C" Battery. Division had finally authorized the battery to move in range of the battle area.

The smoke kept a wall of heavy fog between the enemy and our men—now mainly set up in the ditch, having pulled back several hundred yards from the enemy bunker line. But wounded soldiers being dragged off the battlefield slowed down the withdrawal.

A few minutes later a medevac bird checked in.

"Dust-Off 56, got eight wounded behind that wall of smoke. Want to give it a shot?"

"Affirm, Hardcore 6. Tell 'em to pop smoke."

Sergeant Miles from Battle Company popped smoke and in a few minutes Dust-Off 56 was in and out, en route back to Danger. Ten minutes later the bird swooped in again, picked up another load and took them directly to the 3rd Surgical Hospital at Dong Tam. Just before dark the last load went out.

After the Dust-Off was completed, Tamale 11, our FAC, immediately put in his eighth air strike, scorching the bunker line where the machine guns were with napalm. He then walked four sets of fast burners with 500-pound bombs into the heavily treed area behind the enemy's bunker lines.

BOOM. BOOM. BOOM.

It looked like a burned waffle and smelled like a huge tire fire. Good, I thought, this is just the beginning.

I hated to leave the fireworks, but my bird had to break off to refuel. In my absence, Hayes would again take command. Before leaving, I briefed him on the tactical situation as we both circled the battlefield in our C&C choppers. We agreed there was still a good chance to trap the enemy—who'd be getting on his track shoes, ready to run at first dark. We knew we needed to pin Charley by air and artillery fire and get Battle Company reorganized, get Winston replaced and out of there and bring in other sealing units—my Claymore and Dagger Companies standing by on PZs at Danger and Dong Tam and at least one more attached company.

Thirty minutes later, back over the fight, I relieved Hayes, who flew to

Danger to organize the required airlift. While he got that together, I started working on a plan to put in a good seal and punish the shit out of our opponent. Hayes would give me all the men and lift he could get so we could put forces where we needed them, then repeat what we did on the twenty-third and twenty-fourth and do these guys in. We were going to turn the battle around and win in the final inning.

It was almost too dark to pick LZs for the pile-on companies, but I had the C&C chopper swing over to the southwest of Battle Company's position where the vegetation opened up into rice paddies so I could recon an LZ for the company going in there.

Suddenly machine-gun slugs ripped through the belly of our chopper and punched through the cabin. Then...THUMP! My leg felt as though it had been whacked by the Terminator. But strangely, it didn't hurt.

The back of the chopper was awash in gore, and I realized it wasn't only mine. Captain Reynolds, sitting next to me, had been hit by several slugs. He'd already turned that pale white dying color I'd seen too many times and he was clammy cold to my touch. Going back to Danger would do him no good—without immediate and top-notch medical attention, he wasn't going to make it, he was only minutes from checking out of the net. I told the pilot to take us to the 3rd Surgical Hospital at Dong Tam at max speed.

Murphy's Law chose this moment—the worst possible time—to throw us a clinker. Smoke filled the chopper. The crew chief shouted, "Fire, fire." The pilots fought the controls, radioing "Mayday, Mayday, Mayday."

I called the Battalion TOC, gave them a Sitrep and asked Colonel Hayes to take command of the Hardcore and take over the fight. The ground was coming up fast. I figured Saint Pete was about to receive some fresh recruits.

FIFTEEN

Dong Tam
25 MARCH 1969

The smoked-filled chopper fell from the sky like an air-dropped cannon with a bad chute. Figuring we were about to become one of the 10,000 choppers that bought the farm during the Vietnam War, I went into a weird hyper-alert yet hyper-relaxed kind of autopilot, totally focused and ready to deal. I'd been there before.

But one hundred yards from a fast-approaching chunk of what looked like very hard rice paddy, the engine stopped sputtering. The smoke cleared from the crew compartment and we started gaining altitude. Bruce Palmer and his super-competent crew worked their miracles and somehow not only got our sick bird airborne but then nursed that shot-up sucker all the way back to Dong Tam.

It was dark when we wobbled into the 3rd Surgical Hospital's pad. As soon as we hit the ground, a medical team tossed Reynolds and me on litters and hustled us to triage. A Doc rushed Reynolds to surgery, saving his life, while I got a compress slapped on my wound to stop the bleeding along with a shot of morphine that sent me flying to the moon.

The bullet had entered my left leg about six inches up from the ankle and punched out about four inches higher, leaving an exit hole the size of a fist. That leg, thumped by hot steel twice in Korea and once earlier in Vietnam, had already taken so many hits there were hardly any places left for new scars. Now this mean little mother.

Somewhere in my daze, I could hear Dong Tam starting to take heavy VC fire, but I was too spaced out to be concerned about the incoming. And when I came to, deep in the bowels of the 3rd Surgical Hospital's underground bunker system, the mortars and rockets were still slamming in—from the sounds outside we could have been on the beaches of Anzio during World War II.* Fortunately, the hospital bunker complex was well built—it would have taken a small nuke weapon to knock it out—and as stoned as I was from the morphine, I wouldn't have cared if we'd gone out glowing in radiated dust.

I drifted in and out of sleep, eventually fixing on Doc Holley—what a time for him to be on R&R. Fortunately Doc Schwartz, his replacement, was made of the same tough stuff. Schwartz had done a brilliant job patching up Wallace's people while the slugs zipped through our bird. His skill saved a lot of lives that day and night. Suddenly a familiar voice interrupted my trip.

"Hardcore Recondo, Sir," Charlie Wintzer snapped, saluting smartly.

Schwartz had sent Wintzer to the hospital to check on the Hardcore wounded. I was glad to see him—every member of the Battalion, myself included, loved Charlie. He epitomized the spirit of the Battalion medics who followed Doc Holley's wild-child example—brave beyond good sense and technically super-proficient. A senior medic deeply dedicated to the men of the Hardcore, he'd taken the year-long medical course at Fort Sam Houston and probably could whack off a leg, pluck out an appendix or deliver a baby alongside any good country doctor.

"You're going to be evacced to Long Binh by chopper once the incoming shit slows down," Wintzer told me.

Not what I wanted to hear. My place was back with the Hardcore. "How's the wound?" I asked.

"The bad news is it looks like you gotta lot of muscle damage. The good news is the Xray shows no broken bones. My guess is you'll be laid up for a month and then limp like Sammy-the-Gimp for a while."

---

*Almost one hundred soldiers were killed or wounded in the VC barrage at Dong Tam, mainly REMFs who for the moment were earning their combat pay in spades, and a dozen helicopters were turned into junk.

A month! No way!

Wintzer's gung-ho "Hardcore Recondo" had brought on a loud chorus of "Hardcore Recondos." I looked around and discovered the bunker was filled with Battle Company wounded, covered in bloody bandages, many confined to litters, unbeatable in spirit. Sure, they were shot up. And for the last ten hours they'd gone through a nightmare that the protected, the privileged and the others who dodged this bad war could never know. But these noble warriors, mainly kids from blue-collar America caught up in a war the United States was fast losing, were awesome.

Lying on that litter three feet off the ground on a sandbagged table and listening to those young heroes sound off was one of the most moving moments of my life. I was so proud of them. Not just for their bravery that day, but also for their fighting hearts and their deep love for their combat brothers.

The cheering increased when Ed Clark invaded the bunker with what seemed like at least half of Dagger Company, still celebrating the medals they'd received that afternoon. To make their hospital call, they'd gone through wall-to-wall VC mortar fire.

"The boys heard yuh were hit, Colonel." Clark drawled, handing me a beer. "We decided to come by 'n cheer yuh up."

The hospital Docs tried to shoo the party crashers out but soon gave up. Probably a smart move. Clearing armed, half-drunk paddy rats from an underground bunker into vicious incoming fire would have been a major tactical mistake. So here they were, drinking beer, shouting "Hardcore Recondo" when suddenly my head started to spin. All that morphine coupled with the adrenaline I'd expended hit me like a giant Mickey Finn. The last thing I saw before I zonked out were the light fixtures swaying back and forth underneath the bombardment, dust falling down from the bunker's heavy-timbered ceiling each time a round came close, the THUMP,

THUMP, THUMP of incoming pounding the earth and the chant of "Hardcore, Hardcore, Hardcore."

The perfect martial lullaby.

While Palmer was flying us to the hospital in his battered bird, Battle Company grunts still out on the killing field were praying for darkness. By the time it arrived, they'd all pulled back to the safety of the streambed. Marty Miles, Rick Hudson, Dan Evans, two grunts from the 3rd Platoon and 3rd Platoon Sergeant Ron Sulcer were the last live round-eyes to make it to that big, beautiful ditch.

"The Dust-Off came and took me to the hospital," Sulcer recalls. "They cut my clothes off and put a little piece of paper over my crotch and then all of a sudden they took me to the operating room and I remember it was as cold as can be before I went under."

When Sulcer, who was twenty-one years old, came out of the anesthesia, he was lying on his back with his head turned to one side. Until he noticed the wounded VC lying in the rack next to him. "I just went ballistic," he says. "I started shouting to get him the hell away. A nurse moved him, but I'll never forget his face. I was sure he was one of the guys who had taunted me."

To the amazement of the doctors, Sulcer didn't need blood. One surgeon said to him, "You must have seen that thing coming and sucked all your guts up inside your chest cavity because it didn't get your liver, large or small intestines, stomach or anything else vital."

"So all it did was make that big old hole in me," Sulcer says.

Back in the bush, Evans found Nev Bumstead "kneeling in the weeds in front of the streambed with RTO Billy McAllister and a squad of grunts." He told Bumstead they were the last ones in and that all the casualties had been pulled out.

"You see anybody else out there, they're VC—so kill 'em," Evans said, pointing to the tree line.

A handful of 1st Platoon survivors were spread out in the ditch. "Once we thought everyone was back we were trying to regroup because we'd been so separated out in the field," "Sugar Bear" Bauer recalls.

"We was all lookin' around for Doc Evans," Arles Brown told me in his West Virginian drawl. "None of us seen him for a while and we was kinda worried about him 'cause he was always takin' care of the wounded with no regard for himself."

At barely five feet six inches, Brown was probably the smallest guy in the Platoon. When he found out his buddies were in trouble, he cut the cast off his broken foot and hitched a ride on a helicopter from the firebase to the fight. He wanted to make sure his best pals made it, especially the Doc.

"We were so relieved when we saw him coming down that ditch with Hudson," "Sugar Bear" says. "Everyone went running up to them like it was some kind of big reunion. Which I guess it sort of was."

"We thought you were dead," "Sugar Bear" said.

"It's news to me," Doc Evans shot back. L. J. Henderson betrayed his excitement by puffing just a little harder on the stub of one of his ever-present cigars. Ron Miller flashed a boyish grin. Mario Sotello thumped him on the back as if to make sure he was really there.

Marty Miles, who'd taken over Lieutenant Keppel's platoon, now found himself sharing the command of Battle Company with FO Ross Sterling. "You handle the infantry stuff," Sterling said, "I'll handle the arty."

Miles appointed Platoon sergeants and put what was left of the chopped-up unit—it had lost about 30 percent of its field strength in the fight—"in good defensive positions."

Almost all of Miles's soldiers were running low on M-16 and M-79 ammo and he needed machine-gun slugs for his M-60s. He had his guys redistribute ammo among themselves, then told his leaders to scrounge more from Alert

Company soldiers. Because of Winston spending the day in Yellow Smoke Land, they still had a full basic load.

"As soon as I hit that ditch and put my squad in position, I took inventory of the ammo," Sergeant Bauer recalls. "I had a total of about fifty rounds of M-60, maybe two full M-16 mags per man and two M-79 rounds. We were hurting."

Miles wanted ammo and M-60 barrels flown in. Most of his machine guns had overheated during the fight and he was afraid the barrels were warped. But no one acted on his request for hours, even though in infantry, combat resupply of ammo should have the highest priority—especially with Alert and Battle eyeball-to-eyeball with a tough, numerically superior enemy force that could attack at any time. As L. J. Henderson put it, "We were down to throwin' rocks at 'em."

It's possible that the resupply delay could have been the result of "shit happens." Dong Tam, where the Jay Hawk—9th Division Aviation Battalion—resupply ships were based, was, as I experienced for myself, under serious mortar and rocket attack at the time. It's possible that the 9th Division Aviation couldn't get a ship off the ground until Dong Tam went all clear. But whatever the reason, failure to get Battle Company soldiers resupplied with ammo left the troops hanging out to die.

Sergeant Dubois remembers scrounging through the web gear of the wounded and dead searching desperately for more ammo. His foxhole was near Major Bumstead's CP in the bomb crater and he observed him in action. "To be honest, he kind of lost it," Dubois recalls. "He kept hearing things and saying stuff like 'Hey, they're coming. You hear that?' Which didn't exactly add to my confidence level."

The battlefield fell quiet while Miles's and Angyal's people dug in. Then Ross Sterling set up with Bumstead in his CP and began clobbering the enemy positions with artillery fire.

"Lieutenant Sterling walked it back and forth all night throughout their positions," Bumsted's RTO Billy McAllister says. "It sure sounded good."

At 0200 hours, a VC squad probed Battle's position, but broke off the attack after wide-awake warriors took it under fire. Miles, worried that it might just be the tip of the VC spear, asked Bumstead how the ammo supply request was coming. Bumstead called the Battalion TOC and found out that at last two choppers loaded with ammo were on their way.

Ten minutes later, the lead supply bird, flying blackout, circled the LZ east of the streambed, which had been used throughout the day for inserts and medical evacuation. Bumstead himself guided it in with a strobe light. It was sledgehammer simple. Easy approach. No trees. Open, level rice paddies. No contact on the ground. The first Jay Hawk swooped in, hovering just off the ground while the crew quickly tossed out the frags and claymores and took off. A detail from Battle Company policed the ammo up and ran it back to the troops.

The second bird with the much-needed machine gun and rifle ammo followed the same west-to-east approach, with Bumstead again bringing it in with his strobe. Bumstead thought the pilot "came in too low and too hot" before crashing about one hundred yards north of the LZ. However, several Battle Company soldiers say they heard an RPG fire and saw a round hit the chopper. Sergeant Dubois, who spent almost four years in Vietnam as a grunt and as a helicopter crewman, swears he saw an RPG round hit the chopper when it was "maybe twenty-five feet off the ground."

According to Dan Evans, "The helicopter came in and I saw these sparks coming off the tree and then the thing just tilted to the right and went straight down and started burning immediately."

RPG round or accident, the chopper exploded in a ball of fire that lit up the battlefield. "It was like a football victory bonfire," said Marty Miles with the attitude of a hardened grunt. "I wasn't worried about the crew, I was worried about lighting up my positions and my guys losing night vision."

In the glare of the fire, "You could actually see the silhouettes of the pilot and a crew member jump out and start running away," Evans said. Supporting gunships, flying cover, swooped in and policed them up.

But the right door gunner—William W. Schoth—was pinned inside the bird. And soon the ammunition aboard the burning chopper started cooking off.

"You could hear him screaming as he died," Bauer said. "It's sad to say, but we were so hardcore, it didn't faze me at the time. It was a very long night, nobody slept, that's for sure. You might say we had other worries on our mind. Now when I think back on it, I have a very hard time not choking up."

Evans felt totally helpless. "His screams echoed around the perimeter. It was horrible. The fire was too hot to get close to. There was nothing we could do."

Another explosion rocked the burning aircraft and the screams mercifully stopped. A little later, another crew member wandered into Battle Company's lines. The rest of the night was quiet.*

At first light, Battle Company's search parties recovered the remaining bodies of their fallen comrades and policed up their weapons and gear. At 0710 hours, four armed VC walked into Alert Company's position and were cut down, then Battle and Alert Companies were lifted out and flown back to Danger. And that was the end of almost twenty-four hours of horror.

My next memories are of waking up in a medevac chopper on my way to Long Binh, not sure if it was the cold wind that snapped me to consciousness, the moans from the kid in the litter above me or the violent buffeting the chopper was taking from the concussions of the shells exploding around us. The VC had scored a direct hit on the huge ammo dump I'd worried about when I first flew into Dong Tam two months earlier. It had been cooking off

---

*In 1995, when Ed Clark and Doc Holley revisited the battlefield, locals who said they were VC soldiers or supporters and that they were there on 25/26 March, told them that an RPG round hit the chopper just as it was landing. They pointed out the place in the paddy where the chopper had crashed and burned, which tracked exactly with Clark's memory. They explained that on the day after the battle they found C-Rations and other U.S. supplies and equipment around the crash site. One elderly woman, who according to Clark described the battle well enough to have been an eyewitness, said a friend of hers still had a watch recovered from "a dead American." A runner was dispatched and soon returned with what Holley and Clark suspected was helicopter crew chief William Schoth's watch. Almost thirty years later, according to Doc Holley "it was in perfect running condition."

for hours and we were right in the middle of a barrage of red-hot metal.

Larry Faulkenberg has never forgotten those explosions: "When I woke up, the ammunition dump was getting hit and the tables were shaking around and I thought, We're going to get it again. I really got scared then too because I didn't know how bad it was. I seen ole Slim Holleman and he was on the side in the aisle with me at the hospital and I saw he had like a big old white bandage around his head and I started hollering at him and I said, 'Slim, Slim' and he wouldn't answer and after a few minutes they came in and covered his head up and I can still see that now. He had died right there. That was really scary. I was nineteen years old."

The sky lit up like one of those multimillion-dollar Fourth of July celebrations. Hundreds of thousands of shells from tiny M-16 slugs to huge eight-inch artillery rounds triggered each other off, filling the night with red-hot shrapnel. Even in my state, I couldn't help thinking how glad I was to be a grunt. I'd never liked flying in aircraft over hostile skies—never mind that in this case the shells were ours. That thin sheet of metal covering the floor of the flying machine never seemed like enough protection for my most vital body parts. Many grunts, this one included, sat on their steel pots while making helicopter assaults—the ultimate in covering your ass. Whenever I flew, I yearned for the safety of a good, deep foxhole.

Finally, we landed at the Long Binh Evac Hospital. And the next time I awoke, a doctor was looking at my leg. "Colonel, you're in luck," the surgeon said. "If that bullet had been a hair closer to your shin bone, we'd be taking off that leg."

"Yeah," I said, slowly looking down to make sure there were two legs under the sheets. "I've always been lucky."

He examined the wound and put on a fresh bandage. "Your medical records indicate this is your seventh wound. With that much metal cut out of you, I'm not sure lucky's the right word. Anyway, at least you won't be getting any more Purple Hearts. Rules are, you can stay here for only four days. Then you're off to Japan."

Not on your life, I thought.

"Hold on, Doc, there are eight hundred kids in my Battalion I'm trying to keep from ending up here. This is nothing—the Battalion Docs can look after it."

"Impossible," he said. "That leg needs a month to heal and it'll probably be another month before you can return to limited duty."

The doctor told me he'd been a rifleman in the "Big War," Normandy to Belgium, where a chunk of shell sent him home. So he knew about the brotherhood of infantry, a great break for me. A different Doc might have decided I was crazy to choose the Delta over Tokyo and sent me to Japan for other reasons—like joining Billy Winston in an Army psycho ward.

On the morning after the fight, a sergeant had brought Winston to Doc Schwartz. "He was fully alert but did not seem to be in contact with reality," Schwartz recalls. "The sergeant said to me, 'Doc, you got to help me out, you got to do something for him. I don't know what's happened to my captain.'"

"I put Winston in the back of the aid station on one of the bunks," Schwartz says. "It was a tricky situation. I asked the sergeant what happened. He told me Winston just lost it. The orders he was giving weren't making any sense, he had lost contact with reality."

The sergeant went and sat on a bunk across from Winston. "He was a neat guy," Schwartz says, "he loved and respected Captain Winston and it was breaking his heart that the Captain had flown over the cuckoo's nest. Then suddenly Winston turned to the sergeant and said, 'I want to continue dictating my memoirs.' So the sergeant took out a notebook and Winston started dictating in a kind of grandiose manner. It was like Napoleon describing the whole grand campaign and how it should be run.

"I didn't know what the hell to do 'cause he'd obviously lost it. I thought,

I don't want to medevac this guy out of here as a psycho case, so what I'm going to do is the easiest possible thing: I'm going to stall and see what happens. I'd gone way beyond what the Army would allow, but I really didn't give a damn what the Army would allow. I had some totally optimistic idea, he'd snap out of it and we'll be able to get past the whole thing. Finally, I couldn't go any further and I was going to have to move him. I figured I might even have to do it with a straitjacket, but it was not at all necessary. I just called the medevac and the sergeant took Winston onto the aircraft. That was the last time I saw him."

Knowing that I sounded bonkers myself, I still pressed my case with the doctor, even though he was looking very skeptical. "Look, I can run the Battalion on crutches. In Korea, I went AWOL from a hospital with my arm in a cast to get back to my Raider unit. You're not gonna make me go AWOL again, are you?"

"I might chain you to your bed."

I could see he was trying not to smile. Good—I had wiggle room.

Another Doc stuck a needle in my arm and I was wheeled into surgery. After sleeping for almost twenty straight hours, I came to the next day to the voice of John Hayes talking to a nurse. Standing next to him, grinning ear to ear, was Chum Robert, now Hayes's Artillery LNO.

"Hi, Sir," I said a bit blearily. "How're the boys?"

"Good enough to be worrying about you. I picked up an NCO during the fight who was hit in the shoulder and leg and the first thing he said to me was 'How's Colonel Hackworth?' In most units of the 9th Division, the soldiers don't even know the name of the battalion CO, let alone worry about him."

"Well, I'm worrying about them, too. How's Battle Company?"

"Everything's good. Nothing big went down after you were hit. Battle Company's back at Danger, fixing to go out on ambush operations tonight."

Hayes's words were the best medicine I'd received since I'd been hit.

"Look," I said, "you gotta tell General Ewell to lean on the medical folks and get me out of here."

"I know Ewell wants you back, Hack. The Hardcore's his best performer. You can bet I'll ask him to shake a few trees. But you take your time and get healed. George Mergner's doing a good job, he's one hell of a soldier. Big balls. Saved a lot of lives last night. I put him in for a DFC. And the rest of your boys are out there killing the Cong just like you taught 'em."

"Battle Company's got to be kept busy," I said. "Lee Dyment should shoot a platoon of replacements into them ASAP. If they sit around Danger licking their wounds, they'll just feel sorry for themselves and never get back on their horses."

"Gotcha, Hack. Mergner's got them cleaning weapons and jumping through their asses. I was out at Danger this morning and Battle Company was policing up cigarette butts and paper as if they were back at Benning. Gonna get you some officers, too. Mergner told me he had only seven officers left in your four rifle companies, and you're authorized twenty-four. Now, what do you want to do about Alert Company?"

"No way Winston's coming back. Too bad—he was one of my best until he cracked. Reckon we should leave Frank Angyal in the saddle. I got Trent Thomas with the Aussies and he was scheduled to replace Winston next week. Frank will run things damn well until Trent gets back."

Hayes asked Chum to leave so we could talk privately. "I hope you're gonna tear Winston a new asshole on his efficiency report," Hayes said.

No way was I going to do that. "I've been in a lot of fights with him both here and in the 101st and he's a good man. His bottle just filled up. Some people have bigger bottles than others. I don't think because he temporarily went bananas his career should go down the drain."

Hayes crossed his arms across his chest and gave me that hard-ass look of his. "He's just the spoiled son of a three-star general."

"Oh, come on, John, this has nothing to do with his old man. Let's cut him some slack."

"Hack, if I go with your call, you gonna save Bumstead, too? After you were hit I tried to get something going, but that joker did nothing. He just froze and whispered on the radio. Formed a perimeter and hunkered down all night. Gotta tell you, Hack, my instinct says he lost it—that's if the fucker ever had it."

"Your instinct's right—he was the wrong guy to put on the ground. I really screwed that one up. Let me chew on it and come up with a recommendation. Meanwhile, let him help George Mergner. This isn't the time to break in a new S-3."

Hayes turned to go. "Gonna get Lee Dymant working on decorations," he told me. "There were some incredible acts of heroism out there. I want 'em recognized. Know there's at least one Medal of Honor, three or four DSCs and a truckload of Silver and Bronze Stars."

The Army, true to form, shortchanged the Hardcore on Hayes's list. But Doc Evans, Eugene O'Dell and Marty Miles were awarded the Distinguished Service Cross. Sergeant Wallace, who deserved the Medal of Honor, and Lieutenant Sterling, who was put in for the DSC, were given Silver Stars, along with the valiant "Sugar Bear" Bauer and Doc Schwartz.

After Hayes and Robert left, I continued refighting the battle as I had every waking moment since I'd been hit. How did Battle Company get caught in an open field? Why didn't Turner use a route where his soldiers would have concealment and cover? What happened to the Battalion SOP, which called for a point element to precede the main body, thus preventing the whole unit from being chain-sawed to ribbons? Christ, we'd learned this the hard way at Qui Nhon, where Bumstead had been a platoon leader, and at Dak To, where he'd skippered the Tigers. I'd stressed always to use a point over and over in the *Vietnam Primer,* my Hardcore leader's book, and repeatedly face-to-face with every leader from squad up in the Hardcore.

The questions bit at me like Delta ants, but I knew I wouldn't find answers until I got back to the Battalion. In the meantime I had to live with the hard fact that if I hadn't gone to Dagger's award ceremony, I'd have been where I should've been: fighting my Battalion. And I knew this bad call would go with me to the grave.

Battle Company had taken six KIAs—Frank Joseph G. Ellis Jr., Earl Marshall Hayes, Joe Earl Holleman, Dennis R. Richards, Bradley James Turner and Tiger Scout Doi and nineteen WIAs. Alert Company had no casualties less one very shell-shocked captain. Jay Hawk, who flew the night ammo resupply mission, had one KIA—William W. Schoth II—in the chopper crash.

There were twenty-three counted enemy dead. USAF Tac Air, Army gunships and artillery put enough steel in the ground that day and night to sink that tiny part of Vietnam. Experience tells me their fires zapped a lot of VC, but like in poker, at the end of the game, it's only the chips in front of you that count. Once I returned to the Hardcore and found out the battlefield was not swept the morning after the fight, I was one pissed-off hombre. But I could also understand John Hayes's decision: He had two leaderless units on the ground led by a fumbling incompetent who'd long ago run out of combat gas. As bitter as it tasted at the time, in retrospect he was right.

Guilt tormented me the entire time I stayed at Long Binh. But then my surgeon and the doctor who ran the 3rd Surgical Hospital worked out how they could reverse-evacuate me to the front instead of the rear, so I got my ticket back to Dong Tam.

"They'll keep you there and when your wound is OK you can rejoin your unit," the surgeon told me. "I'm sending you back because when I got hit I didn't want to leave my platoon either. Later this afternoon, you'll be issued a set of crutches and instead of sneaking beer in bed, you can hobble over to the club. Might join you later myself."

I was elated. I felt a rush of affection for this great Doc, who understood how I felt about my men and why I needed to get back to them. We were all brothers, regardless of color or creed, forged in the hottest furnace known to man: infantry ground combat.

That's why I've always believed accounts of racism in Vietnam are wildly distorted. In the heat of battle, there was no white or black, only Army green. I'm not saying that racism didn't exist—particularly away from the killing fields—but not out where the bullets ripped through bodies and every man's life depended on the man right next to him. I don't want to sound naive. Out in the bush, there was also a very practical antidote to racism. As Claymore Company's Ken Scott, a rifleman from Trinidad, put it, "If you're a black man and you have a loaded weapon in your hand and it isn't on safety, nobody's going to show their colors or whatever racism they have with 'em. They might have it, but no, it's not going to show in the field."

The truth is that few in the Hardcore, myself most definitely included, fought for the United States of America, the flag, Richard Milhous Nixon or the 9th Division. We fought for each other. We'd have died for each other as Dennis Richards did for the fatally wounded Bradley Turner and as Sergeant Don Wallace almost died for Joe Holleman. Our allegiance was to our Hardcore brothers. We hung in there for each other. Our biggest fear was to let a buddy down.

SIXTEEN

Fire Support Base Danger
05 APRIL 1969

I became a commuter. Each morning I'd fly from the hospital at Dong Tam to FSB Danger in a Brigade LOH, clump around on my crutches, then shuttle back each evening. The 3rd Surgical Hospital Docs were so concerned about keeping the wound clean that they actually ordered a bed check on me every night to make sure I kept my word and didn't go AWOL.

Being at Dong Tam, which ironically means "united hearts and minds" in Vietnamese, was like living downrange of a shooting gallery. General William C. Westmoreland, who personally picked the name, got it as wrong as he did his infamous 1967 "We are prevailing" speech to Congress. Every night I spent there the place was rocketed and shelled by the very folks whose "hearts and minds" Westy wanted to win.

When my leg was better and I got the green light to return to Danger, I couldn't have been happier. As far as I was concerned, I'd never call those REMFs motherfuckers again—nor bitch about their getting combat pay. Every soldier in the Hardcore I talked to felt the same way—they would have taken Danger over Dong Tam any day of the week.

George Mergner was doing a great job commanding the Hardcore. When I made my day hops, I tried to stay out of his hair and let him handle the tactical side of things. All the Hardcore gang knew George was temp help, but a unit can have only one skipper. I remembered how I'd felt about

Hunt sticking his nose in my business, bit my tongue and did my damnedest not to interfere with George's operation while he was acting CO.

From the time I was hit until my first visit to Danger ten days later, the Hardcore under Mergner recovered from 25 March and began functioning like a new German machine gun. During those ten days, the Battalion had 136 confirmed VC killed and the Air Force reported twenty more probable kills. Hardcore casualties: twenty-one wounded, mostly by booby traps. VC to 4/39th kill ratio was 157 to 0. Now, that was a ratio I could live with—and one the VC couldn't tolerate.

There were no big actions, just little ankle-biters. Most of the contacts came from Tahler's Night Hunter and Sniper operations and the rifle companies' small unit ambushes. But add them all up, and we were doing quite a number on the enemy. Much as I hated to admit it, Mergner's brilliant performance made me feel redundant. To rub salt into the wound, I heard that while I was in the hospital, the Sergeant Major began announcing, as George slipped into my old commander's chair at the morning briefing, "Gentlemen, the CO, XO and S-3."

The Hardcore log for 31 March shows how things were progressing:

TIME	INCIDENT
0535	C-66—Platoon from Claymore Company—blew a Claymore on three VC walking down the trail toward their position. Three VC BC.
0545	C-66 blew a Claymore on four VC moving down a trail. Four VC BC.
1616	Two KBA—killed by air—by Apache—7/1st Air Cav (Black Hawk).
1830	C-66 kills one VC on trail.
2245	Night Hunter: Three VC*
2250	Night Hunter: Four VC*
2301	Night Hunter: Five VC*
2325	Night Hunter: 6 VC*

*All kills made in sampans; six sampans destroyed.

Controlling the battlefield meant we were also disrupting the VC commo system. Because the VC didn't have too many fancy radios and those that did knew our radio intercept guys were monitoring their nets and reading their mail, most VC messages and orders were delivered by courier system the same as during our own Revolutionary War. If we kept up the pressure, I knew they'd have to either abandon Base Area 470—a huge psychological blow to the Communist effort in our little chunk of the Mekong Delta—or move in more Main Force units to try to regain lost turf. Which would mean more 23 and 24 March – type victories for the Hardcore.

As for the troops, Battle Company was already back in the game. Craig Tessau, a good man who'd been a Battle Company platoon leader—followed by a stint in Battalion supply and then in operations—was the perfect guy to hold the reins until Knapp returned. DeRoos was sitting firmly in the saddle of Claymore Company. His ambushes tore ass almost every night. Clark had Dagger in great shape and they, under his close and continuous supervision, were getting even stronger every day. Once Trent Thomas replaced Frank Angyal, who was more than happy to go back to running his Red Platoon, and got the long-range ambushes clicking again, Alert Company hit their stride as well.

Thomas was a gung-ho Military Intelligence officer who'd worked with Clark at Brigade. His heart was Infantry, but he was so damn smart his MI bosses wouldn't approve his many requests to branch transfer. But he and I eventually prevailed over John Hayes and the Division G-2, Lieutenant Colonel Spirito, who traded Hayes his best MI officer to free up Thomas for the Hardcore. He already had OJT'd with DeRoos for a week and spent two weeks with the Australians, where he'd learned firsthand from masters how to ruin Charley's day.

Captain Don Meyer had also reported in. He'd been one of my company commanders in the "Stay Alert, Stay Alive" Battalion at Fort Lewis and one helluva of a platoon leader in the 101st until he stopped a bucketful of shrapnel with his face and chest. After his two-week Hardcore-sponsored tour with the Aussies, he reported in to Claymore Company to understudy Gordy DeRoos.

After I graduated from crutches to cane and resumed command, Mergner's competence meant I could concentrate on deconstructing the details of the battle of 25 and 26 March and figure out how that rat-fuck happened and the lessons to be learned. I hobbled around the firebase talking to the troopers and leaders of Alert and Battle Companies, the Battalion staff, chopper pilots and anyone else who could give me an eye-witness account.

But Platoon Sergeant Ron Sulcer, who miraculously lived through that fight, cut to the chase when he summed up the battle of 25 March with his usual Texas-farmer good sense: "If you had your shit together, the VC didn't screw with you. And that day we didn't—and they screwed with us big time."

After talking to the troops, there was no doubt in my mind that on 25 March Bumstead was enough at fault that he too should have had his head lopped off for not stopping Turner in his tracks instead of ordering him to attack and for not realizing the truth about Winston early in the game and relieving him.

But Bumstead was into such serious denial that he was as decomped as Winston in terms of performance. While I was recovering, Mergner initially took Bumstead on his chopper during operations with him—until he decided the man was worthless. "He fell asleep and mumbled over the radio in his sleep," Mergner recalls.

He quickly followed my example and began leaving Bumstead behind in the CP to tidy up the paperwork, but by then even this taxed the man's capabilities. Mergner informed Hayes that Bumstead couldn't hack the job and requested that Chum Robert, loaned by Hayes to Mergner to fill in as his Fire Control Officer until a replacement for Captain Reynolds came in, be assigned as the S-3. Hayes told Mergner to wait until I got back.

By the time I finished my review, I concluded that the only difference between Bumstead and Winston was that Bumstead never called for yellow smoke or claimed his in-laws were out to get him. But all the same, Bumstead was one battle-rattled piece of work.

So I fired him.

Fall out.

The truth was that I should have sacked him during our first week with the Hardcore, when I saw he couldn't do the job. Keeping him on was one of the worst decisions of my Army career—and one I unfortunately let ride even after I knew he couldn't handle the fast pace in the S-3 saddle. He was my boy after all and I guess I thought I could will him into becoming a capable S-3. The combination of his ineptitude and my ego made for a lethal cocktail. Seven good men died and nineteen more were wounded on 25 March as a direct result. I had to make sure he'd never command again.

On the other hand, perhaps the reason I covered for Winston and not Nev in my efficiency reports was that I didn't actually see Winston spinning over the edge the way Tom Aikens and Jimmy Hux had. And I did see Nev—not pacing himself, not getting enough sleep, drowning himself in minutiae, then screwing everything up and endangering the men.

Perhaps I was wrong in calling Winston's medical evacuation a "change in command," no different than if he'd been hit by a slug, but he was a smart, talented officer with a great future. At Fort Campbell, where I'd first met him, he was a new lieutenant fresh out of West Point doing the job of a seasoned major better than most. In the Hardcore Battalion, I'd considered him my "horse" company commander—I gave him the toughest missions and he always came through. He was so good that I had all future company commanders OJT with him in the field where he passed on the tricks of the trade exactly as Don Schroeder had mentored me back in January.

Maybe I felt guilty I'd worked Winston so hard. Maybe I felt responsible for his crackup. It didn't occur to me at the time that by not reporting his breakdown, I'd done nothing to prevent him from getting another command. One day, as commander of a division, a corps, or an army, he could just as easily lose it all over again and to protect the troops I should have let that be known.

He did stay in the Army and through his own extraordinary ability commanded a battalion and then a brigade. By 1989, he was on a star glide and then something happened—I have no idea what—and he suddenly retired as a bird colonel. Just as well. Hayes was right that he was potentially as dangerous as Bumstead—he could have commanded a division during Desert Storm and had 15,000 men popping yellow smoke.

On 12 April, John Hayes diplomatically transferred Bumstead to Brigade as his Civil Affairs Officer, a job where he could use his Vietnamese language skills and excellent knowledge of the Vietnamese people toward helping win hearts and minds without putting one more American soldier in harm's way. I wrote a godawful, career-killing efficiency report saying he was a disaster and shouldn't be promoted, and of course, I didn't recommend him for further military schooling. He never did command troops again.

After I finally fired Bumstead, Don Meyer took over Claymore Company and Gordy DeRoos became the S-3. With Bumstead's departure, a long-standing black cloud moved from over the Battalion's head and most of our operational problems disappeared. It helped that Gordy brought twelve good months of company-level command experience to the job from his two tours in Vietnam. He understood what the units went through, the enemy, terrain and conditions and how far the troops could be pushed.

Doc Holley returned from a Hawaiian R&R, but without his sidekick, Bobby Knapp, who'd climbed off the plane and collapsed with malaria. According to the good Doc, "Shithead" wouldn't be back for at least a month. Doc Holley told me Knapp had probably been sick for weeks but gutted it out because he loved the men of Battle Company so much.

Knapp's loss was a heartbreaker. Battle Company desperately needed their old skipper back. His leadership magic would have had the boys of Battle charging again within a few weeks. As Platoon Sergeant Dale Fite put it, "If Bobby Knapp said, 'OK, guys, let's go all the way to Hanoi,' I would've said, 'All right, let's do it.' He was that type of guy."

But much as I loved Bobby, neither the men of Battle nor Tessau nor I could wait that long. My search for a new Battle Company commander moved into high gear.

While I was in the hospital—on the theory that if things are running smoothly, the Army will do everything it can to fuck it all up— Division G-1 (Personnel and Administration) assigned us Major Ronald Hopper.* He'd been a staff officer at Ewell's headquarters, and since he was senior to Mergner, by regs he should have been made the acting CO.

"No way will that guy take over the Hardcore," Hayes had announced, and somehow he got G-1 Lee Dyment to fiddle the regulations, which left Mergner in command until I got back.

Hayes didn't want Hopper in the Hardcore at all, but he couldn't get Dyment to reassign him, so Hopper became Battalion XO; Mergner took Gordy DeRoos's job as S-3. I was pissed. With Mergner as XO and DeRoos as S-3, things had never worked better. Worse, Gordy had been passed over on the recent captain-to-major promotion list, the same shafting I'd experienced in 1962 when I was first up for major. An efficiency report rendered on me eleven years before, when I was a twenty-year-old lieutenant, had correctly labeled me "impulsive and impetuous." It turned out a decade later to be a near career-killer. So I well understood how DeRoos must have felt.

I explained the situation to Hayes, who agreed that if DeRoos's performance as S-3 was as spectacular as the job he'd done as skipper of Claymore, we'd give him a "he's-God's-second-son-and-he-walks-on-water-too" special efficiency report after thirty days on the job. This, along with his distinguished combat record with Claymore Company, would hopefully give him a better shot on the next promotion board. But now Hopper was a spoiler.

"We can't have two S-3s," Mergner warned. "Division will eat us alive."

"George, we won't have two S-3s," I said. "We'll have two XOs. We'll keep Gordy in the S-3 slot for a month, but you'll be S-3 in real life. Gordy will be your high-priced assistant and once he's put in thirty days, we'll give him Battle Company and return Tessau to the staff. For the record, you and Hopper will both be in the Battalion XO slot."

Mergner didn't buy it. "Lee Dyment's guys will close us down in five minutes."

"Screw 'em. By the time they catch on—if they ever do—Gordy will be on his way to major and everything will be Jake."

The scheme worked. Gordy got his oak leaves on the next promotion list, went on to make lieutenant colonel before retiring to become a millionaire stockbroker in Iowa and now lives the good life in Hawaii.

Things didn't go well for XO Hopper. It was bad enough that he was, as the troops said, "an FNG"—a fucking new guy—and nobody trusted him. But he was also a by-the-book man and by April, the Hardcore team forged in fire during the previous three months had morphed into the sort of organization that wasn't much into the bullshit of bureaucracy. Witness Mergner's response when told we'd used up our entire monthly allocation of artillery rounds before the month ended and weren't getting more until the first of the following month: "Then send us the allocation from a battalion that isn't killing as many VC."

When Hopper whipped in with his straight-arrow ways, some of the old-timers called him "arrogant," some said he was "prissy." And although he stayed in the Battalion until after I left, I never developed any faith in him, whereas I'd instantly trusted Mergner. Whenever I was out on an operation, I'd make up a reason for Hopper to go to Dong Tam so that it would be Mergner running the show in case I got hit again. He was the best S-3/XO I ever had and under his command when I was busted up the Hardcore never missed a beat. Unfortunately, his first-class job skippering the Battalion was never recorded in his official record and although he retired as a full colonel, Mergner never got another command. The guy should have gone to general.

By mid-April, I was back in charge but still "Sammy the Gimp" as Wintzer had predicted. Mergner stayed with the "follow-me-into-the-trenches" stuff, and the guys, seeing no change from the way I operated, continued to fight proudly by his side.

While I was recovering, every day precisely at 1600 hours, Bill Casey, the medical platoon leader, would report to the Battalion TOC to clean my wound and change the bandages.

One day he said, "Colonel, something's been bothering me. Mind if I ask you a question?"

"Fire away, Bill."

"About a month ago a sniper was firing by the bridge down the road at the firebase, and you grabbed your rifle and ran down there and shot him. It seems to me that you have a thousand guys to do that kind of thing."

"You're right. What I did had nothing to do with the sniper, but every-thing to do with showmanship. Remember Patton? He turned a 100,000-man Corps in Africa from sick to strong in a few weeks—and showmanship played a big role in his success. Once I went after that sniper, I'll guarantee you before the day ended the guys in the Battalion were saying, 'Hear about the old man? He killed twenty snipers today.'"

But also, moments like that were what made my blood flow. Phil Gilchrist, the guy who recommended me for a commission in Korea, wrote when I was promoted to colonel, "Hack a colonel! You'll always be a rifleman in my book." I think old Phil hit pretty close to the mark. I'd chosen to return to FSB Danger rather than cool my heels in Tokyo General because I truly loved being an Infantry commander—there's no bigger challenge than leading a group of fighting men, forging them into a precise and capable weapon—and I loved the grunts in the Hardcore. Together we were proving the enemy could be beaten with the tricks of his own game.

I also enjoyed the time I spent with Frank Gunn, the assistant Division commander who ran the tactical side of the show for Ewell. Whenever we got into a fight, Gunn was the old pro commander with a lot of combat experience under his pistol belt who kept us out of trouble and served as a great role model. He'd led a platoon and company in Africa, was a Battalion XO in Sicily, commanded a battalion at Normandy and ended the war as the Regimental Commander of the 39th Infantry—all by the time he was twenty-four years old. Like me, he couldn't stay away from the forward edge.

All I wanted to do was stick with my boys as long as I could, then maybe get a Brigade. I didn't give a rat's ass about getting the War College punch or any other holes on my career ticket. My leg was almost healed—it wouldn't be long before I could toss my cane and get out there and run with the Hardcore.

SEVENTEEN

Between battles, I wasn't the only guy in the Hardcore doing some limping around. We also had more than our fair share of noncombat casualties, which according to Doc Holley almost always involved two parts of the body: feet or dicks.

Treating VD was a constant. "The longer we operated in an area, the higher the VD rate would go up," Charlie Wintzer recalls. "Holley had the medics line up all the girls once a week and loade them up with penicillin."

"It was far more efficient to treat the whores than have a Platoon of grunts lined up at the aid station every morning with drippy dicks," Holley shrugs.

About once a week, Holley left the Battalion Forward and went back to Dong Tam to care for the guys bringing up the rear. He held sick call at the Battalion Aid Station in Dong Tam on those mornings from 0730 to 0930. "We also used to hold unannounced 'short-arm' inspections," he says. "The most common thing we found was the clap—AKA gonorrhea—although a lot of these kids got a more serious type of VD which caused the lymph glands in the groin to swell up as big as sweet potatoes. The affliction was so painful they sometimes couldn't walk with it. We'd have to put them in bed and give them IV antibiotics."

One day a soldier came in, unzipped and plunked his dick right down on the desk in front of the Doc.

Sergeant Robert Ashley, one of the Big Band-Aid's most trusted medics, rushed out from behind him and drew a line on the floor.

"See that line?" he told the grunt. "You go stand behind it and you stay behind it. And if you ever come in here again, that's where you stand. The Doc can see your dick just fine from there."

Spring of 1969 was ground zero in the sexual revolution era. In the Hardcore, the troops were as into free love as any other guys, though in Vietnam, unless they were "milking the snake," more often than not, they had to pay for it.

At every village, bridge and traffic jam, the whores lined up beside the road to hawk their bodies: "Hey, GI! You want boom-boom? Five dollar."

Boom-boom was big business. Once the Vietnamese realized they had something almost every GI wanted, there were hooches everywhere filled with girls hustling for a Yankee buck. Fathers sold daughters, brothers sold sisters or mothers, mothers and daughters sold themselves. They were a very entrepreneurial people.

"A low price for a prostitute in the village was a sure sign that Americans hadn't operated in the AO before," Dan Evans remembers. "The longer we stayed the higher the prices would go. When we'd first hit an area, a C-Ration candy bar was good for a quickie. Some girls would throw themselves on their backs in exchange for a wooden ammo box."

Now I know why the Hardcore artillery and mortar guys used to whistle and walked around with smiles on their faces: Their ammo came in wooden boxes. But inflation soon struck big time everywhere around Danger. Even the prices at the friendly neighborhood whorehouse began escalating out of sight. Major Mergner solved the problem in a hurry—he buzzed the house in the C&C chopper and sent the word, "Tell Mama-San to knock it off, or I'll blow up her goddamn whorehouse."

The prices fell immediately. A clear case where air power did the job.

It was Doc Holley who felt the brunt of this capitalism. "There was just so much available sex and so little hygiene—as far as non-combat-related illness, VD was it by far. And I don't particularly remember the Army sending in prophylactics. It was like the problem was just ignored. No one ever wondered why we were using so much penicillin. I'd see all these horny nineteen-year-olds lined up—five or six guys standing there waiting their turn at some shack just off the road—and I knew soon they'd be lined up waiting for me."

Jim Robertson concurs. "You couldn't go anywhere without being propositioned." One day as he drove through the village of Ben Tran—not an easy chore since the streets were always mobbed with foot traffic—the surging crowds forced him to slow to a crawl. In the seat next to him, Sp-4 Larry Freer, Robertson's sidekick, was riding shotgun. Suddenly, Freer leaned out the window and waved to a kid.

"Hi, Jesus!" Freer yelled.

The boy grinned and waved back.

"What was *that* all about?" Robertson asked Freer, who said with a shrug, "That kid tried to sell me his mom the other day. It was like, 'You wanna fuck my momma, GI? She numbah one virgin.' I been calling him Jesus ever since.'"

Speaking of miracles, Jerry Sullivan still remembers the time a convoy of jeeps pulled up to Firebase Claymore, the little fort in the bush where his squad stayed while standing down. "Out stepped three or four sensational-looking, scantily clad round eyes from some hot TV show," he says. "We're talking micro-miniskirts, halter tops, minimal cover—along with a couple of captains, a major and several NCOs. These weren't Donut Dollies—they were absolutely beautiful, airbrushed, *Playboy* quality. We're talking totally surreal, totally crazy. Here we were in this world of gray mud and funky green shit, and it was like they were like hanging fresh meat in front of a bunch of hungry animals.

"The women hung out with us, chatted us up, even rubbed against us—they really fucked with our minds—and immediately we all completely lost our focus, which was trying to stay alive. Suddenly we're all running around with our dicks dragging in the dirt and here we are trying to fight a war. It's a wonder we didn't just hog-tie the jerks who brought 'em in and gang-bang the girls. I mean, we were armed and dangerous—and extremely lonely."

Anywhere American soldiers spent time, the whores showed up, so the troopers never had to be lonely for long. And when cash was scarce, there was barter. Cigarettes, soap, mosquito repellent, C-Rations, candy bars, wooden crates, cardboard boxes, scraps of corrugated steel, anything of any use at all could be traded for sex. The price varied with the vendor's and the buyer's immediate needs but if a deal could be struck, which was almost always the case, the women stayed.

The area surrounding the Division base camp at Dong Tam consisted of a string of shantytowns, and if you took a census, you'd find hookers made up 75 percent of the population. Whenever the Army ordered a change of military payment certificates—scrip that was used as a substitute for greenbacks to curtail black market activity—it was always a big secret. But within hours the word would be out and so would the panicked prostitutes, all trying to barter thousands of dollars in scrip that was fast becoming worthless. The women weren't the only whores in town. Some of the REMFs made small fortunes by giving the girls five cents on the dollar, then laundering the scrip through the troops coming in from the field.

Where there was a will, there was always a way. When Carl Ohlson first arrived in-country, he learned the ropes when he got the platoon's first SP pack—a large cardboard box full of cigarettes, cigars, soap, toothpaste, mosquito repellent. "SOP was to have the guys draw lots to establish the picking order," he remembers. "But no matter who won, soap and mosquito repellent always went first. I couldn't figure out why until Sergeant Perry, one of my sergeants, took me aside and told me the going rate to get bopped down in the ville was six bars of soap and two bottles of mosquito repellent.

"'What about money?' I asked.

"'Nope, they won't take military scrip—they don't think it's worth anything.'

"After that, I started noticing that guys would leave Danger, saying they were walking down to the bridge. They'd go charging down the road holding their bars of soap and mosquito repellent, and they always came back smiling."

"I saw guys get laid for as little as three or four cans of C-Rations," recalls Tom Aiken, a straight arrow himself. "But the prostitutes were picky. They couldn't read but they memorized the numbers and knew which cans were good. If they didn't like what you gave 'em they'd throw it back at you and yell, 'No fuckin' number ten!' which was a can of the awfullest bread you ever put in your mouth—we were all always tryin' to get rid of number ten. They knew how bad it was and weren't havin' any of it."

As soon as the troops realized the women were willing to trade sex for stuff that was being thrown away, garbage dumps became a favorite place for hookers to set up shop. While the security detail looked the other way, the mama-sans—as the madams were known—and their baby-sans, the whores, would comb a mound of rubbish and emerge with all sorts of useful things they'd accept in exchange for their favors. They must have thought Americans were the most wasteful people on the planet.

The whole Delta was an equal opportunity fuck-for-pay zone. One night Marty Miles was pulling security right next to a little hamlet of thatched hooches just outside Dong Tam. The VC had blown the bridge over the inlet leading into the small harbor that fed the base. A road led up to the ruins of the bridge. On the other side was Dong Tam. Miles was guarding the western flank and harbor on a routine security mission. "Anytime you've got a hamlet like that with GIs on easy duty you've got whores," he recalls. "There was one girl, much more generously endowed than the others. She was black. A lust object for all of us. The first time I talked to her, I mumbled a few words in English and I was totally shocked when she replied matter-of-factly, 'You want bang-bang, GI?' Then I realized that her father had to be a French soldier from Africa."

Given these laws of supply and demand, the more experienced, more savvy troops lost no time in getting down to business. "My best friend Rollins sure loved the whores," Aiken remembers. "He'd get two or three at a time and go in a bunker. He asked a buddy or two to stand in front of the door and guard it. "Don't let any of them out," he told us. "I'd hear some weird and wild sounds, but Rollins meant what he said and I knew if I let any of them out he'd whip my ass and whip it good. I'd seen him in action and I swore I'd never get on his bad side. When he came out of the bunker he'd be laughin' his ass off.

"The man played hard, but he fought even harder. If you had to go to battle, he was who you wanted to go with—he didn't give a shit about Army protocol, just about keepin' his men alive. You want to talk about tough, he invented tough—when he went to the field he wore a towel around his neck that he placed over his face at night to keep the mosquitoes off and he carried no food and no water, just two canteens of white rice whiskey and ammo, lots of ammo. He was a mountain hillbilly from Mont Eagle, Tennessee, and he really knew the score. He died gettin' six men to a Dust-Off area. That's how he got hit. I'll never forget him. I woulda done anythin' for him. Beginnin' with guardin' that bunker door."

Not many nineteen-year-old draftees could keep up with Rollins. And some of them had other priorities like sleep and food. After too many days in the bush, a good time could be a glass of milk.

"Right after Hack took over we went up to Moc Hoa," Aiken recalls. "I remember when we first got up there somebody sayin' there was a little whorehouse and that Hackworth had made sure everyone was inoculated. I was busy drinkin' milk that day, it was the only day I ever saw real milk in Vietnam, quarts of it that Hack got in there somehow and I couldn't get enough of it. Normally we had only the powdered stuff and that's why I kept drinkin' and drinkin' until I was sick, actually vomitin'. That milk was a whole lot more important to me than almost anythin' else at the time."

The whores who serviced these boys were as varied as they were plentiful. Some were strikingly attractive and some were as ugly as a box of volcanic rocks. One of the women hanging around Firebase Danger looked like she'd taken a load of double-ought buckshot full in the face. Strangely enough, she made a living. A grunt from Claymore Company spent some "short-time" with another young woman in a whorehouse outside of Dong Tam. When he came out to give his buddy a chance, he said, "Pass this one up, man. She's jailbait." When his pal asked him what he meant, he said, "I'm ashamed of myself; she's just a kid."

"How do you know?" said his buddy. "You can't tell a gook's exact age. They're either old or young."

"She got no hair down there. Can't be more than twelve."

His friend laughed all the way into the whorehouse. He knew something his friend didn't—that Vietnamese women have little or no pubic hair.

On a sweeter note, Toby Hager recalls a story he "never told to anybody before" that happened when "we were over at a place we called Tombstone Territory, Alert Company's little camp about a mile down the road from Danger where the pagoda was. It was pouring rain. I had a coupla sick guys I'd put back at my Platoon CP so they'd be out of the wet, and Tom Aiken, another kid from Illinois name of Grant and I were on the perimeter pulling duty for them.

"Right outside the perimeter, there was that little pagoda, maybe about twenty yards from us, where some of the locals used to come. And this night there were these two Vietnamese prostitutes who came walking over to us with ponchos on. Grant knew them and said they were cool. So I was set up to have a session with this lady. I'm all ready to go and she takes off her poncho and she's pregnant. So I'm thinking, If you have sex with a lady who's pregnant won't you hurt her or the baby? Now I'm maybe twenty, twenty-one years old, really naive, really, really worried.

"You didn't kiss women over there, it just didn't happen, but suddenly this girl leans over and gives me a nice sweet kiss, which led to many more of these long, sweet kisses. We were together there for about an hour and every so often I'd try to tell her she had to be careful and try to convince her to give up sex until she had her baby. I can remember being really concerned, so scared and worried that someone would kill her baby and hurt her. I mean, like where was Doc Holley when I needed him? He'd of gone, 'Fool—it's OK.' But he wasn't there to tell me what was what, so all we did was kiss away. It was actually very touching, there was a connection."

Other one-night stands had their own innocence as well. Sullivan still remembers what happened to him one night at Moc Hoa Special Forces camp. "A real pretty girl walked straight up to me at the LZ as I was getting off a helicopter and took me by the hand. We walked behind a steel conex and made love on a poncho liner. I don't know why she chose me or who she was or where she came from—all she seemed to want was me, our time together, she asked for nothing else. We made love and lay there wrapped in the poncho for quite a while and to this day it remains one of the strangest, most touching events of my life. It was very personal, very real and very true—like we found each other for a moment. She needed to be held and I did, too. I was nineteen, she was maybe sixteen—we were just two lost kids."

But Marty Miles seems to have been born streetwise. "Out at Danger, the Permanent Party knew where the local places were and had the time to go there," he says. "As for the rest of us, you could say we were usually too beat to get beat. But I remember an instance when we had security duty, where we were set up right by the bridge that was still intact and I had the pleasure of sleeping with the proverbial farmer's daughter, although in this case he was a merchant. My sense was that this family would take in a GI for a week, scarf up all the cigarettes and other stuff they could get from him while he did the same with the lovely daughter of the house. When his tour was up and he moved on, so did they."

Other times pussy patrol could get pretty grim. One night, two or three klicks down the road from Danger at the little French compound where Claymore stayed, Sullivan ran into an old man selling his daughter. "At best she was seventeen or eighteen," he says. "Probably a hell of a lot younger. There were at least twenty soldiers standing in line, but I don't think I had much of a wait before it was my turn at bat. I went in, she was lying there in this ratty little room, obviously distressed. I began to assume the position. But I was so disgusted that there was no way anything was going to happen. I couldn't zip up and get out of there fast enough."

Something similar happened to Larry Tahler. "We were somewhere on ambush out in the boondocks, when a young kid about ten years old asked me, 'You want to fuck my sister?' At first, I said no, but he kept bugging me and bugging me and bugging me until finally I said, 'OK, let me see your sister.' He dragged me to his sister's hooch. It turned out that she was at least six months pregnant, really showing. I just couldn't do it. There was no way."

About a month or so after we'd set up FSB Danger, Aiken's company set up at Tombstone Territory and started running long-range ambushes. "One night when I was leading a patrol, there was a little South Vietnamese soldier who came walking out there on a dike with a girl who was about seven months pregnant. It wasn't quite dark yet, and everybody could still see. I guess he was the girl's pimp. He wanted to come back after dark to sell the girl to anyone who wanted her. I told him, 'Show up and I'll blow your brains out.' If it was after dark, as far as I was concerned, he was fair game."

Most of the boys got their ashes hauled whenever they could at the local Steam 'n Creams. It was considered reliable and efficient, the old wham, bam, thank-you ma'am with no complications. "You'd choose your 'attendant,'" Marty Miles recalls. "Then you'd go into this big steam room, where you could stay, in theory, for as long as you wanted. But let's face it, none of us were much interested in cleaning our pores.

"That was all a pretense for the hand job which was the real reason we were there. It was hilarious. All these hulking American warriors and these tiny Vietnamese women. They led us off with our cocks in their hands, pulling us along as we shuffled lamely behind them. What they'd do was get you on your stomach for the massage, then ask if you wanted 'something special.' I mean, Who didn't? You rolled over for the 'Happy Ending.' Pretty much the only place in Vietnam where you could find one guaranteed."

No problem in getting off, but a Steam 'n Cream trip was definitely no-frills all the way. "I remember being on the table," Toby Hager says, "and a couple of girls actually ducked through the curtain to ask my girl questions. At least two popped in at different times. The questions were short and the answers even shorter. I mean, it was like I was in an office with people sticking in their heads and saying, "You got those figures?""

Once, as the moment of truth approached for Marty Miles, a girl in the adjoining stall stood on her own table and peered over the curtain bar down at him. "She started having an animated conversation with the tender maiden who was taking care of my business," he recalls. "I always wondered if she was commenting on my equipment or what. Most likely she was discussing washing her hair or what she was fixing for dinner. I thought, 'Ah, the joys of young love. We have truly won their hearts and minds!'"

"I'd say 90 percent of sex happened at the Steam 'n Creams," says Tahler, a Night Hunter in more ways than one. "If you were an enlisted man, you didn't have enough time alone for whacking off. If you were out in the boonies for a few days a lot of the guys would be checking out the villages for a girl willing to go "boom boom." Most of the guys wanted to get laid, but I always preferred blow jobs. Those girls were dangerous—who knew what they carried?

"So the relief typically was a Steam 'n Cream. We even had an Army-approved Steam 'n Cream in Dong Tam and there were a good number of others—at least three or four—in the villages surrounding the base. Most of them had two or three girls. You'd pick the one you liked and get a steam bath and a massage and then you'd bargain for a blow job."

At least Tahler did, since according to Marty Miles the women at the Steam 'n Creams were normally only willing to do a hand job. When he heard he'd really scored, Night Hunter 6 said, "I guess those guys just didn't know how to negotiate."

My own view was that I'd never begrudge a grunt for reducing his white count as long as it didn't dull his edge for combat—especially since a few hours after unzipping to get off he might be zipped up in a body bag. But as Aiken puts it, "When we were out in the field there was no such thing as sex, we were too busy humpin' and tryin' to stay alive. I'd say our next priorities were sleepin' and eatin', and when Hack took over we were out on ops so much more of the time there was a whole lot less than before. Not that it made a whole lot of difference to me. I was married and I always took my vows seriously, although I can't say I wasn't tempted. When we got home from Vietnam and Toby Hager met my wife, Marcia, he told her, 'You have some husband there. Take it from me, he was Mr. Clean.'"

The Mr. Dirties were left to Doc Holley, who finally in desperation decided to launch a one-man anti-VD crusade to scare everyone into cleaning up their act. His first move was to make up a fictitious disease he called Black Syphilis.

"I told all my medics the deal," he recalls. "We began a rumor campaign about the dread scourge, how it was so bad that anyone who caught it would have to be immediately quarantined on an island off the coast of Vietnam. 'Well,' I'd say, 'I sent a guy off last week...' and I told them Black Syphilis was so hard to cure it would take two or three years to get the victim to the point where it would be safe to send him back home.

"I'd feed the flames to keep them afraid. But I don't know if I stopped many of them—they probably figured if they were going to die anyway, they'd prefer it be from the Black Syph. At least they would've bought it having a good time."

One day Larry Tahler came in with a dose.

"Lieutenant," said the Big Band-Aid, "if you get the clap one more time, I'm going to have to put you in the hospital and give you penicillin intravenously."

"It was back to blow jobs," Tahler shrugs. "Which was just fine with me."

For those who had little or no experience with women before they entered the Army, it wasn't that easy. Jim Robertson still remembers the kid who caught gonorrhea his first time with a hooker behind Firebase Danger's garbage dump. When he confided his outrage to another soldier, the buddy asked him if he knew the woman who had done it to him.

"Yep," he said, "the bitch at the garbage dump."

"Well, hell," his buddy said, "give it back to her."

This angry young man caught the clap eight more times before he rotated home.

Under the Uniform Code of Military Justice, you could be court-martialed for Drippy Dick, the logic being that if a soldier was put out of action due to an ailment he'd brought on himself, he was negligent in his duty.

But in Vietnam, the Army, male-dominated and practical, established an unwritten addendum to the regulation—don't tell and we won't ask. Soldiers knew they could get treatment from medical personnel without dire consequences as long as they didn't let their maladies interfere with their duties. Many a warrior endured "the drip" as the price to be paid for carnal relief.

The issue of soldiers and the clap, of course, has been around a lot longer than gunpowder. Back in Italy at the end of World War II the word was "If you're drippin' you're not shippin.'" Meaning you wouldn't be going home anytime soon.

This wasn't just the Army's problem. Jim Robertson tells of a squad leader he knew who picked up a dose just before he was due to go home. The guy extended his tour. "I asked him if he thought risking his life for another six months wasn't a little bit much," says Robbie. 'You don't know my old lady,' the squad leader said. 'If I go home with the clap, I'm definitely a dead man.'"

That was probably an exaggeration but fortunately he didn't need to find out. He had the ministrations of the Big Band-Aid and his trusty medics to save him from a fate he obviously considered worse than death.

EIGHTEEN

Giao Duc General Hospital

The Hardcore was blessed with fine medics led by a great Battalion Surgeon. Most were draftees like Doc Holley, Dan Evans, Rick Hudson and Charlie Wintzer; and many were conscientious objectors like Wally Nutt, who refused to carry a rifle and gave his life while looking after his wounded Dagger Company buddies on a fire-swept field. Though few if any wanted to be in the bloody swamps of Vietnam, these selfless Hardcore medics looked after their flock in a most extraordinary, caring way.

Combat medics rank among the bravest of the brave and ours were no exception. More often than not, they were the most visible targets—running or crawling out in the open on the same dangerous ground where their comrades just took a slug or tripped a mine.

The Hardcore medics didn't wait for a miracle to pull the wounded out of a dangerous place—they provided the miracle, pulling, sliding, dragging and packing shattered bodies out of view of an enemy sniper's scope. And while bullets were snapping all around them, they sealed a punctured chest, administered morphine, got IVs going to pump life back into broken fighters. Stopping the bleeding, arresting shock, they provided powerful encouragement: "You got it made." "Million-dollar wound." "Only a scratch." "Hang in there." "Dust-Off's on the way."

"The guys looked at the medic as sort of a father and mother figure combined, as the guy that would save you when you got wounded," Doc Wintzer recalls. "If someone got a Care package from home, the medic would be the first who got to share it. All the troops wanted to make sure I knew their names. Believe me, the troops took care of the Docs. Kind of like paying a premium on a life insurance policy in advance. The troops well knew a lot of people came home because a medic was there."

When he first joined the 4/39th, Doc Evans remembers one of the veteran medics telling him "not to form bonds with the men in my platoon as it would be very hard emotionally when they became wounded or killed. This is impossible to do when you live with a group of men twenty-four hours a day for months. Very strong bonds form the camaraderie that the Platoon shared as a result of the brotherhood of a battlefield and the dangers and hardships we endured. Every member of my platoon was wounded except two, one or more times while I was their medic. They never told us in training that the casualty rate for grunts was so high."

Doc Evans is now a veterinarian with almost thirty years of medical experience. Recently reflecting on his combat medic training at Fort Sam Houston, he observed, "I can't believe how much us medics did with just ten weeks of medical training. Had we known how little we knew, we would have been too paralyzed with fear to treat anyone."

Besides life-and-death responsibility, the Docs also carried a heavy emotional load. They saw the damage up close, witnessed the smashed bodies and young men—many not old enough to drink in bars back home—covered in ponchos and plopped onto the floors of choppers.

The month of March was particularly hard on Doc Evans and Battle Company's 1st Platoon. "After 25 March, I never did get that close to the replacements the way I did with the men in the platoon before that. Two men I worked on that day died on the battlefield. That wasn't supposed to happen. Us medics were to keep all the wounded alive. I let two families down. To this day I don't know the names of anyone who joined the platoon after 25 March 1969."

I've always wondered what made these men so special. Was it the title of medic, their training at Fort Sam Houston, their terrible responsibility and knowing how vitally they were needed—or was it some extra issue of courage that compelled them to keep going into the line of fire to care for their men? Leadership certainly played a big part; and in the Hardcore, Doc Byron Holley and his assistant, Lieutenant Bill Casey, the medical platoon leader, set one hell of an example. Both men went out with the rifle platoons on combat missions, enduring the same conditions and horror as their medics.

Holley was a doctor, an M.D., but I always thought he would have made one damn fine combat commander. He fought for his guys like a lioness looks after her cubs. In the Hardcore, no one screwed with Doc Holley's medics, including me. And my arrival didn't exactly thrill him or the rest of the Medical Platoon. "We probably had an attitude problem when you checked in," Charlie Wintzer recalls. "You came with a heavy reputation. I remember Doc Holley and I sitting in the aid station and his saying, 'God, this is going to be hell—we've got some GI Joe lifer out here who's going to just ruin us.' It looked as if somebody was going to come in and kick ass and make career soldiers out of us."

Early in the game, Doc Holley informed me that I didn't know jack shit about doctoring and field sanitation. "If you don't fuck with my medics," he told me, "I'll keep your troops in fighting shape." I heard him loud and clear. As far as he was concerned, he didn't have to prove anything to me. I was the one who had to prove something to him.

If Holley demanded the max from his medics, he demanded more from himself. Even when cold beer was available, he'd limit himself to one can a day, because he considered himself on duty round the clock. "Doc Holley would refuse to let his hair down even when everything was cool," Wintzer says. "He told me, 'If I have more than one beer, I won't be in control and maybe I won't do the right thing.' I used to get so pissed off when he insisted on sewing up every wound—even minor scratches—even though he was bone tired. Hell, I wanted him to get some rest, but I also wanted to practice sewing people up."

"Seeing what my medics were doing out in the field was truly amazing," Holley remembers. "Imagine taking kids fresh out of high school, give them ten weeks of infantry training followed by another ten weeks of medical training and then arming them with medicines capable of killing a grown man if given in excess or at the wrong time—and then sending them off to the field to take care of other high school kids who've been blown to pieces. On paper it won't work. In reality, it happened over and over again during the Vietnam War.

"I was in awe of their performance, but I'm not sure they ever knew just how I felt. I was the fatherly type who always tried to put myself in their shoes and give the best advice I could, knowing that sometimes even the best advice could not save the life of their dying patient. We agonized over many situations together, but I don't ever recall a tear being openly shed by any of my medics or me. We cried a lot on the inside but felt we always had to be upbeat and strong as we were the only hope of survival for all our comrades."

The heroism Dan Evans and Rick Hudson displayed on 25 March '69 is the stuff of legend among Battle Company warriors, many of whom wouldn't be alive but for their skill and courage.

"I was one of the first to get hit, "Larry Faulkenberg recalls. "The VC were stitching the field with machine-gun fire, but I didn't have to lay there long. I really praised God when Doc Evans got to me through all them bullets. With a collapsed lung, I wouldn't have made it without him."

After long and dangerous tours as platoon Docs, both Evans and Hudson were offered cushy REMF jobs. Both refused. They preferred staying with their boys.

"Medic. Medic. Medic. Doc, I'm hit."

Every cry is imprinted in a medic's brain. Claymore Company Medic Dave Anderson will never forget his first fight: "Machine-gun fire, tracer bullets flying everywhere. It was total chaos. I crawled back where the three wounded boys were calling 'Medic.' The first guy I came to was lying still on the ground. I took off his steel pot, and the top of his head came off. That's when I said to myself, 'Son, you're in too deep.' I crawled to the next guy. He was shot in the lower leg. Lord, I was scared. I got my scissors out, cut off his boot, and I put a pressure bandage on. He said, 'Doc, the bullet went through my leg. You only bandaged one side of it.' I was thinking, In my shape, you're damn lucky that I got it half right. All the training in the world didn't prepare a man for the shock of battle."

Medic Billy Scott was one of the Hardcore's most unlikely heroes. "I didn't think I was big enough or strong enough or brave enough to be a combat medic," he recalls.

Doc Holley had his doubts, too. "Oh, Lord," Holley said to himself the first time he first saw Billy. "Where are they getting these kids? He's such a sweet little kid, almost a mama's boy. Why isn't he back home teaching Sunday school?"

When Billy first checked in, the Battalion was still at Dong Tam. He hid in the Division chapel for two days until Holley tracked him down and found him sitting on a pew praying.

"Billy, you have to come out," he said. " You can't stay here forever."

"Dr. Holley, I'm scared to death just bein' in Vietnam. I can't help it. I've prayed over it. I believe with all my heart I'll be killed if I go to the field."

Holley couldn't help remembering his own baptism by fire and told Billy how when he heard the bullets snapping by barely a foot above his head, "it was the first realization I had that, hey, a guy can get killed pretty easy over here. I looked up at the moon and prayed, 'God, please don't let me die in this hellhole.' And it was just like I heard a voice saying: Relax, everything's going to be just fine, just remember what you learned in basic training—when the lead's flying, get your butt down. It was like a protective shield came around me and I lost any fear. And I learned fast that you can cover a lot of territory crawling."

Holley kept Billy in the aid station and built up his confidence. Gradually he settled down. The nightmares of combat, the visions of a ten-foot-tall VC tearing his chest cavity open and ripping out his heart faded.

Then came the day Dagger Company needed a platoon medic to replace Ernest Osborne, who was headed home. Holley felt that Billy was ready. But there was still one problem. Where Billy was a small, deeply religious man and never uttered a curse word or packed a weapon, Osborne, who swore up a blue streak was the exact opposite. A rugged man, big, profane and macho, he packed an M-16 and a slingshot, which he used to fire steel balls with the same deadly accuracy as with his automatic rifle. He was one mean mother.

"We liked Billy, but weren't sure he could do the job—we had a confidence problem with him," Mike Kidd recalls. "He was nervous and small, and his medical aid bag was almost as big as he was. We just didn't know how he'd perform in a bad fight."

That night Dagger Company got clobbered. Instead of looking after himself, Billy repeatedly exposed himself to enemy fire looking after his boys. The morning after the fight, General Gunn pinned a Bronze Star medal for valor on his skinny chest. "He won us," Kidd says. "After that night, there would have been a mutiny in the Platoon if someone tried to take Little Billy from us. He was our Doc, and we were proud of him."

Like most medics who joined the battalion in 1969, PFC Joe Cannon, a medic from Queens, New York, was a conscientious objector. His rifle

Platoon Leader, Lieutenant Carl Ohlson, worried because Cannon, like many medics, refused to carry a weapon.

"The VC don't care if you're a Quaker from Queens," Ohlson told him. "They'll kill you in a heartbeat." After much persuasion, Ohlson got Cannon to carry an empty .45-caliber pistol. "I carried the loaded clips in my pack, figuring if we got into a tight spot I could toss them to him," Ohlson remembers.

After an ugly fight in April, Cannon gave Ohlson back his pistol. "I don't want to carry an empty .45," he said. "I want a loaded M-16. When these cats are shooting live bullets at me and they're flying over my head, my conscientious objector feelings disappear. I want to shoot back."

"You know, Cannon became one of my best riflemen," Ohlson says. "The next thing I know he's packing an M-79 grenade launcher."

"Where'd you get that hog?" Ohlson asked.

Cannon grinned at him. "I traded a little penicillin for it."

"Cannon walked right behind me, and whenever we got into a firefight, he popped off more rounds than anyone else," Ohlson says. "He became one of the best shooters I ever had."

The Docs not only had to worry about bullets, booby traps and bugs, they had to deal with other ugly surprises like the Two-Step Snake—take two steps after being bitten and you were as dead as an empty bottle of whiskey.

One night an urgent radio message woke Doc Evans in the bush. "Doc Hudson needs help," Bobby Knapp said. "Something's bitten one of our guys. His eyes are swelling shut, his lips are big as balloons, and he's having trouble breathing."

Evans rushed to medic Rick Hudson's Platoon, where he found Hudson working hard to save the stricken soldier's life. "He was having an anaphylactic allergic reaction that could puff up his brain, close off his trachea and suffocate him to death," Evans recalls.

Evans suspected a spider bite. He knew the soldier was going to die unless he and Hudson pulled off a quick miracle. "Hudson was a great medic," Evans says, "but neither of us was adequately equipped to handle a problem like this. We didn't have epinephrine or antihistamines, which should have been given by IV for an attack like this. We had Benadryl capsules, but we figured oral antihistamines were probably of little value at this stage."

Working way out in the middle of bandit country with a red filtered flashlight held by company commander Bobby Knapp, Hudson and Evans forced a capsule down the stricken soldier's throat. "His throat was so swollen it was like trying to push a bean into a mouse's ass," Evans says. "Every muscle in his body was strung as tight as drying rawhide. His body arched off the ground as he tried desperately to suck air into his starved lungs. Neck muscles stood out like cords. Veins popped out of his forehead, ready to explode. He sounded like a rooster trying to crow."

The soldier died three times that night. Each time Evans and Hudson brought him back with CPR.

"I've got a pulse," Hudson shouted just as the Dust-Off landed.

The chopper flew to the Hardcore firebase, where Doc Holley and Wintzer were waiting at the pad. An hour later the word flashed to Lieutenant Knapp from Holley, "Tell my two medics they did a damn good job. Their patient's fine. He'll rejoin you all once he's had some rest."

Over the aid station PRC-25 radio, Doc Holley frequently got such emergency calls. "Usually the medic had done as much as I could personally have done under the circumstances," he says. "Occasionally, I was able to suggest something they'd not tried to keep the patient alive until the Dust-Off chopper arrived. These were monumental decisions to place on the shoulders of such young soldiers with such limited training. But time and again they proved their grit and skill by doing just what they had to do. Always with little regard for their own safety."

Battle Blue Platoon medic Mike Hill, who took a bullet on 25 March while rushing to the aid of a wounded soldier, says his first casualty four months earlier was a boy who probably killed himself because he was stoned. Hill had just seen him smoke a joint, then pick up a booby-trapped grenade.

"The instant he touched it," Hill said, "it went off."

It blew him to smithereens.

"I worked frantically on him," Hill said. "I was covered in his blood. I knew he was dead, but to keep the men's morale up, I just kept working on him. Finally, the Dust-Off came in."

As Mike figured, the soldier arrived DOA at Dong Tam's 3rd Surgery Hospital. "I realized while working on him that we weren't there to win the war," he says. "We were there to keep each other alive."

"There were times you felt so inadequate," medic Rick Hudson recalls. "We didn't have a lot of training back in the States, and frequently we were faced with problems that a medical doctor wouldn't have been able to cope with, especially out in the mud when the bullets were flying. There were times I felt so frustrated and so inadequate, like when you're holding somebody who's dying in your arms—or who is already dead and you can't bring them back to life. Those moments live with me day in and day out."

Hudson's closest friend in Battle Company was Nigel Frederick Poese. Both were very religious. They read the Bible together. Because of Hudson's religious beliefs—he was also a conscientious objector—he initially chose an aid bag over an M-16. During one operation, RTO Poese's radio antenna tripped a booby-trap wire in a tree—a favorite VC trick. Hudson rushed to his side.

"I remember holding him in my arms, giving him mouth-to-mouth and patching up his chest wounds," Hudson says. "All of his buddies were standing around saying, 'Come on, Doc, save him.' A kid trying to save a kid. That's hard, and I couldn't save him. I'll never be able to get over that." Poese died in the Dust-Off en route to the 3rd Surgical Hospital.

In another fight, Hudson hit in the leg and the wrist from the flying steel of an AK-47 round that ricocheted off his rifle, refused evacuation. "I need to stay out there with the guys because I'm the only medic," he said. His platoon leader had to order him onto the Dust-Off.

He spent a week or two back at the Battalion aid station "going nuts with worry for my guys, and wasting my time treating VD and handling routine sick call."

Air assaults were another hairy part of a medic's job. One time while Dan Evans was airborne with his Platoon, their slick suddenly plunged toward the ground. "The door gunner said we were going to crash," Evans says. "I looked down and saw some streams and had this idea I was going to jump into one of them. It beat riding the thing down." Evans got out on the skid, and seconds before the ship creamed into a rice paddy, he bailed out, but missed the stream. "I kinda swan-dived into the wet rice paddy right next to the stream and just slid forever."

His problems were just beginning. Evans and the chopper had come down near a VC base camp. "Bullets started flying, and then our circling gunships started blasting. The VC took off. What saved us was that the ship crashed right next to a VC hospital, and they weren't prepared for shooting there."

Miraculously, he didn't get a scratch; but from then on, whenever Evans climbed into a bird, he was one white-knuckle flier.

For some of the medics, the load finally became too great to bear. "One morning, we had a couple men pretty badly wounded from a booby trap, and our Doc—who'd mended his share of broken and torn-up troops—was patching them up while we waited for the medevac bird," Captain DeRoos recalls. "I was out checking the security for the Dust-Off PZ when the Doc ran over to me, knelt down, grabbed my hand and started sobbing his heart out... said he couldn't take it anymore. Then he lost it completely, asked me if he could use the radio to call his mother, and then started mumbling. He was totally off the planet. He'd just seen so much. I knew exactly how he felt. I sent him out on the Dust-Off. He was evacuated to the States."

Sergeant Mike Simmons, the Battalion PIO and our own "Ernie Pyle," loved Doc Holley's setup. When he wasn't out in the field with the troops getting stories, he wisely crashed at the Battalion aid station. There he could always hustle a litter for a bed and, with a little luck, scrounge a cold beer. The aid station was the only place in the Battalion that normally had ice—to keep the whole blood chilled. Sometimes, just sometimes, a six-pack would somehow fall into the blood container and get cold, too.

The Medical Platoon sergeant was an old soldier whose snoring sounded like a battery of 155mm howitzers firing on full automatic. "No one could sleep when Sergeant James D. Aleridge was sawing logs inside the Battalion aid bunker," said Wintzer. "So Holley made him sleep outside, where he always made sure to rig up a mosquito net."

On the nights Simmons spent at the aid station, he slept outside next to Sergeant Aleridge, whose snoring reverberated even through both men's sandbagged metal culverts. Oddly enough, the next morning Simmons would wake up well rested, while the old sergeant would be red-eyed and moaning about how he couldn't sleep because the mosquitoes ate him alive.

After Sergeant Aleridge went home, Simmons confessed: "I'd flip open one corner of his mosquito net, the mosquitoes would do their thing, Aleridge would start moaning. I could sleep through almost anything, but not that godawful snoring." One more page from the Hardcore manifesto of out-G-ing-the G.

Then there were G moments when you'd realize all over again just what you were up against. Once Wintzer was filling in for a Battle Company medic when the company found a VC hospital. The VC had flown the coop, leaving empty cots, pots and pans and a bunker full of medical supplies.

Wintzer was sorting through the supplies, when he came upon containers that looked familiar. "It was scary to find stuff with my handwriting on the boxes," Winzer said. "A lot of the medicine I found in that VC bunker I'd handed out to civilians when we'd treated them in the villages. This convinced me that the VC were everywhere—and they were really playing us for suckers."

When Major Hopper arrived at the 4/39th and started throwing his weight around, it didn't help his FNG image when he got into a pissing contest with Doc Holley, by far the most beloved man in the Battalion, the night before Holley was shipping out to join the REMFs he'd been damning at a Saigon hospital. With the Doc's combat tour up and his replacement on board, it was party time. His medics put up a big sign made of cardboard from a C-Ration box over the aid station's bunker door, reading "GIAO DUC GENERAL HOSPITAL, 'DOC HOLY' IN RESIDENCE." There was a halo above "Holys'" name. The sign also sported a logo from *Ben Casey*— a popular 1960s TV show—along with the symbols for death, life, infinity, male and female—and, of course, the arrowhead emblem of the Hardcore Recondos.

And then Holley's Docs threw a major bash—we're talking endless cold beer, 180 proof medical alcohol, music, the works. I stopped by early in the evening, had a beer, listened to Tom Aiken play his hot country guitar, thanked Doc for his great work and repeated heroism and disappeared back to the TOC. Around midnight, Hopper decided the now-roaring celebration was too loud—which it was—and that the party animals should hit the sack. But instead of asking Mergner or one of the old-timers to deliver the word, he did it himself. You know, new broom. Get everyone's attention.

"Knock off the noise! Don't you know you're in a combat zone?" he screamed to the drunken revelers.. Among them were more Purple Hearts than Hopper had years sucking air.

Holley told Hopper to get out of his aid station. Hopper pulled rank. The wrong thing to do with the good doctor anytime, but especially when he was certifiably shit-faced. Doc jumped up, chewed out the XO to the cheers of the crowd and when things heated up even more, he booted the major in the butt and out of his bunker.

Hopper reported Doc's insubordination to me. "Captain Holley should be court-martialed!" he ranted.

To pacify the major, I sent Mergner over to the aid station—where he had a beer while he calmed Holley and his band of merry men. Then finally all was quiet at FSB Danger.

The next morning I took Hopper aside and told him to cut the crap. You don't court-martial heroes.

NINETEEN

Fire Support Base Danger
13 APRIL 1969

Throughout the month of April, under the company skippers' fight-smart leadership and new tactics, the Battalion regrouped from the beating on 25 March and started kicking ass. There were no big battles like in March, just small actions executed by small-unit leaders becoming increasingly proficient with the Hardcore's counter-guerrilla techniques. The Battalion stats for the month of April—including all supporting elements such as TAC Air, gunships, Air Cav and artillery—say it all:

US WIA	US KIA	VC KIA
62	6	698

By 9 April, I'd assumed full duty with only a slight limp from my 25 March wound. Mergner had cranked the Battalion to a new high and the S-2/S-3 sections were humming like a Mercedes dealer's own car. The S-1 shop was well manned by former rifle platoon leader Lieutenant David Risley, a Silver Star recipient and top administrator whose grunt experience taught him well how to take care of the soldiers.

We scored big time with a new S-4, an extraordinarily capable and experienced Hawaiian captain named Morio Takahashi who kept the lash-up well supplied. Another outstanding Hawaiian National Guard Captain, Fred Debusca, replaced Bob Johnson as CO of Headquarters Company when, after ten hard infantry months, he returned to the engineers. It was their gain and our deep loss—Bob had done a great job both as the S-4 and later as the Headquarters Company CO.

Another downer came when Division G-1 issued the Battalion Sergeant Major Dwight Overstreet, who outranked Bob Press. Even though I fought the assignment with all my energy, I lost and Bob Press, my right hand and dear friend, was reassigned to E/75th Rangers as Top Kick—lucky for them but a terrible loss to the Battalion and to me personally.

Sergeant Major Overstreet, on his second Vietnam tour, had asked for an infantry battalion. He turned out to be an old pro and a damned good man. If we had to lose Press, we couldn't have gotten a better replacment. Overstreet and I never clicked the way Press and I did, but maybe that was because Press and I had been through so much together over the previous decades that he'd become like a brother to me.

Alert Company was now rocking and rolling with Captain Trent Thomas sitting firmly in the driver's seat. His experience as a Brigade intelligence officer had really paid off. "At Brigade, I had had the chore of tracking, reporting on and targeting the VC for several months and now I got the opportunity to do something with the information."

Thomas inherited a finely tuned killing machine from Winston. "Alert was like a well-coached football team," Thomas recalls. "Every member knew the plays and the players. Platoon leaders Frank Angyal and Fred Meyer were warriors who fully bought into the idea of a long-range ambush company. The soldiers reflected their leadership: daring, proficient pros. Each new guy had an experienced mentor to teach him the ropes. "Normally, we spent three days out of six on ambush, with two of the others on Airmobile Ops—the remainder on drying out, maintaining and training. We generally were inserted outside of our artillery coverage—the VC knew our range fans. We'd slip into an ambush position just as dark fell, then moved into our actual ambush site after dark. Charley never knew what hit him."

During the previous month, we'd walked through fire and made it to the other side without too many burns. John Hayes told me, "General Ewell is as pleased as punch with the Hardcore's transformation."

The Battalion's Log for 13 April 1969 gives an idea of just how active the Hardcore was during a busy April day.

ITEM NO.	TIME IN/OUT	INCIDENTS, MESSAGES, ORDERS, ETC.
1	0001H	Journal opened.
2	0300H	Sitrep negative for all elements, 0100H, 0200H, 0300H
3	0417H	C66 engaged 4 VC in sampan; they heard metallic Clicks and there was a secondary explosion. Sampan headed south. VC were armed. Will check in morning. 4VC (BC) WS949413.
4	0445H	Flashy 32 reports he had to shut down due to power
5	0500H	A56 reports quite a lot of sampan across the blue too far out of range to engage. WS915400.
6	0535H	D6 reports that he got movement around his psn and west; arty called in.
7	0553H	Resupply ship due at 0830H tail #956; LOH
8	0608H	C76 engaged 8 VC across the blue from them.
9	0657H	From D Co: Roster #115 has shrapnel wounds and slight AK wound and will stay in field; D6 wants to be sure he gets a Purple Heart. Roster #19 has old wound infection and will also be on resupply. All result of 1753H firefight.
10	0700H	Jayhawk 868 on station for insertion of Snipers.
11	0727H	Plans for 14 April sent to Bde.
12	0728H	Change from Bde-CAV.
13	0730H	3 VC KBA while inserting Snipers; taking evasive action WS974444; black PJs.

ITEM NO.	TIME IN/OUT	INCIDENTS, MESSAGES, ORDERS, ETC.
14	0802H	Syn #2 975450; Syn #4 949448-0710 to 0735H.
15	0900H	Resupply slick on station, tail #956; off at 0940H
16	0950H	Snipers kill 1 VC vic WS97145; Scooter with 1 rd at 600 Meters; black PJs, hiding in wood line.
17	1015H	AHC on station. Anteater 4 on station at 1020H.
18	1023H	A56 starting to move SE from night location.
19	1103H	14 blade hours at this time.
20	1125H	Night locations: C76 WS990430; C56 WS999442; A56 XS) 16437: D6 WS923407.
21	1130H	A56 spotted 3 VC taking evasive action vic WS917495; called in arty with negative results.
22	1142H	A6 & 76 made leaflet drops at 1045H WS960430 & WS990450.
23	1147H	A VC (BC) for John Wayne with 2 rds at 500 meters; black PJs, vic WS983450.
24	1205H	D6 found and destroyed 2 sampans and 4 lean-to fighting positions vic WS943422.
25	1218H	Both Sniper teams are receiving probing AK fire WS979452 & WS972452; D72 receiving AK fire at this time.
26	1226H	D6 engaged 2 VC vic WS938432 w/AKs; black PJs; 2 VC (BC).
27	1240H	Snoopy has 1 VC (BC) with 3 rds at 150 meters with black PJs; killed at 1205 vic WS975449.
28	1242H	Ar 1210H received AK fire (4 to 5) at WS930400. Arty put into area; 2 VC (KBA).
29	1250H	At 1240H D76 engaged and killed 1 VC with black pants and blue shirt. 1 VC (BC).
30	1302H	Sniper team 4 receiving AK fire again.

ITEM NO.	TIME IN/OUT	INCIDENTS, MESSAGES, ORDERS, ETC.
31	1303H	At WS94238 D66 killed 1 VC (BC) with blue shirt and black pants.
32	1304H	At WS93400 A56 killed 2 VC (BC) w/black PJs; also 1 VC (KBA) same coordinates.
33	1317H	A56 receiving small-arms fire and calling in arty; contact broken at 1319H; was est. 3-4.
34	1323H	Stogie 13 reports activity WS878439; 10-15 bunkers and 8-10 people; negative results as yet.
35	1327H	A56 reports a lot of fire at WS923493; arty and gunships requested.
36	1355H	Stogie engaged and killed 2 VC (BC) trying to wade a river; black PJs.
37	1355H	1 US urgent Dust-Off for Co.A, bullet in leg and shock WS923403. Stogie on station. Dustoff 56 on station 1415H, complete 1423H. Roster #126, #17, #124, and LOH observer.
38	1425H	Stogie reports LOH down WS923493 as he was going in for Dust-Off. He has extricated uninjured pilot; injured observer on ground with A56.
39	1432H	At WS981471 D6 engaged and killed 1 VC(BC) w/black PJs w/weapon (AK-47).
40	1440H	Stogie engaged and destroyed hooch vic WS925405; also hit bunker with rockets to no effect. Hooch destroyed was where the fire that downed the LOH came from. 2 VC (KBA).
41	1500H	A56 had found 8 VC bodies KBA (arty) and has engaged and killed 2 VC w/small-arms fire; 2 AKs captured.
42	1545H	D6 found and destroyed 1 BT (trip wire) at WS928405. Many TU DAI signs in the area.

ITEM NO.	TIME IN/OUT	INCIDENTS, MESSAGES, ORDERS, ETC.
43	1610H	Snoopy got 1 VC (BC) with a two rounds at 400 meters. Taking evasive action in wood line, no weapon WS974448.
44	1625H	Night Search AOs: 1, X17, 16, 15, 14, 13, 12, 11-H45, 44, 43, 42, 5-41, 39, 38, 37, 32, 31, 30, 29, 26, 25, 24, 23, 22, 18, 17, 16, 12, 11, 10, 2, H1, 2, 3, 4, 5, 6, 7, 9.
45	1635H	Stogie released at this time.
46	1715H	D6 receiving sniper fire at WS923409; putting in arty.
47	1820H	D Co's point man engaged 4 VC in sampan wearing blue shirts and black PJ bottoms taking evasive action vic WS928408. VC had weapons—everything sank. 4 VC (BC).
48	1825H	A56 is at the Ferry Point and is ready to be picked up. They were picked up at 1826H.
49	2030H	D6 is in NL at 2025H. C56 in at 2035H, A56 at 2100H C66 in at 2230H.
50	2038H	Flare ship on station at 2038H kilo 83.
51	2100H	A76's Fat Cat for tomorrow's opn is 39.
52	2135H	Plans for 14 April have been called in.
53	2030H	Night Hunter 6 is up at 2030H, down for fuel 2125H. NH guns and C&C off station at 2316H.
54	2120H	Warning order to D6 has been turned in.
55	2240H	At XSO349 NH engaged and killed 2 VC (BC) in sampan.
56	2300H	Negative sitrep for all elements.

Darkness brought an end to the fast pace but didn't stop the contacts. At 2330 hours, an Alert Company ambush killed five VC in a sampan and captured two AK-50s, giving us a grand total of forty-three VC dispatched to Buddha Heaven that day.

The next morning, 14 April, Craig Tessau's Battle Company got into a sharp firefight with a platoon of VC. Tessau's boys had caught them with their pants down and they took off, leaving four of their comrades with rigor mortis setting in. After Battle checked the area, the company moved out. But since the VC might be back to collect their dead, a squad-size Stay-Behind force remained in place. Bingo! Two hours and two short M-16 bursts later, two more VC soldiers joined their now stiff comrades.

Stay-Behinds became the Battalion's SOP. We hammered into everyone's heads that the VC were always watching us; we were on his turf and he knew it as surely as a topless dancer knows her body. He constantly studied us looking for weak points and patterns—and when he found a soft spot, he'd strike.

Our Stay-Behind elements zapped the VC scouts as well as their scrounge parties sent to pick through abandoned U.S. overnight positions for the goodies untrained and undisciplined GIs left behind. Charley turned everything he found—empty C-Ration cans, spent radio batteries, commo wire—into weapons or devices to use against us. Except that now we used his scrounging against him.

Veteran commander Captain DeRoos explains the Stay-Behind technique he used so successfully this way: "Proper camouflage and radio procedure, i.e. break squelch—using the press-to-talk button as a voiceless code: break squelch once when settled in place, twice for half-hour negative sitrep, three times for VC sightings, open commo when ambush triggered. Each man with the Stay-Behind squad knew exactly where the guy on the other side was and had to be able to see those positions. The site had to have 360-degree coverage, no exceptions. Piss-in-place, no smoking, no personal radios, no talking or moving around were the rules. If no ambush was triggered after a couple of hours, they'd rejoin the company. Pretty basic stuff, but if not constantly checked, the troops would ignore it. All of the men followed this procedure and after we'd done it a couple times, word got around to the rest of the troops, so going over the checklist didn't take all that long to wrap up.

"The ambush site was picked out before the main body left the area. Standard Procedure was a rifle squad reinforced with a medic, extra ammo, grenades, an M-79, a couple LAWS, smoke grenades and claymores. The squad leader was given a map, compass, his position coordinates, planned join-up location and our artillery concentrations.

"Deciding whether or where to leave a Stay-Behind was often more of a gut feeling than anything. Some places just begged for one, though—like a river crossing point or a trail junction with well-worn paths, Tu Dai mine warning signs posted here and there, smell of cooking fire smoke in areas without hooches.

"When we ran across an area that looked promising while we were on the move, and if there was good concealment nearby, we'd drop off a Stay-Behind. Once the Stay-Behind wasted two VC while they were coming toward them, talking up a storm. Normally the VC were church-mouse quiet. Not this time, though, so they couldn't have had any idea we were still in the area. Hell of a morale booster for the troops, especially after being shot at and booby-trapped so often. It proved to them that even tough Charley, a formidable opponent, didn't always have his shit together."

Battalion SOP called for the Stay-Behind force to always be in radio commo with the main body and never to be more than a twenty-minute distance from a reinforcing element. When using the column formation, the Stay-Behind element always peeled off from the front of the column and took up a hide position without slowing down the main body's advance.

On 17 April, Claymore Company conducted a Search and Clear operation with an ARVN unit. The two outfits had infiltrated behind a VC village and set up platoon-size ambushes. The plan was for the South Viet unit to sweep through the village, hopefully flushing some R&Ring VC soldiers into Claymore's waiting guns. As the South Viets got closer to Claymore's positions, their small-arms fire smacked into Lieutenant Travis Lee's Platoon's position. Lee tried to shut off the fire by calling the American adviser who was with the ARVN for that very purpose, but couldn't raise him on the radio. Next he tossed a smoke grenade to mark his platoon's location and when that failed, he tried to shout above the roar of the firing. Finally, he ran forward between his men and the advancing ARVN, shouting to them to cease fire—and was instantly cut down by their fire.

A few weeks before, George Mergner had interviewed Lee, an engineer officer detailed infantry to relieve the shortage of grunt lieutenants, when the new replacement reported into the Hardcore. "He told me he wasn't telling his parents he'd been reassigned. He was afraid they'd worry," Mergner said.

"It was one of the bravest acts I heard of in Vietnam. He literally died for his men," squad leader Sullivan says. "He was a wonderful leader who cared for his troops. Had he been infantry-trained he'd probably still be with us. He died before he learned the dos and don'ts."

Later that day, Claymore Company trapped a small VC element in a heavily wooded area and clobbered them with artillery. After the barrage lifted, a Tiger Scout heard a VC soldier say, "We are surrounded by U.S. soldiers."

"Then they took off like squirrels going up a tree," Sullivan said. His Tiger Scout reported that the enemy wore greenish-blue uniforms with backpacks and pith helmets. From other bits and pieces of information collected from around the battlefield, we figured our opponent was definitely not local village VC or from any of the other VC Main Force units we'd tangled with—these guys seemed like they couldn't walk and eat rice at the same time. Later that day we took two POWs from the same outfit; they squealed like Mafia turncoats bucking for the Witness Protection Program, identifying their unit as the 309th Main Force Battalion. Both POWs fell for my time-tested battlefield interrogation technique: POWs would be blindfolded, then told loudly in Vietnamese to talk or die. Of course they'd refuse so I'd shoot into the ground next to one of them, simultaneously kicking that POW in the side and producing a loud grunt. I'd go back over to his blindfolded mate and ask if he wanted a dose of the same medicine. Then you couldn't shut the guy up.

This time around we learned that we'd nailed a green unit, fresh out of Cambodia. The 309th didn't know the battlefield as well as the Hardcore and paid the price.

The next morning, Mergner and I were flying in our LOH when Claymore Company's Don Meyer called and said he had an emergency: Platoon Sergeant Richard Onisk was stuck in the middle of a canal. We landed and as I jumped out on the canal bank, Onisk, sunk up to his chest in mud, saluted and shouted, "Hardcore Recondo, Sir."

I tossed him a rope, which he tied around himself, and a dozen men from his platoon tried to pull him out. We couldn't budge him—he was stuck fast. Next, Mergner, still in the chopper, tied the rope to the skids and lifted—and failed again. Then, with Mergner holding the Sergeant's LBE—Load Bearing Equipment—while Onisk held tight to a skid with both arms, the chopper lifted once more. The suction was so great that the chopper shivered and shook from the strain. Finally there was a loud slurping sound as Onisk popped out with enough mud clinging to his body to build an adobe house.

Even in the Vietnam bush, there were moments when you'd suddenly be splitting your sides laughing.

On another one of those occasions, Carl Ohlson was out sloshing around with a unit on a search mission tasked with finding some buried VC weapons.

That day he had a couple of men from the South Vietnamese National Police working with him. It was hot, swampy and the men were dehydrating fast. At one point, one of the cops—they didn't speak English—came running back from the point signaling with his hands that he'd found something interesting. Ohlson looked up the track and saw a tiny opening in the jungle that led to an overgrown plantation. "There was fruit all over the place," he recalls. "Pineapples and mangoes, coconuts—everything."

Ohlson went back and made a deal with the machine-gunners to cover the two avenues of approach to the hidden Garden of Eden. "Then I pulled out my knife and yelled, 'FRUIT ORGY!' The police were swinging machetes, we were shoving mangoes down our throats, our uniforms were stained with little seeds, we were walking around, burping. And right at that moment, Hack flies over and asks for a sitrep.

"'Oh, yeah,' I said. 'Haven't found anything yet. Still looking.'

"Hack said, 'OK, keep up the good work,' and left.

"About an hour or so later everybody started developing the trots. We ran out of toilet paper, and I've got this platoon of eighteen people with the galloping runs and just then Hack turns up again telling us he has a new target and we gotta get out to an LZ. So I'm trying to stall: 'Hey, this trail's still hot, we think something is buried down here,' anything to delay. Oh man, it was funny."

Despite the mud and mangoes and eighteen cases of Ho Chi Minh's revenge, our ambush operations were tearing up the VC's infrastructure. Tom Aiken tells the way it was running long-range ambushes "out there at the sharp end of the stick" with Alert Company. "My Platoon Sergeant Toby Hager's SOP was to move a small recon team into an area just before dark to have a good look at possible ambush positions. If he thought the area would be worthwhile, we'd sneak back after dark and set up.

"On one operation in April, Toby, me, and another squad leader were reconnin' an ambush position," Aiken recalls. "Two VC came toolin' down the river. They parked their sampan no more than five yards from us. Toby whispered to the other squad leader, 'Take the one in back and I'll take the one in front.' Well, as soon as they pulled up, Toby rose up from the bush alongside the river and one of the VC saw him and said somethin', which was probably 'Oh shit.' Toby wasted him, but the other Squad Leader with us froze. I dropped the VC just as he was fixin' to cut down Toby. I blew him out of the boat.

"On another ambush, the CP alerted me that three sampans were comin' down the canal," Aiken says. "I woke the guys in my squad that were sleepin'.. By the time we were set, the sampans were right in the center of the Company kill zone. There were three VC in each sampan. On Captain Thomas's order, the whole company opened up. Eighty guys doing the mad minute just riddled them. I didn't fire. I figured one more rifle wasn't gonna matter, so I tossed two grenades into the canal. The next day, Captain Thomas came up and said I was the only one in the company who used grenades, and if we had missed any of them, those grenades would have gotten them in the water. But I don't see how eighty guys could miss three sampans, all lit up by a full moon. It was like shootin' fish in a barrel.

"One night we pulled off two ambushes, one right after the other. We were initially set up in an old VC bunker complex, when fifteen or twenty VC walked into us. We wasted eight of them and the rest took off. We slipped south a few hundred yards and a few hours later, six more walked into our ambush. We didn't fire one round—just popped our claymore mines. Six more VC bit the dust.

"We had a guy named Reggie Shell who was blind as a bat at high noon. Believe it or not, he carried an M-60 machine gun. I remember him walkin' up on a couple of gooks that weren't twenty-five yards from him. He let fifty rounds go in one long burst and never hit a damn one of them. They scattered like quail. I took the M-60 away from him and gave him a grenade launcher, you know, an area fire weapon. About two hours later, we'd crossed a canal and started movin' east along the side of the blue. Shell was the last man in line. He turned around and out of nowhere came a sampan with three VC. They had AKs and they were raisin' them up to fire at us. We was all lookin' straight ahead, but Shell, who was the last guy and responsible for watching the rear, saw 'em. He snapped off one M-79 round and it landed smack in the middle of that damn sampan, killin' all three of 'em. This was pure blind luck by a blind gunner, but he sure saved our sorry asses."

On another good night, Claymore Company air-assaulted deep behind the target, moved by stealth and set up an ambush. "We caught the VC moving out," Lieutenant Rex Fletcher recalls. "All three of our platoons were positioned on canals and trails, which we figured the VC would use. They didn't have a chance."

Claymore's 1st Platoon, led by Platoon Sergeant Richard Onisk of mud-bath fame, nailed seven VC during the same operation. He said, "We were spread out to cover both the canal and the trail close to it. One VC, apparently the point man, walked by our first element and shortly behind him was six more. One squad sprang the ambush on the six VC and another squad further upstream got the lone VC."

Sergeant James Bonshock, a Claymore Company acting Platoon Leader, set up with a small element along a canal when he heard a sampan putting toward his ambush position. "It was so close I tossed two grenades right into the sampan. I heard one rattle around on the craft's bottom before it exploded," he said. "The explosion killed two VC and sank the sampan—which was loaded with supplies."

"The success of our ambush operations was due to the improvement of our guys in quietly and quickly moving to and setting up our ambushes," says Platoon Sergeant Harry Hanson. "One of my squads let a VC walk right into their position and captured him before he knew what happened. Most of our ambushes were triggered no farther than twenty yards away."

"The Company's short-range-ambush concept gave our soldiers more confidence and also helped kick up morale," says Gordy DeRoos. "They got more rest, walked less in the rice paddies, but still tore Charley's ass. One soldier described the technique as being like bomber pilots. We quickly move to our targets, take 'em out and come home.' I agree. It's a smart way to fight the war. It made the men feel like they were part of an elite, specialized team with a doable mission, as opposed to just another outfit tromping through the boonies, losing buddies to mines."

Hanson, a savvy, hard-charging NCO, always looked out for his soldiers. "When I first took over the company, I had a long talk with Sergeant Hanson, who'd been in the unit for a long time," DeRoos recalls. " I learned right away that he didn't much trust anyone above Platoon level and that included me. He told me, 'I've seen too damned many eager-beaver missions that did nothing but tear my guys apart.' I knew he could help swing things around if he sensed I'd change the tactics and stop the tripping-through-the-minefields insanity. He was a natural leader who pretty much reflected the mood of the troops, so I knew if I could get him behind me the men would pick up on it and fall in line. It worked. It was a case of the old story: Get to know your people, listen to your noncoms and get them working with you."

Being out there with a squad was dangerous and scary business. "When we were setting up in any kind of ambush," Dagger Company's Tommy Pye remembers, "we'd normally have one man awake and two guys sleeping. I always moved about twelve feet away from the group and when it was time to wake me up, if you didn't call my name you didn't want to put your hands on me."

Battle Company's 2nd Platoon was spread out alongside a riverbank when

Carl Ohlson got word from his rear security element that three armed VC were following the Platoon. "I gave my machine-gunner a signal—three fingers extended toward him and then I made like I was slitting my throat with my hand, meaning there were three of them and to take 'em out," Ohlson said. "They were in black pajamas and had AK-47s and an RPG."

His gunner, an American Indian the guys called "Chief," was a dead shot. "My main, number one guy," Ohlson said. "Chief quickly set up and the VC walked right into our hasty ambush. All three were women. Chief fired, wounded one and missed the others."

Later, Ohlson asked the "Chief" how he could have missed from point-blank range. He replied, "I was upset because they were women. In my society women are held in high esteem. Women are earth, mother of man." "Chief" admitted to Ohlson he fired high. "I picked the wrong man for this ambush," Ohlson dryly noted.

Day and night, night and day, our ambushes were destroying the VC. During the magic month of April the VC lost initiative and the Hardcore grabbed the ball and ran with it.

Yet, over the long haul, even if the Army had adapted the Hardcore's tactics, we'd never win the war until the folks up at the top understood Bernard Fall's golden rule: *In revolutionary war, the people and the military must emerge on the same side.**

Nearly a quarter of a century later, when I met with former VC General Bao Cao in 1994, he said, "When I was Vice Commander of Military Region Eight, movement of our soldiers and supplies almost came to a stop in your sector because of the ambushes and your night helicopter attacks.

"Once in 1969, I escaped one of your ambushes by minutes," he went on. "I was moving by sampan, when local people warned me by beating paddle on the water. I was no more than 300 meters from the American ambush position when I turned around."

---

*Bernard Fall, *Street Without Joy* (Mechanicsburg, PA.: Stackpole Books, 1961), p. 375.

"General," I said. "That's the fate of war. We could have talked earlier under far different circumstances."

Bao smiled and nodded. "Yes, but in the south we continued without one airplane, one submarine or one warship and we beat you."

I couldn't fault his logic. With all our high-tech gear and superpower muscle, we were outdone by stouthearted, determined people wearing sandals made from discarded American tires, carrying AKs and outwitting us with paddles.

TWENTY

Fire Support Base Danger
28 APRIL 1969

Twenty-eight April started with a bang. We were busier than an Army Drill Sergeant on day one of basic training. At 0246 hours Tahler's Night Hunters painted eleven VC red and the fury continued nonstop for the next twenty-four hours.

Early that morning, four Hardcore Platoons air-assaulted into separate LZs behind a South Vietnamese Force made up of local Regional Force units. Our joint mission was to sweep and clear an area where intelligence indicated a VC buildup. The tactics called for the Hardcore Platoons to drop deep behind the enemy, then, using stealth, to infiltrate into ambush positions along Charley's probable escape routes. The Hardcore would act as the anvil, the South Vietnamese troops as the hammer, pounding the VC into our waiting ambushes.

The operation fell apart faster than a five-buck pair of shoes. The minute the VC fired on the South Vietnamese, they went to ground. For the rest of the day our so-called "hammer" hid behind rice paddy dikes waiting for dusk, and then scurried back home before dark to secure their village and the villas of their brass.

Which left the Hardcore elements without a mission, playing with themselves. Long before the South Vietnamese fucked the dog, we moved a Dagger Platoon by chopper from Danger to fill a critical hole along the anvil line. They immediately made contact. Dagger White Platoon leader Lieutenant Joe Formachelli reported that he'd locked onto "at least a company-size element."

Formachelli was super gung-ho, the kind of leader who didn't need a boot in the butt. You had to hold him by the back of the belt or he'd charge in where wise men fear to go. I told him to cool it, hold in place and put artillery and gunship fire on the enemy.

A few days earlier Formachelli's platoon had been moving through heavy brush about three miles north of Danger. "It was so thick you couldn't see three feet in front of you," Ed Clark recalls. " It reminded me of that kid's book *Br'er Rabbit in the Briar Patch.*"

Leading from up front as was his style, Formachelli was walking just behind his Tiger Scout when suddenly the VC blasted the point from low, damn near invisible bunkers. Formachelli, a giant of a man, charged through the brush, ripping vines apart as if they were tissue paper as he emptied his M-16 point-blank into the bunker firing ports. He killed at least one VC and drove off the others.

He had just tossed a grenade into a bunker aperture when an AK-47 round struck his helmet dead center, entering between the steel pot and the helmet liner. The round didn't touch him, but it knocked him down and split his steel pot as if an ax had hit it. "It was a clean shot that went from the front of his helmet to the back," Squad Leader David Wagner recalls. "Didn't even scratch him. It didn't surprise us. He was Superman and we all loved him."

"Joe got to his feet with a sheepish 'aw-shucks' grin on his face," Clark says. "He reminded me of a big ol' lovable teddy bear. He jumped up and he and his boys soon cleaned up the enemy positions. Joe's quick and bold action saved the life of his point man and perhaps others. But for the next coupla days, he complained about having a 'terrible headache.'"

"Lieutenant Formachelli became a changed guy after that head-shot thing," David Wagner says. "He was no longer the happy-go-lucky super-gung-ho guy anymore."

Clark disagrees. "Joe was still happy and gung-ho, he just got smarter. I had a little talk with him about how I needed live lieutenants to run my platoons and if he kept charging bunkers he'd get himself killed."

A few weeks later back at Danger in front of his Company, I had the pleasure of pinning a Silver Star on his massive chest. I even showed the gathered troops his ruptured pot. He was my kind of leader and I was proud of him, as were the men of Danger.*

But I needed a leader on the ground more experienced than Formachelli, whose enthusiasm might just get us into trouble, so Ed Clark choppered in along with his small CP group. With Clark on the ground, I figured if things got hotter I could reinforce him with two more of his Platoons on standby at Danger.

By 1550 hours, Clark and his boys were inadvertently right in the middle of a large VC force. Charley had probably been concentrating on the South Vietnamese Regional Force units to their front and not noticed Dagger slipping through the bush to their rear.

"The 2nd Platoon was awesome," Clark says. "It moved silently and professionally. We unknowingly slipped through a large VC force without detection. We didn't see them or they us."

Mergner and I got a LOH and flew out to make sure Clark was doing OK. Just as we got over him, his element again made contact.

"We'd been chasing and fighting the VC since early morning and I was worried that we were running low on ammo," Platoon Sergeant Kidd remembers. "I'd just asked Captain Clark to get us resupplied, when a new sergeant got into red ants. This guy stood up right in the middle of the firefight and started ripping his clothes off. One of the guys tackled him and several others held him down. That fool almost got himself killed. Believe me those red ants would just drive you to do such crazy things."

"The colonel's helicopter came down almost on top of the VC, at treetop level—approximately thirty or forty feet above the ground—duking it out," Kidd said. "I couldn't figure how they kept from shooting the chopper down, unless they were too busy laughing at the GI doing the striptease in the middle of the paddy, I know that's mostly what had our attention. We would shoot a couple rounds and then look back to see what clothes the Sergeant had left and if the two guys with him had managed to pull him to the ground. Then out of nowhere, Hack's bird showed up and we had our real-life 'Duel in the sun.'"

I'd seen a bunch of Charleys hightailing it away from Clark's forces. Carroll went into a tight circle and we spotted an entire platoon, all looking good in pith helmets, khaki uniforms, load-bearing equipment and toting AK-47s. One of the few times in Vietnam I ever saw so many enemy soldiers in the open. While I called for gunships and told Clark to try and move a force behind them, Carroll gave chase and they instantly scattered—all, that is, except one really brave dude.

Far from running, every time we made a pass this character would take up a perfect firing position and shoot at us with his AK-47. On one knee, foot pointed toward the target and elbow under his weapon, he didn't even flinch as our chopper barreled at him. A snapshot of this guy would have made a great NVA recruiting poster. He was totally determined to get us; we were equally determined to get him. When we made a pass, he'd fire a burst and I'd get off a couple of 40mm rounds. But no matter how close we came in, that VC just knelt there in his marksman-of-the-year position coolly firing his weapon at our chopper. It was some shooting match.

Finally, I got a close hit, which knocked him over, but after only a second he got up, squeezed off another burst and then hauled ass into the bush. He was one courageous soldier—probably the platoon leader—willing to take us on against near-impossible odds, buying time so the rest of his platoon could escape.

By the time the gunships arrived, the VC had disappeared. At the time I remember thinking, How can you beat such fighting spirit? One man against a war machine. In a small way, his stand symbolized the war: a small backward country taking on a superpower and winning because its people believed their cause was right and stubbornly refused to give up.

Mergner was sitting directly behind me. "You got as excited—in a happy way—as I had ever seen you," he says. "You were hooting and hollering over the radio—'It's like World War III up here'—and that guy was shooting back at us as rapidly as we were shooting at him. The green tracers from his AK would come straight for the LOH and flare out all around. While you were shooting I was thinking, One of those tracers could hit me square in the forehead."

When we got back to Danger we noticed a bullet hole in the LOH housing immediately below the main rotor. Don't know what kept it in the air. I'm sure we must have heard from Hayes on that later, particularly since in the middle of the shoot-out, Hayes called and asked if we were below one thousand feet. I told him no, cheating by eight or nine hundred feet.

During the same fly-around, we spotted a VC in a sampan heading in a hurry for a tree-lined canal bank and I yelled, "Get him!"

Mergner pulled his M-79 with zero confidence. "Seemed like any time I fired an M-79 from a helicopter, the round would go in the aimed direction and then sharply break in the direction the helicopter was moving," he says. "Physics! I got the shot off just as this guy's sampan hit the bank nose-first and he had started to scamper from the rear to the front of it. The round hit the sampan immediately behind him. Good-bye! Total luck."

On the ground, Clark knew he'd probably bitten off more than he could chew, but he also knew he had surprise on his side. His boys were making good, small contacts, killing two here and four there. The terrain, criss-crossed with canals and irrigation ditches, thick jungle with tall trees, vines and dense thickets, favored Clark's counterguerrillas.

Everything got very quiet. "We knew the VC were all around us," Clark remembers. He also knew the 2nd Platoon and his CP group, which totaled twenty-five men, were not up for a mano-a-mano with an enemy force four or five times their size.

A few hours earlier, Division had pulled out all of our choppers for a higher-priority mission. Reinforcing Clark with his two platoons sitting at Danger was no longer in the cards. According to Sun Tsu—"When the enemy is strong, retreat"—his only common-sense course of action was to get out of there.

"The tide had come in and we couldn't get across a big blue to our front," Sergeant Kidd recalls. "We sent out a four-man patrol to find a ford."

Only a minute or two after the patrol moved out, a VC force across the canal, firing from the foundation of a destroyed hooch no more than twenty meters away, ambushed the recon patrol. Point man Roger Lee Ward was immediately killed. The Hardcore soldier behind him, his slack man, Melvin Grayson Ehrhart, blasted M-16 rounds into the VC. Before Ehrhart could take cover, he was hit, falling into a ditch that fed into the main canal. The good news was the ditch provided good cover from small-arms fire; the bad news was there was no way to get to him without taking more casualties.

"As soon as the patrol got hit the fighting became close," Sergeant Kidd says. "The enemy was suddenly all around the Platoon. They had us good. The recon patrol had moved out about forty yards when they opened up on them, and at first all the fire was directed there—as if Charley figured that this was our whole unit and not just four men. It took him a while to wake up and get to our position, especially with the suppressing fire we were putting out on the burnt-out hooch."

After setting up a tight perimeter, Clark had FO Lieutenant William Kilpatrick pommel the enemy position, laying down a wall of artillery fire around his element. Then he led another patrol around to the enemy's flank, attacking with LAW rounds and small-arms fire. "We got their attention fast," Clark says. "They must have thought we had them surrounded rather than vice versa."

When the enemy's attention was diverted, Walter Lee Nutt III, the platoon medic, a new Doc who'd been with the platoon for only a few days, rushed forward under heavy fire to patch up the wounded. Clark and three riflemen tried to lay down covering fire, but the enemy had more guns. As soon as Nutt dove into the ditch, Clark spotted four more VC, one carrying an RPG and two carrying a wounded soldier. But before he and his guys could take them under fire, they disappeared behind a hedgerow wall paralleling the canal on the other bank.

A minute later, Clark heard gunfire and then an RPG fired in the direction where Nutt was working on Ehrhart. Nutt and Ehrhart were instantly killed.*

Sergeant Bill Vandermay, whose squad had rear security, heard the shooting up at the front of the column. "We got down and took up firing positions and kept our eyes peeled on the trail," he recalls. "Three VC walked right into us. We shot them and that started a hell of a firefight. We were firing our weapons and tossing grenades in our own little war separate from the platoon."

As the firefight raged, Sergeant Kidd sent word to Vandermay that he'd have the main body lay down covering fire and to rejoin the platoon with his

*Walter Nutt, a deeply religious conscientious objector who refused to carry a weapon, was found dead next to Ehrhart with his bandages and scissors still in his hands. He was posthumously awarded the Distinguished Service Cross. Years later, Nutt's father, a combat doctor in World War II, sent Clark a letter describing how his wife woke on 27 April 1969—it was 28 April in Vietnam—with a sharp pain in her neck, shaking from a vision that she'd been shot.

"Dr. Nutt examined her and didn't find a bruise," Clark said. "As the day wore on she became very weak and had a burning desire 'to depart and to be with Christ.' While resting she told of seeing the hands of the savior outstretched toward her through the open heavens. As she reached out her hands to him to be received, the vision retreated. She then saw that she was holding Walter's head in her arms and there was blood on it. Three days later the Nutts returned home to find an Army officer in their driveway. The officer informed them that Walter had died from a bullet in the neck."

Squad ASAP. Kidd wanted maximum people in his main perimeter and no sideshow firefights to worry about. "Vandermay had the other M-60," Kidd says. "Ours was jammed. We were working frantically to fix it and we needed his people and that gun."

About the same time, Clark hit the VC from the sky. Vandermay directed four air strikes. "The bombs were dropping real close," he remembers. "The shrapnel was just singing through the trees and the bombs were dropping right where the enemy fire was coming from. One of our guy's eyes glazed over and he went into shock. He was worthless from then on."

Clark got on the radio to the TOC. "Send me my platoons and a resupply of ammo."

But Mergner couldn't get any choppers to lift Dagger's two reaction platoons—the 9th Division birds were still tied up. Finally, Mergner fast-talked two U.S. Navy Seawolf gunships to come to Clark's assistance. They got on station in record time, darting in and out of friendly artillery fire and air strikes, putting effective rocket and machine-gun fire on the enemy.

"Stingray 26 arrived exactly at the most critical moment of the fight and saved the day because our asses were really hanging out there," Clark says. "Dusk was setting in, and the battlefield was still a roar of gunfire, grenades and artillery explosions. Bright flashes lit the jungle and gun smoke hung low to the earth. Just when we thought the VC were going to assault, they broke off. Perhaps it was the air strikes and artillery and the gunships combined. Whatever it was, we were damn glad they broke off. Next, I shifted the artillery to their likely avenues of escape and brought in the Navy Huey gunships to work the area in close to us with machine-gun fire."

"Then it was quiet," says Kidd, "except for the artillery shells crunching in and the thump, thump, thump of the Navy birds flying over us."

"We had to slip out of there just like we slipped in—with maximum stealth," Clark adds.

Fortunately, Clark and the men of Dagger had been operating throughout that area for weeks. So Clark was able to war-game the best way to Route 4, where they could be picked up. But there was no way the going would be easy. They had four dead—Denny Lynn Asher, Melvin Grayson Ehrhart, Walter Lee Nutt III and Roger Lee Ward—who would be difficult to pack through the jungle while evading the enemy.

Trees forty to seventy feet high surrounded the battle area, leaving just enough room to bring in a single Huey helicopter—if it came straight down and left straight up. One of the Navy gunship pilots told Clark he'd give it a try. Down he came in near darkness, clipping small limbs with his rotor blades, VC bullets snapping around him. As soon as he landed, he off-loaded his door gunners, machine guns and ammo, then lifted out Clark's seriously wounded. On the second trip, he took Dagger's extra gear and the dead. On his third extraordinary landing, he dropped off ammo and water Takahashi had thrown on at Danger, recovered his crew and weapons, lifted off and rejoined the second Navy gunship, whose crew had been putting down suppressive fire throughout this incredibly difficult feat of flying.*

"Had the Navy not taken out our dead, which really tied us down, I'd have had to opt for waiting it out till light," Clark says. "I already knew where I'd go—north behind the VC and into a thicket. They wouldn't have expected that."

Thirty-two years later, Clark still refights that battle. "If only we'd gone behind the hedgerow rather than take the easier path alongside the canal, I know we'd have gotten the enemy first and four good men who were killed in that encounter would've lived," he says.

Only those who've walked that walk of life and death can understand a soldier's "If I'd only" replays of events. How "had we just gone to the left" or "if I'd only waited and softened the objective with more supporting fire"

---

*Clark and the men of the 2nd Platoon recommended the pilots and crew of "Stingray 26"— the Navy chopper that landed and saved them—for awards for heroism. Theirs was an incredible series of acts of extraordinary bravery. Imagine how those two sailors must have felt down on the ground with the grunts, surrounded by the VC, watching their bird fly away.

haunt the brain.

Clark and his Hardcore soldiers warily picked their way through the black night to the rendezvous point on Route 4. Just as the platoon was fording the last blue before reaching the highway, a short soldier named Wren lost his footing and disappeared under the brown, mucky water. Sergeant David Wagner was just behind him in the column and saw him go under.

"I ripped off my LBE and gave it and my rifle to the fellow behind me," Wagner said. "I dove and went to the bottom, but I couldn't find him. I swam a bit downstream and there he was on the bottom weighed down by all his equipment and ammo. I grabbed him and got him up just in the nick of time. Another few seconds and he'd 'a been a goner." Sergeant Wagner was later awarded the Soldier's Medal for his bravery.

Clark and his brave and bone-tired warriors closed Danger at 2030 hours and filled in their foxholes around the firebase's perimeter. On that single day, the Hardcore team killed fifty-five enemy soldiers while taking four dead and four wounded. The price was not worth the gain. As far as I was concerned—in spite of the 14 to 1 ratio—the enemy had won the round. I was heartbroken.

TWENTY-ONE

Dong Tam
2 MAY 1969

A snakebit day. First, the choppers scheduled to insert Tahler's Snipers were canceled. "No birds available," Division claimed. Then I got a call from Major Galbus at Division Headquarters:

"Colonel Hunt wants to see you ASAP."

I would rather have filled my fart sack with rattlesnakes and crawled in barefoot than to have spent five more minutes with that sonofabitch.

"Can't come," I replied. "No chopper."

"No problem," Galbus shot back. "Colonel Hunt's sending his. It'll be there in three zero. The meeting's important."

I flew to Division in Hunt's spiffed-up bird, pondering why if we couldn't get a Huey to insert our Snipers, one could suddenly materialize to chauffeur me to this rendezvous.

When I reported to the Prince of Darkness in his spacious, spit-shined office, he fawned over me like a Lockheed lobbyist schmoozing the Secretary of Defense. Hard to believe this was the same guy I'd threatened to kill only two months before. He was all "Hack" this and "Hack" that and "Would you like something cold to drink?"

Just warm, gracious Hunt and paranoid me—there were no witnesses.

He jawed about how we'd had some tense moments in the past but that was to be expected under the stress of combat between two strong warriors.

I had to stop myself from asking whom he was talking about, since it couldn't have been himself. He said the past was the past, he wanted to tidy up last-minute projects prior to shipping home at the end of the month and just needed to "confirm a few details" with me.

Then came the sucker punch. He passed me a thick draft document titled "The Battle of Thanh Phu."

"Here's the Division's report on our 11 and 12 March fight," he said.

That nightmare fuckup immediately jumped front and center in my brain: My guys dead center of a shooting gallery full of friendly fire. Our own choppers, directed by Hunt, pouring fire and steel into Alert and Claymore Companies.

I flipped through the pages. Slick, well-written copy. Charts. Sketch maps. Time lines. Spot reports. The mother of all glory reports. A breathless description of a perfect combat action. All of it even phonier than Hunt himself.

He had, of course, sponsored the puff piece. Here's a sample, Hunt's teaser for the main attraction:

It was determined that an enemy battalion had been encircled and had been almost annihilated. This story has been carefully recounted by Prisoner of War Phan Xuan Quy, Headquarters Secretary (Battalion Adjutant) of the 261B Main Force Battalion, Dong Thap I Regiment of Military Region II. The account of the 9th Division participation in the battle has also been described by Colonel Ira A. Hunt Jr., Commanding Officer of the 1st Brigade. The parallelism between the two accounts is striking—time of insertions, weapons locations, bunkers, troop maneuvers—all relating very closely. The only major difference is in the box score. When the U.S. statistics are compared to the VC claims, glaring inconsistencies are noted. These, too, tell a story: the conservatism of the U.S. forces versus the exaggerations of the Communists. In the pages that follow, the prisoner of war's story, the 9th Infantry Division's depiction and the lessons learned from the operation are provided. It is believed that the Free World Forces can learn much from the analysis of the Battle of Thanh Phu.

BOX SCORE — BATTLE OF THANH PHU

Combat Statistics	Reported by U.S.		Reported by VC	
	U.S.	VC	U.S.	VC
Forces in Contact	630	150-200	1500	298
Helicopter Insertions	101	NA	84	NA
Killed in Action	3	72	150	203
Wounded in Action	20	--	--	--
Weapons Lost	0	7	--	UNK
Aircraft Lost	1	NA	3	NA

The reference to Lieutenant Phan Xuan Quy, the VC POW who practically co-wrote Hunt's report, gave the game away. Around Division Headquarters, this fink was known as Super P. for good reason. Several weeks after Hunt's "battle," the 7th ARVN Division had captured Lieutenant Quy. When Hunt heard about the prisoner, he quietly arranged to have Quy turned over to him for "interrogation."

According to Captain Hugh Atwell, the 9th Division Stockade officer in charge of the POWs, neither he nor his boss, Lieutenant Colonel Phillip Ash, the Division Provost Marshal, ever saw Quy. Atwell says, "Super P. was never on my books, but there were rumors of his existence. He was never logged in as required by international law."

A 9th Division staff officer explains this special arrangement. "Quy was not handled as a POW, but as a VIP. He was treated better than anyone in the headquarters except for Hunt himself and General Ewell. Quy sat around Hunt's office eating Hunt's special ice cream and being treated like Westmoreland's kid brother."

When the Lieutenant Colonel told me this story I wondered if they shared the same bowl along with Hunt's passion for ice cream. As Hunt told Hayes when John was understudying him, "I don't know how I'd get through this war without ice cream."

"Super P."—who said he was the adjutant or S-1 of the 261B Battalion—must have thought he was in Viet Cong Heaven. Instead of being hunted, he was living in the lap of luxury. Pumping up the report sure beat cooling his heels in an ARVN POW camp waiting to be tortured and—if he didn't cooperate—possibly shot. He probably would have signed a statement that Ho Chi Minh's mother was a Wall Street Capitalist Pig if Hunt had suggested it.

A former 9th Division senior staff officer observed, "Super P.'s perspective is no doubt the result of early recognition on his part that life would become mighty comfortable if he gave the Colonel the testimony he needed to bolster his account."

That was POW Quy's purpose in Hunt's grand scheme—to testify that the report was dead on target. And the good life around the 9th Division flagpole must have inspired Quy to jack up the body count yet again. The latest figure was 203 KIA out of his 300-man battalion. Remember, forty VC were initially reported killed in the fight even though we found barely half that number on the battlefield—but by the end of the battle Hunt had pumped the number up to fifty-seven. Then it inexplicably rose to seventy-two and now, according to Super P., it had skyrocketed to an awesome 203—even though only seven weapons were reported captured.

Super P.—who validated so many of Hunt's claims and whose own account made the report in Hunt's words, "an historical document of some significance, because the opportunity did not arise too often for such an exercise"—was more than eager to help Hunt fiddle the books. Amazing what a little ice cream can do for a fellow's imagination and ability to add, especially with a little help from Hunt's infamous body count formula: 2 + 2 = 20.

Nothing in Hunt's report adds up. What, for example, happened to all the enemy bodies? Using the "seventy-two enemy soldiers killed" figure and the time-tested three-wounded-to-one-dead rule, the estimated 300-man 261B Battalion would have had twelve effectives left. Each VC soldier would have had to haul ass somehow toting at least twenty-four dead or wounded comrades' bodies along with their twenty-four individual weapons!

Even applying Quy's 203 figure—which ended up in Hunt's "I-Am-the-Biggest-Cong-Killer-in-Vietnam" Report—would mean eighty-eight wounded survivors would each have been humping at least two dead comrades plus all their weapons. And remember, this Herculean task would have been accomplished while moving on swampy terrain with two reinforced U.S. battalions firing everything but atomic weapons as they ran a gauntlet of fire.

Such an obviously false report could never have been submitted in any other division in Vietnam. But in this unique situation, Hunt, the then acting Brigade CO, wore two hats: he was also the Division Chief of Staff. Lord of all he surveyed, he could write the report as CO, approve it later as Chief of Staff—and not one of his cowed subordinates would dare challenge its truth.

Nor would the previous CG, General Ewell, over whom Hunt seemed to have Rasputin-like power. It was not uncommon for Hunt to ridicule, demean and chew out the two brigadier general assistant division commanders in front of Ewell and his staff and actually get away with it. According to eyewitness division staff officers, Ewell never said a word when such incidents occurred, he just let his boy Hunt tear general officer ass. It was almost as though Hunt had something on Ewell.

Brigadier General James S. Timothy, a former 9th ADC and a frequent recipient of Hunt's lashings, told me, "In thirty-five years of service, I never saw a more unusual command setup. Imagine a colonel chewing out a general."

Lieutenant Colonel John Milani, who was on the Division staff, offers this explanation for the bizarre arrangement: "Ewell always let Hunt be the bad guy. His personality didn't allow him to chew out people. He always let someone else do his dirty work. He would talk to someone in glowing terms about how he was hand-picked to be in the Division and when the interview was over and the officer had left, Ewell would bend his wrist effeminately. 'Get rid of that guy,' he'd say."

Hunt, on the other hand, told Milani, "I owe Ewell for everything I have and I'm not going to stop riding that horse until I make general."

This tracks. A 9th Division staff officer calls Hunt "obsessively ambitious," his style was "intimidation and belittlement" and confirms that he had an "unexplainable rare and close relationship with the CG."

I didn't exactly make Hunt's day when I told him I'd never before seen such an elaborate snow job—and that he'd better believe I'd seen more than my share of phony after-action reports.

Hunt blew off my insult, then tried to sweeten the pot. He said the Hardcore, now the Division's best Infantry Battalion, deserved consideration for a recommendation for the Valorous Unit Citation for the 23 and 24 March fight and also for its incredible battlefield performance during the months of March and April.

If I endorsed this fake report, he suggested, my Battalion of brave warriors had an excellent chance of receiving this coveted and distinguished award. But Hunt was turning honest credit honestly earned into his own private extortion scheme. So much as I wanted my men to get the credit that was due them, I told him he could stick the report and the Valorous Unit Citation up his fat ass.

Hunt's face flushed red, veins popping out like purple ropes.

"I'll get you, Hackworth," he hissed. "You're dismissed."

I was not the only guy Hunt tried to suck in. Bill Hauser, the artillery commander during the fight, had the same request laid on him. And also refused. About the same time a clerk from Division Awards and Decorations walked into Jim Musselman's office and informed him, "I'm here to assist you to write a DSC for Colonel Hunt." Musselman threw him out on his ear. Colonels Hayes and Sullivan both, according to a 1971 Department of the Army Inspector General's report, were asked to sign off on a recommendation for an award for heroism for this action as well. Both refused.

Even Ewell could be skeptical of Hunt at times. One day at Division Headquarters when Hunt wasn't around, Ewell called an officer who witnessed the fight aside to talk to him. "Colonel," he said, "Hunt's exec has put him in for the Distinguished Service Cross. What do you think of that?"

"Sir," he answered, "you're putting me on the spot."

"That's my intention, Colonel. Answer the question."

"Well, Sir," he said, "I don't think Colonel Hunt's actions during the battle warrant a valor of that magnitude."

"What magnitude do you think they warrant?"

And he said, "Well, actually, none."

And Ewell said, "I thought so, too. That's how I feel about it."

But there were no further ramifications for Hunt—and he did get even. No Valorous Unit Citation recommendation was ever submitted for the Hardcore Battalion.*

Once I told Hunt to piss off, he tried to get still other officers who fought at Thanh Phu, both on the ground and in the air, to endorse his overblown version of what went down, but as with his grab for the DSC, Mr. Popularity couldn't find a taker. Captain Sherman Williford, who retired as a brigadier general, and whose rifle company was knee deep in some of the heaviest fighting at Thanh Phu, was also summoned to Hunt's office. "I was asked to

---

*Although I didn't know it at the time, John Hayes recommended the Medal of Honor for my actions on 25 March 1969, which was somehow buried at 9th Division headquarters when it was merged with a DSC I received for the action on 23 March. Mergers are against regulations, which specify that valor awards are given for a specific heroic action, not a series of actions over several days like a meritorious award. The MOH recommendation still sits under a big rock at Department of the Army in somebody's let's-hope-this-goes-away Inbox.

read over and sign a witness statement describing Colonel Hunt's great feats of combat leadership, exposure to danger and bravery. I refused to sign."

Another potential witness to the great "victory," Captain Gordon DeRoos, was flown in from a combat operation in the field, given the VIP treatment, shown the report and "asked" to "sign off." Gordy told Hunt, "I was just a captain in the battle. A small bit player who never got the big picture. Sorry, I can't help you." Good old silver-tongued Gordy.

The whole sorry episode says it all about the accuracy of official reports signed by general officers during the Vietnam War. And remember, the White House and Pentagon made national security decisions such as reinforcing or withdrawing from the war based on the veracity of these very reports.

A former 9th Division officer writes that the "Thanh Phu after-action report was all about enhancing Colonel Hunt's file. It had nothing to do with reality."

But the U. S. Army, not unlike the Catholic church when dealing with a wayward priest, couldn't admit that one of its senior officers was a liar—that like so many other great U.S. "victories" in Vietnam, from Hamburger Hill to Ripcord, the Battle of Thanh Phu was as make-believe as a paper moon. But at least the Army Inspector General who investigated the battle had the guts to write concerning the report that "the account of the Battle of Thanh Phu [My Phouc Tay], while perhaps not entirely accurate, cannot be considered a false report," which may sound mild but considering the Army's Honor System, is close to an accusation.

At least I didn't have to hitchhike home that day. Major Galbus was waiting outside. He escorted me to Hunt's chopper and flew me back to Danger.

TWENTY-TWO

Cai Be
06 MAY 1969

"Hardcore 6, I have some big news for you. Recommend you fly in so we can powwow."

Ed Clark was radioing from out in bandit country. Dagger 6 was so revved up, he sounded like he'd captured Ho Chi Minh himself. Clark and the men of Dagger were executing a mission in a patch of bush nine miles west of Cai Be. The first day, the trip had been uneventful. Then things got real interesting. As Clark puts it, "What started as a sneak-and-peak guerrilla-type operation ended up as a bang-and-bomb job."

Since early April, Battle Company, Division LRRPs, our Snipers and recon aircraft working this particular area had all been reporting VC activity. Clark's mission was to ID the VC unit operating there and get some hard evidence on what we were up against—documents or a POW.

A few weeks earlier, Battle Company had checked out the same turf and found a lot of abandoned VC structures—base camps, defensive bunkers, a large mess hall capable of feeding several VC companies—a fair amount of supplies and, of course, booby traps and Punji stakes galore.

Craig Tessau, Battle Company skipper at that time, says, "The place hadn't been used for several months, but someone was keeping it in good shape." Before Battle pulled out they blew up most of the installations. "All the time we were in there, we had that eerie hair-standing-straight-upon-the-back-of-your-neck feeling that someone was watching us."

Now Dagger Company had slipped back in to follow through. Once Clark set up a base and ran out patrols, he made immediate contact with three VC and dropped one. The newly deceased was from a Main Force unit—steel helmet, green uniform with red scarf, boots, new AK-47 and pack. Platoon leader Mike Kidd, the patrol leader, described him as "one squared-away dude."

Clark, who could smell trouble ten rice paddies away, formed a defensive perimeter and put his boys on 100 percent alert. Within an hour, the VC attacked his position in broad daylight and three more Charleys bit the dust. For the next six hours, the men of Dagger had their hands full.

He called in Tac Air and gunships, and the howitzers from Danger rained down shells. By the time the smoke cleared at 2150 hours, twenty VC were stretched out dead in front of their positions. It had been a lopsided victory with no U.S. casualties until a Tiger Scout tripped a booby trap, killing himself and wounding Sergeant David Roy Schaefer, who died on the chopper medevacking him to Danger.

While Clark and his guys banged away, Tahler deployed all of his Sniper Teams to the west of Dagger's operation, hoping Dagger's activity might cause Charley to move into his killing zone. In short order, "John Wayne" and "Red Baron" each zapped a VC as they were hauling desperate ass to get away from the warriors of Dagger. As darkness fell, Tahler concentrated his Night Hunter operations in support of Clark and nailed fourteen more.

Since the contacts and medevac had already blown Dagger's cover, we re-supplied the company with ammo and rations by chopper and they moved to a previously reconned night position after topping off. At midnight Dagger had finished setting up and was in position. "I knew the VC were there in strength," Clark said. "We stayed on 100 percent the whole night."

Dagger had been down this dangerous road many times. Its hardened veterans knew that when you twist a tiger's tail in his own lair, you'd better stay alert and expect trouble.

Just before daylight the company shifted to yet another position and formed a tight perimeter. At dawn, Clark put the company on 25 percent alert so the men could get some rest and sent out recon patrols under Lieutenants David Crittenden and Pat Hughes.

"Snoop around," Clark told them. "But don't get engaged unless you have a clear target of opportunity. I don't want you in a big fight."

Just as Crittenden's boys were about to move back to the patrol base, they hit pay dirt, ambushing two sampans with several VC in each. "We zeroed out the first sampan, but a couple guys jumped out of the second sampan and hightailed it into the bush," Crittenden recalls. "Three or four of my guys and me went after them. We went across the canal and almost chased them into what we found out later was a VC regimental headquarters."

Crittenden zapped them. And then he found the mother lode that made Clark get on the radio and call me: a pile of documents including tactical plans from the body of what Crittenden believed was a regimental XO. Whatever they were, the VC didn't want to let them go.

"Things were pretty hairy for a while," he remembers. "We had to fight our way back to the platoon."

By the time I could scratch up a LOH, it was completely dark. Mergner opposed my going because he figured the risk of flying in there didn't outweigh the gain—and as he pointed out, there wasn't much we could do with our "breaking news" until first light.

I allowed his careful nature to win over my impulsive side—which probably saved my life and Ken Carroll's. Just about the time we would've landed, the VC hit Dagger with a barrage of RPG and mortar fire followed by an infantry assault. In the skirmish, Dagger took six wounded and killed eight VC.

When we found out, Carroll was the spirit of happiness and I wasn't too sorry I'd stayed home either. Mergner didn't say anything to rub it in. He didn't have to—no one could miss that I-told-you-so look."

Dagger stayed in contact on again, off again throughout the night. "The VC were thicker than fleas on a wild dog, probing the company from every direction," Sergeant Rich Polak recalls. Tahler's Night Hunter operation racked up an additional nine VC. His Snipers also added six more VC scalps to their belts.

At first light, Dagger got another shower of RPG fire, which wounded six soldiers. By the time I flew in, yet another six men had been taken out by RPG fire and evacuated to Danger. "My Tiger Scout checked out the captured documents," Clark told me. "He says the VC are planning a big attack."

"That might just explain why these little shits have been giving you such a hard time," I said. "You might be stumping around their assembly area and fucking everything up."

"We've got 'em," Clark said, his voice resolute. "I know this ground. Give me two more days and another platoon and we'll send 'em back to Hanoi DOA."

"Settle down. Right now all the advantages are the enemy's. He knows you're here, so you've lost your major weapon, surprise. He's well dug in and you're hunting him out in the open. Sure you killed eighty-eight gooks—counting supporting element kills from artillery, gunships, Tac Air and Tahler's boys. But you've lost twenty-one soldiers, one U.S. KIA—David Schaefer—one Tiger Scout KIA and nineteen U.S. WIA. It's time to go back to the barn and dry out."

"Let us stay here," Clark pleaded. "Hell, no one knows the terrain out here better than my boys. If you give us just two more days, I'll give you another 24 March win."

Clark had the 101st Airborne Division Hamburger Hill fever. He thought if he just kept attacking he'd win.

"You're getting out of here in the morning," I said. "And I want you to just sit tight until then. Only run out local patrols. Have your artillery guy get with Allison and work out a fire plan—artillery and Tac Air—and blister the shit out of the area where the VC base camps are."

Clark, a true warrior and one stubborn hombre, didn't want to back off. But after methodically recapping why he should be allowed to stay and getting turned down, he replied, "Wilco, Sir." Disappointment was written all over his face.

"Look," I said, "go back to Danger and rest and refit. John Hayes will have his people look over these documents and figure out what the VC are up to. I promise you, Dagger will be right in the center of the action when we come back, which will be when we're ready, on our terms and at the time of our choosing."

"Roger that," Clark said.

"Charley doesn't defend dirt unless he's up to something," I said, thinking out loud. "My bet is he's probably guarding a cache he's squirreled in here for a little party down the road. Or he just wants to suck us in and make us bleed. Remember, this war isn't about ground. The French held both Hanoi and Saigon, and still lost the war."

Ground, of course, was a big deal in all of America's previous wars, but in Vietnam—where there weren't any Romes, Berlins or Tokyos to capture—it never meant shit. How I wished our generals, who believed that after the fight if they held the ground, they'd won, could get it through their heads that the enemy's objective was to make us bleed. Giap knew that our men's blood pouring out of the tube every night back home would eventually kill support for the war—that was how he planned to win.

I flew to Brigade, gave John Hayes the documents, and told him about the Tiger Scout's warning. Hayes said he was glad I'd hand-carried them. If they'd come in routinely, by the time they were translated they might not've done us much good. I flashed on Tet 68—when all that unread intell telling us in advance that a big VC offensive was coming down sat in the spooks' In boxes, but no one looked at it until after the enemy attacked.

Clark returned to Danger without further enemy contact and his soldiers settled in for a well-deserved rest as firebase security. And after our little venture, I hung a do-not-disturb sign on that area.

On 11 May, Carroll, Allison and I flew back there to pop in some artillery rounds as cover while I scoped things out. Ken and I were like Frank and Jesse James. Just a few weeks earlier, as we flew to Moore, Carroll was powering along on the deck, zipping down the canals, having good fun in his flying machine, when he spotted three VC bopping along a trail. He dropped down on them like an eagle going after salmon. The result: three VC KIA. We lifted off and flew for about five minutes when Gordy De Roos, who was sitting in the back, spotted a sampan hidden under some bush at the edge of a canal. We again dropped with Gordy's M-16 and my M-79 barking—and there was one more VC KIA with the recently departed enemy's sampan now sitting at the bottom of the canal. By the time we landed at the Brigade pad, we'd sunk two more VC sampans.

When the Hardcore TOC proudly reported the contacts to the Brigade TOC—"All kills made by Hardcore 6's chopper"—John Hayes went ballistic. He rang Mergner at the Battalion TOC:

"I told you to keep him at Danger!"

"How do you expect me to control him?" Mergner shot back.

Besides, how could Hayes keep me at Danger when he wanted me to attend a target meeting at his headquarters at Moore? The trip from Danger to Moore traversed Indian country and by my way of thinking, it was a waste of "blade time" not to do a little search and destroy along the way. I took every opportunity when flying over the battlefield to do a little hunting, especially with Carroll.*

Once we finished our recon, we dropped Allison back at Danger and since we still had thirty more minutes of light and no one at Brigade screaming for the bird, Carroll and I decided to check out the battlefield. We made our SOP run around the outer barbwire of Danger and continued to make overlapping concentric circles away from the base until we hit the main canal that ran north of Danger. Next we zipped up the canal, skimming at treetop level over the water.

Carroll saw the sampan first. "Two armed gooks at twelve o'clock," he snapped. I could hear the note of glee in his voice as he slipped the bird to the right so I could get an M-79 shot out of my left door.

BAM. And before I could break open the weapon to reload, Carroll handed me a fresh round. I whacked it in as he turned the bird in a tight arc. When we came back over the sampan, it was sinking and a well-ventilated VC soldier floated in a spreading circle of red water, looking mighty dead.

"Where's the other guy?" I asked, but before Carroll could reply I saw a muzzle flash behind a bush at the edge of the canal and simultaneously, as I heard thudding sounds coming from the chopper's belly, I felt a sharp blow to my left leg. While Carroll maneuvered I snapped off a round at where I'd seen the muzzle flash, plastering the area with a half dozen more 40mm rounds as Carroll made another tight circle. Blood spurted out of my leg from what looked like the exact spot where I'd been hit before.

Shit, what if it went in the same hole? I thought.

---

*Carroll received six Distinguished Flying Crosses during his one-year tour with the 1st Brigade for above-and-beyond stuff such as when he flew into a hot LZ to pick up two wounded Hardcore troopers after Dust-Off choppers passed because of too much incoming enemy fire. Or when he landed, almost out of fuel, on a small naval patrol boat and scooped up a seriously wounded soldier. As he put it, "the critical mission took priority over my 'yellow light,'" indicating he was running on empty. Or when he flew through fierce enemy fire to sink a large sampan carrying VC soldiers and a load of ammo. Or when he used his chopper to block a squad of enemy soldiers from bugging out of a bunker until gunships could zap them. After the bunker was destroyed, he landed and policed up their weapons.

When we came back over the area I'd whacked, I saw the gook stretched out behind a nipa palm bush. He looked dead, but just to make sure, I cut the sonofabitch in half with another round.

Carroll quickly checked out the bird. "Nothing wrong 'cept a few holes in the floor," he softly said in his Missouri accent. "You want me to land and police up that AK?"

"Let's make it back to Danger."

"Wilco, you want me to report the two kills?"

"Nope. No sense giving the prosecution the evidence to ground us—we'll stick 'em in the count during the next Hardcore firefight."

"Roger, Sir."

When we landed at Danger, before I unassed I had a look at the damage to the bird—three neat holes right under my seat. "Tell your mechanics to fix these on the sly and keep their traps shut. If John Hayes hears about this, our ass is grass and he's gonna defoliate us. Got it?"

I limped over to the aid station and since I was still a gimp from wound number seven, anyone looking on was none the wiser.

Wintzer was on duty. "Charlie, check this out for me, will you? And keep in mind I'm not going to be evacuated."

Charlie looked at my leg. The slug had punctured the big muscle at the back of my left calf just behind where I'd been previously hit. The entry wound was no bigger than the circumference of a wooden pencil.

"Could be a bullet or a piece of metal from the chopper floor," Charlie said.

He fished around with forceps trying to find the slug but just couldn't clamp onto it.

"Charlie, you can root around until that sucker starts hurting. If you can't get it out by then, forget it."

When the pain came, Wintzer stopped digging, put a wick in the wound so it would drain, shot me up with penicillin and bandaged me up.

I swore Charlie to secrecy and decided the slug would stay. I'd seen enough men do a good day's work with a lot more scrap metal in them than that little sucker. Thirty-three years later, it's still in my leg, the size of an M&M—and it frequently sets off finely tuned alarms at airports. From a recent Xray, it looks like half of an AK-47 round.

That might have been the end of it except that even though Mergner warned me not to have the Doc sign off on the paperwork, I really wanted that Purple Heart. To me it was the only award still not commonly abused.

Mergner was certain it would set off alarm bells. "All Battalion commanders' wounds are reported to Abrams."

"Relax, George, would you? Hundreds of guys get hit in Vietnam every day. My paperwork's gonna get buried in the bureaucracy."

The next morning John Hayes flew into Danger. "Hack, you want the good news or the bad news first?" he asked with his usual great smile.

"Let's wash the bad news down with the good."

"I know you got yourself shot up again and poked a bunch of holes in one of my dearly beloved birds. You OK?"

"I'm fine, just a little scratch. Your bird was hardly dented. What would you do if you saw two VC right out in the open just begging to be zapped?"

"I'm in the U.S. Army, Hack, so I'd follow my Brigade Commander's standing orders. You know, that little ole rule about you staying at a thousand feet and no more hunting trips. Abe's heard the news too. I hear he's more than a little pissed at you, and General Hollis thinks you're nuts. No small thanks to your pal Ira Hunt for that impression, I'm sure. You can bet your boots you made his day."

"What's the good news, boss?" I cut him off, hoping to change the subject. I was not at all happy that Abe (General Creighton Abrams, COMUSMACV) had gotten the word about Purple Heart number eight.

"The documents Crittenden scooped up are hot," Hayes said. "It was an order from the Dong Thap 1 Regiment. The VC are planning a two-battalion attack on Giao Duc District Headquarters and Fire Support Base Danger. Your old adversary the 261A is fixing to hit Danger."

This was the battalion we destroyed just two months before—and now they were rebuilt and ready to go for a little payback. The VC were amazing—they could rebuild faster than an ant colony.

"Do we know when?" I asked.

"No, but I'd say soon."

"Reckon Ed Clark spoiled their neat little plan," I said. "Dagger killed a bunch, destroyed a lot of heavy weapons and ammo. Charley will need to get his shit lined up again before he attacks."

"I agree. The Hardcore's made them lose a lot of face. Hurting you and ripping up a District Headquarters right under your nose will even the score and tell the people they're still the baddest asses in the valley."

We decided the VC would need time to recover from Dagger's recent damage. In the meantime, we'd keep a sharp eye on the VC base area we'd uncovered and buy a little more time by beefing up District Headquarters with a U.S. rifle platoon, a section of M-41 Dusters which had twin 40mm guns and Tahler's Snipers along with a Pink Filter night vision device. We figured once Charley saw this reinforcement, he'd go back to the drawing boards.

"I'll have Don Meyer concentrate Claymore's ambushes along the most likely avenues of approach into District Headquarters and Danger and at the VC's probable supporting weapons and assembly positions," I said.

"OK, Hack. Double the number of OPs and LPs at Danger and kick up your alertness level to the max and I'll have our LRRPs keep an eye out on that base camp."

"Wilco. Give us a week. We'll let Charley build up a big pot and we'll go back in there with a royal flush."

"Figured you'd see it like that. Let me know what you need. And, Hack, stay at 1,000 feet or the generals are gonna take you out of here in a strait-jacket—and probably me along with you. I'm serious. Hollis tore my butt over your fun and games yesterday."

"Wilco that, Sir," I said. I displayed my most sincere and obedient look.

TWENTY-THREE

Fire Support Base Danger
18 MAY 1969

The next morning I visited Giao Duc District Headquarters, where the Battalion's kitchens were located along with our 4.2 Mortar Platoon. Captain Medlock, the American district adviser, and I walked the perimeter, which was in a typical state of ARVN dysfunction. The fighting positions were as neglected as the raggedy-ass barbwire barrier belt surrounding the camp. I told Medlock we had intelligence the camp might get hit and that for the next week we'd keep a rifle platoon in the camp along with Dusters and our Snipers.

The adviser promised to try to get the ARVN Commander to strengthen his positions, which was exactly what I wanted him to do and the only reason for our conversation. I wanted the VC to get the message via ARVN special delivery that we knew he was coming. I thought he'd delay his attack until our augmentation was out of there and he figured our guard was down. That suited me just fine—I planned to hit him in his attack position just before he struck us.

Next I moved Tahler's Combat Support Company CP along with all of his Snipers into the camp. Larry wasn't happy.

"What are we, bait?" he fumed.

"Yep, the VC just love to munch on skinny little Jewish boys. I'm dropping leaflets giving them your new address. You're probably number one on their Most Wanted List for all the incense your boys have made 'em burn."

I wanted Tahler there so I had a solid commander on the ground with good commo to me. I knew he'd build a tight position. I told him to set up all of the Hardcore guys—the rifle platoon grunts, cooks, mortar men, Snipers and the rest of the Battalion's ash and trash—in their own sector of the ARVN perimeter and to organize an inner perimeter inside the camp composed of all Americans, a fall-back position in case the camp was overrun. I didn't trust the South Viets any more than their guerrilla brothers and cousins.

The next morning Tahler rang from his new location. "Hardcore 6, you got to come here right away. Over."

He wouldn't tell me why over the radio but stressed the urgency. We didn't have the assets that day and everything was cool at Danger, so I jumped in my jeep and sailed for ten dusty minutes down Route 4 to District HQ.

When I pulled into the ARVN compound, there was Tahler talking to my old friend John Paul Vann, now the civilian Chief of Pacification for the Delta Military Assistance Command, a brigadier general's billet.

"Damn, John, what a surprise," I said as I snapped him an airborne salute.

"I'd have visited you at your firebase, but we knew we wouldn't be allowed in," he said.

"What the hell are you talking about? You know you're always welcome."

"Heard you wouldn't let a South Vietnamese anywhere near the place," he said with a shit-eating smile on his face.

"Now, that's a fact. But last time I looked you were still a West Virginia boy."

"Been over here so long some people think I'm a Viet and others think I'm a 'combat bum.' You know that's what most Saigon generals are calling anyone who stays over here more than a coupla tours."

"What combat bum could stay away?"

John Paul Vann and I went back a long way. He'd been my company commander in early 1951 in the Eighth Army Ranger Company in Korea. When I reported in to the Rangers, Headquarters Section Sergeant Jim Kohlbecker, now a Florida Federal Marshal, assigned me to be Vann's bodyguard. In the weeks we were together, I was seldom more than a few yards from him and I'd developed a lot of respect for this straight-shooting leader. He was a savvy, hard-driving, no-bullshit-style soldier.

By 1969, Vann was a legend in Vietnam. He'd been a division adviser to the Vietnamese in 1962 and 1963 and after one of the pivotal early battles of the war—Ap Bac—he ended up blowing the whistle on all the lies our generals were spinning about how ARVN was winning the war, a courageous act that ended his promising career. He retired from the Army in disgust with twenty years' service.

But Vietnam—the people, the war and the fact that he believed it could be won—obsessed him. So he returned in 1965 as a low-ranking civilian adviser to the pacification effort and soldiered his way up the ranks. I'd met with him many times during my previous tours in Vietnam and always found him upbeat, full of good ideas.

"Hack, just drove here from Dong Tam and never saw security better or the people happier. TV antennas everywhere. We're winning this war."

I loved his optimism, but I told him he was a damn fool to drive all over Vietnam. "You got a helicopter now, John. You're a big wheel. Use it. If you don't, one of these days you're gonna get wasted."

"C'mon, Hack, you're not my bodyguard anymore. Besides, I've gotta get out and visit the villages and hamlets, be out with the people. I gotta see things for myself—I've been here too long to believe any of these bullshit reports." He was one gutsy sonofabitch. Had he been COMUSMACV from the onset of the Americanization of the conflict, the outcome might have been remarkably different.

"Since I've been at DMAC I've been watching the stats on your Battalion," he said. "Boy, you are burning up this area. But I worry that your body count includes a lot of civilians."

"Sad to say, it includes too many," I replied. "We try to be careful, but our ambushes take out civilians who violate curfew and we've definitely hit civilians who were mixed in with the VC or just got in the way during a fight."

That was the problem in the Delta, he said, and for that very reason, he'd opposed sending the U.S. 9th Division to fight there right from the get-go. He was working on getting President Nixon to pull the 9th out of Vietnam first.*

"Once the 9th's out of here, I reckon that 80 to 90 percent of the Delta's population will come to our side. You guys have been the VC's biggest recruiter. You kill a boy's mama, which side do you reckon he'll join?"

I had to agree. When soldiers' homes are destroyed and their families slaughtered, they get into wanting an eye for an eye. We had a blood feud going on in the Delta. It was a lot simpler fighting in the Highlands.. There, a movement behind a tree was either an enemy soldier or a monkey. We could shoot first and ask questions later.

"Here it's a flat bitch," I said. "First fight I'm in, we spot some people running. No weapons. Looked like kids to me. The aviation CO, an old vet in the Delta, wanted to zap 'em. I had him check fire, then I inserted a rifle platoon. You know what? They got shot up. The pilot was right. It's a motherfucker telling the good guys from the bad."

Just a few days earlier, Jerry Sullivan had been on an ambush in a free-fire zone that blew away a Vietnamese family at 0230 hours, well past the 1900 hours curfew. "We killed a whole fucking family and the ones we didn't kill we maimed," Sullivan recalls. "They might've been a VC family, but they were still women and kids. It broke my heart to hear a little baby scream, mama-san wailing, crying, caught between hysteria and death."

*A few weeks later it was announced that two Brigades of the 9th Division would be the first U.S. units to quit the war under the phony new Nixon/Kissinger Vietnamization Program. Maybe he had a red phone to Tricky Dick. With Vann, anything was possible.

"I was scared and shaking that night," Rifleman Vic Henry said. "A sampan came down the canal and our ambush blew it away. It was well past curfew. Suddenly people are screaming and crying. We'd ambushed a sampan full of civilians. It was grisly. We kept it to ourselves. It was part of everyday life."

We were fighting mainly at night in a frontless war where the enemy was often impossible to identify. Most of the Viets we encountered actively or tacitly supported the VC, perhaps not always by choice, and most were either Communist soldiers or supporters who were out to kill us. They came in all sizes, sexes and ages, many led double lives and few followed the rules of conventional war.

The VC and their NVA brothers from the North—feverishly fighting for their independence—believed that every Vietnamese citizen was first and foremost a soldier in their civil war. General Giap wrote; "The entire population participates in the armed struggle, fighting—according to the principals of guerrilla warfare—in small units."

What made it an even dirtier war was that both the VC and NVA refused to acknowledge they were bound by the Geneva Convention. So everyone had to be considered the enemy: The pretty girl waving on the side of the road might shoot you in the back of the head or detonate a mine that would zap a dozen of your mates; the old man tilling the field set out booby traps when we looked the other way; and the little kids begging for goodies acted as scouts.

Shame and constant pressure from everyone in the command, including me, to score big on body count caused the guys down in the trenches to report civilians killed as enemy soldiers. As Henry says, "It was part of everyday life."*

*The unfair way CBS beat up on Senator Bob Kerrey in August of 2001 brought this issue back again to the American people and most assuredly to those of us who gave orders, dropped bombs and napalm, squeezed triggers, popped claymores or called in artillery fire missions on an enemy that too often turned out to be civilians caught in the crossfire. These incidents were the most common whenever U.S. forces were fighting in heavily populated areas such as the Mekong Delta. I think it's safe to say there's not a soldier, sailor or airman who fired a weapon in such areas who can guarantee he didn't kill a civilian by mistake. War is always hell, but fighting in this sort of twilight zone makes it even harder to rationalize.

I knew Vann was right. Americans should never have been deployed in the Delta—especially under the command of "The Butcher of the Mekong Delta," with his insatiable appetite for body counts.

"Ewell's crowing about killing 22,000 VC in the last year was pure bullshit," Vann went on. "A lot of the dead were civilians. I told him to look at the weapons-to-body ratio. Flat ridiculous. Two hundred to one." He paused, a sardonic smile flickering across his lips, but his eyes stayed serious. He started in on Harris Hollis, a tanker who'd just taken over for Ewell.

"Once Hollis found out we were old friends, all he wanted to talk about was how well your Battalion was doing. I told him your tactical innovations are the best coming out of the war. Any other U.S. or ARVN battalions copying you?"

"Only the Sniper concept," I said. "You know how Army leadership is. They don't like change. They're still fighting World War II. Reckon they'll switch to Korean War tactics in about twenty years."

"You should know that Hollis asked me if you've always been so reckless, kind of implyin' you had a death wish," Vann said. "Thinks you're takin' too many chances. You might just back off and cool it for a spell."

And with a bear hug and a salute, he and the other civilian adviser he was traveling with took off out the gate all by themselves—without any armed escort—headed for Route 4 to Cao Lanh.

A few years later, John Paul Vann, then advising in the equivalent of an Army two-star billet, was killed in Vietnam leading from the front as the II Corps senior adviser. Ironically, he didn't buy the farm bopping down a muddy road in a Landrover or holed up in a hamlet bunker under attack, but in the very machine—a chopper—I'd suggested he start using.

As John sailed out of sight, I turned my mind back to zapping Charley. The idea was to put Alert Company, the Battalion's Long Range Ambush Company, into the game first. In early May, Trent Thomas asked to stand down Alert Company and take them back to Dong Tam. "They've been on the go since February—the men need a break," he said. "We need four or five days just to train. We need to sharpen up on the basics and go over our SOPs."

"Good thinking, Trent, leave in two days. Have a steak fry and some cold beers while you're there, the boys need that, too."

Then I told him I wanted Alert Company rested, retrained and back at Tombstone before the eighteenth.

Thomas was doing a great job with Alert, as was Don Meyer with Claymore. I'd given each an AO—they collected their own intelligence and decided on the locations of their ambushes. I'd learned first hand in the Raiders way back in Korea that a staff officer in a remote headquarters could fuck things up royally and get a unit in a real jam. So I gave them carte blanche to operate the way Larry Tahler did with his Snipers—maximum freedom to do their own thing. Both completely ran their own operations and coordinated their plans with Mergner and me at daily meetings twenty-four hours in advance of their missions.

There was little micromanagement in the Hardcore. I was a firm believer in mission-type orders that wouldn't strangle the unit skippers with detail imposed from above. I wanted the Hardcore leaders to be able to do their thing without having to deal with any extraneous bullshit. If I didn't trust a subordinate leader, it was simple—he wouldn't be there. And I felt the same way about loser soldiers. Losers were DXed—read fired—immediately. Both practices had a positive effect on the real soldiers.

And then Hayes flew in. No big smile. The news wasn't going to be joyful. I immediately thought Hollis had canceled the operation we were cooking up for 22 May. Wrong.

"Hack," Hayes said, "General Abrams has ordered that you be relieved. You can have any job in Vietnam as long as you're not in direct combat.

I'm really sorry, old buddy. I know you love the Hardcore, but the word is you're too valuable and you're still taking too many chances."

I was floored. How could General Abrams—of all people—do this to me?

The man was a cigar-smoking tiger who'd practically invented the word attack. As a reconnaissance battalion commander in Europe during World War II, he was always up front in the thick of it. He got a DSC for extraordinary heroism for leading the breakthrough force into the surrounded 101st Airborne at Bastogne. How could the guy who lived by the maxim FOLLOW ME fuck with me like this? It made absolutely no sense.

But Abrams was also a guy with an iron will—when he made a decision, it stayed. I was screwed. You can't argue with the boss, especially when he's a two-fisted, hard-charging four star.

John saw my face. He quickly tossed me a bone.

"Look, the glass is half full—it took some heavy lifting, but you're gonna be here for the main event."*

Without missing a beat, we got back to planning what Mergner now tagged "our going-away party," since he was scheduled to return to the States in early June. We thought Charley would make his final recon on the twenty-first, then make last-minute preparations—such as leader briefs and moving his assault troops into their forward assembly areas—the day before the attack. We figured he'd come at us on the night of the twenty-second or twenty-third, when there'd be no moon, so we planned to catch him in his assembly areas before he crossed his line of departure.

I gave Mergner my guidance: Employ max stealth and start moving units out on the nineteenth. Hayes agreed we'd pull our reinforcements out of Giao Duc on the nineteenth as well. The endgame was that by the wee hours of the twenty-first, the Hardcore would be wrapped around the VC assembly area tighter than a chastity belt around a medieval virgin.

---

*John wasn't exaggerating about the effort he'd had to make to keep me there. Years later, an old pal, retired Colonel Harry Hellmuth, who was on Abe's staff and was responsible to keep him informed of "sensitive casualties"—sons of VIPs and Lieutenant Colonels and above—said, "I sent your name into General Abrams when you collected your eighth Purple Heart. An hour later my buckslip came back. Abe had scrawled across the report, "Get him out of there ASAP."

Mergner got busy putting the plan together.

On the morning of 17 May, Battle Company got into a stiff firefight about five klicks from where Crittenden captured the Dong Thap 1 Regiment's attack order. DeRoos and boys killed five VC. RPG fire thumped down all over his 3rd Platoon, killing Douglas Edward Lohmeyer and wounding three other soldiers. But there was a consolation prize.

"May have a good one," radioed DeRoos, reporting that he'd taken two VC prisoners. "My Tiger Scout says one is a VC Company Commander from the 261A Battalion. Ornery little bastard. Wouldn't give me shit. Watch out, he'll spit in your face."

Scooping up the POWs along with our wounded, I headed back to Danger.

The VC company commander was a first lieutenant in his late twenties, mean as a shedding rattlesnake and covered with scars. The worst was a hole in one of his legs almost as deep and wide as my fist where a huge chunk of flesh had been blown out and never sewn up. It would have been a bad wound even if medical attention had been available. Still, it had healed and this bad-ass had gone back to duty.

He didn't want to talk to me so I pointed to the old wound on his leg.

"No hospital?" I was trying to soften him up.

The prisoner shook his head. Then I showed him some of my wounds, which provoked the first bit of interest from the guy. He asked if they were from Vietnam.

"No, no," I replied. "Before. Korea. But this one"—I showed him one of my leg wounds—"this one came from the VC here in the Delta."

The wound was still red and raw, with big, vicious-looking stitch marks.

"Maybe I did it," he said, and roared with a huge belly laugh.

"Yeah, maybe you did."

We'd found a common bond, laid down our swords, put the war aside.

"Look," I said, "I know you're one tough sonofabitch. I know you'd like to grab a hand grenade and blow us all up. I know you're not going to tell me anything about your unit because I know you wouldn't get anything from me. So I'm not going to ask. But I'm a soldier. I admire your Army's skill. I want to know more about your Army, why you believe as you do and what makes you fight so hard."

For the next three nights, when I came in from the field, the prisoner, an interpreter and I would get together and talk. I learned a great deal about his cause and how the VC operated.

"All right, my friend," I told the POW, "the word is I've got to evacuate you. I'm going to send you to my division headquarters, where you'll be interrogated, and then they'll turn you over to the 7th ARVN Division. Now, the first thing ARVN is going to ask you is to *Chieu Hoi*—change sides. If you do, they'll send you to a reorientation camp and when you come out you'll have a South Vietnamese uniform, an M-16 and be assigned to a South Vietnamese unit or maybe you'll even come back here as a Tiger Scout and we can work together. So when you go to the 7th Division, tell them you're going to *Chieu Hoi*"

"I'll never do that."

"But you've *got* to do it," I said. "Do you know what they do to people who don't *Chieu Hoi*? They shoot them!"

"Then I will be dead. I expect to die anyway, fighting for my cause, the freedom of my country, Vietnam. I believe in my cause," he said, and began pointing to his leg and his many other raggedly healed wounds. "I believed in it through all of this. I will never surrender. I will fight until I'm dead. If they ask me to join their side I will spit in their faces."

The numbers crunchers at the Pentagon didn't factor this kind of fierce patriotism into their estimates. Their formula was: so many tons of bombs, so many rounds of artillery, so many dead VC equaled victory. Between January and March 1969, the 9th Division fired 311,083 artillery rounds—

more than it fired in the same period in 1945 during the Ardennes campaign in Europe. So we had to be winning. At least according to the stats.

After my session with this guy, I knew that besides fighting the war with a new set of tactics, we had to stoke that same fire in our soldiers' bellies. This guy totally focused on winning, while the average American grunt concentrated on not becoming the last casualty in a war that most believed couldn't be won.

On the night of 18 May, Claymore Company sprung an ambush, killing three VC. At first light Jerry Sullivan, who was the ambush leader, got stuck in the canal while searching a dead VC. "My Tiger Scout always razzed me about being beaucoup kilos because I was so tall," he recalls. "I'd already learned never to stop when you're in the mud and when you're out there in that mud, walk on your toes and if you can, throw brush such as nipa palm branches down and walk on it. But I got so involved checking this dich out, I forgot my own rules. Before I knew it I was in the mud up to my waist. I threw my M-16, the captured documents and his AK to my guys on the bank and did the only thing a man could do in that tidal quicksand: lean forward and claw and crawl out like a damn mud crab, which when I look back on it, that's exactly what we were. Hardcore mud crabs."

While Jerry mixed it up in the mud, another Claymore Company ambush taught the VC a costly lesson about the importance of noise and light discipline when a squad of VC sauntering down a trail stopped about fifty yards away from where SP-4 James Fitzgerald was set up as part of a platoon-size ambush.

"I told our platoon leader. The lieutenant put everyone on 100 percent," the M-79 grenadier recalls. "I couldn't believe it. The next thing the VC did was to string up poncho shelters and then light up and sit there jabbering and smoking."

"We continued to observe the group for about half an hour thinking perhaps a larger element would link up with them," says platoon leader Lieutenant Edmund Csefalvay. "We didn't even need our Starlights because of their cigarettes."

Csefalvay quietly moved an M-60 machine-gun team and two more M-79 gunners from his rear security squad to the canal bank. When everyone was in position he triggered the ambush with every man tossing a frag grenade and then blasting away.

"It was almost over before it started. We counted ten VC dead through our Starlight Scopes and the gooks didn't get off a round."

Not all ambushes were without a price. Battle Company Carl Ohlson's platoon was setting up an ambush alongside a canal the night before this action, when his guys spotted three VC bopping down the trail.

"We took 'em under fire, killing the lot of them. Our location was compromised by the firing so we moved to set up in another position and while doing so one of my guys tripped a booby trap, wounding two soldiers. Doc Christiansen rushed through the mined area and patched up the wounded. We dusted 'em off and then moved again."

Nothing else happened for the rest of the night. At first light while the platoon was still "hunkered down next to a rice paddy dike and a row of banana trees, we were hit by two RPB rounds which came from out of nowhere," Ohlsen said. "The VC must have been aiming at my antennas. The rounds exploded right in my CP, killing our fine medic, Thomas Lee Christiansen. He died instantly of a head wound. And the VC disappeared."

By mid-May 1969, 110 days after I took command, the Hardcore boys really had their shit together. They were confident, their morale was high, their leadership at every level had instilled a will to take the fight to the enemy. In my bones, I knew for certain we were on our way to one helluva finale.

TWENTY-FOUR

Five Klicks North of Danger
22 MAY 1969

D day was set for 22 May. The plan called for selected Hardcore units to wrap around our target by 0600 hours, after which Battle Company would be picked up at Danger at 0800. They'd fly south before doing a 180 and heading due north, right on the deck just above the paddy dikes; then they'd plunk down in a large field just north of the enemy base camp. Mergner's and my thinking went that the VC would look up, see the birds and say, "Well, here they come. We'll haul ass and fight another day."

Battle Company, under Gordy DeRoos, would be the beaters while the rest of the Battalion would be the bushwhackers, employing the VC's own favorite tactic: the ambush. George and I carefully worked out where they'd probably run by studying aerial photographs and talking to Hardcore leaders who knew the ground and to Division Rangers whose LRRP teams operating out of Danger had worked the area.

On 19 May, we started positioning our units to move to those choke points. Alert Blue, under Lieutenant Fred Meyer, was sent deep—ten klicks northeast by chopper—and told to ambush their way slowly south. On 21 May, Don "Lank" Meyer's Claymore would move out of the little fort they'd set up in an old French schoolhouse and head north. The night before the steel jaws of our trap snapped shut, Ed Clark's Dagger, which was operating southwest of the objective area, would start moving to its ambush sites. At first light on D day, the platoons from A, B and C running security back at or near Danger and Claymore's base would be on PZs ready to chopper in to reinforce their respective companies or be popped into any VC escape holes that Mergner and I might have missed. At Danger's main LZ, Trent Thomas with Alert Red would be configured for chopper pick up as the Battalion reserve/reaction force.

Tahler and his Snipers would go out by truck with Claymore, drop off and set up in a wood line just south of the enemy base area. We didn't think the VC would try to get out that way because they'd have to boogie across a wide-open rice paddy while under fire, swim a deep canal then drip their way across another paddy. But if they did, the Snipers would be patiently waiting.

Tac Air was laid on as well as Chum Robert's Redlegs, standing by back at Danger with plenty of 105mm ammo stacked up by their guns. Both would blast and burn Charley out of his bunkers when he went to ground after realizing that this time around running wasn't going to work.

There would be no prep fires. Surprise and stealth would be our immediate weapons.

Boomerang, Bounty Hunter and the Air Cav from "B" Troop 3/17th Cav—Stogie—would provide the guns and chopper lift. We even lined up a Psych War chopper to try to coax the VC out of their holes during and after our little firepower demo.

The VC base camp, located in a jungle area about five klicks due north of Danger, was about an eight-square-click area bounded on all sides by four different blues—which made for easy VC movement by sampan. Setting up that close to Danger was clever. Who looks for terrorists living in an apartment above an FBI SWAT office?

We carefully concealed all our preparations, knowing Charley always watched our bases for any changes in activity. We made everything look like business as usual: no increase in artillery fire or ground recon patrols or helicopter recons in or over the objective area. To enemy spies, Alert was just running its usual long-range ambush, Battle and Dagger their Ranger ops. Around Danger, Claymore continued to conduct their short-range ambushes at night, in addition to working with the local Viet RF units during the daytime on Cordon and Search Ops.

Before the operation, I talked to all Battalion leaders, a company at a time. This was going to be their graduation exercise, I told them, and I'd be leaving a few days after they got their diplomas. I was damn proud of them. What had once been a dud outfit was now full of studs. "It turned into my going away party, too," Sergeant Steve Elgin says, "even though it wasn't exactly how I planned to spend it—I was supposed to process out to go home the next day. First Sergeant McDonald got into my face about my not going out on the mission, so we got into a little hassle. I grabbed my rifle and started walking away from him. He said, 'Where are you going?' I said, 'Out with my squad. I'd rather be dodging bullets than hanging around here listening to your shit all night.'"

Early in the morning on 19 May, Dagger went out to jitterbug and conducted six false insertions ten klicks north of our target. Choppers rolled in to an LZ, then lifted off with the doors shut and the troops lying on the floor. From a distance, it looked as if we'd inserted troops.

On the real inserts, Dagger killed five VC. But instead of returning to the base at the end of the day, per routine, Dagger went into a hide position south of the objective area. After dark, a single platoon returned to Danger—spread out on all the choppers so that, to an enemy observer, it would look as if the entire company had returned.

The Dagger platoon withdrew to Danger, then secured the firebase with the help of the headquarters and artillery folks. We also put the Battle platoon in ops all around Danger to give additional depth to our security in case Charley came calling while we were light on infantry defenders.

On 20 May, we tightened the noose. During the night, units carefully moved toward their ambush positions. Alert and Battle racked up four kills, while Ken Carlton's Bounty Hunter guns and Chum Robert's cannons whacked five more VC.

The next day, Battle began operating two klicks south of the objective area. The Company had six small contacts, killing seven VC and capturing five new AK-47s. It also recovered a map and documents from one of the newly departed enemy soldiers. Then, at 1540 hours, a Tiger scout tripped a booby trap, killing himself and wounding two soldiers.

Clearly, the VC didn't want DeRoos to move any farther north, so we accommodated them. At 1740 hours, we lifted out two platoons and DeRoos's company headquarters by chopper. Then we did a fake pickup with his other platoon, enabling it to go into a hide position.

During the same period, Tahler's Snipers and Claymore Company moved by truck seven klicks to the east of the target area, where Claymore conducted a Cordon and Search with an RF company. After the op, the trucks returned in the dark to Claymore's schoolhouse base, but again with only one platoon spread out among all the vehicles. To our local neighborhood VC spies, it looked as if everyone had come home. But in reality we now had the Snipers and two platoons from Claymore in hide positions.

By the night of 21 May, according to the map and documents taken off the dead VC the day before by Battle, the 261A Battalion was inside our trap. Time to shut the door. Battle CO Gordy DeRoos briefed his platoon leaders on the operation. "Clearly something big was going down," Lieutenant Carl Ohlson says. "We were told to make sure our guys took cover once we took our initial objectives and not to do anything foolish. Most of what I'd dealt with until then was no more than a VC platoon and here we were going up against at least a reinforced battalion. The fact that we had a lot of friendlies going in was comforting. I get a lot of comfort in numbers and here we were going to have all this support, gunships and other heavy stuff, and it made going in a lot more palatable."

In the darkness all units deployed around the target started moving to their final objectives. "At three in the morning the word came down to saddle up," recalls Jerry Sullivan. "Walking through that area in the dark was very difficult and slow, it was very difficult to navigate. So now they were saying get your shit on and move out, and it was like, 'Wow.' Gotta be something big."

Throughout the night, Night Hunter and the PPS-5 ground radars we'd set up in nearby RF and PF outposts checked the enemy base. "There was movement but my guys reported no change to enemy activity inside the target area," Larry Tahler recalls. "The enemy was playing right into Hack's plans."

By first light on the twenty-second everyone was in position. The 261A was a Red goose waiting to be roasted.

"We were sitting on the PZ by Danger with ten slicks and about eighty folks waiting to go," says Lieutenant David Diefendorf, Battle Company FO. "There was a big squabble—probably it was the tension—one guy was upset at the whole world because he'd been carrying an M-60 machine gun ever since he got in-country—but we got him to calm down. Then Hardcore 6 called up and said, 'Battle 6, I have decided to commit you.'"

"I did not like his choice of words. It sounded like 'Look out, here we go.' All I could think was holy cow, what have you got in mind for us now?"

The choppers lifted off. "It was a tremendous way to go to work. The most exciting thing I've ever experienced was to climb into those helicopters and go zooming off to who knows what. Even though I was scared, I loved it."

Sergeant Gary Dubois, a Battle Company squad leader, didn't love it at all. "Every time you went out on those choppers, you knew there was a really good chance you might get killed. You were just hanging out in the air and even if they weren't shooting at you yet, you were waiting for it to happen at any moment."

The Hardcore grunts scrambled out of the birds and had complete surprise. "It didn't take the VC long to wake up," Gordy DeRoos recalls. "The LZ quickly turned hot. We were still moving into the tree line when the shit hit the fan. There was a lot of wild shooting, especially in my direction. We took one WIA, a new lieutenant named Mitchell who was with me in the command group getting in some OJT. Shot in the leg. Guess all my antennas sucked in the fire."

"As we were coming off the LZ, here's Mitchell in front of me looking at a map as if he was reading the *Wall Street Journal* on his way to the office," Diefendorf remembers. "The dude who hit him was only about seventy-five yards away. I sprinted over to this square water-filled septic pool, where I went over the lip and scootched down. The bank was steep enough that I could keep my head out of range and my feet out of the water, a tricky deal since I was humping the radio, rifle and tin pot. The company CO was beside me and the bullets were flying pretty fast and pretty heavy over our heads."

Captain DeRoos looked over at his FO, who'd turned chalk white.

"Haven't you ever been shot at before?"

"Yeah, sure I have," said Diefendorf, who was only in his third week with Battle Company. "But this is something I'll never get used to."

Diefendorf lasted another three weeks before he got blown up. He was one of the lucky ones—he lived to talk about it. FOs and infantry platoon leaders especially green lieutenants—weren't very good insurance risks in Vietnam.

Before the operation, I'd stressed to the squad leaders, especially Battle Company's people who were making the air assault, that they should always be looking for cover for their elements—protection from direct-fire weapons—so that when the slugs started snapping they'd be able to move quickly to a protected spot. "Looking for cover is like looking for mines," I reminded them. "An infantryman does it always and automatically. You've got to constantly ask yourself, When the bullets fly, where will I dive?"

Battle Company Squad Leader Sergeant Tim "Sugar Bear" Bauer took me at my word. "As the choppers were coming in," he recalls, "I spotted a canal bank that I could get my guys behind in case things got hot. As soon as the firing began, we moved there from the LZ—with L. J. Henderson covering us with his machine gun. Then we all laid down covering fire so he could get back to us. We spotted an enemy bunker and destroyed it and then I realized I was missing two guys. Two newbies had frozen up on the LZ and were glued to it. I told Henderson to cover me while I ran out and got them.

"'Forget it, "Sugar Bear." You're nuts. They're not worth it,' Henderson said.

"'Cover me, L. J. Maybe one day, that'll be us out there,' Bauer replied."

Bauer went out under heavy enemy fire and brought the men back. Then DeRoos told him to check out an area deeper in the woods.

"I thought I saw movement and I had the point man take cover while Henderson blasted the spot," Bauer says. "There were a bunch of VC, but before they could get a round off, Henderson and the rest of my guys had done major damage to them. My platoon didn't even take a scratch."*

Diefendorf tried to bring in arty support, but because Allison—the Battalion artillery liaison officer—was hammering the deep VC positions, nothing was immediately available. So DeRoos used gunships to suppress the VC fire, and the guns stopped it immediately.

"The VC had hauled ass. Rice was still cooking on fires and their gear was scattered everywhere. It wasn't what you'd call an orderly withdrawal," DeRoos recalls.

The VC beat feet right into the arms of Ed Clark and Dagger Company. During the first fifteen minutes after Battle landed, Dagger mowed down ten

---

*Sergeant Bauer was awarded his second Silver Star for rescuing the new men and for later triggering the ambush while Henderson was feeding the VC a steady ration of 7.62mm ammo.

VC. "Battle Company pushed them into us," Clark recalls. "The VC were flat panicked and didn't know we were there. It was a Kentucky turkey shoot and the turkeys weren't shootin' back."

Trapped between Battle and Dagger, the VC had no place to hide. "At first they were running away from us, but then the guys waiting for them from other companies would fire at them and they'd come running back," Sergeant Gary Dubois says, "so they just kept running back and forth and we kept cutting them down."

"We just decimated them," Dagger's Sergeant David Wagner remembers. "They had no cover—they couldn't go across the rice paddy because we could see them and when some tried to jump in the river, they were shot or fragged. We took a POW and got him right back to Captain Clark for interrogation. One guy came running toward my squad and we shot him and his head came off. It was about fifteen minutes before I went out and took a beautiful Chinese pistol off this guy. His brains and everything were already crawling with ants. I was thinking how coldly efficient mother nature was— this gook goes from probably a guy with a family, an officer, to nothing in such a short period, being recycled into something else almost before my eyes. But the pistol was beautiful, wrapped in oilskin and then in a plastic bag. We just sat there all day, from dawn to dusk, shooting them. Didn't lose a man. I kept thinking payback for 13 March—revenge for that and for all booby traps."

By now Charley was running in every direction. We'd blocked his main escape routes along the canals and high-speed trails with our stay-behind-and-hide forces. From a few minutes after Battle Company air-assaulted in until almost twenty-four hours later, Claymore Company had continuous light contact. "They started running toward our ambush position and we were just waiting," recalls rifleman Vic Henry. "They didn't see us hiding like Indians and we mowed them down. It was like shooting fish in a barrel.

I kinda spent my day shooting and picking up enemy weapons. Reckon we policed up fifteen or twenty AKs."

From 0959 on D day until 0705 hours the next morning, Claymore ambushed and killed thirty-five enemy soldiers. There were no big contacts. Small disorganized groups of VC first ran toward Dagger, got whacked, bounced off, then ran to Claymore, who smacked them, and then to Alert, who cut down twelve VC over ten hours.

"This mission was simple compared to Hunt's chaotic battle of Thanh Phu," USAF Brigade FAC Captain Joe Connor, the brilliant Air Force FAC who'd been running the air strikes when the op kicked off, observes. "The troop positions were clearly marked, the enemy was contained and there was no panic on the radio. The fighters had picked up the battle area from observing where the Army gunships were directing their fire. I also marked the specific targets with white phosphorous rockets. Since we were delivering lethal ordnance close to our troops, the pilots readily accepted my directive to fly a restrictive bombing run repeating the same heading. This exposed them to more ground fire, but it dramatically lowered the chance of a 'short round.'"

"Napalm splashed in front of my squad, flushin' three VC out in the open," says Tom Aiken.* "Me and my guys cut them down. It was as easy as swipin' watermelons when I was a kid. And when they fell, I couldn't help thinkin' of my buddy and the day he was killed by VC mines. 'These guys are for you, Glenn.' What a day! I remember wishin' Toby'd been there to see it, leadin' us and all. Only time I've ever been mad with him was when he got hit four days before and had to be medevacked out—I was pissed off at him for leavin' me. He'd a loved this. What a difference between now and bein' in the Rocket Belt last November, getting' the shit blown out of us."

When the VC saw that all the waterways and trails were blocked, they completely panicked, scattering in every direction like al-Qaeda from a B-1 strike.

---

*Alert Company Sergeant Aiken was awarded the Bronze Star for valor for his part in the operation.

Captain James Mukoyama, Mergner's assistant S-3 who was with Mergner and me in the C&C chopper, said he'd never seen anything like it. "The VC bounced off one ambush after another. Each time they ran panic-stricken into one ambush, they'd lose a dozen or so men and bounce off, only to hit another blocked escape route. I saw a wounded VC throw his weapon into a canal with his last bit of strength just before he died. I figured he did it so we couldn't retrieve the AK. This taught me an important lesson about the courage, discipline and dedication of our foe."

Battle's platoons now set up in front of the VC's vacated positions. DeRoos had his boys grenade and demo all the bunkers and heap all the VC weapons and equipment in a big stack.

"It was eerie," Carl Ohlson says. "After we got a couple hundred yards into the wood line, there was no enemy movement in our sector. You could hear muffled firing to our front and flanks. Captain DeRoos stressed that we had friendlies out beyond us and to be careful with our fire. We kept popping smoke so the choppers flying above us had a fix on our forward trace. Last thing we wanted was to get hit by our own stuff."

From the air the battle was like watching a giant pinball game. The VC were the ball and they'd bounce off one ambush and it would light up and then they'd bounce off another. Boomerang air mission commander Ken Carlton looked down and saw a dozen or so VC lying dead in a field. "They were real close together with their weapons lying next to them," he says. "Our friendlies popped up and waved. Reckon they were worried we'd hose them. They'd kicked ass."

The helicopter assault, designed to confuse the enemy, more than did the job. "We could hear the VC running back toward us hollering and scream-ing," Ohlson remembers. "They got within range, and they ran smack into my platoon. You don't actually get to see them too often, most of the time they were hidden, and here they were running around right out in the open.

You could hear the crack of the M-16s and the deeper thud of the AK-47s. I controlled one half of the ambush and my platoon Sergeant the other—both of us had M-60s—and you could hear a burst from the left gun and a burst from the right gun. It was a shooting gallery like at the arcade. Really wild. The guys were going nuts—really getting confident. It was pretty cool, it was payback, the guys were getting very psyched. When the smoke cleared there were about a dozen enemy soldiers stretched out in front of my platoon and a pile of weapons. This was my first big fight and I gotta tell you, it was like being at the movies. My boys were magnificent."

Dagger Company Platoon Sergeant Richard Polak and his men had been sitting for quite a long time when, he recalls, they "started hearing gunfire and a whole lot of stuff going on off in the distance. All of a sudden we had all this movement out in front of us and it was like being at a shooting gallery on the Atlantic City boardwalk. We didn't have the same sense of unease we usually had—it was actually kind of refreshing once we got the idea that it was going very well. Nobody was getting hurt except them. I'm not saying the guys were having a great time, it wasn't like a carnival or anything, but we weren't taking casualties and we were kicking butt."

By 1100 hours, Claymore had three broken M-60 machine guns, the rifle companies needed topping off with ammo and the Stay-Behind elements that had been in the bush for several days were running low on everything.

Because Captain Morio Takahashi, our old Hawaiian S-4 had his act together, a Boomerang slick started running resupply missions.

When new machine guns and ammo were flown to "Lank" Meyer at an LZ south of his position, the six-foot-four paratrooper Captain took one gun to machine-gunner Robert Runnebohm. "Let's see if this one works," Meyer said, picking up the machine gun and firing it from a standing position like a rifle.

"I was amazed—never saw anyone fire a gun like that. Damn thing would knock most people down just firing from the hip," said Runnebohm, a big six-footer himself. "He fired about twenty rounds, handed it to me and said 'this one's a keeper."

"'Keep hosing down this sector and keep a sharp eye on that canal,' Meyer said. Count on it, they'll be trying to float out.'"

A few minutes later, Runnebohm saw a tube sticking up through the water like a periscope, moving down the canal. "I gave it a short burst," he said, "and a VC floated up to the surface."

Lieutenant Rex Fletcher, Runnebohm's gutsy platoon leader, jumped in the water and pulled the dead VC out to search for documents. A few minutes later, Fletcher was checking his positions, when six VC ran down a path parallel to the canal. They were met with a wall of fire and six more VC were added to the Dich Board—adding to a total running higher than seventy, matched against three friendly WIAs.

Now the VC were caught right in the middle of our trap. Joe Connor put eight air strikes with surgical precision in the center of the VC base camp. From 1000 to 1800 hours, napalm and 500-pound bombs pummeled the enemy. Connor placed his bombs and nape perfectly—just far enough from our ambushes not to singe any friendlies.

"The bombs were landing no more than 600 meters from my platoon and you could hear the fragments sing through the bush," recalls Jerry Sullivan. "Bet your boots we kept our positions well marked with smoke. You could see the shock waves from the explosions and feel the furnace heat from the napalm. The pilots flew so low you could see their faces and easily see the silver napalm canisters darting down. They were scorching the earth."

"The Hardcore kept the Air Force busy on 22 May," Connor says. "That day, all four of the Brigade's Tamale FACs flew continuously from dawn to dusk—Major Ray Medina, Tamale 10; Captain Joe Nuvolini, Tamale 11; Captain Larry Mink, Tamale 12; and myself, Tamale 14."

"The aging 'Hun,' as the F-100 was affectionately called, was the perfect airplane to support 'troops in contact' in the Delta. That day each fighter carried two canisters of napalm and two 500-pound high-drag bombs. They got to us in a hurry out of Bien Hoa Air Base, had the endurance to orbit till the troops were ready and routinely delivered the 'big hurt' while flying fifty feet above the enemy. Their 20mm cannon was a welcome bonus.

"The Tamales and Huns became very proficient in supporting our troops when they were in close proximity to the enemy. Tamale's job was to fly our O-1 Bird Dogs over the battlefield assessing the situation, marking the friendly and enemy positions and coordinating the air strikes with the artillery and the gunships.

"After directing a couple of air strikes that morning, I got low on gas and turned over the FAC mission to Larry Mink. At this time, there was a pause in the operation as Hackworth called in a Psychological Warfare helicopter to offer the enemy an opportunity to surrender. Not that they'd be standing in line to take him up on the offer. You had to admit they were tough."

Back at Danger, Chum Robert's battery filled in when Connor was out of fighter aircraft, walking the fire back from one ambush site to the next. "I remember thinking it looked good when it left my guns and I just prayed that it got where it was supposed to go—on the bad guys, not the good guys," Chum says. His prayers were answered. He and his boys fired over 500 rounds of 105mm HE and 100 rounds of Willy Peter. And it was all on target.

"The air show gave us all a shot in the arm," says Jerry Sullivan. "Everyone in our platoon was beat. We'd humped all night to get into position whereas the other platoon was taxied in. We had a great position in a burned-out ville. Good cover. We just hunkered down behind the foundations and popped away whenever they showed."

In the middle of the fight, a chicken came walking out of the rubble of the hooch. Sullivan's Tiger Scout, a tough little guy named Fee, shot it. "We took some water, put it in a steel helmet, took some C-4 out of a claymore mine, boiled the water and more or less cooked the chicken. We were so hungry by then, just the fact it was dead was good enough. The other guys were looking at us and saying, 'What the fuck are you guys doing?' We said, 'Hey, we're having lunch.' We felt like cavemen, sitting there, rubbing our bellies and grinning. We had blood and chicken feathers all over us."

At that moment, they got word that a resupply chopper was coming in. "Someone yelled, 'Here's our supplies,'" Sullivan said. "We knew the pilot didn't want to sit out there—you know, whoop, whoop, whoop, chop, chop, chop—any longer than he had to. He came in hot on our smoke and just as he started to flare, Fee and I broke cover and started running toward him. We just wanted to get the shit off the bird and let him get out of there before he got shot up."

BA-BOOM!

Rifleman Ken Scott heard the tremendous explosion. "I saw Sully go up in the air, at least twelve feet up—Sully was light in them days, couldn't of been no more than 120 pounds. When he came back down everybody had to stop, you couldn't move no more. If one man trips a booby trap, it means there's more than one in the area and you have to stop and check what you're standing on so I couldn't just go rushing over to him like I wanted to."

A black cloud of smoke swirled up around the fallen squad leader. Sullivan felt something warm, looked down and saw his boot had been blown off his foot and his pant leg was smoldering. Snuffing out the fire, he saw that his leg was pretty well shattered from the knee down. "I went, 'Whoa, that's bad,'" he says. A couple of pieces of shrapnel had torn into his groin. "I distinctly remember reaching down to make sure everything was still there. Then I lay back and thought, 'Well, that's it for me.' The whole time, Fee was holding me in his lap, crying like a baby.

"They cut my pants off and wrapped me in compresses and tossed me in the helicopter. It was like 'Hey, your taxi's here.' The guys said, 'We'll see you back at Dong Tam.' I was sitting up and when I looked down at the extent of the damage, I knew I was fucked. I knew I'd never see those guys who I loved so much again. We flew out of there real low over the paddies. I had my head hanging out the door watching the paddies and the water buffalo and the tracers flying under me, and I'm thinking, Man, what a ride. I wish this guy would get some altitude before we get our asses shot down."*

From the time Jerry Sullivan was evacuated, the rest of the fight centered mainly on the Bounty Hunters and Stogie gunships. The VC, knowing all the doors were nailed shut, tried to bug out cross-country in small groups. Above them the gunships circled like hungry hawks in search of prey, picking off kills mostly in twos and fours. But now and then, the gunners caught several large groups running across an open field and killed as many as twenty VC at one whack.

We were lucky that Bounty Hunter platoon leader Ken Carlton, a master of orchestrating gunships and slicks, was in the front seat of our command bird on the op. Carlton's Bounty Hunters—along with the Air Cav Stogies—killed over fifty VC.+

"We caught 'em in the open and went down there and kicked ass," Carlton said. "Even my door gunners blistered them and the Colonel and the Major in the back were shooting their fucking rifles out the door. When my guns were off station, the artillery guy in the back hammered them with 105 stuff. I was in a lot of fights in Vietnam before and after this shoot-'em-up, but I've never seen the enemy so cut up or screwed up than on this one."

Throughout the battle, George Mergner flew with me in my C&C. He confirms the pain we inflicted on the enemy. "Little blue-shirted people were

---

*Sully's 1430-hour battlefield medical assessment was accurate. Even though he spent more than five years in various hospitals, the explosion effectively ended his promising Army career and he was eventually medically retired. "In many ways I was lucky," he said years later. "Had I stayed in Vietnam, I'm sure I woulda gotten myself killed somewhere along the line." Over thirty years after the event, Sully was awarded the Bronze Star for valor for his part in the operation.

+Ken Carlton was awarded the Silver Star for his daring.

running everywhere. One gunship that was flying right down at paddy level caught three VC running across the field. He rammed a missile up their ass and they just disappeared. I ran out of space on my map board, noting with grease pencil the rapidly changing body count and tactical situation. The coordination of fire support—Tac Air, artillery and gunships—was masterful.

"In the early afternoon, just as the fight was heating up, we got a call in our C&C from the Brigade TOC officer—one of those usual 'be advised' calls, telling us we had just about consumed all our blade time," Mergner recalls. "Hack and I looked at each other with a what-the-fuck expression and I gave them a curt, 'Thank you, out.'"

Blade time be damned. We continued swooping down, picking up the company commanders and flying them over the fight to let them see what was happening from the air. This way they got a bird's-eye view of the big picture so when they were back on the ground they could plan their next moves with a better, more integrated sense of the battle.

"About midday, Hack swooped down and picked me up in his helicopter," recalls Alert Blue Platoon leader Lieutenant Fred Meyer. " He just came right down behind me and said, 'Get in, Stud.' I said, 'Yes, Sir.' That was pretty cool to have him come down like that to take me up and show me where each company was and how the battle was going. He just wanted me to understand the nature of what I was doing. Circling around with him like that gave me an instant view of the whole deal and was a big help once I got back down on the ground with my men."

The m.o. did result in a couple of ass-chewings from John Hayes and more than a couple of admonishments to remember his 1,000-feet rule. "Yes, Sir," I agreed—until the next time we needed to pick up a commander or dispose of a target.

I had prepared for this battle for twenty-three years. And, thank God, Hayes let me fight it. All I had to do now was sit in my chopper and call down to the Hardcore leaders: "Heads up, Fred Meyer and Ed Clark, they're coming your way, let 'em have it," followed soon after by "All right, DeRoos, they'll be back in your position in about twenty minutes" or "Lank, make sure you're set, they're headed your way." Or tell Ken Carlton to get his guns over to the south where Tahler's Sniper screen was reporting "beaucoup enemy movement." Or—because my map reading sucked at best and was beyond hopeless at 100 MPH—constantly ask George Mergner, who did a brilliant job putting and keeping the show together, "Where the fuck are we?" Or tell Bob Allison to "get an air strike over there" or "put arty on that section of jungle."

Except for—rightly—nibbling away at my tender ass when my bird got too low, Hayes told me he was there for us, to holler if we needed anything—and he let us get on with the job. But this wasn't the case with the rest of the brass. As the battle unfolded, it seemed as though every general in Vietnam was hovering over the fight wanting to play combat warrior: two lieutenant generals, two major generals and what seemed like a fire team of brigadiers, most of them falling over each other trying to put in their own two cents' worth. It was like having a dozen Ira Hunts micromanaging the show.

I wanted to skip rope. Jim "Mook" Mukoyama recalls, "Finally, Hack got on the horn and told the brass he was fighting a battle, not running a side show and that he didn't have time to answer their questions. He bluntly told them to stay off his command freq and get the hell out of the airspace before there was an accident."

General Hollis got on the radio and ordered me to land and give the brass a briefing at Danger. When I came back at him that I was too busy and why didn't I drop off Mergner, Hollis said no—it would be me.

I threw a temper tantrum in the chopper. George and Mook* hosed me down, I put Mergner in charge and they dropped me off at our busy LZ at

_____

*As a Reserve major general, Mook stood tall and blew the whistle over corruption in the National Guard to a congressional subcommittee and as a consequence was forced to retire prematurely.

Danger, now filled with simonized Hueys. George says I must've given them the shortest briefing in history, since I called him to pick me up ten minutes later—and from what I recall, I'm sure he was right. The brass—starched and fourteen stars strong—stood around my Situation Map in the Battalion's briefing tent really getting off on 'being there." It was clear that Hollis had pulled me from the fight to do a show-and-tell as a self-serving PR ploy. I was pissed and didn't try and hide it. With one foot out the tent door I gave them a quick overview of what was going down and said, "Gentlemen, if you don't mind, I have a battle to fight. I suggest you hold your questions until it's over." Bet the war stories flew at that evening's cocktail parties.

Once I got back over the fight with Mergner we put together our plan for that night, starting with scooping up Dagger and bringing it back to secure Danger. The other companies also moved to LZs. And just as the sun fell out of the sky, the Boomerang slicks landed—covered all the way in by Bounty Hunter guns. While the guns circled, the troops rushed to the waiting aircraft. Then, with doors shut, the slicks lifted off and landed at Danger in the dark.

But no one disembarked. Because "A,""B" and "C" Companies' Hardcore troopers were lying in the PZ grass. Once darkness settled in, the platoons moved to their previously reconned night ambush positions. We would teach our unconventional opponent a lesson learned…from him.

That night Claymore observed repeated enemy movement and called for artillery fire. Machine-gunner Runnebohm says, "As evening turned to nightfall, I think the few VC that survived thought we'd completely pulled out. About two A.M., a small group of VC tried to escape using sampans to cross the river. We let them get into our trap and gave them everything we had. It sounded as if there was an entire battalion opening fire when in reality it was less than twenty of us."

At first light, after three more contacts, Claymore grunts found twelve dead VC. Battle Company was equally busy that night. "As evening was getting there I remember signs of them all over the place," Sergeant Dubois says. "We caught one alive, but because it was getting dark the skipper didn't want to bring in a bird. I don't know who was watching the prisoner, but he got away and jumped into the river. Several guys opened up, but nobody really knew if they got him or he got away. We moved to a different spot to set up our perimeter and you better believe I stayed awake that whole night. There was a big Vietnamese grave there and we set up behind it. They buried their people on top of the ground so it was a big mound of dirt. I remember taking all of my hand grenades off my LBE and laying them down beside this grave where it was easy to get them real quick. They were all around us, you didn't know what direction they were coming in."

In the middle of the night DeRoos spotted movement on the other side of the river. "One of my guys saw a bunch of soldiers moving through his Starlight scope," he says. "They looked like a litter party. We took them under fire and slapped a lot of artillery on them. We picked up seventeen kills."

"The whole Battalion was engaged at one time or another," Diefendorf remembers. "Oh, we cleaned their clock, absolutely, that's for doggone sure."

Battle Company rifleman Donnie Cline will never forget 22 May—because he still regrets missing the fight. He was at Danger pulling security when the Hardcore came back covered in victory. "It was one of the best morale boosters for the company I ever did see, and I had to miss it!" he says. "When my buddies got back they told me, 'It was just like shootin' fuckin' ducks in a gallery.' Everybody's morale was up and they were sayin' stuff like 'Well, I know I got at least four of 'em.' Somebody said, 'They were jumpin' into the water and we were pumpin' 'em as they were jumpin' into the water while the rest of 'em were tryin' to fade back into the jungle.'"

"Yeah, yeah, you feel like you're the stud of the earth, it's a great thing," Carl Ohlson says. "Oh, I was elated. I think every time you have a victory like that you can't help but feel good because you get into that battle-soldier mode. The adrenaline's flowing, your mouth is dry, your hands're sweaty and you're always watching out for your guys, making sure everybody's covered and you're concerned about people being hit but when you have the upper hand, you're feeling battle-high. Everybody was just going bonkers."

"It felt absolutely wonderful," Tom Aiken recalls. "That's probably a sad thing to say about war, but I'd seen the damage they'd done to us on so many occasions that it was tremendously satisfying to turn things around."

Very few times in the recorded history of war does a fight go exactly as planned, but 22 and 23 May was one of those rarities when the enemy played right into our hands. Never did a commander ever have better troops or small-unit commanders. Not to mention a lot of input from Lady Luck.

Lieutenant David Crittenden, who scooped up the VC battle plans that triggered the victory, remembers it all this way: "Capturing the documents was the blind good luck of a young lieutenant who didn't know better. Everyone was excited that we had a plan and the plan worked. One of the biggest things that the guys felt good about was that we sustained very few casualties, which wasn't the case with the VC—that was the end of that battalion battle group."

That night I went into my little bunker back at Danger and fell into my sack feeling as if it had been ten thousand years since I'd taken command of this lash-up. No, that's wrong, I told myself, it had been only four months. And over that time, the good men of the 4/39th had traveled a million miles from hopeless to Hardcore. I fell asleep to the bark of Chum Robert's 105s and the music of the TOC's busy radio—and slept like a stone.

TWENTY-FIVE

Fire Support Base Danger
25 MAY 1969

Our lopsided victory hit page one of newspapers right across the USA. The Hardcore had deactivated the VC's 261A battalion, the 514X Mortar Company and 522nd Rocket Company. In the *Washington Post*, reporter Ward Just called the battle "a textbook illustration of how to fight the Viet Cong, which is altogether logical because the American field marshal, a lieutenant colonel named David Hackworth, has in fact written a manual on how to fight guerrillas in South Vietnam." With equal accuracy, Ward also said, "It is not a manual that has been widely read."

The day after the battle, the TOC phone started jumping off the hook with calls from Saigon-based reporters looking for a quick quote. Besides the press, stars galore fell on FSB Danger.

For starters, there was four-star General Bill Rosson, a wonderful combat leader I'd served under in Germany who understood the importance of sitting in the mud and shooting the breeze with grunts or pulling on a jacket without any stars and going through the chow line with a mess kit like the rest of the troops. This soldier's soldier was well-known for keeping everyone on their toes, from lax leaders at the top to sloppy, uncaring cooks at the bottom.

We gave him the sort of no bullshit briefing I would have wanted. When we finished, he praised the Hardcore's performance and then walked the firebase perimeter, talking to Ed Clark's boys about the fight and how they'd out-G'd the G.

I'm not exactly certain how many VC we killed during the battle. Our Battalion operational logs reflected 147 for the two-day period. Division reported 172 and the *Washington Post* 134. AP reported 164. Whatever the final number, we'd put the hurt on three VC units for a good spell, and the Division intelligence folks now rated all three units as combat ineffective. So we'd chased Charley's sorry ass all over our AO and fertilized a lot of ground with dead VC. For sure, Charley was burning a lot of incense.

During my months with the Hardcore, the Battalion—along with its combined arms team—had dispatched more than 2,500 VC KIA by actual body count in exchange for twenty-five Hardcore lives. The ratio: 100 to 1. Even with fudging the numbers, the Fog of War and civilians killed by mistake and counted, these were damn good numbers. Over the long haul, General Giap would never have been able to sustain such losses. If every Allied infantry battalion in Vietnam had followed the model set by the Hardcore, Westmoreland's goal of winning the war by attrition would have been fulfilled.

Never happen—as the grunts always said.

We'd fought my last battle with the Hardcore exactly as I'd planned to fight my first in Vietnam four years before. At least this time around, thanks to John Hayes, I fought it my way. Then, as Brigade S-3, my 101st Brigade Op Order for Operation Gibraltar called for rifle platoons from the 2/502nd Parachute Battalion to maneuver independently, covertly sealing the enemy's escape routes—backed up by a big firepower pounce on him when he tried to escape. But a timid battalion commander who believed in safety in numbers got cold feet and chose to operate in a battalion-size formation—like Normandy, two up and one back and feed 'em hot chow—and only brave troopers and massive firepower saved that battalion from having its ass handed to it by the VC.

The Hardcore proved how the war should be fought: mixing guerrilla tactics with our big firepower stick and mobility—beginning with well-led, well-trained and well-motivated troops. Our experience reaffirmed what I'd written for *Infantry Magazine* after my first tour in Vietnam:

> The most important lesson to be drawn from the war in Vietnam is that a lightly equipped, poorly supplied guerrilla Army cannot easily be defeated by the world's mostpowerful and sophisticated Army, using conventional tactics. To defeat the guerrilla, we must become guerrillas. Every insurgent tactic must be copied and employed against the insurgent. The marvels of modern technology have caused some to believe that exotic gear has replaced the man with the rifle. It is not true. Never in the history of modern warfare has the small combat unit played a more significant role...and the brunt of the fighting falls squarely on the platoon. The outcome of the war will be determined, in large part, by the skill, guts and determination of the platoon leader.

The next visitor was a three-star out of Long Binh, one of the kibbitzers who'd pulled me out of the battle to brief the generals at Danger. No warrior like Rosson, he was a staff smoothie without a clue, his head still somewhere on the Plains of Europe refighting World War II along with most of his superiors.

After this fool came three-star Ewell and two-star Hollis and a squad of lesser lights. Not one of these starched and polished gentlemen showed the slightest interest in how we'd done our number on the enemy. Not one even visited the troops. All they wanted to hear was BODY COUNT.

Uniformly, the brass praised our win, but only Generals Rosson and Gunn were even listening, let alone computing—only they bothered to dig into the details to learn from them. The others regarded the battle as a sporting event; not much more than "Army beats Navy—and now that we've spent time up on the forward edge with the brutish gladiators, we'd better get back to our headquarters or we'll miss Happy Hour."

This happened even though by the end of May 1969, the Hardcore was driving the train. The enemy was so busy running, hiding and trying to stay off the tracks that he didn't have time to mess with ARVN and the South Vietnamese people. And if we could have stayed together as the Hardcore team—the grunts, Tac Air, arty and other nonorganic supporters—we'd have become even better at killing VC at an even lower cost in friendly casualties and lower aircraft and equipment losses.

Forget about it.

One day after the battle, General Hollis flew to Danger for the change-of-command ceremony. I passed the Hardcore colors to Major Jim Taylor, a good man who fought to put the Battalion to full use. The Hardcore performed well during the next six weeks but then as part of the drawdown, it was the first U.S. Infantry Battalion shipped home—where it was deactivated. And all the hard lessons learned for which we'd paid so dearly in blood were flushed down the drain.

For the change of command exercise Captain Joe Connor, our great Tamale 14 FAC, arranged a surprise: Two of his F-4 Phantoms buzzed Danger, then did a magnificent flyover. Sniper leader Larry Tahler caught me looking at the sky. He remembers the moment this way: "It was a totally different unit from the one Hack took over the night he overheard me calling him an SOB. Well, four months later he was still an SOB, but our SOB—and we loved him. The day he left, the troops were without graffiti and hippie beads and soldier-straight. And my Sniper's eye actually saw tears running down Hardcore 6's cheeks."

Gordy DeRoos spotted me as I headed for the chopper pad and the bird that was waiting to fly me off to Saigon. Until Gordy reminded me, I'd forgotten that I didn't make it all the way on my own feet. As he tells it,

"The troops from Battle Company, who'd put a price on Hack's head in February, hoisted him on their shoulders and carried him to the chopper. Hack looked like he wasn't all that comfortable about it, but I could see he appreciated where they were coming from and went along with it. That gesture by the troops pretty much echoed the mood of the rest of us as we watched him leave. I personally had an empty feeling in my gut."

So did I. Not long ago, Sniper Jones sent me the letter he wrote his mom from Danger on 25 May 1969. The letter goes like this: "The most terrible thing happened today. Colonel Hackworth left. You remember the one everyone hated, and wanted shot? Now there's another bounty out for him— to anyone that can get him back."

As the troops in Vietnam used to say, "There it is, m'man."

EPILOGUE

Greenwich, Connecticut
11 SEPTEMBER 2001

None of us will ever forget where we were or what we were doing on 11 September 2001. That morning, Eilhys and I came into the kitchen from our usual morning hike. As we started breakfast, she turned on the television and I heard her say, "Oh no!"

The first plane had just rammed the World Trade Center—and obviously this wasn't some pilot with a cinder in his eye who'd lost it on his descent into La Guardia. Then, like a perfectly aimed incoming round, the second plane exploded in its fireball.

And so it began. And none of our lives will ever be the same.

The first thing that flashed in my mind as I watched the horror was how little difference there is between Vietnam and the prolonged global conflict—the war against terrorism—that now confronts us. The second thing that came to me was that the older I get, the clearer it becomes that the fundamentals of warfare don't really change. With technology, everything just comes faster, smarter and meaner. But the basics remain the same.

The lessons we learned in the Hardcore are more relevant than ever to our country's success or failure. Back then, what we concentrated on was Combat 101—the blocking and tackling, not the big fancy stuff—and that same approach is equally valid today. Star Wars missile shields are not going to defeat terrorists. Victory will come only through the mastery of combat basics: agility and speed; good intelligence and security; patrolling and ambush techniques; sound defensive tactics that stress alertness; and marksmanship—being a good enough shot to kill the sonofabitch with the first round.

What the Hardcore and other good units in Vietnam also did was internalize and live by a warrior ethos that's been around at least since Joshua blew his little horn at Jericho:

Rule 1: Stay alert, stay alive.

Rule 2: Keep your weapon clean, right at hand and ready to fire.

Rule 3: Trust no one except the guys on your right and on your left.

Rule 4: Always take care of your troops.

Rule 5: Know your enemy as well as you know yourself.

Rule 6: Don't forget nuthin'.

In Afghanistan early on, the most serious incident, the one where we took the most casualties, happened because a Special Forces operator on the ground gave his own coordinates to a bomber crew, who then executed their mission with sublime perfection—dropping their bombs directly on top of him and his team! Human error. The same sort of sloppy stuff that went down in the Argonne forest, Normandy, Pork Chop Hill, Dak To. When people don't have their heads together, you better believe shit happens. And the higher tech the ordnance, the greater the price the ground-pounder has to pay.

The first American soldier lost to hostile fire in Afghanistan was Sergeant First Class Nathan Chapman, who was killed in an ambush near Gardez. A fourteen-year-old boy shot Chapman in the back, then escaped while anti-Taliban leaders were debating what do with him.

Chapman wasn't wearing an armored vest.

Why the hell not? The question outraged me because something similar had happened in Somalia to Casey Joyce, a Ranger I'd known since he was a little kid. His vest was too heavy and inflexible—he figured he couldn't move around quickly enough to do his job. So, he compromised by taking off his back armor plate, which left his chest protected but his back exposed. He dropped seven pounds and the decision cost him his life.

The Rangers, the men who invented "Don't forget nuthin'," thought their mission in Mogadishu that day would be a wham-bam-thank-you-ma'am walkover. So they didn't take sufficient ammo, medical supplies, water or night vision devices. When they got stuck in an all-night stand, they couldn't see, they had to ration ammo and Ranger James Smith died of a relatively minor wound because a Doc couldn't do a cut-down. Had the proper medical gear been available, Smith would have lived to fight another day instead of bleeding out.

When I learned about Chapman's vest, I touched base with a buddy in SF Command and raised hell. He denied the story.

"Hey, everyone has a vest," he said. "We issued them."

Bullshit, I told him. Then he checked around.

What really happened is that some 10th Mountain Division ration-stackers at a staging base in Uzbekistan broke into the Special Warfare supplies meant for the SF teams in Afghanistan and made off with a basic load of it, including vests. The truth came out after some SF operators spotted REMFs wearing the special equipment back in the rear.

"Hey, motherfuckers," one of the SF studs said, "you stole our stuff and left us without any vests." They then wiped the floor with the scroungers and recovered what they could of their gear.

How do I know this? Not through any genius detective work on my part, just by listening to the troops. In Vietnam it was the grunts. Now it's the Special Forces guys and the Rangers.

The Army went to hell and back trying to cover up. But eventually I got a call from a reluctant truth teller who admitted, "My God, it turns out you were right. We issued 5,000 but only 4,000 got there—the REMFs stole the rest. We're gonna issue more and make sure they get where they're supposed to."

Tell that to Sergeant Chapman's wife and kids.

Where is the Army's institutional memory? REMFs always ride high at the expense of the grunts. When I went to Vietnam for the first time, my outfit, the 101st Airborne, landed wearing herringbone twill fatigues and Corcoran leather jump boots. Three weeks in the jungle and our boots were so rotten we had to hold them together with Army-issue green tape.

The 101st was also General William Westmoreland's old outfit. The first time Westy came out of Saigon to visit his boys, he and his entourage were all wearing tropical fatigues that breathed and jungle boots. As soon as he saw the tape, he had his people take off their boots and give them to us right on the spot. And when he got back to headquarters, he ordered the boots peeled off every REMF in sight and sent us duffel bags full of the good stuff. Maybe the best thing he did in-country.

Now we spend more time fussing over al-Qaeda detainees—painting little green arrows on the floors of their cells so they know which way to pray toward Mecca—than worrying about the men guarding them.

But Afghanistan shows us we've learned a good deal despite the friendly fire screw-ups and deaths like that of Nathan Chapman. In the success of our Rangers, Marines and SF "A" Teams—our Quiet Professionals—you can see what we've got going. We've just got to take it further. The war on terror, unlike the Gulf War, has to be fought by small teams, well led, properly trained and highly motivated. We can be sure we're beginning to get it right when a ten-man "A" Team kills fifteen hundred enemy soldiers at one thunderous crack.

These are the pros who've managed to resist the political correctness that's infected most of the rest of the U.S. military. Beginning with taking a stand and saying, "You want to put women next to us in this kind of combat, we're outta here."

In the Hardcore, I made the troops into that kind of animal. They took pride in being tough, fierce—and the baddest asses in the valley. Whether we're comfortable with it or not, up against the dedication of terrorist fanatics, touchy-feely, politically correct Armed Forces won't cut it.

Since 1989, the men of the 4/39th have been gathering for a yearly reunion and over the past four years many of them have been closely involved with this book. Their hope is that the story of the Hardcore will drive home the hard lessons of Vietnam and help protect our present and future grunts from repeating the mistakes of the past.

The children and grandchildren of the men who fought in the Hardcore are serving their country today. This new generation needs to be prepared now so they don't needlessly repeat old—fatal—mistakes. Their bosses must be made to prepare them correctly, which can happen only if there's an end to denial, beginning with: WE DID NOT WIN THE WAR IN VIETNAM. And then, WHY?

In two major battles and hundreds of minor ones, the Hardcore Battalion proved it could beat the VC at their own guerrilla game at a low cost in U.S. casualties, that the tactics and techniques we developed were sound not only in this war but in the unconventional wars to come, and that American soldiers, although mostly draftees and badly trained in the U.S. for the Vietnam War, were the best in the world—if they were properly motivated, trained, cared for and led.

After our "Going Away Party," we were applauded, commended, had our backs scratched like so many pets—and it was then I began to realize that all those stars circling in their choppers above would never understand the nature of the Vietnam War. Or what made the Hardcore tick. Nor did they intend to learn from our experience—to apply the example we'd given them on the battlefield.

Had all U.S. units replicated the Hardcore's techniques and tactics, the threshold of pain for the enemy would have been so terrible that he'd have crawled back in his hole. Instead, after the fight too many generals went back to their plush out-of-touch headquarters and drank martinis and told war stories about "their experience" in battle that day. The lessons disappeared like the olives in their drinks. It was Field Marshal Douglas Haig and World War I all over again: the mud, the futility, the blinkered mind-set.

The Hardcore sent to Hawaii as part of the Nixon Vietnamization con game titled "Peace with Honor," was soon deactivated. I went to the advisory outfit up at Pleiku led by my old 101st Brigade CO General James S. Timothy, where my first real hands-on experience with ARVN confirmed my gut feeling that the South Vietnamese Army was a terminally sick outfit still fighting as the French had taught them—and as we kept reinforcing—with World War II tactics certain to produce defeat. After Pleiku, I went to the ARVN Airborne Division, the elite unit of the South Vietnamese Army. There, the "best" leadership, the "best" equipment, the "best" soldiers, were nearly as incompetent. Hell, I thought, if this is the best they've got, don't expect the average Viet combat units to do any better.

I tried to make the brass understand the nature of the war, that all the bombs and shells American industry could produce would not help us prevail in Vietnam. Everywhere I went I talked about the tactics necessary to "out-G the G"—the same tactics that led the Hardcore to knock the VC on their butts and dominate the battlefield. Yet I was shouting into deaf ears. To change course would have been an admission by the stars—to say nothing of our politicians—that they'd had their heads up their collective asses since the early 1960s and were responsible for thousands of needless American deaths. Ironically, the grunts' own bitter summation of Vietnam had hardened into the military mind-set all the way up to the top of the chain of command. With, of course, its own bizarre spin and incalculably bloody ramifications.

"You look back and laugh at some stuff and can't even figure out how other stuff happened," observes Gary Stevens, a draftee wounded during the Hardcore's 22 May victory. "After guys got hit, obviously you would feel bad. We had a saying over there when we got back to the firebase. After a few beers, we'd tell each other, 'Don't mean nothin.'"

But it's got to mean somethin'. If the top brass don't start acknowledging the past, our kids will continue to pay.

In the spring of 1970, General Creighton Abrams offered me the job as the senior adviser of the 44th Zone down in the Delta, right where the Hardcore had fought so valiantly, probably because I knew the terrain and the enemy so well there. The job this time was to advise ARVN Ranger and other Zone regular units. The U.S. Special Forces units spread along IV Corps' Cambodian border were also under my operational control as were two U.S. aviation squadrons, including my old pals the Blackhawks. I took the gig even though by then it was obvious there was no way the war was going to be won unless the Saigon government was unwound and the new crew found itself a South Vietnamese General Vo Nguyen Giap.

By March 1971, when I became the youngest combat arms full Colonel in the Army, I'd lost all heart for moving on to the Army War College, an essential pit-stop on the road to general. I wrote to the Pentagon and told the Army brass that I didn't want go to War College or to be a general. As I told a buddy, "I've no aspirations to be a general because I have known only a few good ones. ...I'd rather be a bird colonel who doesn't give a fuck and who everyone is afraid of because his shit is straight."

Around that time Colonel Harold "Ace" Elliot, a great airborne leader, a soldier's soldier with four combat jumps in World War II, nailed me. "You've changed," he told me. "You're not the bubbling kind of guy you once were, you've got a chip on your shoulder." Ace Elliot was a dear friend of mine— he knew me really well—but even he didn't get where I was coming from.

"I just don't like your attitude," he said. "You're not the old gung-ho David Hackworth."

He was right.

Finally, after doing everything I could to make the Army listen, I sounded off to the press and the American people about how the politicians and the brass had screwed up the war. But nothing changed—no one in power, soldier or civilian, got off their butt to set things right. The body bags just kept piling up as we went on lying to ourselves. And losing.

So I left the Army, went off to Australia and began a new life. While I was down under, Saigon fell and the Army became even more resolute in its denial. We're never going that route again, the generals concluded, we're going to get ready for what we're good at: conventional war. Fighting the Soviets on the German plains, fighting Saddam in the desert, using air power to pound the enemy into submission. In other words, going back to what they were comfortable with, refighting the Big Kahuna—World War II—any way they could.

In 1988, now retired Lieutenant General Hank Emerson and I went to Hawaii to brief the top Army brass, their staff and subordinate COs on our experience. Colonel Horace Hunter, the operations officer who invited us, had pulled two tours in Vietnam. He said, "Hack, these guys are sucking this up like Vietnam never happened. They must not have learned a thing from that war even though most of them served multiple tours there."

As usual, Hank Emerson went one better: "Christ, just eighteen years ago at LZ Ripcord, the 101st Airborne lost almost five hundred soldiers because nothing was learned from our eight years' prior experience in Vietnam," he said. "There's no institutional memory."

Hank was dead right, and his words motivated me to write my military memoirs. Because of the success of *About Face,* I returned to the States and became a contributing editor for *Newsweek,* covering wars around the world.

Other unconventional wars were bubbling on the horizon and I knew what we'd learned in Vietnam—like it or not—could help us understand the new face of war. And the tactics I'd come to employ there could help us fight and win.

Ironically, Desert Storm obscured the real danger that lay ahead of us. The operation was a tremendous victory because not only did we have total observation through our satellites, air supremacy and armored formations that were the best in the world, we were also facing a punk enemy headed by a master of miscalculation. But it was a conventional war, conventionally fought. Little we did in Iraq, less logistics, could have applied to Vietnam or our next insurgent shoot-out.

In December 1992, *Newsweek* sent me to Somalia. Here the conditions— on a much smaller scale—were like those in Vietnam: Snipers and mines and booby traps were picking our soldiers off and we couldn't see the guerrilla-type enemy, masters at hiding who fought only on their terms.

This time I was looking at the battlefield as a war correspondent, but there was no way to take the young soldier out of the old warhorse. My style of reporting was to hang out with one of the rifle platoons for four or five days at a clip and then send in my copy. Pretty soon, to the young troops, I became the "Old Sarge." Eating and sleeping with the grunts, I became just another old pro who'd been around a war or two, and they forgot I was a retired Colonel. Pretty soon, it was "Hey, Hack, does this machine gun have a good field of fire?" and "What do you think of this patrol formation?"

Major Martin Stanton, Operations Officer of the 2/87th, the Infantry battalion I was tagging along with, was an old friend. He asked me to give a class to the battalion leaders on how we used choppers in Vietnam.

"Are you sure?" I asked. "Remember, I'm a leper as far as the Army's concerned. What's the Pentagon going to say when they hear you've got me teaching a class on the battlefield?"

Stanton was sure. I gave a two-hour lecture on airmobile operations in a nonconventional environment. "This is how we did it in Vietnam," I told them. Most looked at me with blank faces as though I were speaking Somalian.

I realized with an electric shock that it was as if Vietnam never happened. These fine young soldiers were like explorers in an unknown land without a map or compass, and a single two-hour cram session on airmobile operations in an insurgency environment wasn't going to be much help.

After I left, the Ranger Force in Mogadishu—some of the best warriors going—was specifically tasked to take out Mohamed Aidid, a major clan leader, and got chopped up. They conducted six helicopter operations—all identical, all by the book and all fruitless. They'd go out on helicopters, drop into the objective, conduct a raid, return to base. What they didn't factor into the equation was that Aidid and his guerrillas were watching, the way good terrorists do, and on their seventh raid—3 October 1993—instead of grabbing Aidid, they ended up surrounded and trapped and but for their courage and fighting skill would have been destroyed to the man.

The general in charge, William Garrison, had no go-to-hell plan to deal with the mess when the operation turned to shit. Nor any tanks to break through to the besieged Rangers—even though Marine tanks were close, the Army didn't want the Marines to ride to their rescue. And so our fine young men were seriously fucked. Eighteen dead and over a hundred wounded. A defeat. A disaster that caused the sole surviving superpower to beat feet out of Somalia in total disgrace.

Casey Joyce, the young warrior who died for lack of lightweight, flexible body armor, was the son of a lieutenant I soldiered with when I was a captain stationed in Germany. Wanting to be like his dad, a true stud, Casey joined the Rangers and went to Somalia as a member of the "get Aidid" mission. I kept flashing on this blue-eyed, blond-haired brave boy in a body bag.

It was as if my own son had been killed. He and his brother had played with my kids when they were growing up.

Determined to find out what happened, I went to Walter Reed Hospital to talk to the wounded, then to Fort Benning to meet with some of the Rangers who'd been in the fight. They all told me the same thing—how they'd been sucked in and then out-guerrillaed, outmaneuvered, outsmarted.

Like most executives or bureaucrats in large organizations, as today's top military leaders go up the chain, they develop the disease called CRS—Can't Remember Shit—and forget what it was like to be at the bottom. Somewhere along the line they stop listening to the ordinary grunts, the ones who do the actual fighting and dying, the ones who know what they need to defeat our enemies.

To ignore them is criminally stupid. These days, I get hundreds of e-mails a day from warriors in all branches of the military, many still in the nation's service, some retired, all of them passionate about making sure we get it right the next time out. Most of them make a lot of sense.

Of one reality, all of them are certain. Getting it right is the last thing on the mind of the Military Industrial Congressional Complex, where an F-22 fighter goes for mega-bucks a pop and the Star Wars II Program will come in at a $60 billion minimum. But gold-plated monuments to pork won't help the counterinsurgent or counterterrorist get a gun that doesn't jam.

The best way to prevent a war is to be so strong and so well prepared for the right kinds of war that no adversary will dare take us on. Yes, we must be primed for high-tech conflicts with superpower types, the People's Republic of China for example, but we must be as ready for insurgency fights and terrorism. As we continue to purchase mainly big-ticket toys, we're again pumping up for only one kind of war, probably the wrong war, and again young men and now sadly young women will needlessly suffer and die.

And, count on it, the wars of the immediate future will be nonconventional—in fact, they're already going on now. Two years ago, we gave Columbia, a dangerous guerrilla-infested country where our Seals and Special Forces are now operating, $1.3 billion to fight a war of insurgency. Peru, Bolivia and Ecuador are in serious enough trouble that we have military missions there as well. The instability in the region can only be expected to spread, not diminish.

Look what happened to the USS *Cole*—a billion dollar high-tech missile platform capable of horrendous mass destruction crippled by two insurgents in a skiff because the top brass continue to operate as conventionally as they did in Vietnam. Even though the members of the security detail on the *Cole* were at their posts on high alert—in an extremely dangerous port where they'd already been warned that a terrorist attack was highly probable— not one of their weapons had a round in the chamber. The security detail gave the small craft that killed seventeen sailors and almost sank the *Cole* a big, friendly American wave, and the terrorists waved back—just before they rammed their human torpedo into the ship. The Rules of Engagement had stated that our weapons were to have no rounds in the chamber.

From the *Cole* to the 9/11 World Trade Center attacks was one small step for terrorists and one huge defeat for mankind. Obviously, we need to change the rules fast. Obviously, we've hesitated too long.

Five years ago, I was walking with Eilhys in Central Park, when a car backfired. Several seconds after I'd thrown her to the ground and rolled with her under a bush, she asked shakily, "What's going on?"

So I told her that New York was at the top of the terrorist hit list. As a student and survivor of my wars, I could see it all coming down as clearly as I saw that we'd lose in Vietnam unless we fought that war with the correct counter-guerrilla tactics.

My wife loves New York City more than anyone I know, yet within the year, at her insistence, we moved to Connecticut. But we can't all get out of town. In fact, there isn't a place left to go where we can ever be far enough removed from the physical and emotional fallout of terrorist attacks. There's no longer any safe spot for Americans except what we mindfully make for ourselves.

Our very survival depends upon our no longer letting the Military Industrial Congressional Complex keep trying to fight today's battles with yesterday's war machine. Instead, we must quickly punch into the bottom line of common-sense counterterrorism and stop buying pricey hardware that's more about pork than war-fighting.

This time around, as in Vietnam, we're once again hunting and then slugging it out with an unconventional opponent, and most of the tactical advantages are his. The terrorist is like the audience in a theater, while we're the actors on the lighted stage. He sits shrouded in darkness, checking out our weaknesses and strengths, and when his attack plan is perfect, as on 11 September 2001, he strikes at the moment the target is most vulnerable. And then he runs away to plan an even bigger and better attack for another day.

We now need to fight smart as much as we need to get even.

There is no other choice. We do it right or we lose. We win—or we die.

AFTERWORD

The Weakest Link

Soon after I left the Hardcore I scratched down my thoughts on the biggest-problem I had while skippering the Battalion: green lieutenants.

From my post-Vietnam scrutinizing of a lot of units and a lot of lieutenants from every service, I believe the lieutenants of today can profit from these updated observations.

Pleiku, South Vietnam

June 1969

I never could figure out Army logic. The command of an infantry or tank platoon is the most demanding and dangerous job in the Armed Forces, yet the Army's senior brass consistently fail to recognize this reality and provide lieutenants with the practical, hands-on training they need. As a result, platoons too frequently wind up under the command of the least qualified, most inexperienced leaders in the military.

The average infantry lieutenant who joined the Hardcore in 1969 was simply not prepared to lead a rifle platoon. Because the Army's approach to training had failed to ready him for the reality of combat in Vietnam, he was extremely weak in troop leading, practical knowledge and small unit combat operations—and was almost without actual field experience.

The old saying "Good judgment comes from experience and experience is gained from bad judgment" was certainly applicable in the Hardcore. Out of sixty-eight infantry lieutenants who joined the Battalion while I was there, only two had ever stood in front of a Regular Army platoon; the rest were fresh out of service schools and/or training centers. As a result of having no experience in the art of handling men in tactical situations, these young and usually well-meaning officers were, with a few fine exceptions like the Tahlers, Knapps, Meyers, Ohlsons, Crittendens, Fletchers and Formachellis, almost valueless as platoon leaders unless they were given at least a thirty-day OJT period with a "stud-type" leader or they lucked out, as Roger Keppel did, by drawing winners such as Marty Miles, Jim Richardson, Toby Hager or Rich Polak as their platoon sergeant.

Besides technical and tactical incompetence, the next biggest shortcomings of new infantry leader replacements were a failure to be demanding and a reluctance to ensure that their men carried out the basics that would keep them alive on the battlefield.

One of the reasons for these deficiencies was that many of the social values were diametrically opposed to what's expected of a combat leader. To take a single a case in point, I had to constantly deal with a basic civilian-instilled value that drastically conflicts with combat leadership: popularity.

By the time these young men entered the Army, they'd been brainwashed for at least twenty years' about the importance of being "a nice guy." After four years of college ROTC/military academy training or about a year of basic infantry and OCS, they were supposed to be well-prepared leaders who always placed the welfare of their troops just below the accomplishment of the mission. Wrong. The average new lieutenant who joined the Hardcore had an almost Pavlovian instinct for being popular, so the definition of "welfare" was up for grabs. Because he had to be a good guy, he'd become a "joiner" instead of an "enforcer."

In Vietnam, good guys let their people smoke at night and take portable radios to the field. Good guys allowed night ambushes to set up in abandoned hooches so they wouldn't get wet and left only one guard by the door so everyone else could get a good night's rest. They let their men leave their boots on for several days and didn't inspect their feet, resulting in immersion foot. They didn't make sure their men kept their weapons and magazines perfectly clean or protected themselves against mosquitoes or took the required malaria pills and salt pills.

Good-guy lieutenants ended up killing their men with kindness.

While the run-of-the-mill lieutenant had a vague idea of what was required, he didn't have the experience or good sense to enforce the rules. When push came to shove, he preferred to turn his head the other way rather than come down hard on slackers. He overlooked deficiencies such as dirty weapons and ammunition, improperly safe weapons and grenades, incorrect camouflage techniques and the improper use of terrain—not using natural cover to provide protection from small-arms fire. And without an ass-kicking company skipper or demanding NCOs, the soldiers' habits became sloppier and sloppier. Carelessness ruled. And of course the result was casualties that could've been prevented had the lieutenant demanded the small things be done well.

My own experience has been that soldiers in combat will do only what's required of them. Under weak, nice-guy leadership, they'll try to get away with everything they can, violate every basic rule in the book. At the same time, because they know they're wrong and that this behavior is placing their lives in jeopardy, they'll respond to the demands of a positive, ass-kicking leader. The result will be fewer casualties and a developing respect for the leader who cares enough for his men to make them to do it right.

Another serious shortcoming was the failure to teach leaders the importance of supervision and the techniques of supervising. The average small unit leader in 1969 seemed to take for granted that his will would be done, that he didn't have to follow up.

The nature of combat in the Mekong Delta and how we operated in the Hardcore greatly extended this problem because small units normally operated on a widely decentralized basis in bitching terrain. This restricted regular visits from company and battalion leaders, prohibiting the more experienced senior officers and NCOs from checking the platoons and passing along "tips of the trade."

Without an experienced, demanding leader, these carelessly led platoons were headed for a world of hurt. The infrequency of heavy combat compared to World War II or Korea in 1950 and '51—and the prevalent all-is-cool attitude—had a tendency to lull soldiers and leaders into a false sense of safety. The more alertness and security went slack, the greater the danger of enemy attack became. We played right into the enemy's hands. As Sun Tzu put it so well: "When the enemy is weak: attack."

I had to inculcate the Hardcore leaders with the burning need to keep their people alert and never let down their guard. I had to instill in them the need to supervise the troops twenty-four hours a day. To make sure that: fighting positions were adequate; soldiers knew the mission, the situation and where the LPs were; proper field sanitation was being practiced; all battlefield debris was destroyed to deny the enemy a source of supply; the troops were all sleeping under cover and protected from "first-round hits" at fire support bases or base camps; subordinate leaders were "heads up" and demanding that their men were alert and tightly controlled. A never-ending list of little things: rifle magazines cleaned, weapons test-fired, grenades "safed," LPs and claymores out, sectors of fire known; salt tablets, malaria pills and "jungle rot" all monitored by the medics; stand-tos frequently conducted.

I had to get every *Leader* to follow this adage: "The best fertilizer in the world is the boss's footsteps...they make things grow."

Whenever I walked with a platoon—it's called a terrain walk—I'd point out to the leader things like good cover, where to set up the machine guns, how to cross a clearing or assault a knob. How to pick avenues of approach, organize supporting fires and employ scouts. I passed on my knowledge and they got the word without losing one soldier by learning battle lessons the hard way.

The principle was to learn so that we didn't keep making the same mistakes again and again. To do this, we copied the VC technique of ruthlessly examining every operation—an exercise that was a lot easier for the VC because they weren't as rigid about rank as we were. When rank rules, people say "Yes Sir" when they should say "no fucking way." I wanted to instill a particular sort of insubordination, but don't get me wrong—when I told the men to do something, I wanted it done. But I also wanted an atmosphere where no one would be afraid to sound off and speak the truth.

After every operation, we'd sit down at the squad, platoon and company level and work up a detailed critique that spared no hard words. It was: "Tom, you had your machine gun in the wrong firing position," "Bill, you triggered the ambush early," "Hank, your go-to-hell plan sucked."

War is so simple, yet the military school system tries to make it so damn complicated. Probably they need to promulgate a mystique in order to protect their turf. But the bare-bones bottom line to winning in battle is simply to sneak up on your opponent and belt the shit out of him from behind as hard and quickly as you can before he figures out you're in the neighborhood—and then beat it the hell out of there.

We should train our small units not in the classroom but in the bush, where warriors can be taught the gut fundamentals of infantry combat. The basics should be instilled by the same instructional techniques as those used in parachute training. Every block of instruction should be reduced to the salient "points of performance," and each soldier should be required to demonstrate his knowledge by ruthless practical examination.

Rommel said, "The best form of welfare for the troops is first-class training, for this saves unnecessary casualties." First-class training means hard work and sacrifice.*

General Bruce Clarke's adage "The more sweat on the training field, the less blood on the battlefield" is an adage I've followed since I was a teenager and I'm convinced it keeps the casualty list short. That's why it was my motto for the Hardcore. And why the new lieutenants were told to listen to their old-hand platoon sergeants, honor graduates not of the Officer Basic Course but of the Battlefield School of Hard Knocks.

Cadets and new leaders who show ineptitude and little leadership ability—such as that walking atrocity Lieutenant William Calley of My Lai massacre infamy—should be immediately eliminated. Calley was recycled three times at Infantry OCS after being found wanting in leadership before finally being commissioned in order to show a "low attrition rate" to higher headquarters. A bad mistake with big consequences. More than any major enemy victory, the shame and horror of My Lai caused the American people to withdraw their support for the war effort. Once they saw what Calley had wrought, they said, "Enough is enough."

Attending Airborne, Ranger and Special Forces courses provides great hands-on training and builds confidence. That and some good OJT—coupled with a keen knowledge of military history—and a caring lieutenant should be on his way to leading well, fighting smart and taking care of his warriors.

In small-unit leaders, confidence, like fear, is contagious. Troopers can feel it, see it and smell it—and it will rub off on soldiers from a platoon to a division as quickly as a good rumor rumbles out of the latrine. Confidence

---

*Besides having experienced noncoms to lead new small-unit officers through the minefields of a combat command, the best way for a new leader to learn his stuff is to read and reread books by combat warriors who've been there. Rommel's *Attacks,* Patton's *War as I Knew It,* and Sajer's *The Forgotten Soldier* are good starters. Don't bother with Clausewitz's convoluted double-talk, but make *The Art of War* by Sun Tzu your bible. Written around 400 B.C., its short and simple lessons of war are every bit as brilliant today as they were then. I've been carrying Sun Tzu and reading it almost daily since I was given a copy of it in Korea in 1950 just after the Red Chinese surprised MacArthur and hit us between the eyes.

produces courage. Most leaders or soldiers aren't born with a double basic load of guts. The average leaders are as scared as the next guy in their first or one hundredth firefight, but if they are confident that they're tactically proficient, that their unit's a squared-away team motivated by a strong sense of duty to accomplish the mission, the courage that's needed to do what many will view as impossible will be there. Mouths may go dry, guts may churn and hands shake, but when the slugs start snapping, the prepared leader will be as cool on the outside as Clint Eastwood. And no one will know he's really scared out of his brain.

Besides being one hell of a job, leading men into battle is the ultimate responsibility. On the battlefield, decisions such as "go left" or "go right" or "go straight ahead" are made in a split second and, right or wrong, good or bad, people get killed. Leaders carry the scars of those decisions for the rest of their lives. Later, battle scenes play back deep into the night like an old movie: "Why didn't I wait?" "Why didn't I bring in more fire?" "Why didn't I go myself?" "Why didn't I go to the left?" Questions that will haunt the blooded combat leader until he's six feet under. Good preparation, hard training, knowing your job and attention to detail will keep the nightmares— and any casualties—to a minimum.

To be a combat leader in the profession of arms is one of the most noble, most deadly jobs going. It's rough and tough and its rewards are few. But if at the end of the day the troops say, "He's a good man"—as opposed to "He was a nice guy"—that's pretty much as good as it gets.

GLOSSARY

ADC - Assistant Division Commander

AG - Adjutant General

AID - Agency for International Development

AIT - Advanced Individual Training, the second phase of a soldier's initial entry training

Airborne - The term used to describe a parachute-trained soldier, a parachute unit or an operation in which parachutes are employed to drop personnel and equipment. Also a salutation between airborne soldiers such as "Airborne, Sir."

Airmobile - An operation in which personnel and equipment are moved by helicopter

AK-47 – A Soviet- or Chinese-made 7.62mm (.30-caliber) automatic rifle—the standard individual weapon for the Viet Cong and North Vietnamese Army

AO - Area of operation

APC - Armored Personnel Carrier, a thin-skinned vehicle used to transport infantry to and around the battlefield

AR-15 - A carbine version of the M-16 rifle

Arc-light – USAF B-52 bomber air strike

Arty – Artillery

ARVN - Pronounced "Arvin," the Army of the Republic of Vietnam (i.e., South Vietnamese)

Assets - Helicopter and fixed-wing aviation support

AWOL - Absent without leave

BAR – Browning Automatic Rifle, the standard U.S. infantry assault rifle of

World War II and the Korean War, and by ARVN during the early part of the Vietnam War. Considered to be the most rugged and reliable weapon going during this period

Basic load – A standard and/or initial issue of ammunition

Basic training – The first phase of Initial Entry Training received by a trainee upon entrance into the military service

Battalion – An Army or Marine Corps unit composed of a headquarters and usually two to five companies or batteries—usually under the command of a lieutenant colonel—with a total of between 400 and 1,000 men

BC– Body count, the reported count of enemy dead

Berm - A wall around a defensive position

Bird - Slang for helicopter or airplane. The term is also used to describe a full colonel (see following entry)

Bird colonel- A full colonel. "Bird" refers to the full colonel's insignia, which is a silver eagle.

Blackhawks – The name of the 7/1st Air Cav Squadron, whose Hueys and Cobras supported the Hardcore

Black pajamas/Black PJs – Lightweight work clothes worn by Vietnamese peasants and associated by Americans with Viet Cong as the VC basic uniform

Blood trail – A trail of blood left by a dead or wounded soldier being carried away or left by an escaping and wounded enemy

Blue – Bodies of water (rivers, streams, canals, etc.)

Blue Max - Slang for the Medal of Honor

Booby trap – An explosive device or destructive charge that activates on contact, meant to kill or maim, concealed, camouflaged and/or set up with a trip wire (e.g., a booby-trapped enemy flag, a booby-trapped dead soldier, a booby-trapped trail)

Boomerangs - The name of the Huey slicks from the 191st Aviation Company that supported the Hardcore

Bounty Hunters - The name of the Huey gunships from the 191st Aviation Company that supported the Hardcore

Brass – Slang for an officer, specifically field grade (major and above) and general officers

Brigade – An Army unit usually composed of two or more battalions of infantry, artillery, armor, engineers, signal or military police—with a total of between 1,200 to 5,000 men

Bronze Star – U.S. military decoration awarded for heroic or meritorious service during combat. Heroism is indicated by a small metal "V" device on the red, white and blue Bronze Star ribbon. The Bronze Star medal ranks below the Silver Star.

Butterbar – Second lieutenant

C-4 - A plastic explosive; its most popular use among grunts on the battlefield in Vietnam was to heat water and C-Rations.

C-130 – Assault four-engine aircraft

C&C - Command and Control helicopter

CG - Commanding general

CH-46/CH-47 - Large troop- or cargo-carrying helicopters

Charley - Slang for Viet Cong or NVA personnel

Charley 4 – Slang for C-4 plastic explosive

Chieu Hoi - Meaning "open arms," a program designed to encourage Viet Cong and NVA to surrender or defect. Individual enemy soldiers who came in under the program were also called "Chieu hois."

Chopper - Slang for helicopter

CIB – Combat Infantryman's Badge, U.S. Army decoration awarded to infantrymen for standing tall in combat under fire

CIC - Counterintelligence Corps

CID - Criminal Investigation Division

CIDG - Civilian Irregular Defense Group, consisting of Cambodians, Laotians, and natives (Montagnards, Nungs) trained and employed in Vietnam and usually under the control of U.S. Special Forces

CINCPAC - Commander in Chief, Pacific

Claymore – U.S. mine, approximately the size of a hardbound book, wire- or trip-wire triggered and laid above ground, most often used for perimeter defense. Packed with C-4 plastic explosives and 8,000 steel pellets—with a range of 300 meters and an arch of 100 meters wide—they were pointed toward the enemy and exploded in a single direction.

Cloverleaf – A patrol pattern: See Vietnam Primer

CO - Commanding officer; conscientious objector

Cobra gunship – Helicopter with multi-weapons systems—rockets, grenades and minigun that would fire 6,000 rounds per minute. The term Cobra was conceived by Specialist Wyley Wright, a member of the 114th Aviation Company.

Commo - Slang for communications

Company – An Army or Marine Corps unit composed of a headquarters and two or more platoons—usually under the command of a captain—with a total of between 100 and 150 men. Generally four to five companies made up a battalion.

COMUSMACV - Commander, U.S. Military Assistance Command Vietnam

Conex – Reusable corrugated metal shipping/storage container 7' cubed (7'x7'x7')—or in half size 7' by 7' by 4'—with double doors. Conexes could be moved, by using special slots on their undersides, via forklift or sling-loaded, by closed-ended posts, via crane or helicopter.

Corps - A military unit normally composed of three divisions as well as supporting units such as artillery, engineer, signal, etc.

COSVN - Central Office for South Vietnam, the control headquarters for all communist activity, political and military, in South Vietnam

Counterinsurgency - Military operations conducted against insurgents

CP - Command post

C/S – Combat support

C-Rations – Military canned food, twelve individual boxed meals per case. Each meal contained a canned main course, canned bread or crackers, canned peanut butter, canned dessert, packaged individual instant coffee portion, three cigarettes, P-38 can opener, napkin and plastic eating utensils.

Def com – Artillery defensive fire

DEROS - Date Eligible Return from Overseas

DFC – Distinguished Flying Cross, an award for heroism or extraordinary achievement while participating in aerial flight. Bronze metal "V" device is worn by Navy and Marine Corps to denote valor

Dich - Pronounced "dick," this was one of many slang terms for enemy dead used during the Vietnam War.

Division - A military unit traditionally composed of three regiments/brigades as well as supporting units.

DMAC - Delta Military Assistance Command

DMZ - Demilitarized zone

DoD – Department of Defense headquartered at the Pentagon in Washington, D.C. A term to describe the U.S. Army, U.S. Navy, U.S. Air Force, U.S. Coast Guard and the Marine Corps collectively.

Dog robber – An officer or enlisted aide to senior brass; an errand boy or girl

Door-gunner – Helicopter crewman whose responsibilities included aircraft defense and supporting fire through the use of a single- or multiple-flex machine gun mounted on each side of the Huey aircraft

DSC - Distinguished Service Cross, the U.S. Army's second-highest valor award

Dust-Off - Slang for medical evacuation by helicopter

DX – Supply term meaning direct exchange. Also used in slang as to DX—get rid of—a loser.

Eagle flights – a helicopter-borne infantry raid aimed at a specific target

E-1 (recruit)—**E-9** (sergeant major) - Enlisted pay grades

FAC - Forward Air Controller

Five by Five — Expression used by radio operators indicating good commo reception

FNG — Fucking New Guy, a term used by grunts applying to replacements of all ranks

FO - Forward Observer. The FO accompanied infantry in the field and adjusted artillery and mortar fires.

Foot mobile — Infantry troops ready to move out on foot at a moment's notice

Frag - Slang for a fragmentation grenade. In Vietnam, the term also referred to a mutinous solder's killing, or attempting to kill, a leader with a frag grenade.

Friendly fire — An accidental attack on U.S. or allied soldiers by other U.S. or allied artillery or air

FSB - Fire support base, a permanent or semipermanent installation that housed artillery, infantry, command and control, and supporting facilities. Its purpose was to provide indirect artillery support to infantry units within its AO.

FTA — "Fuck the Army," a common expression in Vietnam

G-3 — Operations staff section or operations officer

GP — General purpose. Applied to most pieces of military equipment, e.g., GP tent, GP strap

Grunts — Infantrymen

Guerrilla - Also referred to as an "insurgent," a member of an irregular unit that employs unconventional tactics, usually in fighting a war of resistance

Guerrilla warfare - Low-cost, economy-of-force, unconventional military operations conducted by irregular (guerrilla) and/or regular military personnel, generally against an established government or order

Gunship - A helicopter designed as a firing platform to place supporting fires (machine gun and rocket) on the enemy

GVN - Government of South Vietnam

H&I – Artillery and/or mortar harassment and interdictory fire

Halizone tablets – Water-purifying tablets used to make local water safe to drink

HE - High explosives

Hooch – Slang for any dwelling in rural Vietnam and for housing in a military camp; plural, hooches

Huey - Slang for any of the UH-series helicopters

I&R - Intelligence and Reconnaissance platoon, also known as the eyes and ears of the pre – late 1950s U.S. Army regiment

Immersion Feet/Paddy feet – Serious skin deterioration as a result of continuous rubbing under consistent damp conditions

INCOC - Infantry Noncommissioned Officer Course, an acceleration program designed to produce NCOs during the Vietnam War. Also known as Shake and Bake and "instant NCO"

Incoming - Indirect enemy artillery, mortar and rocket fire that falls on friendly positions

Insert - Deployment of infantry maneuver elements by helicopter

Insurgency - Armed activity directed against a constituted government

Jitterbug flights - Infantry raids from choppers at scheduled targets or targets of opportunity

KBA – Killed by air

KIA - Killed in action

Klick - Slang for kilometer

KP – Kitchen police, or kitchen duty

LAW – Shoulder-fired M-72 Light Antitank Weapon

LD - Line of departure

Leg - A nonairborne soldier

Line doggy – A grunt

LMG - Light machine gun, in World War II and the Korean War the .30-caliber Browning and, in Vietnam, the 7.62 caliber M-60

LNO - Liaison officer

Local G – Local guerrilla or village guerrilla

Lock and load - To place a weapon on safety, then ready it to fire by placing a round in the chamber

LOH - Light observation helicopter, pronounced "loach"

LP - Listening post, an early-warning element of a few grunts deployed in front of the main positions

LRRP - Long-Range Reconnaissance Patrol. Members of the LRRP teams are also called LRRPs, pronounced "lurp." Most LRRP members were also known as Rangers.

LZ - Landing zone

M-1 - U.S. .30-caliber semiautomatic rifle used during World War II and the Korean War and by ARVN in the early days of the Vietnam War

M-16 - Unquestionably the worst infantry weapon ever forced upon America's fighting men. By 1969, most of the major bugs were ironed out and it became the standard U.S. and ARVN infantry rifle employed in Vietnam.

M-60 - A 7.62-caliber U.S. light machine gun used during the Vietnam War

M-79 grenade launcher – A single-shot, break-open, breech-loaded shoulder weapon that fired 40mm shells and weighed 6 _ pounds when loaded. It had a sustained rate of aimed fire of five to seven rounds per minute and an effective range of 375 meters.

MACV – Military Assistance Command—Vietnam, organized 8 February 1962, reorganized 15 May 1964, and departed Vietnam 29 March 1973

Main Force – Regular Viet Cong units equipped and structured similarly to the NVA

MASH - Mobile Army Surgical Hospital

Medal of Honor – The highest military award, for conspicuous gallantry and intrepidity at risk of life, above and beyond the call of duty, in action involving actual conflict with an opposing armed force

MEDCAP - Medical Civic Action Program. Combat medics would visit villages and hamlets and care for the local people.

Medevac - Medical evaluation by helicopter, also known as "Dust-Off"

MI – Military Intelligence

MIA - Missing in Action.

Mikes – Minutes. For example, ten mikes are ten minutes.

MO – Mode of operations

Mobile Riverine –U.S. Army 9th Division units, which based off naval ships

MOS - Military occupational specialty

NCO - Noncommissioned officer

Noncom - Slang for noncommissioned officer

NVA - North Vietnamese Army, technically "Quan Doi Nhan Dan Viet Nam," also known as the People's Army of Vietnam or PAVN

OCS - Officer Candidate School, a program designed to quickly produce mass lieutenants from within the enlisted ranks. Also known as "Ninety-Day Wonders" or Shake and Bakes.

OJT - On-the-job training

OP - Outpost or observation post

Op or Ops – Short for "operations"

OPCON - A term used to designate the operational control of a unit over a subordinate unit

OPLAN - Operations plan (a contingency plan)

Out-G the G – Out-guerrilla the guerrillas; i.e., use their tactics to beat the "G" at their own game

Pacification - A MACV program designed to win the hearts and minds of the local populace to our side

PF - Popular Forces, the village-level South Vietnamese militia

PFC – Private First Class, one enlisted pay grade E-3. Approximately 17,909

privates first class soldiers were killed in Vietnam.

PIO – Public Information Officer or Office, flacks, folks who wrote or told the Army story and did damage control.

Platoon - A military unit normally composed of forty soldiers and in Vietnam averaged about twenty soldiers

PLF - Parachute landing fall

Popping smoke – Using colored smoke grenades to mark a LZ, PZ or location

POW – Prisoner of war

PRC-25 - Pronounced "prick twenty-five," the standard U.S. infantry FM radio used in Vietnam

Pre-Tet – Before the NVA/VC attack in February of 1968

Punji stake - The ultimate in low-cost antipersonnel weapons: a sharpened bamboo stake, partially buried by the VC in wait for unsuspecting counterinsurgents

Purple Heart - A military decoration awarded for a wound sustained in combat

PX - Post exchange

PZ - Pickup zone (used in connection with helicopter operations)

R&R - Rest and recreation

Range card - A card used by infantry that shows a fighting position's sector of fire and primary direction of fire

Recon – Reconnaissance

Red, White and Blue – The Hardcore rifle platoons. 1st – Red; 2nd – White; 3rd – Blue

REMF – Rear-echelon motherfucker, a solder who keeps as far away from the fighting as possible. Generically speaking, anyone and everyone in the rear of the rifle platoon or at higher headquarters who is (or appears to be) out of touch with the realities of the battlefield or with the field soldier's lot

RF - Regional Forces, the district- and province-level South Vietnamese militia

RIF – Reconnaissance in Force

ROTC - Reserve Officers Training Course

RPD – North Vietnamese 7.62-caliber machine gun

RPG – North Vietnamese rocket-propelled grenade, specifically, the Soviet B-40 antitank, antipersonnel weapon. A smoke bringer

RTO – Infantry or artillery radiotelephone operator

RVN - Republic of Vietnam (i.e. South Vietnam)

S-1 – Officer in charge of the personnel and administration section of a brigade or smaller unit. "S" indicates Special Staff, brigade, regiment, group and below. "G" indicates General Staff (i.e., G-1), Division level and above. "J" indicates Joint Staff (i.e., J-1), integrated units of all services.

S-2 – Officer in charge of military intelligence section of a brigade or smaller unit (see S-1)

S-3 – Officer in charge of operations and training section of a brigade or smaller unit (see S-1)

S-4 – Logistics officer of a brigade or smaller unit (see S-1)

S-5 - Civil affairs officer of a brigade or smaller unit (see S-1)

Sampan – Small craft used in canals and rivers.

Sapper – (1) A soldier specially trained in infiltration and demolition; in conventional armies an army engineer. (2) A VC or NVA commando, usually armed with explosives. (3) An enemy infiltrator whose mission it was to destroy lives or property. (4) An enemy well-versed at penetrating allied defenses who used explosives against parked aircraft, artillery, bunkers or equipment

Screaming Eagles – The 101st Airborne Division's nickname

Script – Military payment certificates used in lieu of U.S. greenback dollars to reduce currency manipulation.

Search and destroy - A U.S. military operation designed to destroy enemy formations and facilities, but not to hold ground

Second balloon - Slang for a second lieutenant, or "L Tee"

Shake and bake – See INCOC

Shake-down cruise – An operation designed to smooth out the kinks of a unit

Silver Star – The third highest award for valor, higher than the Bronze Star W/"V" but lower than the Distinguished Service Cross or Navy or Air Force Cross

Sitrep - Situation report

Six - Originally the radio identification for unit commander; popularly used as shorthand when referring to the CO, as in "The Six wants it done right now"

SKS - A Soviet semiautomatic 7.62 carbine

Slick - A troop-carrying helicopter (Huey)

Soldier's Medal – Award for heroism that involves risk of life to save another soldier or other soldiers under conditions other than those involving combat with an enemy force

SOP - Standing operating procedure

SP-4 – Spec-4 Army rank; Specialist rank 4th Class (the lesser of the specialist ranks – equivalent in pay to Corporal E-4) designated by an Army-green shield with central device of a gold eagle.. Approximately 11,898 Army E-4's, SP-4s and corporals were killed during the Vietnam War.

Spec – Specialist, a technical rank that begins at the E-4 pay level (Spec-4) and ends at the E-7 pay level (Spec-7)

Spooky – AC-130 gun and flareship armed with miniguns, also known as Puff the Magic Dragon. A pee-bringer

Squad – An Army or Marine Corps unit usually made up of six to twelve men. Four to five squads make up a platoon.

Stand in the door - An Airborne term referring to the moment before one steps out of the door of an aircraft; used in popular jargon to signal the total commitment on one's part to a belief or one's determination to stand by one's word or commitment.

Stand-to – All personnel ready to fight at the assigned fighting position

Steel pot - Steel helmet with plastic liner

STRAC - Military perfection and readiness

Studs – Great soldiers or great leaders

Table of Operations – Military unit organizational document which provides personnel and equipment authorization

Tac Air - Tactical air support

TDY - Temporary duty

Tet – The Chinese Lunar New Year, a new year's and religious celebration that takes place in January and February each year. The term Tet became synonymous with the 1968 Tet Offensive when the Viet Cong/NVA attacked hundreds of cities throughout South Vietnam.

TOC - Tactical operations center

TOE - Table of organization and equipment

Top, Top Kick - First sergeant

TRUST – Trieste United States Troops, an elite unit that served in Northern Italy in the mid 1940s and early '50s

Tubes – Mortars and howitzers

Two Niner Two - PRC-25 radio antenna used for long range that is heavy and not organic to the radio. Generally set up in a company-sized night location

UCMJ - Uniform Code of Military Justice, the little Red Book

USARPAC - U.S. Army Pacific Command

USARV - U.S. Army Vietnam organized 20 July 1965, headquartered in Long Binh

USO – United Service Organization, which provided troop entertainment

VC - Viet Cong

VCI - Viet Cong infrastructure

Viet Cong - Vietnamese Communist soldier, unit or party member

Vietnamization - The American program under Richard Nixon to turn the war over to the South Vietnamese so that America could withdraw from the conflict "with honor"

VNAF - South Vietnamese Air Force

War of attrition - The destruction of enemy forces and material at a rate that the enemy cannot sustain

Waste - To kill an enemy soldier

Whitewalls - An Airborne haircut: shaved on both sides and the back of the head, and no more than about a half an inch of hair on top

WIA - Wounded in action

Willie Peter, WP – A mortar or artillery round of white phosphorous.

XM-203 - Over and Under—a combined M-16 rifle and M-79 grenade launcher that puts out M-79 40mm and M-16 slugs simultaneously. A pee-bring of a weapon

XO - Executive officer of a company, battalion and brigade/regiment

Zap - To kill an enemy soldie

ACKNOWLEDGMENTS

The guts of this book come from the personal narratives of the men, most of them now in their fifties, who served in or supported the Hardcore Battalion from late 1968 until mid-1969. We drew augmenting material from U.S. Army records such as Department of the Army published monographs and Inspector General Reports, 9th Division After-Action and Spot Reports, 1st Brigade, 9th Division and 4/39th Infantry Battalion Operations Journals for this period, and participants' memoirs, journals, diaries and letters—well worth their weight in gold because of their detail, exact dates and sense of immediacy. We also checked newspaper accounts of actions and recommendations and citations for individual and unit awards to assist and amplify the memories of the participants.

Human memory can play tricks, especially given the fog of battle, the passage of time—most of the interviews took place more than thirty years after the actual events—and the very nature of war stories. After a tale's been told again and again and embellished with each retelling, the actual event often gets blurred to the point where the latest, most refined version becomes "what really happened." In the interest of accuracy, anecdotal eyewitness narratives were matched against those of others who were on the scene and once again matched against the written documentation to verify dates, firefights and details of operations, units and names of the leaders and the led.

Eilhys, who did the majority of the interviews, talked with most of the participants—some as many as six to ten times—and these conversations were then transcribed and either sent or read to the interviewees for further authentication.

When Eilhys completed the interviews she told me, "They are holy men." Having had the privilege of seeing these warriors perform in combat, I instantly knew what she meant. The young men, mainly draftees, who served with honor and bravery on the killing fields of Vietnam's Mekong Delta, out-G-ing the G and out-Regular-ing the NVA Regulars, will forever bear the stigmata of that terrible misadventure.

We gratefully thank these former comrades-in-arms who over the last four years shared their stories by opening painful doors they'd hoped would be forever sealed and provided us with their letters home, other memorabilia and photographs. They were indeed sanctified in combat. And now it's our most fervent hope that they feel comfortable enough with our book to conclude we got it right.

Special thanks to "Doc" Evans, one of the Hardcore's great heroes—who spent several decades tracking down Battalion members and conducting extensive interviews he drew from for his own very special book, *Doc: Platoon Medic*—for his constant support and assistance, for kindly allowing us to use these transcripts as well as material from his book and for putting us in contact with scores of former Battalion members.

Thanks too to our heroic Battalion surgeon, "Doc" Holley, who also kindly allowed us to use his transcripts and material from his wonderful account—*Vietnam 1968 – 1969: A Battalion Surgeon's Journal*, which has become a guide for combat surgeons the world over—for his selfless efforts whenever we shot up a flare. As on the battlefield, the good "Doc Holy" was always there.

Without the help of ex-Vietnam Green Beret Kevin Gors this work wouldn't have been as complete. Super-sleuth Kev put his mighty private-investigator resources and skill together to track down hard-to-find folks for our interviews—including Hardcore troops the Department of the

Army said were dead! We thank him very much for his generous pro bono contribution to this work.

Thanks to Gordon DeRoos, LeRoy Dyment, Dan Evans, John Hayes, Byron Holley, Robert Johnson, Robert Knapp, Richard Marek, Judy Martin, Bob McMahon, George Mergner, Jim Mukoyama, Carl Ohlson, Emil Robert, Jim Robertson, Jim Silva , Sid Smith, Jerry Sullivan, Mike Suessman and Ben Willis for sweating through numerous editions of the manuscript, giving us guidance and keeping us out of the minefields. Our final product was greatly enhanced by their input, insight, comments and corrections.

We couldn't have even begun to tell the story without our excellent support team—Mike Clifton, Deborah Gonzalez, Jennifer Goodwin, Taryn Greenberg, Fred Heine, Maura Kallaway, Amy Landon-Arnel, Sonia Nash, Dan Matulich and Claudino Weber—the "book grunts" who sweated through the dozens of drafts and much of the pick-and-shovel research and filing, typed the interview transcripts, collected data, kept the computers operating, pounded the manuscript into final form and found the MIA documents Eilhys and I misplaced in the strangest spots.

Tom Mathews, our dearest friend, teacher and mentor, brilliantly cut out the chaff and made this work sing. And many thanks to Tom's wife and partner, Lucille Beachy, for keeping Tom and FSB Mathews up and running during the campaign.

Kudos to publisher Shawn Coyne for having the vision to see the Hardcore story clearly at the Line of Departure, the faith in us that we'd take the objective and for being there in the heat of the fray. Thanks also to his partner, Webster Stone, and Rugged Land's fine production team—Chris Min, Tammy Blake and Alex Selim. And to their legal eagle Elizabeth McNamara and to our own Elizabeth Barad.

Honorable Mention to Sally Allen, Hillary Bibicoff, Jeff Field, Bert Fields, Liz Glotzer, David McKenna, Chris Salvaterra, Martin Schafer,

Michael Schiffer, Tony Scott, Casey Silver and Gail Stayden—and their fine teams—for seeing the story as a movie while we were still struggling to write the book.

Our love to Elizabeth England, Ben and David Joel Hackworth, who selflessly sacrificed time with their mom and dad while we wrestled this sucker onto Shawn's desk. You were ever in our thoughts, dear kids, along with Tony, Laura, Olivia, Cameron, David Scott, Grant and other family and friends whom we hold dear.

And finally, our special thanks to Dr. Gerald Haidak, who saw early on the need for this book and encouraged us to write it. We love you, Dad.

Even with the countless checking there probably are still errors, for which we proffer our regrets and our apologies. We also changed certain names to preclude embarrassing those who didn't always shine and/or to protect their families from any discomfort.

EILHYS ENGLAND
DAVID HACKWORTH

WWW.HACKWORTH.COM

WWW.TEAGLES.HACKWORTH.COM

PO Box 11179
Greenwich, CT 06831

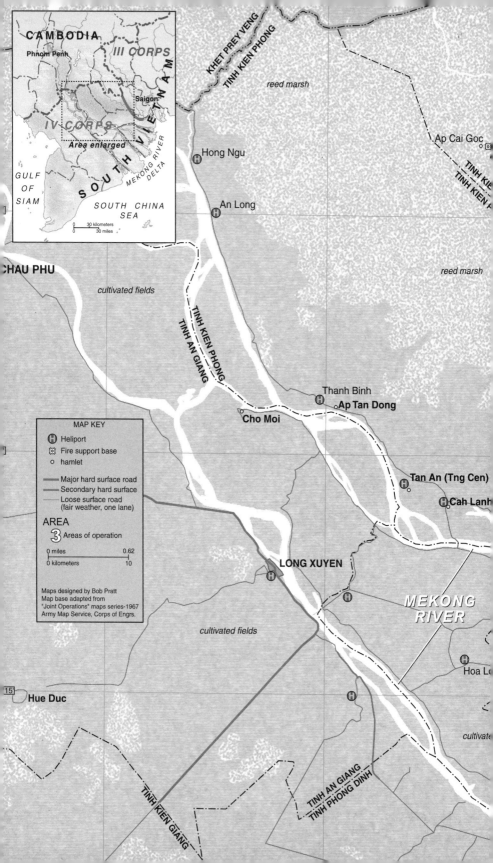

Inset map labels:

CAMBODIA

Phnom Penh

III CORPS

SOUTH VIETNAM

Saigon

IV CORPS

Area enlarged

GULF OF SIAM

MEKONG RIVER DELTA

SOUTH CHINA SEA

30 kilometers
30 miles

Main map labels:

KHET PREY VENG

TINH KIEN PHONG

reed marsh

Ap Cai Goc

TINH KIE

TINH KIEN P

Hong Ngu

An Long

CHAU PHU

reed marsh

cultivated fields

TINH KIEN PHONG

TINH AN GIANG

Thanh Binh

Ap Tan Dong

Cho Moi

Tan An (Tng Cen)

Cah Lanh

MAP KEY

H Heliport

⊡ Fire support base

○ hamlet

—— Major hard surface road

—— Secondary hard surface

—— Loose surface road
(fair weather, one lane)

AREA

3 Areas of operation

0 miles   0.62
0 kilometers   10

Maps designed by Bob Pratt
Map base adapted from
"Joint Operations" maps series-1967
Army Map Service, Corps of Engrs.

LONG XUYEN

MEKONG RIVER

cultivated fields

Hoa L

15

Hue Duc

cultivat

TINH KIEN GIANG

TINH AN GIANG

TINH PHONG DINH